New Materialisms

New Materialisms

Ontology, Agency, and Politics

EDITED BY
DIANA COOLE AND SAMANTHA FROST

DUKE UNIVERSITY PRESS *Durham & London 2010*

© 2010 Duke University Press
All rights reserved

Printed in the United States of America on acid-free paper ∞
Designed by Jennifer Hill
Typeset in C & C Galliard by Keystone Typesetting, Inc.

Library of Congress Cataloging-in-Publication Data appear
on the last printed page of this book.

To our children, Lucien, Simon, and Madeleine, who are growing up in a new materialist world, and to Shirley Margaret Coole (1923–2009) and Michèle A. Moriarty (1952–2009), who did not see the end of the project but live on in memory.

Contents

Acknowledgments

For their enthusiasm and suggestions in early stages of the project, many thanks to Wendy Brown, Bonnie Honig, and Linda Zerilli.

At Duke University Press, we would like to thank Courtney Berger for her confidence in the project as well as her persistence and insight in making suggestions about the shape of the volume and the arguments in the introduction. This book is all the better for her timely interventions and enduring patience. Thanks to Cynthia Landeen for her indexing prowess and also to Timothy Elfenbein, John Ostrowski, and Michael Wakoff for shepherding the manuscript through the production process.

We are grateful to the outside reviewers whose perceptive questions and suggestions helped bring shape to the project at crucial stages.

In a project like this, the position of editor is especially privileged for the perspective it gives on the whole. We appreciate the willingness of contributors to work with us and to participate singly in the ongoing conversation we two have had over the past few years as we pulled the volume together. We are also grateful for their patience as we honed the volume into its current form. We hope that they appreciate the significance of each and every conversation and essay in the quality and import of the volume as a whole.

For their invaluable participation in the "New Materialisms" conference at the University of Illinois, Urbana-Champaign that enabled many of the contributors to discuss and refine their arguments during February 2007, thanks to Ted Bailey, Pradeep Dhillon, Brenda Farnell, Debra Hawhee, Patrick Smith, Charles Varella, Linda Vigdor, and Martha Webber. For especial assistance and encouragement, thanks to Michael Rothberg and his helpers at the Unit for Criticism and Interpretive Theory. For calm and reliable assistance in coordinating the conference, thanks to Jacque Kahn, Theodora Kourkoulou, Lawrence Schehr, Melodee Schweighart, and Aprel Thomas. We would especially like to convey our gratitude to the Andrew Mellon Foundation, whose funding for "State-of-the-Art" conferences made this conference possible.

Individually, we would like to express sincere gratitude for the many stimulating conversations we have had with particular friends and colleagues over the lifetime of the project and for the encouragement they have given us. Jane Bennett, Kristin Cain, Sam Chambers, Alex Colás, Bill Connolly, Tim Dean, the late Paul Hirst, Kim Hutchings, Cécile Laborde, James Martell, Cris Mayo, Siobhan Sommerville, Jenny Bourne Taylor, and Caroline Williams all made special contributions, often in unexpected ways they may not even realize. As individuals, we would also like to acknowledge the mutual support we have experienced from each other as editors, in a transatlantic friendship that has yielded a genuinely collaborative project.

Thanks, too, to staff and colleagues in the Gender and Women's Studies Program and the Political Science Department at the University of Illinois, and to colleagues and students in the Department of Politics at Birkbeck College, University of London, for their ongoing support and interest in our research.

Diana Coole & Samantha Frost

Introducing the New Materialisms

As human beings we inhabit an ineluctably material world. We live our everyday lives surrounded by, immersed in, matter. We are ourselves composed of matter. We experience its restlessness and intransigence even as we reconfigure and consume it. At every turn we encounter physical objects fashioned by human design and endure natural forces whose imperatives structure our daily routines for survival. Our existence depends from one moment to the next on myriad micro-organisms and diverse higher species, on our own hazily understood bodily and cellular reactions and on pitiless cosmic motions, on the material artifacts and natural stuff that populate our environment, as well as on socioeconomic structures that produce and reproduce the conditions of our everyday lives. In light of this massive materiality, how could we be anything other than materialist? How could we ignore the power of matter and the ways it materializes in our ordinary experiences or fail to acknowledge the primacy of matter in our theories?

Yet for the most part we take such materiality for granted, or we assume that there is little of interest to say about it. Even (or perhaps, especially) in the history of philosophy, materialism has remained a sporadic and often marginal approach. For there is an apparent paradox in thinking about matter: as soon as we do so, we seem to distance ourselves from it, and within the space that opens up, a host of immaterial things seems to emerge: language, consciousness, subjectivity, agency, mind, soul; also imagination, emotions, values, meaning, and so on. These have typically been presented as idealities fundamentally different from matter and valorized as superior to the baser desires of biological material or the inertia of physical stuff. It is such idealist assumptions and the values that flow from them that materialists have traditionally contested. It is true that over the past three decades or so theorists have radicalized the way they understand subjectivity, discovering its efficacy in constructing even the most apparently natural phenomena while insisting upon its embeddedness in dense networks of power that outrun its control and constitute its willfulness. Yet it is on subjectivity that their gaze has focused. Our motivation in editing this book has been a conviction that it is now time to subject objectivity and material reality to a similarly radical reappraisal. Our respective researches have prompted our own interests in changing conceptions of material causality and the significance of corporeality, both of which we see as crucial for a materialist theory of politics or agency. We now advance the bolder claim that foregrounding material factors and reconfiguring our very understanding of matter are prerequisites for any plausible account of coexistence and its conditions in the twenty-first century.

Our commitment to editing a book on the new materialisms at this time springs from our conviction that materialism is once more on the move after several decades in abeyance and from our eagerness to help define and promote its new directions. Everywhere we look, it seems to us, we are witnessing scattered but insistent demands for more materialist modes of analysis and for new ways of thinking about matter and processes of materialization. We are also aware of the emergence of novel if still diffuse ways of conceptualizing and investigating material reality. This is especially evident in disciplines across the social sciences, such as political science, economics, anthropology, geography, and sociology, where it is exemplified in recent interest in material culture, geopolitical space, critical realism, critical international political economy, globalization, and environmentalism, and in calls for a renewed materialist feminism, or a more materialist queer theory or postcolonial studies. We interpret such developments as signs that the more textual approaches associated with the so-called cultural turn are increasingly being deemed inadequate for understanding contemporary society, particularly in light of some of its most urgent challenges regarding environmental, demographic, geopolitical, and economic change.

The eclipse of materialism in recent theory can be negatively associated with the exhaustion of once popular materialist approaches, such as existential phenomenology or structural Marxism, and with important challenges by poststructuralists to the ontological and epistemological presumptions that have supported modern approaches to the material world. More positively, materialism's demise since the 1970s has been an effect of the dominance of analytical and normative political theory on the one hand and of radical constructivism on the other. These respective Anglophone and continental approaches have both been associated with a cultural turn that privileges language, discourse, culture, and values. While this turn has encouraged a de facto neglect of more obviously material phenomena and processes, it has also problematized any straightforward overture toward matter or material experience as naively representational or naturalistic. Notwithstanding the capacity of these currently dominant theories to clarify arguments and to alert us to the way power is present in any attempt to represent material reality, however, we believe it is now timely to reopen the issue of matter and once again to give material factors their due in shaping society and circumscribing human prospects. The essays we have commissioned for the current volume are exemplary of some of the new and innovative ways of conceptualizing and responding to this reorientation.

The essays that follow are at the forefront of current thinking about matter; about how to approach it, and about its significance for and within the political. They resonate with our own belief that to succeed, a reprisal of materialism must be truly radical. This means returning to the most fundamental questions about the nature of matter and the place of embodied humans within a material world; it means taking heed of developments in the natural sciences as well as attending to transformations in the ways we currently produce, reproduce, and consume our material environment. It entails sensitivity to contemporary shifts in the bio- and eco-spheres, as well as to changes in global economic structures and technologies. It also demands detailed analyses of our daily interactions with material objects and the natural environment. What is at stake here is nothing less than a challenge to some of the most basic assumptions that have underpinned the modern world, including its normative sense of the human and its beliefs about human agency, but also regarding its material practices such as the ways we labor on, exploit, and interact with nature.

In labeling these essays collectively as *new* materialisms, we do not wish to deny their rich materialist heritage. Many of our contributors indeed draw inspiration from materialist traditions developed prior to modernity or from philosophies that have until recently remained neglected or marginalized currents within modern thinking. From this perspective their interventions might be categorized as *renewed* materialisms. If we nevertheless persist in our call for and observation of a *new* materialism, it is because we are aware that unprecedented things are currently being done with and to matter, nature, life, production, and reproduction. It is in this contemporary context that theorists are compelled to rediscover older materialist traditions while pushing them in novel, and sometimes experimental, directions or toward fresh applications.

If we pluralize these new materialisms, this is indicative of our appreciation that despite some important linkages between different strands of contemporary work and a more general materialist turn, there are currently a number of distinctive initiatives that resist any simple conflation, not least because they reflect on various levels of materialization. What has been exciting for us as editors has indeed been our sense of encountering the emergence of new paradigms for which no overall orthodoxy has yet been established. Our aim in presenting the twelve essays collected here is accordingly to initiate a debate about the new materialism while on the one hand, leaving its future possibilities relatively open and on the other, eliciting key themes and orientations that we judge to be bringing structure and velocity to current arguments. It has been our ambition here to contribute to a broad-ranging discussion that is emerging about the nature of our materially and discursively fast-changing world by bringing together a number of leading scholars who are engaging critically with it. In introducing their work our more specific aims are to explain the reasons for a widespread sense that rejuvenating materialism is necessary, to outline and contextualize some of the principal questions and modes of thinking that are emerging in response, and to make clear our own commitment to a renewed materialism in social and political analysis.

The Context of the New Materialism

In advocating a new materialism we are inspired by a number of developments that call for a novel understanding of and a renewed emphasis on materiality. Of great significance here are, firstly, twentieth-century advances in the natural sciences. The great materialist philosophies of the nineteenth century, notably those of Marx, Nietzsche, and Freud, were themselves hugely influenced by developments in the natural sciences, yet the new physics and biology make it impossible to understand matter any longer in ways that were inspired by classical science. While Newtonian mechanics was especially important for these older materialisms, for postclassical physics matter has become considerably more elusive (one might even say more immaterial) and complex, suggesting that the ways we understand and interact with nature are in need of a commensurate updating. While we recognize that there can be no simple passage from natural to social science theories or from science to ethics, developments in the former do become disseminated among educated publics; they inform expert witnesses who contribute to relevant policy making, and they gradually transform the popular imaginary about our material world and its possibilities. As Stephen White points out, ontology involves not simply the abstract study of the nature of being but also the underlying beliefs about existence that shape our everyday relationships to ourselves, to others, and to the world: "Ontological commitments in this sense are thus entangled with questions of identity and history, with how we articulate the meaning of our lives, both individually and collectively."[1] From this point of view, thinking anew about the fundamental structure of matter has far-reaching normative and existential implications.

A second and urgent reason for turning to materialism is the emergence of pressing ethical and political concerns that accompany the scientific and technological advances predicated on new scientific models of matter and, in particular, of living matter. As critically engaged theorists, we find ourselves compelled to explore the significance of complex issues such as climate change or global capital and population flows, the biotechnological engineering of genetically modified organisms, or the saturation of our intimate and physical lives by digital, wireless, and virtual technologies. From our understanding of the boundary between life and death and our everyday work practices to the way we feed ourselves and recreate or procreate, we are finding our environment materially and conceptually reconstituted in ways that pose profound and unprecedented normative questions. In addressing them, we unavoidably find ourselves having to think in new ways about the nature of matter and the matter of nature; about the elements of life, the resilience of the planet, and the distinctiveness of the human. These questions are immensely important not only because they cast doubt on some of modernity's most cherished beliefs about the fundamental nature of existence and social justice but also because presumptions about agency and causation implicit in prevailing paradigms have structured our modern sense of the domains and dimensions of the ethical and the political as such. Recent developments thus call upon us to reorient ourselves profoundly in relation to the world, to one another, and to ourselves.

In terms of theory itself, finally, we are summoning a new materialism in response to a sense that the radicalism of the dominant discourses which have flourished under the cultural turn is now more or less exhausted. We share the feeling current among many researchers that the dominant constructivist orientation to social analysis is inadequate for thinking about matter, materiality, and politics in ways that do justice to the contemporary context of biopolitics and global political economy. While we recognize that radical constructivism has contributed considerable insight into the workings of power over recent years, we are also aware that an allergy to "the real" that is characteristic of its more linguistic or discursive forms — whereby overtures to material reality are dismissed as an insidious foundationalism — has had the consequence of dissuading critical inquirers from the more empirical kinds of investigation that material processes and structures require. While by no means are all the essays in this volume hostile to constructivism, and new materialists countenance no simple return to empiricism or positivism, we share the view current among many critics that our contemporary context demands a theoretical rapprochement with material realism.

Congruent with these imperatives for readdressing materiality, we discern three interrelated but distinctive themes or directions in new materialist scholarship, and we use these to organize the rest of our discussion here. We do so in the hope of setting a framework for ensuing debate, although we are aware that our three themes are somewhat unevenly represented in the essays that follow. First among them is an ontological reorientation that is resonant with, and to some extent informed by, developments in natural science: an orientation that is posthumanist in the sense that it conceives of matter itself as lively or as exhibiting agency. The second theme entails consideration of a raft of biopolitical and bioethical issues concerning the status of life and of the human. Third, new materialist scholarship testifies to a critical and nondogmatic reengagement with political economy, where the nature of, and relationship between, the material details of everyday life and broader geopolitical and socioeconomic structures is being explored afresh. An important characteristic shared by all three components is their emphasis on materialization as a complex, pluralistic, relatively open process and their insistence that humans, including theorists themselves, be recognized as thoroughly immersed within materiality's productive contingencies. In distinction from some recent examples of constructivism, new materialists emphasize the productivity and resilience of matter. Their wager is to give materiality its due, alert to the myriad ways in which matter is both self-constituting and invested with — and reconfigured by — intersubjective interventions that have their own quotient of materiality.

Towards a New Ontology: Matter, Agency, and Posthumanism

At first glance it seems hard to imagine how we might think about matter differently since its brute "thereness" seems so self-evident and unassailable. It seems literally to provide the solid foundation of existence and to offer itself to an unambiguous ontology. Yet exposing such commonsense and philosophical beliefs as contingent assumptions is a precondition for thinking materiality in new ways. Many of our ideas about materiality in fact remain indebted to Descartes, who defined matter in the seventeenth century as corporeal substance constituted of length, breadth, and thickness; as extended, uniform, and inert. This provided the basis for modern ideas of nature as quantifiable and measurable and hence for Euclidian geometry and Newtonian physics. According to this model, material objects are identifiably discrete; they move only upon an encounter with an external force or agent, and they do so according to a linear logic of cause and effect. It seems intuitively congruent with what common sense tells us is the "real" material world of solid, bounded objects that occupy space and whose movements or behaviors are predictable, controllable, and replicable because they obey fundamental and invariable laws of motion.

The corollary of this calculable natural world was not, as one might have expected, a determinism that renders human agency an illusion but a sense of mastery bequeathed to the thinking subject: the *cogito* (I think) that Descartes identified as ontologically other than matter. In distinction from the passivity of matter, modern philosophy has variously portrayed humans as rational, self-aware, free, and self-moving agents. Such subjects are not only deemed capable of making sense of nature by measuring and classifying it from a distance but are also aided in such a quest by theories whose application enables them to manipulate and reconfigure matter on an unprecedented scale. The Cartesian-Newtonian understanding of matter thereby yields a conceptual and practical domination of nature as well as a specifically modern attitude or ethos of subjectivist potency.

It has been important briefly to sketch this modern account of matter because in many ways new materialists define their materialism as an alternative to it. As mentioned already, we discern as an overriding characteristic of the new materialists their insistence on describing active processes of materialization of which embodied humans are an integral part, rather than the monotonous repetitions of dead matter from which human subjects are apart. It is important for us to make this difference clear because a further trait of much of the new materialism is its antipathy toward oppositional ways of thinking. As such, its exponents generally decline to locate themselves explicitly through critiques of ontological dualism such as one finds in Cartesianism: they prefer a creative affirmation of a new ontology, a project that is in turn consistent with the productive, inventive capacities they ascribe to materiality itself. The prevailing ethos of new materialist ontology is consequently more positive and constructive than critical or negative: it sees its task as creating new concepts and images of nature that affirm matter's immanent vitality. Such thinking is accordingly post- rather than anti-Cartesian. It avoids dualism or dialectical reconciliation by espousing a monological account of emergent, generative material being. It draws inspiration from exploring alternative ontologies, such as that of Spinoza, whose work emerged more or less contemporaneously with Cartesianism in early modernity yet which until recently enjoyed a far more subterranean or subjugated existence.[2] This new materialist ontology is evident in a number of the essays that follow.

Descartes → post-cartesian → vitalism

Given the lively immanence of matter associated with new material-isms, it is unsurprising that they should be emerging contemporaneously with a new vitalism.[3] Gilles Deleuze, whose work has been influential in much of the new ontology, did not count himself a materialist despite his radical empiricism and some evocative descriptions of materialization. But he was emphatic that everything he wrote "is vitalist, at least I hope it is."[4] Hostilities between these respective approaches have traditionally been staged as an opposition between mechanistic and vitalist understand-ings of (dead versus lively) matter. Typically, they were resolved by distin-guishing between the sort of mechanical, inorganic matter described by physicists and the evolving organic systems described by biologists. But new materialists are attracted to forms of vitalism that refuse this latter distinction. They often discern emergent, generative powers (or agentic capacities) even within inorganic matter, and they generally eschew the distinction between organic and inorganic, or animate and inanimate, at the ontological level. Jane Bennett has provocatively labeled this an "en-chanted materialism," ascribing agency to inorganic phenomena such as the electricity grid, food, and trash, all of which enjoy a certain efficacy that defies human will.[5]

Even natural science, whose influence on some of these new accounts of matter is far from nugatory, now envisages a considerably more indetermi-nate and complex choreography of matter than early modern technology and practice allowed, thus reinforcing new materialist views that the whole edifice of modern ontology regarding notions of change, causality, agency, time, and space needs rethinking. Perhaps most significant here is the way new materialist ontologies are abandoning the terminology of matter as an inert substance subject to predictable causal forces. According to the new materialisms, if everything is material inasmuch as it is composed of physicochemical processes, nothing is reducible to such processes, at least as conventionally understood. For materiality is always something more than "mere" matter: an excess, force, vitality, relationality, or difference that renders matter active, self-creative, productive, unpredictable. In sum, new materialists are rediscovering a materiality that materializes, evincing immanent modes of self-transformation that compel us to think of causation in far more complex terms; to recognize that phenomena are caught in a multitude of interlocking systems and forces and to consider anew the location and nature of capacities for agency.

Conceiving matter as possessing its own modes of self-transformation, self-organization, and directedness, and thus no longer as simply passive or inert, disturbs the conventional sense that agents are exclusively humans who possess the cognitive abilities, intentionality, and freedom to make autonomous decisions and the corollary presumption that humans have the right or ability to master nature. Instead, the human species is being relocated within a natural environment whose material forces themselves manifest certain agentic capacities and in which the domain of unintended or unanticipated effects is considerably broadened. Matter is no longer imagined here as a massive, opaque plenitude but is recognized instead as indeterminate, constantly forming and reforming in unexpected ways. One could conclude, accordingly, that "matter becomes" rather than that "matter is." It is in these choreographies of becoming that we find cosmic forces assembling and disintegrating to forge more or less enduring patterns that may provisionally exhibit internally coherent, efficacious organization: objects forming and emerging within relational fields, bodies composing their natural environment in ways that are corporeally meaningful for them, and subjectivities being constituted as open series of capacities or potencies that emerge hazardously and ambiguously within a multitude of organic and social processes. In this monolithic but multiply tiered ontology, there is no definitive break between sentient and nonsentient entities or between material and spiritual phenomena.

So far we have emphasized the extent to which new materialist ontologies are rejecting the presuppositions that underpin modern philosophy and the classical sciences that have been its ontological conjugate. But we also want to draw attention to ways in which the natural sciences have themselves been problematizing the notion of matter and thus undermining classical ontologies while inspiring the sort of radical reconceptions of matter we associate with new materialisms. In order to explain such developments, we need to undertake a brief excursus through modern physics. What we want to emphasize here is the way matter as such has become both less conceptually important and more ontologically negligible, while at the same time its very possibility of being has become more elusive.

When Newton laid the foundations of modern physics in the seventeenth century, he realized that one of the most important properties of a material object is its mass. While for laypersons mass is generally envisaged as equivalent to size or weight, for Newton it was the property of an object or body that makes it difficult to accelerate (its inertia). What sets an object in motion, he concluded, are forces of attraction and repulsion that act upon it. Broadly speaking, it would be the task of classical (mechanical) physics to examine the interactive relationships between bodies and the forces that act upon them. Although physics began with ordinary objects, it developed as a science of forces and movements that are less obviously material yet from which matter is inseparable. According to this mechanical model, when a force moves something, it performs work, and the ability of a system to perform work is measured as energy. Einstein's theory of relativity would show that mass and energy can be converted into one another and are in this sense equivalent: a theory that further subverted the idea that solid matter persists as such.

In 1905 Einstein also produced the first persuasive argument for the existence of atoms (although there were atomists even among the pre-Socratics); gross matter itself now became a more negligible component of the cosmos. For the microscopic atom consists of a positively charged nucleus surrounded by a cloudlike, three-dimensional wave of spinning electrons.[6] And if most of the atom's mass resides in its nucleus, this is itself but a tiny percentage of the atom's volume. The atom is a smeared field of distributed charge whose subatomic particles are less like planets in solar orbit than they are like flashes of charge that emerge from and dissipate in the empty space from which they are composed. Even when vast numbers of atoms are assembled in the kind of macrostructures we experience in the "condensed matter" of the perceptible world, their subatomic behavior consists in the constant emergence, attraction, repulsion, fluctuation, and shifting of nodes of charge: which is to say that they demonstrate none of the comforting stability or solidity we take for granted. While this does not of course mean that the objective world we inhabit is mere illusion, it does suggest that even — or especially — the most ardent realist must concede that the empirical realm we stumble around in does not capture the truth or essence of matter in any ultimate sense and that matter is thus amenable to some new conceptions that differ from those upon which we habitually rely.

On entering the realm of subatomic particles one finds an even more quixotic and elusive sense of matter. In little more than a century, well over one hundred subatomic particles have been discovered (or, as radical constructivists might argue, invented), yet this quantum realm seems scarcely less strange than that of medieval theology. For instance, here matter is described as being composed of two kinds of particle, quarks and leptons, which together compose fermions. In the Standard Model, quarks are the building blocks of the universe, although they are not really distinct or discrete quantifiable "units" because the states that constitute them as "particles" are variable, a variability that produces the electrical charge of which they are composed.[7] When quarks interact inside a proton, it is the massless "gluon" that is credited with holding them together. But while there is no accepted theory about why particles exist in the way that they do or how their characteristics might be rendered more predictable for the purposes of instrumentalization, there is agreement that any account of matter also requires an inference of short-lived virtual particles that flash in and out of existence, clustering around the more enduring particles whose properties they alter. Interestingly, what causes mass remains something of a mystery: a type of particle called a Higgs boson is hypothesized as having the capacity to make space "sticky" in a manner that we experience as mass. A popular science book lyrically declares that the "material world is fashioned from frozen matter."[8] However, the "freezing" mechanism remains an enigma. In sum, "particles" are more like vibrating strands of energy, strings that oscillate in eleven dimensions, than like small versions of the sand grains suggested by their name. In any case, physicists infer that most of the universe is composed of the so-called "dark matter" that is needed to explain the gravitational pull manifest in the galaxy, and they claim that only some 10 to 15 percent of the theoretically required material is visible. Indeed, recent astronomical research suggests that as little as 3 or 4 percent of the universe may be composed of ordinary matter, while something called "dark energy" or "quintessence" is invoked to explain an expanding universe.[9]

The point of this synopsis for new materialisms is to show that theoretical physics' understanding of matter is now a long way from the material world we inhabit in our everyday lives and that it is no longer tenable to rely on the obsolete certainties of classical physics as earlier materialists did. Granted, one can still discern in physics' terminology of fundamental forces and elementary particles the holy grail of discovering the fundamental constituents of matter. But forces, charges, waves, virtual particles, and empty space suggest an ontology that is very different from the substantialist Cartesian or mechanistic Newtonian accounts of matter. And while scientific theories cannot simply be imported into philosophy, the tropes and rhythms they suggest can transform theoretical discourses. In fact, it is evident from new materialist writing that forces, energies, and intensities (rather than substances) and complex, even random, processes (rather than simple, predictable states) have become the new currency. Given the influence of classical science on the foundations of modern political thought, it is germane for new materialists to ask how these new conceptions of matter might reconfigure our models of society and the political. Furthermore, the practical applications of the new physics, such as the ones scientists anticipate in nanotechnology or quantum computing, may soon have significant material effects upon our bodies and our working or recreational environments.

While particle physics has radically changed our sense of the composition of matter, other currents within physics, notably chaos and complexity theory, are also transforming our sense of the patterns or characteristics of matter's movements.[10] They, too, are undermining the idea of stable and predictable material substance, hastening a realization that our natural environment is far more complex, unstable, fragile, and interactive than earlier models allowed. Complexity theory is playing an increasingly significant role in understanding sociomaterial processes, too, because it appreciates their inextricability from a wider natural environment.

During the 1970s scientists turned their attention to nonlinear dynamic systems that seem structured yet unpredictable and which mainstream physics had tended to ignore because they are inexplicable in mechanistic terms. As James Gleick remarks of chaos theory, "fractals and bifurcations, intermittencies and periodicities . . . are the new elements of motion, just as, in traditional physics, quarks and gluons are the new elements of matter. To some physicists chaos is a science of process rather than state; of becoming rather than being."[11] While for chaos theory apparently random effects have an extremely complex, nonlinear provenance, for complexity theory the emphasis is on unpredictable events that can catapult systems into novel configurations. For both, the physical world is a mercurial stabilization of dynamic processes. Rather than tending toward inertia or a state of equilibrium, matter is recognized here as exhibiting immanently self-organizing properties subtended by an intricate filigree of relationships.[12] Tumbleweeds, animal species, the planetary ecosystem, global weather patterns, but also new social movements, health and crime, and economics are all amenable to the kind of explanation developed by complexity theorists.[13] Such phenomena are now understood as emergent systems that move with a superficially chaotic randomness that is underlain by patterns of complex organization, which in turn function as foci for further organization and development. Such systems are marked by considerable instability and volatility since their repetition is never perfect; there is a continuous redefining and reassembling of key elements that results in systems' capacities to evolve into new and unexpected forms. Their logic of proliferation is again resonant with new materialist senses of contingent, immanent self-transformation.

If such patterns of organization are not predictable or determinable, this is in part because there is no longer a quantitative relationship between cause and effect. For any emergent material configuration, infinitesimally small causes can transform successive conditions for interaction among elements such that they end up having massive but unanticipated effects.[14] What is famously known as "the butterfly effect" in weather patterns, for example, refers to the possibility that a slight disturbance of air precipitated by a flapping of diaphanous wings could set off a succession of complex meteorological and atmospheric changes that trigger a hurricane in another hemisphere. In such cases it is not, as John Urry explains, that "the sum is greater than the parts — but that there are system effects that are different from their parts. [The] components of a system through their interaction 'spontaneously' develop collective properties or patterns. . . . These are non-linear consequences that are non-reducible to the very many individual components that comprise such activities."[15] Because innumerable interactions between manifold elements that produce patterns of organization successively *transform* those elements, it is impossible either to predict outcomes in advance or to repeat an event.[16] Since, moreover, determination within dynamic systems is nonlinear, terminal effects cannot be construed as possibilities that were already latent in some initial moment.[17] Again, one can discern in such material productivity a posthumanist sense of material agency and a limitation of humans' agentic efficacy.

In outlining elements of a new materialist ontology in this section we have drawn attention to the vibrant, constitutive, aleatory, and even immaterial indices that characterize the new senses of materiality and materialization evident in current scientific and philosophical thinking. At this level we have alluded to indirect implications that we believe such dynamic ways of conceptualizing matter have for our most basic ideas about humanity and agency and thus for politics and society. We believe there is much work for politically minded materialists to do here. In considering a second direction of the new materialism in the next section, we examine more directly some of the already urgent political and ethical challenges presented by recent developments in the natural sciences and their application. Our attention shifts here from the physical to the biological sciences of matter.

Bioethics and Biopolitics

There is something unprecedented about our contemporary situation in which the prefix "bio-" proliferates. Molecular biology and its cognates are achieving the sort of privileged status previously reserved for theoretical physics, fuelled by a revolution in biomedicine and biotechnology. This is in turn propelling an unprecedented range of issues concerning the nature and status of living matter onto the agenda of critical thinkers and defining what we see as a second major strand of a *new* materialism. While there are many relevant initiatives developing here, we draw attention to four in particular. These are the spillover effects and applications of complexity theory, a new focus on the body and its role in politics, a number of bioethical controversies that again touch on some fundamental questions about the distinctiveness of the human and of moral agency, and biopolitical concerns regarding new possibilities for and configurations of biopower that are also shifting perspectives on and definitions of politics.

In the previous section we considered the importance of complexity theory for new ways of understanding dynamic physical systems. We now draw attention to some of the broader ways this approach is affecting the treatment of biological organisms and their relationship to other aspects of their material environment. In the life sciences as well as in physics, material phenomena are increasingly being conceptualized not as discrete entities or closed systems but rather as open, complex systems with porous boundaries.[18] Such theories challenge earlier distinctions between physical and biological systems, drawing attention to their interaction and transforming the way scientists think of biological matter and its imbrication in the social. Whether we are talking about unforeseen mutations, trajectories of illness or distress, patterns of global climate change, or the vagaries of the international economy, the open systems or ecological perspective provokes us to consider (and find better ways to think about) the interactions between socioeconomic and environmental conditions and biological and physiological or physical processes.[19] As with postclassical physics, the new biology facilitates new ways of thinking about matter and its effects on our visceral-social economy; these in turn pose significant challenges for our modern conceptions of moral and political agency.

Approaches to global warming offer one example of such thinking as well as exemplifying a new emphasis on the material dimensions of social existence. As instances of the deleterious effects of rapid climate change mount, there is increasing attention to the way seemingly insignificant daily activities work synergistically to produce effects that devastate the global environment. The enormous macroscopic impact of myriad mundane individual actions provokes critical, political, and legal reflection not only upon the nature of causation but also upon the nature of the responsibilities that individuals and governments have for the health of the planet. The unequal effects of occurrences such as rising sea levels and drought associated with climate change also pose serious questions for advocates of social justice, especially in light of the mismatch between actions, intentions, and consequences. Questions regarding the definition, the ethical value, and the moral and political culpability of the human, the nonhuman, and the virtually human become especially vexed as concerns about environmental degradation and dwindling natural resources acquire an urgency unimaginable just a generation ago. Such questions not only prompt reflection upon who or what should be taken as the subjects and objects of ethical, legal, or political action; they also suggest a need for new ways of theorizing risk and accountability as humans meddle more vigorously in natural processes and thus become more materially, if not yet ethically, responsible for outcomes.[20]

A rather different example of the blurring of clear boundaries or distinctions between bodies, objects, and contexts is evident in the myriad biotechnological and digital technological developments that are changing the landscape of the living. Genetically modified organisms now feed much of the world and fuel its vehicles; they seem destined to change forms of agricultural production and energy use irrevocably. Wondrous medical and digital prostheses, too, now enable, enhance, and enrich our physical and social lives in many ways. Whether it is pacing the heartbeat, dispensing medication, catching the news on a podcast, elaborating an internet-based community, finding directions via the web or GPS, or sending family love via wireless communications, digital technologies have become a part of our lives and of who we are. It is not merely the case that more people are becoming something akin to Donna Haraway's cyborg (a fusion of human and technology).[21] More radically, as N. Katherine Hayles argues, our saturation with networked and programmable media shunts us out of the realm of the human and into the realm of the post-human: "an informational pattern that happens to be instantiated in a biological substrate."[22] Such changes have significant implications for our understanding of the human as a distinctive biological or moral entity.[23]

A further example of the way new materialists are being obliged to recognize the interactions of different orders of matter is evident in genetics. For some geneticists, insight into the porosity of organisms' boundaries has been prompted by the discovery that there is a considerably smaller number of genes in the human genome than was initially anticipated. Before mapping the genome, many had imagined that each gene produces a corresponding protein that is responsible for a specific trait: a distinctly mechanistic conception of the work of genes.[24] The assumption that followed was that once all the genes were known and mapped, humans might be able precisely to predict and control their organic life process. The unexpectedly small number of genes that geneticists actually found compelled them to abandon the explanatory framework of simple genetic determinism and to acknowledge that an organism's particular properties and susceptibilities are produced through complex interactions between genes and a host of other factors such as hormones, neurochemical stimuli, dietary intake, and environmental conditions. This has in turn prompted a reappraisal of organisms as discrete, autonomous units with relatively tidy, bounded causal patterns. It has also provided an incentive to study gene behavior using more complex ideas of "systems-biology," epigenomics, and gene-ecology.[25]

While such conclusions reinforce some of the new physics' challenges to older Cartesian-Newtonian conceptions of matter and to correspondingly Promethean ideas of human mastery over nature, they also suggest that previously separate fields such as those of medical and political science must work together more closely since in such models the body is also understood as an open system and one whose interactions with its environment significantly shape its neurochemical functioning and the trajectory of disease and health. Indicative of such cooperation is the way exponents have used an "open developmental systems approach" to examine the effects of successive social contexts on differential health outcomes over time[26] or to reconsider patterns of social behavior, for example, by pointing to suggestive correlations between the demographics of criminal behavior and the geographic distribution of industrial pollutants. Inasmuch as the aggregated effects of environmental toxins can be shown to have deleterious effects upon judgment and behavior, the implication is that cleaning up the environment or changing diet may be more efficacious than incarcerating disaffected urban youth.[27] Such examples show the important policy-making implications of new ways of understanding the internal dynamics of material processes as well as suggest how social stratifications such as class affect and cycle through apparently natural processes.

Biotechnological developments may also have more indirect political repercussions whose complex unfolding it is difficult to predict or control. At issue here is the complex interrelationships between open systems that enable events in one "ecodomain" to precipitate events in another. For instance, petroleum is not only a pillar of the global economy but also, and consequently, a central feature of current foreign policy and international relations. Accordingly, recent efforts to create synthetic bacteria that might produce biofuel could generate considerable macrolevel effects: to end dependence on fossil fuels might not only catapult a different configuration of economies to international prominence, but such a shift in the balance of economic powers might also transform the imperatives that guide international diplomacy and foreign relations, shift the direction of capital flows, and reconfigure the topography of economic migration.

Insofar as politics is understood as an ongoing process of negotiating power relations (a perspective, we suggest, that is particularly congruent with materialism) rather than as a merely formal constitutional, institutional, or normative edifice, political analysts cannot afford to ignore the way biotechnological developments and their corporate owners are implicated in the entire geopolitical system. Clearly, too, developments in biomedicine and biotechnology prompt renewed reflection on the relationship between science and politics. If, for example, biotechnological developments have potentially far-reaching political, economic, and ethical implications, is there not a need for more public, political dialogue about the goals, uses, and ownership of research? Yet if science is brought explicitly into a public forum, what kinds of arguments are to be accorded merit: those informed by secular science, or economic interest, or religious faith?[28]

We have noted that complexity theories and developing technologies are rendering bodies less discrete qua organic entities distinct from physical, environmental, or technologically refabricated matter. As a consequence, when researchers use complexity theories in their consideration of biomatter, they are very quickly led to incorporate into their analyses a host of ethical and political issues. However, a second aspect of the new biomaterialism that we wish to draw attention to is an increasing acknowledgment within theories of politics — and especially in theories of democracy and citizenship — of the role played by the body as a visceral protagonist within political encounters. We suggest not only that this emphasis on bodily processes and corporeal capacities is a notable element within some of the new materialisms but also that it is indispensable to any adequate appreciation of democratic processes.

For new materialists, no adequate political theory can ignore the importance of bodies in situating empirical actors within a material environment of nature, other bodies, and the socioeconomic structures that dictate where and how they find sustenance, satisfy their desires, or obtain the resources necessary for participating in political life. This is in fact something that feminists and class theorists have often insisted upon, and we would add in this context only our concern that such material dimensions have recently been marginalized by fashionable constructivist approaches and identity politics. Of course, the latter have had a good deal to say about the body and its imbrication in relationships of power, but we are not convinced that they pay sufficient attention to the material efficacy of bodies or have the theoretical resources to do so. From this perspective we draw attention to a new materialist predilection for a more phenomenological approach to embodiment. In addition to focusing on the way power constitutes and is reproduced by bodies, phenomenological studies emphasize the active, self-transformative, practical aspects of corporeality as it participates in relationships of power. They find bodies exhibiting agentic capacities in the way they structure or stylize their perceptual milieu, where they discover, organize, and respond to patterns that are corporeally significant. Such theories thus introduce elements of creative contingency, meaning, difference, efficacy, and a limited freedom for improvisation or resistance into nature before cognition begins. In other words, they complement ontologies of immanently productive matter by describing how living matter structures natural and social worlds before (and while) they are encountered by rational actors. Again, they give materiality its due.

This emphasis on corporeality further dislocates agency as the property of a discrete, self-knowing subject inasmuch as the corpus is now recognized as exhibiting capacities that have significant effects on social and political situations. Thus bodies communicate with other bodies through their gestures and conduct to arouse visceral responses and prompt forms of judgment that do not necessarily pass through conscious awareness. They are significant players in games of power whenever face-to-face encounters are involved, such as in deliberative models of democracy. Paying attention to corporeality as a practical and efficacious series of emergent capacities thus reveals both the materiality of agency and agentic properties inherent in nature itself.[29] Both have important implications for the way we understand political processes.

In this emphasis on corporeality, we also glimpse one of the most distinctive characteristics of the new materialist ontologies: their avowed posthumanism. They displace what Giorgio Agamben calls "the anthropological machine of humanism."[30] While new materialists' conceptualization of materialization is not anthropocentric, it does not even privilege human bodies. There is increasing agreement here that all bodies, including those of animals (and perhaps certain machines, too), evince certain capacities for agency. As a consequence, the human species, and the qualities of self-reflection, self-awareness, and rationality traditionally used to distinguish it from the rest of nature, may now seem little more than contingent and provisional forms or processes within a broader evolutionary or cosmic productivity. If human perfection or redemption is no longer understood as the destiny of history, neither is it the goal of evolution. While it does not follow that cognitive capacities for symbolism or reflexivity are no longer valued, the new materialism does prompt a way of reconsidering them as diffuse, chance products of a self-generative nature from which they never entirely emerge. It further invites acknowledgment that these capacities are manifest in varying degrees across different species of being, that they are indelibly material in their provenance, that human intelligence emerges within a spectrum of vital materializations, and that rights — for example in the case of animals — can no longer automatically be understood solely as human rights.[31] From this perspective, the difference between humans and animals, or even between sentient and nonsentient matter, is a question of degree more than of kind. Recalling the earlier quote by Stephen White, it is clear both that thinking in these new ways will have a significant impact on our normative assumptions and that normative theory itself needs to become more engaged with the changing material context in which it considers concepts such as social justice.

The third biodimension we recognize as a vital element of the new materialism concerns a range of specifically bioethical challenges that arise from the way living matter and its definitions are being materially and discursively transformed. At a practical level, biosciences and biotechnologies yield gene therapies, microsurgeries, assisted reproductive technologies, life-saving prosthetic devices, and pharmaceutical mood and behavioral adjusters, as well as cloning, genetically modified crops, and gene hybridization. All such biotechnological developments purport to enhance, extend, or give us control over the hidden depths and minutiae of life, and in this sense they contribute only to a modern will to dominate nature. Yet their negative externalities and their inability to control the forces they unleash are also apparent, opening up a minefield of ambiguous ethical and political possibilities (such as biodisasters and bioterrorism). As both promises and threats, such developments summon new materialists to confront pressing bioethical and biopolitical questions about the nature of responsibility and property ownership, the relationship of humans to the world, the very definition of the human in relation to the nonhuman, and the way shifting definitions of nature and life affect subjective experiences of selfhood or the forms and domains of politico-juridical regulation. For as Nikolas Rose points out, while biotechnologies bring new tools and procedures for classifying, measuring, monitoring, and modifying biological stuff — genes, carbohydrates, amino acids, cholesterols, cell structure, facial profiles, heart rates, and so forth — within our daily routines, so individuals' experiences of themselves as subjects and agents of their own lives are also transformed.[32] This, too, raises significant questions regarding the distribution of material resources and of access to new biotechnologies that literally promise more life, in terms of longer, healthier life spans, to the privileged.[33]

At the same time, it is becoming evident that changes in living matter are rendering obsolete many of the conventional ethical categories used to evaluate them. As scientists succeed in bridging species, artificially creating and extending human and animal life, and manipulating and synthesizing genes to create new life forms, they muddle the concepts and boundaries that are the ground for much ethical and political thinking. Smart synthetic life forms, for example, challenge our very conception of ourselves as persons since distinctions between intelligent and unintelligent life have been crucial in efforts to distinguish humans from other animals and to justify humans' instrumental appropriation of material resources.[34] If scientists have the capacity to create life from matter, and if such life forms can take the form of intelligent agents able to carry out specific tasks, then previously essential distinctions are rendered less viable, and the norms that depend upon them become less intelligible. This raises questions pertaining to life forms themselves. What kind of ethical value should we attribute to synthetic life forms and according to what criteria? If synthetic life forms act in unexpected and unacceptable ways, we need to consider who is, should, and can be held responsible. In this domain, science fiction may well be ahead of mainstream ethics.[35]

The final aspect of new biomaterialist inquiry that we see as important concerns the emergent modes of biopower afforded by biotechnological developments. To be sure, some of these questions center on the ownership of the new patents and the considerable power accumulated by global corporations which have no accountability to the world's population beyond their own shareholders but which are acquiring extensive control over the food, water, and energy that are the very condition of human survival. This is one reason why in the next section, we advocate renewed attention to international political economy. But our particular interest here is to identify the importance for new materialists of the unprecedented micropowers that biotechnology is engendering. As Rose warns, theorists need to be alert to the ways in which the culture and norms of the contemporary biopolitical context provide opportunities for controlling groups and individuals in new ways. Readers of Foucault, such as Rose, are well aware of the biopolitical interest the modern state has taken in managing the life, health, and death of its populations since the eighteenth century. The state's management of fertility rates, marriage and funeral rites, epidemics, food hygiene, and the nation's health is not new or even necessarily malign. But there has until recently been a dearth of attention paid to this material aspect of power that justifies incursions into the most intimate habits of daily existence and thus warrants critical investigation. Similarly, while the bevy of new biotechnological capacities, as well as movements to ameliorate environmental degradation, are to be welcomed in many ways, the tools, practices, policies, and regulations they occasion must also be considered critically in terms of their capacity to facilitate and encourage more intensive interventions in the everyday minutiae of our material lives. For even as we might welcome a broad transformation in lifestyle according to an ecoethos, the norms, incentives, and identities people adopt inevitably become part of new disciplinary formations whose contours need to be specified and traced.

Biotechnological developments also raise specifically political questions about what life is and how far it can or must fall under state control. According to Agamben, contemporary history has witnessed the "growing inclusion of man's natural life in the mechanisms and calculations of power."[36] As we see in debates about fetal rights, abortion, stem cell research, and euthanasia: medical, scientific, or religious accounts of the boundary between life and death are currently becoming further enmeshed with issues surrounding sovereignty because increasingly the state must legislate on matters that were formerly left to God or nature. Seemingly technical questions about biological life processes enter the political order because the state must frequently make decisions about the worthiness of different lives. Assisted suicide, for example, demonstrates how the very definitions of life and death are thrown into the political arena once decisions about survival rely on medical expertise.[37] Agamben himself explains how the condition called *coma dépassé* (a state in which vital functions cease but life-support machines maintain the comatose, artificially surviving body in a limbo between life and death) has obliged legislators to redefine death by shifting the final border of life. In the face of this "bare life" that is sustained and controlled by human technologies, nature is no longer a reliable guide to the difference between life and death. Instead, the distinction becomes a scientific, medical, and ethicopolitical question.[38]

The current interest among social scientists and policymakers in demography similarly demonstrates how scientific innovations and their widespread social uptake in areas of formerly unregulated natural processes — notably reproductive technologies facilitating the reliable management of fertility and medical advances extending life expectancy — may have unexpected but extensive macrolevel consequences to which political actors are increasingly obliged to respond. Aging and even declining populations pose significant political and economic challenges for the welfare state, as well as potentially engendering widespread structural shifts in the balance of global power as developed and developing regions exhibit differential demographic momentums that affect the relative sizes of workforces and armies, ethnic groups and electoral age profiles, and ecological footprints.[39] The sheer materiality and mass of bodies — their numbers, their needs, their fecundity, their productivity, their sustainability and so on — is becoming a key dimension of political analysis and intervention.

In this section we have sketched a number of directions that we discern within new biomaterialist thinking and whose importance for ethico-political inquiry we are especially eager to foreground. Our main argument here has been that new ways of thinking about living matter are radically and rapidly reconfiguring our material world — both empirically and conceptually — not only transforming our most basic conceptions of life and the human but also intervening in the very building blocks of life and altering the environment in which the human species — among others — persists. While these reconfigurations pose huge ethical and political questions with which many new materialists are engaging, we are also aware that from a materialist perspective normative questions cannot be treated adequately in isolation from a well-informed understanding of new scientific and technological developments or from their material implications and context. In turning now to the third main direction we see a new materialism taking, we emphasize this renewed attention to material context in terms of its economic and political power relations.

Practicing Critical Materialism

The final major trend we identify as a component of renewed materialism is the most explicitly political as well as, sometimes, the most theoretically polemical. It encompasses approaches for which materialism means practical, politically engaged social theory, devoted to the critical analysis of actual conditions of existence and their inherent inequality. This focus orients it toward a methodological realism that is at odds with some more radical, and especially linguistic, forms of constructivism as well as with dominant trends in abstract normative political theory. What we see as new in this aspect of materialism is twofold. First is its practitioners' reinvention of materialism in response to criticisms that radical constructivists and deconstructionists rightly made of earlier critical materialisms and realisms, Marxism in particular; second is this cohort's ongoing invention of new concepts and theoretical frameworks in order to understand the complexities of global capitalism (in its broadest sense) and its diverse, localized effects on everyday lives. Through this creative and sometimes experimental form of materialism, critical social theorists are analyzing current events and developments in a way that is congruent with the pluralist, contingent rhythms of materialization noted within new materialism's other main strands.

There are a number of indications that critical social theory is reorienting toward more realist approaches to political analysis. For example, Axel Honneth complains of "a growing tendency today for social criticism to be practiced as a form that is without a component of sociological explanation."[40] Ian Shapiro calls for a more realist, problem-solving approach to overturn the assumption that ideas or beliefs are elemental and constitutive of reality.[41] Margaret Archer advocates a mode of social realism that "makes our real embodied selves living in the real world really load-bearing."[42] David Harvey warns against the "serious danger" of proceeding as if "material and absolute space did not matter." Harvey concedes that evocations of the proletariat or multitude in motion, or of the effects engendered by postmodern spatial constructions, are illuminating. But he also points out that "no one knows what any of that means until real bodies go into the absolute spaces of the streets." Harvey thus cites approvingly the materialist claim that rights "mean nothing without the ability to concretize them in absolute space and time."[43] From this materialist point of view, it is ideological naïveté to believe that significant social change can be engendered solely by reconstructing subjectivities, discourses, ethics, and identities — that is, without also altering their socioeconomic conditions or tracing crucial aspects of their reproduction to the economic interests they unwittingly serve. Similarly, John Smith and

Chris Jenks observe that paradoxically, "radical constructivisms rest on the over-estimation of *human* construction and authorship." They argue that to claim that something is constructed often has the unintended effect of recentering the human subject as the locus of agency despite the intention to undermine such claims.[44] In other words, a constructivism that presumes matter's passivity or plasticity in the face of power may echo an earlier ontology for which matter is inert stuff awaiting cultural imprint.

Yet what sort of materialism is being retrieved, reinvented, and advocated here? Is it primarily a *methodological* or *epistemological* reorientation toward more realist, sociological analysis? Or is its principal concern a different *focus* that catches more material (and specifically, political-economic) aspects of society and power in its sights? Surely, it is both. For, from a methodological perspective, although a turn to more realist, empirical modes of investigation implies a rejection of the more radical aspects of recent constructivism, it by no means entails any definitive antithesis. In light of critiques leveled at crude empiricism's ignorance of the relationships that subtend facts and at representationalist beliefs that knowledge is a mirror of nature, new materialist realisms can hardly ignore the role of *social* construction. For example, when Peter Berger and Thomas Luckmann published their pathbreaking *The Social Construction of Reality* in 1966, they drew on a phenomenological ("'empirical' but not 'scientific'") approach to everyday life in order to explore how commonsense meaning emerges through intersubjective interaction. Understanding society as emerging through an ongoing dialectic between objective and subjective reality, they had no qualms about referring to social reality.[45] Similarly, when Marx developed historical materialism as a critical advance over metaphysical materialism, it was in order to show that things which seem natural and thus unassailable — such as markets, the bourgeois family, the liberal state, or the free, autonomous self — are actually social, historical constructions which are amenable to social change, yet whose collective and systemic logic renders them difficult to recognize and, a fortiori, to transform. Indeed, it is this insight that more recent constructivists have radicalized in order to contest a broader series of constitutive processes inherent in language and discourse. Yet, new materialists stubbornly insist on the generativity and resilience of the material forms with which social actors interact, forms which circumscribe, encourage, and test their discourses. They dwell on the particular salience of economic and state power in shaping, constraining, and constituting life chances and existential opportunities. The challenge for them is thus to track the complex circuits at work whereby discursive and material forms are inextricable yet irreducible and material structures are simultaneously over- and underdetermined.

It is entirely possible, then, to accept social constructionist arguments while also insisting that the material realm is irreducible to culture or discourse and that cultural artifacts are not arbitrary vis-à-vis nature. Even as the most prosaic or carnal lifeworld unfolds within a socially constructed milieu, it does not follow that a) material objects or structures are devoid of efficacy in the way they affect either our moods or well-being, or our concepts and theories, b) matter is without recalcitrance or directedness in its own brutish way, or c) acknowledging nondiscursive material efficacy is equivalent to espousing a metaphysical claim regarding the Real as ultimate truth. For critical materialists, society is simultaneously materially real and socially constructed: our material lives are always culturally mediated, but they are not only cultural. As in new materialist ontologies, the challenge here is to give materiality its due while recognizing its plural dimensions and its complex, contingent modes of appearing.

We now turn to the second aspect of a new critical materialism, where returning to a more materialist mode of social analysis suggests a shift of perspective or focus within social theory. Alongside ethical concerns about subjectivity, normative concerns about social justice, cultural concerns about postmodern diversity, and discursive concerns about the construction of gender or ethnicity, this entails paying attention to the material, historical, and sociological structures of international political economy that lend context as well as practical inertia to identities that entail unequal life chances. It calls for a detailed phenomenology of diverse lives as they are actually lived — often in ways that are at odds with abstract normative theories or official ideologies.

What we have in mind in referring to a critical new materialism is a range of approaches in which interest is currently being rekindled in the wake of poststructuralism and which complement one another in a fairly pragmatic way. They include the Weberian insights of critical theory regarding the bureaucratic state, whose tentacles reach increasingly deeply to control ordinary lives through governance and governmentality, and aspects of Foucauldian genealogy that describe *how* the minutiae of power develop and practically manage embodied subjectivities. They are manifest in a resurgence of interest in sociologies of everyday life, such as those developed by Pierre Bourdieu, Henri Lefebvre, and Michel de Certeau, and in a renewed interest in phenomenologies of ordinary, and particularly corporeal, experience such as those developed by Simone de Beauvoir and Maurice Merleau-Ponty. And they are apparent in new forms of nondogmatic (for example, autonomist) Marxism, too, especially in the turn to critical international political economy and critical geographies of space. In bringing them all under the umbrella of a new materialism, our aim is to discern what they have in common, namely, their interest in the emergent materialities of contemporary coexistence.

Bringing biopolitics, critical geopolitics, and political economy together with genealogies and phenomenologies of everyday life is an especially fertile development in critical materialist analysis. With this eclectic combination of approaches, scholars pay attention to the production and consumption of goods, to the uneven effects of globalization on differently located citizens, to the management, distribution, and legitimization of unequal life chances, and to the operation of power at state and quotidian levels. They examine the way identities are inflected through the circuit of markets and the ways diversity is managed in the reproduction of global capitalism. They explore the differential and often visceral effects of war, violence, climate change, and poverty, and also the relationship between biopolitics, changing demographic patterns, and biocapitalism. In short, the renewal of critical materialism after the cultural turn foregrounds an appreciation for just what it means to exist as a material individual with biological needs for survival yet inhabiting a world of natural and artificial objects, well-honed micropowers of governmentality, and the more anonymous but no less compelling effects of international economic structures.

Characteristic of such efforts is the way they echo elements of the new materialisms we remarked upon earlier: they insist upon the openness, contingency, unevenness, and complexity of materialization as an ongoing process within which social actors and theorists are irremediably immersed. Thus, these "new" critical materialists situate citizens, ideas, and values (as well as theorists themselves) within the fields of material forces and power relations that reproduce and circumscribe their existence and coexistence. They trace the various logics of, and interrelationships between, broad political and economic structures and critically interrogate the complicated causalities that link them to everyday experiences. What is crucial here is detailed, evidence-based knowledge of domestic and international politics and of shifting geopolitical relations. For while there is no question of indulging in economic reductionism or determinism, critical materialists pay close attention to global and regional market economies whose workings have such immense consequences for the survival and opportunities of ordinary but manifestly unequal people.

With these new critical materialisms, the capitalist system is not understood in any narrowly economistic way but rather is treated as a detotalized totality that includes a multitude of interconnected phenomena and processes that sustain its unpredictable proliferation and unexpected crises, as well as its productivity and reproduction. In other words, new critical materialists, including those working with new forms of open Marxism, envisage a dense, inexhaustible field that resists theoretical totalization even as they investigate its complex material structures, trajectories, and reversible causalities. This renewed attention to structures of political economy complements new materialist sensitivities to the resilience of matter in the face of its reconstruction, the agency of nonsubjective structures, the importance of bodily experience, and the myriad interrelated material systems needed to sustain citizens before they can vote or deliberate. That is, the new critical materialisms are congruent with new materialist ontologies inasmuch as they understand materiality in a relational, emergent sense as contingent materialization—a process within which more or less enduring structures and assemblages sediment and congeal, sometimes as a result of their internal inertia but also as a manifestation of the powerful interests invested therein.

Further, these theoretical approaches are consonant with complex systems theory in their recognition that particular effects are the outcome of intricate interlocking systems whose interactions and dynamic processes are variable and, for the most part, unpredictable. Indeed, markets play a significant role in explaining and shaping the outcomes of bio- and ecosystems. For example, as we noted earlier, biotechnological developments that pose significant ethical and political questions also cycle through the market. They facilitate the commodification of body parts or microbes within the bioeconomy, encourage elective health procedures, and promise to reconfigure the carbon-based economy that is central to contemporary capitalism and its distribution of rich and poor nations. The state's biopolitical interests in the nation's health also circle through the food and pharmaceutical industries, while private companies profit from a market in carbon trading and organic food fuelled by ecological anxieties. Whatever passes through these economic circuits is redistributed to the material advantage of some rather than others, while entering into systemic relations that outrun the comprehension or intentions of individual actors. Questions about livable lives are thus as economic as they are ethical and political.

As should already be clear, the renewed critical materialisms are not synonymous with a revival of Marxism. Yet, this legacy does remain important, not least because traditionally Marxism has been the critique of capitalism par excellence. A critical understanding of global capitalism and its multifarious effects remains crucial for contemporary critical materialists, for some of whom a Marxist label has helped to signify their opposition to dominant neoliberal trends. But coming after poststructuralism and its criticisms, no workable version of Marxism can advance a historical metanarrative, aspire to the identification of determining economic laws, valorize an originary, pristine nature, or envisage communism as history's idealized material destiny. As a method that facilitates and orients an ongoing critical analysis of emergent economic and geopolitical structures, revised versions of Marxism accommodate novel approaches and perspectives that help them forge the conceptual and empirical tools needed to gain insight into the intricacies of twenty-first-century global capitalism. In its more authentic modes, a dialectical approach calls, after all, for appropriate theories and concepts to be engendered out of an interrogation of the material conditions of the times, not to be imposed as a rigid formula aiming for accurate representation.

Work by the Regulation School is one example of such a living Marxism construed as ongoing, critical analysis of the material conditions of the times.[46] This is a Marxism that takes seriously the political in political economy and that sees the state, governance, and production as entwined. This view encourages its exponents to incorporate Foucauldian analyses of governmentality, biopolitics, and the role of discourse in maintaining social order, while taking heed of the state's enduring importance for maintaining conditions conducive to capital accumulation. Focusing on regimes of capital accumulation and the regulative structures that help reproduce them, it takes into account the intersectionality of social relations while still recognizing the importance of class. If it examines every-day customs and practices as well as the broader geopolitical developments they sustain or disrupt, this is because it is aware of the complicated, reversible relationships that link micro- and macrolevel processes. It investigates the emergence of new social and economic forms, such as post-Fordism, examines potential sources of rupture immanent to the system and its reproduction, and also remains sensitive to global developments that are uneven, contingent, and pluralist.[47]

From the vantage of the new recessionary phase of capitalism that commenced in 2008, it is abundantly clear just how important is such ongoing analysis and identification of its material elements. For example, if there is a lesson to be learned from recent events associated with sub-prime lending and the consequent banking crisis, it is how few people any longer grasp the complexities of the deregulated financial system, and yet how many are affected, in so many places worldwide and in such imme-diately material ways, by any hiatus in financial markets.[48] Among social theorists it has been fashionable to talk about deterritorialized, dema-terialized capital flows. Yet it is the poverty of individuals induced to take on mortgages they could ill afford that remains the material bottom line underpinning the elaborate but fragile structures of recent financial growth. Spasms in the convoluted flows of capital and futures causes immense and immediate material hardship for real individuals. People lose their life savings, their pensions, their homes, and their jobs; indus-tries are brought to a standstill and national economies to their knees. Indeed, the effects of neoliberal financialization have included the dis-possession of peoples from their land, the privatization of services and commodification of formerly free or communally owned goods, internal migrations into cities without jobs but with burgeoning slums and mass poverty, and external migrations by those seeking better standards of liv-ing far from their indigenous homelands.[49] These are some of the eco-nomic and political conditions sometimes eclipsed in the celebration of pluralistic immigrant cultures: it is surely incumbent on social theorists to study the differential effects of world population growth, the reasons for mass migration, the social and economic backgrounds in which divergent immigrant cultures were nurtured, and the broader effects on global pop-ulation movements of a volatile global economy.

In summary, we have associated new materialism with renewed attention to the dense causes and effects of global political economy and thus with questions of social justice for embodied individuals. We have also noted the affinity between the rhythms of materialization discerned in the socioeconomic processes of global capitalism and those described in the previous sections of our analysis. Commensurate with these dimensions of the new critical materialisms is what we are calling a multimodal methodology, one congruent with the multitiered ontologies, the complex systems, and the stratified reality we have been describing. In particular, we emphasize here the way new materialist analysis traces the complex and reversible causalities that run between different levels of the social system and especially between the microlevel or everyday, and the macrolevel or structural. Indeed, there is currently a surge of interest in everyday life, one that is elaborated through a combination of phenomenological, anthropological, and ethnographic studies on the one hand, and genealogical and sociological studies on the other.[50] Interestingly, some indication of how new materialists might investigate both the quotidian and structural dimensions of late capitalism can already be found in work by Althusser and Foucault. Here we present a few aspects of their ideas that we find salient and provocative for a multimodal materialism.

While Foucault's work has been widely used to study the powerful effects of discursive constructs and to pose posthumanist questions about agency and ethics, what we emphasize here is the concrete material analysis genealogy encourages vis-à-vis the prosaic details of bodily existence. This is the aspect that has often commended itself to feminists eager to investigate the construction of female flesh.[51] Of particular significance is Foucault's insistence that genealogy requires "a knowledge of details": that it documents a discontinuous, "effective history" of the body that is "broken down by rhythms of work, rest, and holidays . . . poisoned by food or values, through eating habits or moral laws"; a body that also "constructs resistances." In its emphasis on "the body, the nervous system, nutrition, digestion and energies,"[52] such an approach takes seriously the material intricacies of existence and the way bodies are constituted as productive but docile matter through disciplining, enhancing, and redirecting their visceral capacities.[53] This in turn opens the way to understanding a more general field or economy of power relations in which bodily capacities are rendered determinate. Foucault describes the kind of micropractices that are at stake in pacifying and reproducing social regimes in order to demonstrate how thoroughly our ordinary, material existence is affected by, and saturated with, power and how protean yet banal many of its tactics remain. While he insists that the development of such powers is not to be explained simply as an effect of, or as functional for, broader structural changes associated with capital, demography, or state building, he does show that these micro- and macromodalities (the everyday and the structural) are mutually interdependent. In other words, he recognizes the multimodal materialist analysis needed to explain the production and reproduction of the modern social order. The matter whose materialization Foucault describes is malleable, socially produced, and inscribed with its histories; paradoxically, it is obliged to acquire (additional, redirected) agentic capacities as an aspect of its subjection.

This attention to material detail and to the plural dimensions and power relations in which such details are to be understood is elaborated in Althusser's essay "Ideology and Ideological State Apparatuses (Notes towards an Investigation)." Althusser's work attracted considerable attention when it first appeared because of the way it developed a materialist alternative to more reductionist or teleological forms of Marxism that rejected its then dominant mechanical and humanist modes. Althusser claims in this particular essay that Marx had envisaged social structure in terms of levels or instances, each with their own "indices of effectivity" and ways of relating to other levels.[54] From this perspective, it is insufficient to regard the state as simply functional for reproducing the social relations of production; one needs to examine its complex, differential elements that are both repressive and ideological in their operations. Similarly, it is necessary to pay attention to "all the direct or indirect forms of exploitation" and to the "subtle everyday domination" whose material details are redolent, we suggest, of Foucault's descriptions in *Discipline and Punish*.

Althusser goes on to distinguish between the Repressive State Apparatus (RSA) and the Ideological State Apparatus (ISA), but he acknowledges that both utilize a mixture of coercive and ideological means: "Very subtle explicit or tacit combinations may be woven" and these need to be "studied in detail" (19f.). Thus parts of the ideological apparatus, such as the church, school, or family, use symbolic modes of discipline that include various forms of punishment, expulsion, or exclusion. And while "the relations of production are first reproduced by the materiality of the processes of production and circulation," ideological relations are also "immediately present in the same processes" (22 n. 12). Habits of working or practices of consuming help to stabilize the system as something that is daily renewed as the familiar, material horizon of ordinary lives and maintained through their routinized performances. As such, the capitalist economy, the juridico-political domain, and the material quotidian are interrelated but not in any fixed or formulaic way. It is these different levels and their shifting interconnections that a multimodal materialist analysis investigates.

Of especial interest here is Althusser's insistence that despite its apparently ideal forms, ideology "has a material existence" (39). "Of course," he adds in a caveat that is crucial for our appropriation of his argument, "the material existence of the ideology in an apparatus and its practices does not have the same modality as the material existence of a paving-stone or a rifle. But, at the risk of being taken for a Neo-Aristotelian, . . . I shall say that [in Marx] matter is discussed in many senses, or that it exists in different modalities, all rooted in the last instance in 'physical' matter" (40). This recognition of different modalities of matter allows Althusser to explain that for the complicit subject, "the ideas of his belief are material in that his ideas are his material actions inserted into material practices governed by material rituals which are themselves defined by the material ideological apparatus from which derive the ideas of the subject" (43). He accordingly draws attention to the way "ideas" are inscribed in actions whose repetitive, ritualized performances are borne by concrete individuals who are thereby practically constituted as compliant or agentic subjects. While such performances are institutionalized in rituals and ceremonies, they also become sedimented at a corporeal level, where they are repeated as habits or taken for granted know-how: lodged in the bodily memory that Bourdieu calls *habitus* or which phenomenologists refer to as a lifeworld. It is indeed this nonreflexive habituality and the way it imbues objects with familiarity that makes artifacts, commodities, and practices seem so natural that they are not questioned. It is in this sense that ideology or power operate most effectively when embedded in the material, practical horizons and institutions of everyday life. Althusser's materialism here is surely exemplified by Foucault's insistence that an analytics of power must focus on its "real and effective practices"; that "we should try to discover how it is that subjects are gradually, progressively, really and materially constituted through a multiplicity of organisms, forces, energies, materials, desires, thoughts, etc. We should try to grasp subjection in its material instances as a constitution of subjects."[55] In conjunction with the broader system dynamics and ecological perspectives mentioned earlier in this essay, such interventions suggest to us a multimodal analysis that is post- rather than (as in Althusser's earlier work) antihumanist.

This last point is elaborated by a final aspect of Althusser's work that we cite here because of its affinity with some of the new materialist ontologies discussed above. It emerges elusively, scattered across a few brief texts (1982–86) that were published posthumously and whose recent publication is only now prompting an engagement with Althusser's later allusions to an aleatory materialism.[56] In these essays, Althusser refers to materialism as the hardest question of all. Aleatory materialism, or a "materialism of the encounter," refers to an underground current in the history of philosophy that he finds running from Epicurus through Spinoza, Marx, and Wittgenstein, to Heidegger and himself. It is distinguished by its nonteleological principles and its consequent ignoring of origins or ends. Instead, it emphasizes emptiness, contingency, and chance. Althusser implies that materialism might itself be no more than a temporarily convenient label and that its aim might be to engender a certain sensitivity — a theoretical practice — rather than to define an ontology as such.

The idea of the encounter alludes to a chance conjuncture of atoms, the event, whose consequence may be the provisional configuring of facts or forms. History emerges here as the continuous transformation of provisional forms by new, indecipherable and unanticipated events, with the corollary lesson that an aleatory intervention may be more efficacious than the patient understanding of trajectories and working through of continuities whose internal logic of development is assumed to endure. In politics, this means that the state is always inscribed with the possibility of its imminent collapse or reconfiguration, where the utter indifference of the people to rule and their unresponsiveness to interpellation by the state apparatus yields the permanent possibility of a revolutionary event capable of halting the political machine. Such events occur in what Althusser calls the void: the space in which the encounter occurs that reconfigures the current conjuncture's elements. However, although the constitution of new phenomena (such as western capitalism) is now viewed as entirely contingent rather than as the destiny of forces maturing in an earlier phase, such phenomena may still have necessary effects and persist for a greater or lesser period of time. While the choreography of the encounter suggests an affinity with chaos theory, Althusser's own approach suggests that he was not equating aleatory materialism with a new set of theoretical, systemic abstractions but with an empirical, concrete analysis of the forms and forces at work. What we would like to emphasize here is that in a multimodal materialist analysis of relationships of power, it is important to recognize their diverse temporalities by examining their more enduring structures and operations as well as their vulnerability to ruptures and transformation—all the while acknowledging that they have no predestined, necessary, or predictable trajectory.

If we have found it useful to cite some of Althusser's and Foucault's more materialist pronouncements in concluding this section, it is not in order to advise fidelity to their theories as such. Rather, it is because we find aspects of their work provocative in suggesting how ordinary material practices might be critically investigated. They encourage us to explore the complex ways in which such familiar practices are effects of more distant power relations that they also help to reproduce. And contra Foucault's insistence on his own nonnormative positivism, what makes such analyses grist for the critical materialist is the recognition that such dense networks of relationships support socioeconomic structures that sustain the privileges and interests of some rather than others, that these advantages are not randomly, much less fairly, distributed, and that understanding how they operate and are maintained is a crucial task for the engaged social theorist, especially one who eschews any lingering faith in the inevitability of either the present or the future.

The New Materialisms: A Collection of Essays

The essays in this volume explore many of the themes and questions we have considered in this introduction. Indeed, in identifying what we have categorized as three principal directions of analysis in the new materialisms, we have been immensely indebted to the way the essays' evocative insights resonate together, sometimes reinforcing but at other times challenging one another. As we had anticipated when we solicited them, the essays are richly diverse both in their understanding of what the new materialisms might be or portend and in the philosophical traditions and conventions they elaborate and contest. Yet collectively, they offer something more than simple diversity. Broadly, the authors concur in their recognition that new materialist ontologies demand a rethinking of, and renewed attention to, the dynamics of materialization. They also share an acknowledgment that such a project demands, as a corollary, a radical reappraisal of the contours of the subject, a reassessment of the possibility and texture of ethics, an examination of new domains of power and unfamiliar frames for imagining justice, and an exploration of the sources, quality, and dimensions of agency. Indeed, as editors, what we have found so striking is that each essay is both profoundly philosophical and also insistently politically engaged: even without our explicit directive, each writer endeavors to link ontological and metaphysical questions with their ethical and political correlates and implications. The essays' convergence on this point binds them into a coherent yet multifaceted constellation.

At the same time, the themes and questions that emerge and reemerge in the essays make it difficult to separate, group, and order them in a definitive way. Drawing on what we learned from the essays as well as our own researches for the project, we decided to divide the text into three sections whose topics — "the force of materiality," "political matters," and "economies of disruption" — rehearse the themes that organize the distinct sections of this introduction: ontology, bioethics/politics, and critical materialisms. Since the authors all engage questions about the forms of subjectivity, power, agency, and ethics opened up by new materialist ontologies, it would have been entirely possible to place most of the essays under any of the rubrics that divide the text. We must acknowledge, then, that there is a respect in which the ordering of the essays is somewhat arbitrary, and we invite readers to reinvent the collection by reading the essays in whichever order commends itself to them. For us, this has meant grouping the essays in a way that allows the discordance and resonance produced by the textual proximity of sources, framings, and focal questions to provoke illuminating reconsiderations and conceptual shifts.

The essays in the first section, "The Force of Materiality," explore the ontologies of the new materialisms, suggesting how we might conceive of matter and materiality outside of the dualism of the material and the ideal. In her comparative study of the vitalist philosophies of Hans Driesch and Henri Bergson, Jane Bennett explores efforts to specify and give a philosophical and scientific language to the liveliness of living matter while also warning of the ways vitalism can be given troubling new life in the political rhetoric of Nazism or the contemporary "culture of life." In tracing Jacques Derrida's and Gilles Deleuze's distinctive projects of figuring materiality outside of the grasping hold of consciousness, Pheng Cheah marks the ways the new materialist ontologies call into radical question some of the foundational concepts in politics. Diana Coole uses Maurice Merleau-Ponty, among other thinkers, to trace the philosophical paths by which phenomenologists have tried to refigure perception and agency by relocating and reimagining the body-in-the-world. Emphasizing and analyzing the impersonal character of both Friedrich Nietzsche's notion of the will to power and Sigmund Freud's account of psychic life, Melissa Orlie explores how we might imagine creativity and freedom from within a new materialist framework.

The essays in the second section, "Political Matters," investigate how the ontological, scientific, and technological dimensions of the new materialisms demand a reformulation of the forms and domains of power, ethics, and politics. Elizabeth Grosz analyzes Henri Bergson's effort to sidestep the "freedom versus determinism" problem that is often posed as an obstacle to political elaborations of new materialist ontologies. She explores the feminist political possibilities in Bergson's contention that freedom is best conceived not as a characteristic of a subject but rather as a characteristic of acts that express the subject. Samantha Frost draws out Thomas Hobbes's materialist analysis of the ways the passions orient subjects in space and time to suggest that fear is a passion through which individuals produce a sense of themselves as autonomous agents. William Connolly weaves together insights about perception and power gathered from Maurice Merleau-Ponty, Michel Foucault, Gilles Deleuze, and contemporary neuroscience to explore how our attachment to the world shapes the texture of political judgment and critique. And finally, situating pain and death in relation to impersonal life processes, Rosi Braidotti reassesses contemporary forms of biopower and sketches the possibility of an affirmative ethics and citizenship.

The essays in the third section, "Economies of Disruption," analyze the relationship between the materiality of the corpus and the materiality of practice, exploring the ways social and economic practices produce and reproduce embodied subjectivity and existential inequalities, as well as the spaces of, and possibilities for, political transformation. Using Alfred Sohn-Rethel, Louis Althusser, and Slavoj Žižek to reexamine historical materialism and its progressivist teleology, Rey Chow considers the potential for terror as well as progress when iterative practices are presented as a model of political agency. Reading Edmund Husserl's phenomenology alongside Karl Marx's historical materialism, Sara Ahmed meditates on the ways the materialization of bodies is bound up with the materialization and objectification of the world(s) in which they live. Sonia Kruks uses Simone de Beauvoir's diagnoses of the infirmities and oppressions of old age to illustrate how the materialisms in existential phenomenology, Marxism, and social constructivism can, in tandem, provide fruitful insights on the genesis, experience, and perpetuation of injustice. Jason Edwards supplements Karl Marx's and Louis Althusser's analyses of the development of capitalism with Henri Lefebvre's studies of the practices of everyday life, in order to propose an expansive and more politically useful conception of the material practices that reproduce global capitalism and structure the geopolitical system.

We conclude by sincerely thanking all our contributors and by reiterating our great pleasure at presenting these essays. We do so in the conviction that, collectively, they set the new materialisms on course to become a significant orientation for social research after the cultural turn. Our hope is that they will not only encourage debate about a new materialist paradigm but also inspire innovative investigations of the fragile, volatile world we inhabit.

Notes

1   White, *Sustaining Affirmation*, 3f.

2   See Israel, *Radical Enlightenment* for a rich elaboration of the history of Spinoza's work. See also Tuck, *Philosophy and Government, 1572–1651* for a historical analysis of the development of Cartesian and non-Cartesian materialist philosophies.

3   See, for example, the special issue of *Theory, Culture and Society*, "Inventive Life: Approaches to the New Vitalism," Mariam Fraser, Sarah Kember, and Celia Lury, eds. Vitalism, the editors contend in their introduction, "matters now" because its attention to "vital processes" assists in current attempts at thinking of process as a mode of being and at introducing "information, knowledge or 'mind' into social and natural entities, making them seem less inert, more process-like: bringing them alive." Fraser, Kember, and Lury, eds., "Inventive Life," 1.

4   Deleuze, *Negotiations*, 143.

 5   Bennett, *The Enchantment of Modern Life*.

 6   Dobson, Grace, and Lovett, *Physics*, 571. We have drawn on this text in constructing this brief excursus through modern physics, along with Calder, *Magic Universe*; Bryson, *A Short History of Nearly Everything*; Smolin, *The Trouble with Physics*; and a useful guide published in the *Financial Times Magazine*, 24/25 November 2007. Also, many thanks to Michael Weissman for assistance in explaining some of the more abstruse details.

 7   There are also antiquarks and, possibly, squarks — quarks' heavier twin — too. Battersby, "Messenger from the Multiverse," 36–39.

 8   Calder, *Magic Universe*, 465.

 9   Lee Smolin writes that no "observation in the last thirty years has been more upsetting than the discovery of dark energy in 1998. What we mean when we say that energy is dark is that it seems to differ from all forms of energy and matter previously known, in that it is not associated with any particles or waves. It is just there." Smolin, *The Trouble with Physics*, 149.

10   Chaos theory and complexity theory are not the same thing, and scholars in the respective fields make the effort to differentiate them. However, because these theories share similar kinds of insights, in this cursory survey below, we ignore the distinctions between chaos theory and complexity theory in order to elucidate a broad trend.

11   Gleick, *Chaos*, 5.

12   Urry, "The Complexity Turn," 10–14.

13   See, for example, Chesters and Welsh, *Complexity and New Social Movements*. For these authors, the application of complexity theory to society is a pre-eminently Deleuzean undertaking.

14   For instance, see Gladwell, *The Tipping Point*.

15   Urry, "The Complexity Turn," 5.

16   Interestingly, John Searle has recently suggested that this particular understanding of the dynamic and transformative relationship between the parts and the whole of a system may be a fruitful way to derive a theory of consciousness within neurobiology. Searle, *Freedom and Neurobiology*.

17   As Monica Greco notes, accounts of complex causation "demand that we acknowledge, and learn to value as the source of qualitatively new questions, the possibility of a form of ignorance that cannot simply be deferred to future knowledge." Greco, "On the Vitality of Vitalism," 24.

18   Thus Fritjof Capra notes that "a living organism is an open system that maintains itself in a state far from equilibrium, and yet is stable." Capra, "Complexity and Life," 37.

19   Latour, *Politics of Nature*.

20   The management of risk has itself become a significant field in areas such as public health and the environment. Much of this follows in the wake of Ulrich Beck's *The Risk Society*, which illustrates its arguments with some stark examples of risks being deemed acceptable by chemical and other companies,

provided those risks were borne by others, notably those in developing countries with little access to legal redress. The case of the Bhopal chemical works in India and the shocking treatment of its victims provides an especially clear example of Beck's argument, while reinforcing the sense in which risk-management requires an intricate systems-wide approach. See Beck, *The Risk Society*; Beck, "The Terrorist Threat"; Franklin, *The Politics of Risk Society*.

21   Haraway, "A Cyborg Manifesto." See also "Annual Review," the special issue of *Theory, Culture and Society*, Mike Featherstone and Nicholas Gane, eds., which includes a series of articles considering the legacy of Haraway's notion of the cyborg.

22   Hayles, "Unfinished Work," 160. See also Hayles, "Computing the Human."

23   Hayles, *How We Became Posthuman*; Fukuyama, *Our Posthuman Future*; Cheah, *Inhuman Conditions*.

24   Wynne, "Reflexing Complexity."

25   Ibid., 72–74.

26   Daniels, *At Women's Expense*; Oyama, *The Ontogeny of Information*; Oyama, *Evolution's Eye*; Fausto-Sterling, "The Bare Bones of Sex."

27   Masters and Coplan, "Water Treatment with Silicofluorides and Lead Toxicity"; and Roger, Hone, and Doshi, "Environmental Pollution, Neurotoxicity, and Criminal Violence."

28   Jasanoff, *Designs on Nature*; Rajan, *Biocapital*.

29   Merleau-Ponty, *Phenomenology of Perception*; *The Primacy of Perception*; *The Visible and the Invisible*. For further development of this phenomenological argument see Coole, "Rethinking Agency," and Coole, "Experiencing Discourse." For a critical realist account that has many points of similarity and which also uses Merleau-Ponty's work, see Archer, *Being Human*.

30   Agamben, *The Open*, 29.

31   Sunstein and Nussbaum, eds., *Animal Rights*.

32   Rose, *The Politics of Life Itself*. See also Sharp, *Strange Harvest*.

33   Goodwin, *Black Markets*; Waldby and Mitchell, *Tissue Economies*; Sharp, *Bodies, Commodities, and Biotechnologies*.

34   MacIntyre, *Dependent Rational Animal*.

35   Such issues have been subjected to serious attention in films such as *2001, A Space Odyssey*; *I, Robot*; and *Blade Runner*.

36   Agamben, *Homo Sacer*, 119. The text of Foucault's he has in mind here is *The History of Sexuality*, vol. 1.

37   Agamben, *Homo Sacer*, 136ff.

38   Ibid., 160–64.

39   See, for example, Jackson and Howe, *The Graying of the Great Powers*; and Magnus, *The Age of Aging*.

40   Honneth, "The Intellectual Legacy of Critical Theory," 345.

41   Shapiro, *The Flight from Reality in the Human Sciences*.

42   Archer, *Being Human*, 2, 4, 9, 22, 44, 111, 121.

43   Harvey, *Spaces of Global Capitalism*, 129, 147. Harvey's reference about rights is to Mitchell, *The Right to the City*.

44   Smith and Jenks, "Complexity, Ecology, and the Materiality of Information," 147.

45   Berger and Luckmann, *The Social Construction of Reality*, 34.

46   For a representative Regulation School approach, see de Angelis, "Neoliberal Governance, Reproduction and Accumulation."

47   David Harvey's commentary is indicative of this open Marxism and its materialist challenges. He observes: "If there has been some kind of transformation in the political economy of late twentieth-century capitalism, then it behooves us to establish how deep and fundamental the change might be. Signs and tokens of radical changes in labour processes, in consumer habits, in geographical and geopolitical configurations, in state powers and practices, and the like, abound. Yet we still live, in the West, in a society where production for profit remains the basic organizing principle of economic life. We need, therefore, some way to represent the shifting and churning that has gone on since the first major post-war recession of 1973, which does not lose sight of the fact that the basic rules of a capitalist mode of production continue to operate as invariant shaping forces in historical-geographical development." See Harvey, *The Condition of Postmodernity*, 121.

48   See for example, Lanchester, "Cityphilia"; and "Citiphobia."

49   Davis, *Planet of Slums*.

50   The editors of a current New Sociology series note that while the discipline had retreated from everyday issues, it is now starting to place "renewed emphasis on the mediation of everyday events and experiences by distant social forces, the intermeshing of the local and global in the production of social practices" and the need to situate "everyday social practices in the broader context of life in a globalizing world." Elliott, "Foreword," viii. New materialists might usefully begin with Henri Lefebvre's introductory words to the final volume of *The Critique of Everyday Life*. Noting how radically everyday life had changed during the course of his investigations (1947–81), Lefebvre ponders: "But what is their significance? Here our problematic emerges, and can be reformulated thus: is daily life a shelter from the changes, especially when they occur abruptly? Is it a fortress of resistance to great changes, or certain minor but significant changes? Or, contrariwise, is it the site of the main changes, whether passively or actively?" Lefebvre, *The Critique of Everyday Life*, vol. 3, 41. See also Certeau, *The Practice of Everyday Life*, which takes its impetus from Foucault's *Discipline and Punish*. What "I really wish to work out," Certeau explains, "is a *science of singularity*; that is to say, a science of the relationship that links everyday pursuits to particular circumstances. And only in the *local* network of labor and recreation can one grasp how, within a grid of socio-economic constraints, these pursuits unfailingly establish relational tactics (a struggle for life), artistic creations (an aesthetic), and auton-

omous initiatives (an ethic). The characteristically subtle logic of these 'ordinary' activities comes to light only in their details." *The Practice of Everyday Life*, ix.

51 While a more poststructuralist use of Foucault's work by feminists and queer theorists has emphasized the construction of discourses, there is a rich field of more materialist feminist studies that examines the material strategies and effects that produce gendered flesh. See, for example, Diamond and Quinby, eds., *Feminism and Foucault*. Biddy Martin's intervention concerning materialism in "Feminism, Criticism, and Foucault" (4–5) is significant, although it is the concrete nature of the analyses to which we especially wish to draw attention.

52 Foucault, "Nietzsche, Genealogy, History," 153, 155.

53 As Paul Patton argues, this way of understanding Foucault's argument does not endorse naturalism but neither does it efface the body's materiality; rather, it understands power "in its primary sense of capacity to do or become certain things" and presents power as redirecting such capacities. Patton, "Foucault's Subject of Power," 65.

54 Althusser, "Ideology and Ideological State Apparatuses (Notes towards an Investigation)," 8f.

55 Foucault, *Power/Knowledge*, 97.

56 Althusser, Philosophy of the Encounter.

THE FORCE OF MATERIALITY

Jane Bennett

A Vitalist Stopover on the Way to
a New Materialism

This essay is part of a larger study of materiality in politics, in which I experiment with narrating events (a power blackout, a crisis of obesity) in a way that presents non-human materialities (electricity, fats) as themselves bona fide agents rather than as instrumentalities, techniques of power, recalcitrant objects, or social constructs. What would happen to our thinking about politics if we took more seriously the idea that technological and natural materialities were themselves actors alongside and within us—were vitalities, trajectories, and powers irreducible to the meanings, intentions, or symbolic values humans invest in them? I'm in search of a materialism in which matter is an active principle and, though it inhabits us and our inventions, also acts as an outside or alien power. This new, "vital materialism" would run parallel to a historical materialism focused more exclusively upon economic structures of human power.

Of course, such a "thing-power" materialism[1] would not be radically new, but part ad hoc invention and part a gathering of elements from preexisting traditions—from historical lines of thought in which materiality is figured not as inert or even passively resistant but as active and energetic, albeit not purposive in any strong sense. According to that tradition—which includes for me Epicurus, Lucretius, Hobbes, Spinoza, La Mettrie, Diderot, the Marx of his dissertation on Democritus, the aleatory materialism of Althusser, Deleuze, and others — the distinctions between life and matter, organic and inorganic, human and nonhuman, man and god, are not necessarily the most important ones to honor.

In addition to these materialisms, I find a rich source of ideas about materiality in the tradition of "vitalism." Especially those early twentieth-century strands called "critical" or "modern" vitalism.[2] These vitalists, who distinguished themselves from the "naive vitalism" of soul by means of their close engagement with experimental science, fought doggedly against one *kind* of materialism — the kind for which materiality is mechanical in operation and thus in principle always calculable to humans. Because the critical vitalists and I share a common foe in mechanistic or deterministic materialism, I devote this essay to one of them: Hans Driesch (1867–1941).

Driesch's Gifford lectures in 1907–8 at the University of Aberdeen on "The Science and Philosophy of the Organism," along with the work of his contemporary Henri Bergson, played a significant part in the popular enthusiasm for vitalism in America in the years before the First World War.[3] Central to this vitalism was the idea that "life" was irreducible to "matter," that there existed a life-principle that animates matter, exists only when in a relationship with matter, but is not itself of a material nature.[4] "The concept of *nature* must be enlarged," writes Driesch, so that it "consists of one completely spatial and one only partly spatial portion."[5] The "vital principle" resides in the latter and provides the impetus for morphological changes in the embryo. But the scope of critical vitalism was not restricted to biology, for the same vital principle was also thought to be responsible for the progressive development of personality and history: insofar as seeds, embryos, personalities, and cultures were all *organic* wholes, there was an isomorphism between physical, psychological, and civilizational orders.

There was some disagreement among vitalists about just how to depict the vital force: Bergson's *élan vital*, for example, competed with Driesch's entelechy. But on the question of "matter," the vitalists were in agreement with each other, as well as with their "materialist" opponents: matter was unfree, mechanistic, and deterministic (though "dynamic" in the sense of capable of undergoing regular changes of state). Whereas the vitalists lifted instances of "life" outside of the reach of this mechanical world, the materialists insisted that every entity or force, however complex, organic, or subtle, was (ultimately or in principle) explicable in mechanical or, as they called it, "physico-chemical" terms.

While Driesch does not go as far as I do toward a materialist ontology, he does insist that the "vital principle" has absolutely no existence independent of "physico-chemical" matter. He makes the relationship between matter and life as close as it possibly can be while still retaining the distinction. I am thus intrigued by Driesch because he pushes the life-matter binary to the limit, even though, at the very last minute, he draws back from taking the plunge into a materiality that is *itself* vibrant or active. It is instructive to see why he draws back: it is for the sake of freedom conceived as a persistent capacity of the natural world to surprise — to produce events not fully determined by their antecedents. This picture of an aleatory world is one that my "vital materialism" too affirms.

Driesch identified a not-wholly calculable, not-quite-material impetus as responsible for organic becoming. Perhaps one of the reasons he, like Bergson, enjoyed popularity in America was because he was received as a defender of freedom, of a certain open-endedness to life, in the face of a modern science whose pragmatic successes were threatening to confirm definitively the picture of the universe as a godless machine. Driesch, a German embryologist, was also one of the first non-Jews to be stripped of his professorship by the Nazis because he objected to their use of his vitalism to justify German conquest of "less vital" peoples. I shall take up the question of the relationship of vitalism to political violence at the end of the essay, where I contrast Driesch's vitalism with that of American evangelical advocates of the "culture of life," a latter-day vitalism conjoined to a doctrine of preemptive war.

But first, I turn to Driesch's entelechy, to his notion of vital force: a life-principle that activated the dull stuff of matter. The haunting association of matter with passivity, which Driesch almost but not quite overcame, is my target. It must go if we are to become more adept at discerning and contending productively with the force of things, with the positive vitality possessed by nonhuman entities and forces.

Entelechy

Driesch was a Kantian, at least at first. Kant, in the *Critique of Judgment*, had repeatedly insisted upon the figure of passive matter: matter "as such" can have no "spontaneity."[6] "We cannot even think of living matter as possible. (The concept of it involves a contradiction, since the essential character of matter is lifelessness, *inertia*)."[7] We must not "endow matter, as mere matter, with a property ([namely, the property of life, as] hylozoism [does]) that conflicts with its nature."[8] Driesch affirms Kant's image of matter to the extent that Driesch affirms the need for a nonmaterial supplement to direct, organize, and animate matter. Driesch also echoes Kant's claim that the vital principle would never become fully transparent to us and could be known only as an invisible presence that performs the tasks that are in fact performed within the organism but which no mechanical matter could ever possibly perform by itself. Entelechy is born in the negative spaces of the machine model of nature, in the "gaps" in the "chain of strictly physico-chemical or mechanical events."[9]

Driesch's case for entelechy proceeds thus, first, by way of transcendental arguments: "x *must* be operative, given the indisputable reality of y." To show how the vital principle cannot be "physico-chemical" in nature, for example, he starts from the observation that, in morphogenesis (the process by which a fertilized egg becomes an adult organism), "manifoldness in space is produced where no manifoldness was." Though on first glance it might seem that this manifoldness in space emerged directly from the spatially uniform, undifferentiated egg, theoretical reason reveals this to be impossible: a *spatial* manifold cannot have a *spatial* unity as its source. Thus, it must be that *some other kind* of "manifold" is present "previous to morphogenesis." Lacking an "extensive character," this prior manifold, the basis of the organism's later differentiation, *must* be an "'intensive manifoldness,'"[10] that is, "an agent acting manifoldly without being in itself manifold in space" (vol. 2, 250). "That is to say, [it is] . . . composite, though not in space" (vol. 2, 316). We have, then, a first definition of *entelechy*: it is the *intensive* manifoldness out of which emerges the extensive manifoldness of the mature organism.

Driesch's negative and indirect case for vitalism proceeds, second, by way of his positive and direct interventions and observations in the laboratory. Indeed, what had initially provoked Driesch to posit the "autonomy of life" was not theoretical reason but experiments on cell-division in the sea urchin. Calculated intrusion into the mechanism of sea urchins paradoxically uncovered the fact that life was inexplicable if conceived exclusively as a mechanism. But the fact that Driesch insists upon the inadequacy of mechanical explanation does not mean that his entelechy is a "psychic" factor: "It is important to grasp the *provisional negativeness* of entelechy, because it will save us from a mistake . . . of regarding the vitalistic agent as something 'psychical.' . . . But the contrary of *mechanical* is merely *non-mechanical*, and not 'psychical'" (vol. 2, 115).[11] For Driesch the critical vitalist, the vital principle must be conceived as *neither* mechanical body nor ethereal soul.

The goal of Driesch's laboratory work and the reason for his strict adherence to the protocols of empirical science was not simply to gain a more subtle understanding of the dynamic chemical and physical properties of the organism but also to better discern what *animated* the machine: "Why then occurs all that folding, and bending . . . , and all the other processes we have described? There must be something that *drives them out*, so to say."[12] Driesch names that something, that animating impetus inside the embryo, entelechy. Neither a substance nor an energy (though active only in relation to those phenomena), entelechy is "the non-mechanical agent responsible for the phenomena of life."[13] Driesch borrows his term of art *entelechy* from Aristotle, retaining its sense of a self-moving and self-altering power but rejecting its peculiarly Aristotelian teleology.[14]

In addition to animating matter, entelechy is also what "arranges" or composes artistically the bodies of organisms. In order to see how entelechy performs this, its "forming" task, *nonmechanically*, we need to take a closer look at morphogenesis, the mode of becoming Driesch says is unique to organisms. Morphogenesis refers both to the process by which a blastocyst moves from a less to a more differentiated form (ontogenesis) and to the process by which a mature organism re-forms itself in response to damage or disease (restitution).[15] While inorganic matter is capable of *change*, only life can *morph*: a crystal formation can diminish or increase in mass, but it cannot become qualitatively more complex and it cannot restore itself by replacing or repairing parts such that the "same" whole endures. "The organism is different . . . from all combinations of crystals, such as those called dendrites . . . which consists of a typical arrangement of identical units. . . . For this reason, dendrites . . . must be called aggregates; but the organism is not an aggregate" (vol. 1, 25). The parts of a plant, unlike the mineral and chemical elements of a mountain, are *members*: when a change occurs in one, the others are not only thereby affected but affected in such a way as to provoke a *coordinated* response.

Developing the contrast between machines and organisms further, Driesch argues that whereas a phonograph "receives vibrations of the air and gives off vibrations of the air" and so "previous stimulus and later reaction are of the *same* nature," in an organism the "impressions on its sensory organs" (for example, sounds) can issue in something (for example, conversations) that belongs to an "absolutely *different* class of phenomena" (vol. 2, 61, my emphasis). Neither can inorganic systems (as mere matter) *learn* from their experiences, says Driesch, for that entails not only "the mere recollection of what has happened, but . . . also the ability to use *freely* in another field of occurring the elements of former happening for newly combined *individualised* specificities of the future which are *wholes*" (vol. 2, 79). Driesch describes the productivity of organisms as following "a curious principle, which may be called . . . *individual correspondence*. That is to say: any real action is an *individual* 'answer' to an individual stimulus."[16] Such individualized action tailored specifically to the situation at hand constitutes the "directing" action of entelechy.

Elsewhere, Driesch describes this "directing" power as the power to allow one of the many formative possibilities inside the emergent organism to become actual. There are always more potential shapes and lines of development for a cell, organ, or an organism than become actual. In (what we would call) the stem cells of the sea urchin, for example, there is "an enormous number of possibilities of happening in the form of difference of 'potential'" in each cell.[17] But if "something else *can* be formed than actually is formed, why then does there happen in each case just what happens and nothing else?" Again Driesch reasons that there *must* be some agent responsible for the singular specificity of the outcome, some decisive agent guarding the entrance to actuality:

> According to our hypothesis, . . . in each of the *n* cells the *same* great number of possibilities of becoming is physico-chemically prepared, but checked, so to say, by entelechy. Development of the system now depends, according to our assumption, upon the fact that entelechy *relaxes its suspensory power* and thus . . . in cell *a* one thing is allowed to

occur, in cell *b* another, and in cell *c* something else; but what now actually occurs in *a* might also have occurred in *b* or *c*; for *each one* out of an enormous number of possibilities *may* occur in each cell. Thus, by the regulatory *relaxing* action of entelechy in a system in which an enormous variety of possible events had been suspended by it, it may happen that an *equal distribution* of *possibilities* is transformed into an *unequal distribution* of *actual effects*.[18]

Note that, once again, Driesch describes the power of entelechy to determine the trajectory of organic growth in negative terms: it acts by selectively "relaxing" its "suspensory power." This capacity for (negative) choice operates in a context of multiple possibilities, and so the actual path of organic growth is not determined in a rigid, mechanical way. Likewise, neither are the individual movements of an adult organism fully determined or mechanically caused by the stimuli of the individual's environment: outside events do affect the individual, but they create only "*a general stock* of *possibilities* for further acting and have *not* determined all further reactions quite in detail."[19] There is thus an "*indefiniteness* of correspondence between specific cause and specific effect."[20] It is in this indefiniteness that "freedom" exists.

In the Gifford lectures, Driesch affirms a qualitative difference between life and matter. Entelechy, that *self-directing activeness* apparent in some bodies, is what distinguishes a crystal from an embryo, a parking lot from a lawn, me from my corpse. But does Driesch also affirm a qualitative difference between human and other forms of life? The question is an important one, I think, because it seems that much of the appeal of vitalism resides in the desire to view man as the apex of worldly existence.[21] Driesch's response is ambivalent. On the one hand, the "directing" power of entelechy (unlike its "formative" power which is distributed equally across all organisms) operates inside man with special intensity. This is evidenced in his greater capacity for "knowing" and "willing." But, on the other hand, Driesch also believes that some analogue of knowing and willing exists in *all* organic processes: "Indeed, as far as morphogenesis and physiological adaptation and instinctive reactions are concerned, there *must* be a something comparable metaphorically with specified knowing and willing."[22]

Close attention to morphogenesis reveals to Driesch a modality of

human and others in terms of entelechy?

change distinctive to "life": this change is *organizing, complexifying, holistic,* and *autonomic* (nondeterministic). But why not model the living systems that entail this type of change as highly complex and dynamic *machines*? If so, then there would be no need to invoke a special vital principle like entelechy to explain morphogenesis. Driesch takes up the question explicitly and finds all mechanistic accounts of morphogenesis inadequate. Here is why: an organism is a working whole capable of innovative action — it repairs injured parts, recreates severed ones, and adapts old parts to perform new roles — all in order to maintain the normal functioning of the whole and to preserve its identity. In contrast, a machine (as a mere aggregation of physico-chemical elements) *"does not remain itself, if you take from it whatever you please."*[23] Because machines cannot self-repair, one must again conclude that there must be at work in the organism some nonmaterial agent that provides "the specific and real stimulus which calls forth the restoring processes."[24]

Neither does the machine analogy hold, says Driesch, for individual organs of an organism. An ovary, for example, emerges from a single, totipotent cell (*"Anlage"*[25]) that "has been divided and re-divided innumerable times," but *"how could a machine . . . be divided innumerable times and yet remain what it was?"*[26] Driesch's experimental evidence for this involves the hydroid-polyp Tubularia, whose cut segments, however small, will regenerate the whole organism. According to the "mechanistic" view of the time, each segment would have to contain a machine, each of which, when cut in two, could still function as a half-size but complete machine. Mikhail Bakhtin, an early critic of Driesch's work, aptly describes the conclusions Driesch draws from his experiments on Tubularia:

> What kind of machine is this which we can divide to our heart's content and which always preserves its normal functions? A number of highly complex, large and small machines with the same function must be contained within our two cm segment. . . . Moreover, these machines overlap one another: parts of one correspond to completely different parts of another. Such a mechanism contradicts the very concept of a mechanism. Thus, the machine theory (in Driesch's opinion) leads to the absurd.[27]

In describing entelechy as the invisible but "real stimulus" for the movement of morphing, Driesch also considers the question of whether entelechy might be conceived as "energy," and thus as a special kind of physico-chemical entity. Again he answers no, rejecting the idea of "vital energy" as oxymoronic, for life is *unquantifiable* and all energies remain for him quantities: "In asserting . . . phenomena to be of the energetical order, we state that there can be a *more or less* of them. . . . *But* entelechy *lacks all the characteristics of quantity*: entelechy *is order of relation* and absolutely *nothing* else."[28]

As I have already noted, Driesch's "critical vitalism" emphasizes the necessarily intimate relationship between entelechy and the regular, observable operations of matter. Entelechy can make use only of "the possibilities of becoming" that are "physico-chemically prepared," for "life is unknown to us except in association with bodies";[29] entelechy always "uses material means in each individual morphogenesis" (vol. 2, 295); entelechy cannot make sulphuric acid if no hydrogen is present, but it can "*suspend* for as long a period as it wants any one of all the reactions which are *possible* with such compounds as are present, and which would happen without *entelechy*" (vol. 2, 180). These formulations display Driesch's struggle to make the life-matter relationship as close as it can possibly be without going all the way over to a (mechanistic) materialism and without implying a metaphysics of "soul."

What intrigues me perhaps the most about entelechy is the way it is a figure of an *impersonal* kind of agency. Like Machiavelli's *fortuna* or the Homeric Greek notion of *psuche*,[30] entelechy is not the unique possession of each individual but rather a vitality flowing across all living bodies. Entelechy coordinates parts on behalf of a whole without following a rigid plan; it answers events innovatively and perspicuously, deciding on the spot and in real time which of the many possible courses of development will in fact happen. Neither is the agentic capacity of entelechy a disembodied soul, for it is constrained by the materiality that it must inhabit and by the preformed possibilities contained therein. But despite this heteronomy, entelechy has real efficacy: it animates, arranges, and directs the bodies of the living, even under changing conditions. It is "an *effective* extra-spatial intensively manifold constituent of nature."[31]

Driesch's invention of entelechy as a creative causality was initially propelled by his assumption that materiality was matter, that is, stuff so passive and dull that it could not possibly have done the tricky work of organizing and maintaining morphing wholes. Sometimes this matter is infused with entelechy and becomes "life," and sometimes it isn't and coagulates into inorganic "machines." Driesch thought he had to figure entelechy as nonmaterial because his notion of materiality was yoked to the notion of a mechanistic, deterministic machine. In 1926, Mikhail Bakhtin rebutted Driesch on this point, arguing that Driesch failed to imagine the possibility of "a relentlessly self-constructing, developing machine [which] . . . builds itself not from pre-prepared parts, but from self-constructing ones." Such a machine, were it to be damaged, would indeed be capable of a self-repair, a restitution prompted and guided by subtle and interactive physico-chemical signals, and thus would have no need for entelechy.[32]

Bakhtin pointed out that Driesch's vitalism depended upon his critique of materialism and that critique depended upon equating materiality with mechanical causality, with an image of machine as a "totally prefabricated" and "fixed and immovable" assemblage.[33] Bakhtin recommended that Driesch rethink what a "machine" can be rather than reject physico-materialist explanation per se.[34] I agree.

But I applaud the way Driesch yokes his vital principle to experiential activities in the lab. This helps him to ward off the temptation within vitalism to *spiritualize* the vital agent. As an example of a vitalism that surrenders to this temptation, I turn now to another figure of vital force, the "soul" inside human embryos produced as a result of fertility technologies.

The "Culture of Life"

At the start of the twentieth century, Driesch was engaged in a public debate that was simultaneously moral and scientific: the vitalist-mechanist controversy combined discourses of freedom and vitality with studies of morphology and matter. At the start of the twenty-first century, many Americans were again participating in a similarly hybrid discourse, as can be seen in debates about abortion, artificial life support, and embryonic stem cell research. One position in these debates might be described as a latter-day vitalism: it is the "culture of life" position advocated by evangelical and Catholic Christians, including then-president George W. Bush. Like Driesch, defenders of the "culture of life" believe there to be something profoundly inadequate about a materialist metaphysic.

But not all vitalisms are alike, and it seems that the "culture of life" is a return to what Driesch rejected as a naive vitalism of soul. Driesch took special pains to distinguish his vital principle from the idea of a disembodied spirit, he explicitly eschewed religious dogmatism in favor of laboratory experiments with sea urchins, and he refused political attempts to link the idea of a vital principle to the idea that some forms of life were more vital than others. The vitalism of the culture of life does none of these things.

In May of 2005, President Bush "appeared at the White House with babies and toddlers born of test-tube embryos" in order to dramatize his opposition to embryonic stem cell research. "The White House event, on what conservative Christians and the president call an important 'culture of life' issue, demonstrated just how far Mr. Bush is willing to assert himself on policy that goes to what he considers the moral heart of his presidency. . . . Tom DeLay of Texas managed the opposition to the bill, also casting it in stark moral terms. 'An embryo is a person, a distinct, internally directed, self-integrating human organism.' "[35] At a National Catholic Prayer Breakfast in April 2007, Bush reiterated his commitment to the life of human embryos: "We must continue to work for a culture of life where the strong protect the weak, and where we recognize in every human life the image of our Creator."[36] Three days later and four years into a preemptive war estimated to have killed between tens of thousands and hundreds of thousands of Iraqis,[37] Bush rejected Senate and House Democrats' attempt to tie $100 billion in additional funding for the war to a timetable for withdrawal of U.S. troops. Said Bush: "We should not legislate defeat in this vital war."[38] Both human embryos and preemptive violence are "vital."

A stem cell is a neologism for a cell believed to be pluripotent, that is, able to become any of the various kinds of cells or tissues of the mature, differentiated organism. The hope is that better understanding of pluripotency will enable scientists to, among other things, induce the production of new nerve cells in damaged spinal cords or new brain tissue in people with Alzheimer's disease.[39] The contested procedure consisted in extracting cells from the "blastula" stage of the fertilized egg, when the egg is changing from a solid mass of cells into a hollow ball of cells around a fluid-filled cavity. The blastocyst may then continue on to the "gastrula" stage, where it differentiates into three germ-layers, whose cells, "channeled into their respective fate paths," are no longer pluripotent.[40] Bush opposes embryonic stem cell research because the extraction halts the morphological process at the gastrula stage. Former House Republican leader DeLay describes this as "the dismemberment of living, distinct human beings for the purposes of medical experimentation."[41] Many Americans agreed with him. Stem cells can also be taken from umbilical cord blood, adult human bone marrow, and fertilized embryos too old to be capable of developing further. The Bush administration does not object to these sources of stem cells, perhaps because blood, marrow, and decayed embryos are conceived as dead matter rather than life and thus pose no threat to the "culture of life."

But what is the "culture of life"? The phrase was the central theme of Pope John Paul II's 1995 "Evangelium Vitae" before it was adopted by non-Catholic evangelicals in the United States to refer to a cluster of theological beliefs linked to a set of public policies.[42] The policies are easy to name: the culture of life, defined in contrast to "the [secular] culture of death," has been invoked to support legislation to keep a feeding tube inserted into a woman whose brain function had ceased, to restrict access by minors to abortion and to outlaw certain surgical techniques of abortion, as well as to oppose federal funding for embryonic stem cell research. The theological or cosmological beliefs within the culture of life are less clearly articulated, but the following four claims seem central:

1 *Life is radically different from matter.* Life is organized, active, self-propelled, and, in diverse registers of the term, "free." Matter is intrinsically passive and predetermined in its operation. Life may be embodied, and when it is, it operates alongside physico-chemical entities and processes. But life is irreducible to the sum of those entities and processes. Life is detachable from embodiment.

2 *Human life is radically different from all other life.* The life of human bodies is not only qualitatively different from matter but also from every other life-form. Like other animals, humans are endowed with a life-force, but unlike all others, this force is "a unique life-principle or soul."[43] "If society loses the sense of the essential distinction of human life from animal life and material things, whether in theory or in the practice of attempting to clone a human embryo, it has lost its stature as a human society. It has lost the compass of humanness and is, instead, laying the foundation for the replacement of a hu-

man living with biological chaos."[44] The ensouled human organism is a quantum leap above other organisms.

3 *Human uniqueness expresses a divine intention.* Human exceptionalism is not a contingent event, an accident of evolution, or a function of the distinctive material composition of the human body. Rather, an omnipotent being ("the Almighty") implants a divine spark or soul into the human individual.

4 *The world is a divinely created order and that order has the shape of a fixed hierarchy.* Humans are not only organic, unique, and ensouled, but ranked at the very top of the hierarchy, in a position *superior* to inorganic matter, to nonhuman organisms, and to the Earth as a whole.

In subscribing to the first point, the belief that life is irreducible to matter, the culture of life qualifies as a kind of vitalism, for it affirms what Driesch said is the central claim *of* vitalism, that is, that the developmental processes of the organism are *not* "the result of a special *constellation of factors known already* to the sciences of the inorganic," but are rather "the result of an *autonomy* peculiar" to life.[45] Insofar as it affirms a soul whose existence is not tied to its relationship to matter, it qualifies as what Driesch called naive vitalism. This "old vitalism" fails to avail itself of the benefit of scientific insight into nature. For Driesch the lab and the reasoning scientist remained the privileged point of access to the life principle, and he insists that it is always "essential to reflect once more with an open mind on the actual biological data."[46] The new vitalism was a falsifiable hypothesis and not a dogma that only immoralists dare contest.

Advocates of the culture of life often do affirm science, in particular weapons technology if it advances the project of American mastery. But science can never contravene the theological verities of ensoulment, human exceptionalism, and the qualitative hierarchy of Creation. To DeLay, for example, no revelation from molecular chemistry or complexity theory about the self-organizing capacity of *inorganic* systems could disprove his conviction that matter is inert and only life is free and open-ended. And no data concerning the differential plasticity of cells at the blastula and gastrula stages could possibly alter the conclusion that the fertilized egg is a person ensouled by the Almighty.[47] What seems to be operative here is a kind of species-narcissism: "life" must remain special—that is, radically other to matter — if we humans are to be able to think of ourselves as the *most* special of its expressions.

The culture of life is also more anthropocentric and hierarchical than the vitalism of Driesch. It posits the cosmos as a rank-ordered creation, at the top of which the Designer has placed his most vital creature, man. Man was given dominion over other earthly creatures because he is the most vital of them, in three conjoined senses of the term: he is the most animate or mobile, the most free or capable of action irreducible to the demands of the body and other material conditions, and the most important to the order because he is the image of God. The allied idea that there exist two ontologically distinct substances (brute matter and spirited life), in conjunction with the idea that man has the most life, helps to render practices of hyperconsumption and exploitation of nature laudable acts of human enterprise and productivity. The idea that the world was originally designed *as* a hierarchy also legitimates a hierarchically structured social order, and it justifies public policies that, because they intensify human inequalities, would otherwise appear unfair or unjust: policies that cut taxes of the wealthy, defend unprecedented levels of corporate executive compensation, and oppose universal health care. The presumption that the principle governing the divine hierarchy is rule by the most free species legitimizes a series of civilizational acts of violence committed in the name of allowing "freedom" to flourish among more and more peoples. Here, the violence of preemptive war, state-sponsored torture, and the militarization of outer space[48] become generous acts in accord with a culture of life where, in Bush's words, "the strong protect the weak, and where we recognize in every human life the image of our Creator." When lodged inside such a divine hierarchy, the culture of and for "life" becomes the righteous domination of the earth by God's most free and vital creatures, that is, Americans. Or, as the post–9/11 bumper sticker announced in the grammar of a command: "God Bless America."

I don't think, however, that there is something intrinsic to vitalism, to the idea of the "autonomy of life," that ties it to militarism, political inequality, insistently wasteful consumption, or civilizational imperialism. Driesch, for example, explicitly dissociated his vitalistic holism from a steep moral hierarchy and the desire for mastery, whether expressed as the view that humans should rule supreme over nonhumans or the view that one group of people has a natural right to dispose of the others. At the end of *The History and Theory of Vitalism*, Driesch goes so far as to reject his own image of nature as divided into dead matter and organic life. He there concludes that everything, whether "inorganic" or "organic," must be entelechial, life-ly, or vitalistic: *"nature is a something in evolution.* All natural becoming is like *one* great embryology." Driesch thus ends his defense of vitalism by "destroying" "the [very] difference between 'mechanism' and 'Vitalism,' . . . which we have established so carefully."[49]

And when the Nazis took up his theory of organic wholes directed by a vital principle in support of their claim that the German nation had to fulfill *its* vital destiny and wage its vital wars,[50] Driesch objected vehemently. "Entelechy recognized no state boundaries and . . . therefore the only biological 'whole' to which one could rightfully belong was 'humanity.' He opposed rising militarism in equally biological language, declaring that the militaristic actions of nature against nation needed to be recognized for what it was: *'the most terrible of all sins'* against the vitalistic principles of life, holistic cooperation and higher development."[51]

As I see it, the important political question that "culture of life" vitalism raises is not "Is the embryo matter or life?" but "How can the figure of life join forces with a celebration of (righteous) violence?" I have tried to illuminate an inner link between, on the one hand, Bush's repeated invocations of life, freedom, and care for the weak, and, on the other hand, his policies of torture, economic inequality, and preemptive violence. The charge of hypocrisy does not quite get at what is at work here. Rather, it seems that faith in the idea of a divinely created *hierarchy* — of the righteous domination of some parts over others — flows into faith in the otherwise inexplicable ideas that the rich deserve to get richer, that war is prolife, and that force can set us free.

Whereas Drieschean and Bushean vitalisms diverge on the question of hierarchy, they share a valorization of freedom or the element of unpredictability and indeterminacy in action. For both, the world contains persistent moments of freedom, despite the comforting regularity provided by natural or divine law. To believe in entelechy is to affirm the freedom of a certain *"indefiniteness* of correspondence between specific cause and specific effect,"[52] a capacity for the aleatory that Driesch extended to the universe as a whole. To believe in the soul is also to affirm a kind of freedom, though one restricted to the "life" embodied in humans: this is the freedom for the sake of which America invades the territories of those humans who "hate freedom" because "they love terror,"[53] but also the free will of a humanity capable of acts worthy of moral credit or blame.

Bakhtin was critical of the way Driesch's ostensibly scientific descriptions insinuated the metaphysical assumption of freedom. Driesch claimed that the blastomere contained multiple intensities, only one of which will be chosen by entelechy, but because at any given time and place there is in fact only *one* possible outcome of morphogenesis, Driesch's "talk of several potentials and possibilities serves only one purpose: it allows for the presupposition that they are all equally possible . . . and that therefore it is possible to *choose* one of them freely. Freedom of choice . . . is the ground of all of Driesch's constructions."[54] Bakhtin, I think, correctly identifies what is at stake in the vitalism of Driesch, and, albeit in a different one of its registers, also at stake in the vitalism of Bush. It is freedom, or faith in the existence of an undetermined world.

This resilient faith may help to explain vitalism's ability to repeatedly rise from the dead, to recur in history despite serial attempts to debunk and dispel it. Vitalism may also draw some of its enduring, or at least periodic, vitality from the fact that there seems to be something inside the practice of experimental science — its pragmatic quest for useful results, perhaps? — that leads it to *understate* or downplay the freedom, the energetic fluidity or surprising creativity of the natural world. This seems to be the case long after mechanistic models of nature have morphed into systems theory and complexity theory, and long after the figure of inert matter has been challenged by fluid dynamics and chaos theory, as well as by the many earlier biophilosophies of flow that Michel Serres chronicles in *The Birth of Physics*. But if there is something internal to scientific thinking that is uneasy about highlighting the idea of an element of indetermination intrinsic to nature, perhaps this is also because, in the West, to admit to indetermination is always to invite its colonization by dogmatic forms of Christian theology. Hence, Bush and the politics of the culture of life.

Vital Materiality

The National Institutes of Health 2001 Report on Stem Cells made two claims that surprised me, a surprise that revealed the extent to which I too had absorbed a machine model of nature. The first claim was that no one

yet knows whether "embryonic stem cells" exist as such in human embryos in the womb, that is, whether they have a presence *before* they are
extracted from blastocysts and placed in a new, laboratory-generated milieu. Though "most scientists now agree that *adult* stem cells exist in many
tissues of the human body (*in vivo*), . . . it is less certain that embryonic
stem cells exist as such in the embryo. Instead, embryonic stem cells . . .
develop in tissue culture after they are *derived* from the inner cell mass of the
early embryo."[55] The second unexpected claim was that it is also uncertain
whether even the stem cells produced in the lab are in fact "homogeneous
and undifferentiated," even though they appear to be and their promise of
pluripotency is premised upon that state of pure, quivering indeterminacy. What?! "Embryonic stem cells" might not even *exist* in the body and
their laboratory avatars might not even *be* an exemplar of undifferentiated
pluripotency?

I would not have been so surprised by this evidence of indeterminacy
unless I had been thinking of my body as a physiological mechanism with
fixed and determinate parts, including stem cells. In contrast, the NIH
researchers seem to be encountering materiality as a continuum of becomings, of extensive and intensive forms in various states of congealment and
dissolution. If no "embryonic stem cells" turn out to exist in vivo, it may
be because an embryo is *not* a collection of discrete parts, perhaps not even
of protoparts or preformed possibilities, and that it is only in the closed
system *of the lab* that a vital materiality allows itself to be sliced and diced
into "embryonic stem cells."

If we think of the term *entelechy* as an attempt to name a force or an
agency that is naturalistic but never fully spatialized, actualized, or calculable, as akin to what Georges Canguilhem described as "des enclaves
d'indetermination, des zones de dissidence, des foyers d'heresie,"[56] then
this vitalist gesture is not inimical to the materialism I seek. This materialism, which eschews the life-matter binary and does not believe in God or
spiritual forces, nevertheless also acknowledges the presence of an indeterminate vitality — albeit one that *resists* confinement to a stable hierarchy —
in the world. It affirms a cosmos of a lively materiality that *is* my body
and which also operates outside it to sometimes join forces with it and
sometimes to vie against it. Despite his great admiration for the wondrous complexity of nature, Driesch could not quite imagine a "material-

ism" adequate to it. Nevertheless, I now locate my "vital materialism" in Driesch's wake. Emerson wrote in his journal: "I have no longer any taste for these refinements you call life, but shall dive again into brute matter." I too go diving there, and find matter not so brute at all.

Notes

1   I develop the idea of "thing-power" in "The Force of Things."
2   The "critical vitalism" of Henri Bergson and Hans Driesch, which contrasted itself to a "naive" vitalism that "allowed for spiritual animation amidst the workings of physical law," emerged "in the nineteenth century transition from a matter-based physics to an energy-based physics." Burwick and Douglass, "Introduction" to *The Crisis in Modernism*, 1. Driesch describes his vitalism as "modern" or "new" in *The History and Theory of Vitalism*.
3   Quirk, *Bergson and American Culture*, 1–2. Quirk also places the works of Willa Cather and Wallace Stevens in this context: "Both Cather and Stevens believed in the 'creative power,' and both . . . linked this power to a vital force, biological in nature and primordial in origin" (8). See also the debates between Arthur O. Lovejoy and H. S. Jennings about vitalism during the period 1911–15: Lovejoy, "The Meaning of Vitalism"; Lovejoy, "The Import of Vitalism"; Jennings, "Driesch's Vitalism and Experimental Indeterminism"; Lovejoy, "The Meaning of Driesch and the Meaning of Vitalism"; Jennings, "Doctrines Held as Vitalism."
4   A 1916 review of Driesch's *The History and Theory of Vitalism* notes that vitalism "will not go down. A consideration of recent literature drives us to this conclusion. One of the most widely read philosophical works of the past few decades (Bergson's *Creative Evolution*) is primarily a defense of this doctrine. The writings of Driesch, both in German and in English, have followed one another with marvelous rapidity and forced themselves upon the attention of even the most unswerving mechanist." Sumner, "Review."
5   Driesch, *The Science and Philosophy of the Organism*, vol. 2, 321.
6   Kant, *Critique of Judgment*, sec. 78, #411.
7   Ibid., sec. 73, #394.
8   Ibid., sec. 65, #374.
9   Driesch rejects a Spinozist theory of "psycho-physical parallelism" precisely because Spinozism, as Driesch understands it, holds "that the physical side of [the] . . . duality forms a continuous chain of strictly physico-chemical or mechanical events without any gap in it." Driesch, *The Science and Philosophy of the Organism*, vol. 2, 115. It is very important to Driesch that his own "proof" of vitalism be understood to be a negative one: "All *proofs* of vitalism i.e. all reasonings by which it is shown that not even the machine-theory covers the

field of biological phenomena, can only be indirect proofs: they can only make it clear that mechanical or singular causality is not sufficient for an explanation of what happens." Driesch, *The History and Theory of Vitalism*, 208.

10   Driesch, *The Science and Philosophy of the Organism*, vol. 2, 144.

11   In Nature conceived scientifically — as here-now-such, there is "no room for 'psychical' entities at all." Driesch, *The Problem of Individuality*, 33. Driesch makes the same point in *The Science and Philosophy of the Organism*, where he says that "there 'are' no souls . . . in the phenomenon called nature in space" (vol. 2, 82).

12   Driesch, *The Science and Philosophy of the Organism*, vol. 1, 50, my emphasis. On this point Driesch echoes Kant's claim that in judging *organized* beings, "we must always presuppose some original organization that itself *uses* mechanism." Kant, *Critique of Judgment*, sec. 80, #418, my emphasis.

13   Driesch, *The Problem of Individuality*, 34.

14   Driesch does not elaborate on his differences with Aristotle and says only that he will retain Aristotle's idea that "there is at work a something in life phenomena 'which bears the end in itself.'" Driesch, *The Science and Philosophy of the Organism*, vol. 1, 144.

15   A blastocyst is the name for the developmental stage of a fertilized egg when it has changed from a solid mass of cells into a hollow ball of cells around a fluid-filled cavity.

16   Driesch, *The History and Theory of Vitalism*, 213. Or, as he puts the point in *The Science and Philosophy of the Organism*, vol. 1, 67: there is an "'individuality of correspondence' between stimulus and effect."

17   Driesch, *The Problem of Individuality*, 38. In the vocabulary of today, it might be said that the stem cells have not yet been channeled into their respective "fate paths."

18   Ibid., 39.

19   Driesch, *The History and Theory of Vitalism*, 213.

20   Driesch, *The Science and Philosophy of the Organism*, vol. 2, 72, my emphasis. The organism's ability to respond perspicuously and inventively to an event (its capacity for "individual correspondence") is not *radically* free: entelechy is incapable of producing that which is *utterly* new, for its intelligent responsiveness remains under the guidance of compacted intensities, which Driesch describes as "a general stock of possibilities."

21   This desire is quite overt in Joseph Chiari's defense of Bergson and Driesch: "Darwin thought that changes and mutations were due to chance; Lamarck ascribed them to the pressure of the environment and to functionalism; Bergson ascribes them to the natural resistance that matter offers to the informing spirit which, through man, evolves into consciousness and therefore gives man his favored position as the goal and the apex of creation." Chiari, "Vitalism and Contemporary Thought," 254.

22   Driesch says he doesn't know just what this "something" is, but though it "may seem very strange" that the most perspicuous "'means' toward [the] . . . end [of maintaining the organic whole] are known and *found*" by every organism, "it is a *fact*." *The Science and Philosophy of the Organism*, vol. 2, 143.

23   Driesch, *The History and Theory of Vitalism*, 210.

24   *The Science and Philosophy of the Organism*, vol. 1, 110.

25   Driesch distinguishes, in his empirical proofs for vitalism (which are better described as disproofs of the sufficiency of a mechanistic account of morphogenesis) between the process of "the *differentiation* of the *harmonious* systems" and the development of the original cell within which differentiation will occur. The latter is "not what comes out of the complex systems, but what they themselves come from. And we shall take the ovary as one instance standing for them all. The ovary develops from one special single cell which is its *Anlage*, to use a German word not easy to translate." Driesch, *The Problem of Individuality*, 21–22.

26   Driesch, *The History and Theory of Vitalism*, 212.

27   Bakhtin, "Contemporary Vitalism," 89.

28   Driesch, *The Science and Philosophy of the Organism*, vol. 2, 169. What could it mean to be exclusively an "order of relation"? Driesch sheds some light on this notion by describing entelechy as an "agent that arranges" elements into a harmonious whole. Driesch sees evidence of this arranging power in instinctive movements: although "physiological factors" play a role in instincts, "there would be something else also at work, a 'something' that may be said to *make use* of the factors" (vol. 2, 51). This "new and autonomic natural factor . . . unknown to the inorganic world" (vol. 2, 114) is also "at the root of the transformism of the species" (vol. 1, 287). In addition, such an arrangement must have been operative in the process of inheritance. A mechanical explanation would speak only of the transfer of material units "localized in the nucleus," but, again, these material conditions cannot be *"the main thing.* Some agent that *arranges* is required, and this arranging agent of inheritance *cannot* be of a machine-like, physico-chemical character." Driesch, *The Problem of Individuality*, 23. Why not? Because, the physicochemical is by definition incapable of the "arranging" agency required. Arranging agency requires both precision and flexibility, an ad hoc judging exquisitely attuned to the singularity of the parts it is to arrange and the singularity of the context in which the organism swims. Physicochemical elements, qua inert matter, are too obedient to generic laws to perform the required juggling, too routinized to arrange artfully.

29   Driesch, *The Science and Philosophy of the Organism*, vol. 1, 16.

30   Psuche marks the difference between a living human and an inactive corpse. It is "composed of a very tenuous stuff, which resides in the body while the individual is alive, flies away through some orifice at death and goes down to

Hades"; it is "simply that whose presence ensures that the individual is alive."
Adkins, *From the Many to the One*, 15.

31   Driesch, *The Science and Philosophy of the Organism*, vol. 2, 326, my emphasis.

32   Bakhtin, "Contemporary Vitalism," 95–96. Bakhtin names this alternative
machine-image "modern dialectical materialism" in contrast to Driesch's
"naive-mechanist point of view with its fixed and immovable machines" (96).
K. S. Lashley makes a similar point in 1923: "The vitalist cites particular phenomena—morphogenesis, regeneration, habit-formation, complexities of speech, and the like—and denies the possibility of a mechanistic account of them. But he thereby commits what we might term the egoistic
fallacy. On analysis his argument reduces every time to the form, 'I am not
able to devise a machine which will do these things; therefore no one will ever
conceive of such a machine.' This is the argument from inconceivability of
Driesch and McDougall, put badly. To it we may answer, 'You overvalue your
own ingenuity.'" Lashley, "The Behavioristic Interpretation of Consciousness," Part 1, 269.

33   Bakhtin, "Contemporary Vitalism," 95–96.

34   So do Deleuze and Guattari. In *A Thousand Plateaus* they describe Nature as a
plane of morphogenesis, which they call a "war-machine." Paul Patton suggests that a better term would have been "metamorphosis machine": "the
'war-machine' . . . is a concept which is betrayed by its name since it has little
to do with actual war and only a paradoxical and indirect relation to armed
conflict. [Its] . . . real object . . . is not war but the condition of creative
mutation and change." Patton, *Deleuze and the Political*, 110.

35   Stolberg, "House Approves a Stem Cell Bill Opposed by Bush," 1.

36   Cole, "Bush Stands against 'Temptation to Manipulate Life.'"

37   The lower estimate is from iraqbodycount.org, the larger one from Les Rob-
erts and Gilbert M. Burnham of the Center for International Emergency,
Disaster, and Refugee Studies at the Johns Hopkins Bloomberg School of
Public Health in Baltimore; Richard Garfield of Columbia University in New
York; and Riyadh Lafta and Jamal Kudhairi of Baghdad's Al-Mustansiriya
University College of Medicine.

38   White House, "President Bush Discusses Iraq War Supplemental."

39   A stem cell, while pluripotent, is not "totipotent" or, as Driesch described it
before the concept of stem cell was invented, is not a "potency" able to "play
every *single* part in the totality of what will occur in the whole system."
Driesch, *The Science and Philosophy of the Organism*, vol. 1, 120–21. See also
National Institutes of Health, *Stem Cells*, ES-2.

40   Maienschein, "What's in a Name," 12.

41   Tom DeLay, quoted in Baer, "In Vitro Fertilization, Stem Cell Research
Share Moral Issues." There is some dispute over whether a pregastrulated
mass is an "embryo." If an embryo is defined as a fertilized egg, then the

answer is yes. But others define an embryo as a dividing egg that has passed *through* gastrulation: "many biologists . . . don't call these early stages of development an embryo, but a preimplantation embryo or pre-embryo. The preimplantation embryo passes through three stages during its week of development: a zygote (one cell), morula (multiple cells in a cluster, all the same), and blastocyst [blastula] (when it develops sections, including a yolk sac, and has an inside and outside but still none of the defined structures of an embryo)." Spike, "Open Commentary," 45.

42   "Evangelium Vitae."

43   Best, "Testimony of Robert A. Best, President, the Culture of Life Foundation."

44   Ibid.

45   Driesch, *The History and Theory of Vitalism*, 1. Driesch defines vitalism as "the doctrine of the *autonomy of life*. . . . I know very well that . . . 'autonomy' usually means the faculty of *giving* laws to oneself, and . . . is applied with regard to a community of men; but in our phrase autonomy is to signify the *being subjected* to laws peculiar to the phenomena in question." *The Science and Philosophy of the Organism*, vol. 1, 143. Although, in the main, by the "autonomy" of life, Driesch is referring to the ability of organisms to self-arrange and self-restore, his use of the term also retains something of the Kantian sense of freedom, freedom from determinism. Henri Bergson affirms something close to Driesch's view; for Bergson, while "analysis will undoubtedly resolve the process of organic creation into an ever-growing number of physico-chemical phenomena, . . . it does not follow that chemistry and physics will ever give us the key to life." Bergson, *Creative Evolution*, 31.

46   *The History and Theory of Vitalism*, 57–58.

47   It is worth noting here that one need not be an atheist to reject the particular constellation of ideas inside the "culture of life": pantheisms of various sorts discern divinity in *all* things, human and nonhuman, organic and inorganic; many "Jewish and Muslim scholars . . . regard life as starting . . . 40 days" after fertilization; some believers affirm that God would approve of embryonic stem cell research as a fuller realization of the potential within the process of morphogenesis. See Maienschien, "What's in a Name," 14.

48   In 2001, Donald Rumsfeld "recommended that the military 'ensure that the president will have the option to deploy weapons in space'"; in 2002 Bush "withdrew from the 30-year-old Anti-Ballistic Missile Treaty, which banned space-based weapons"; and in 2005 General Lance Lord of the Air Force Space Command "told Congress [that] . . . 'we must establish and maintain space superiority.'" New York Times News Service, "U.S. Policy Directive Might Open Door to Space Weapons."

49   Driesch, *The History and Theory of Vitalism*, 223–24.

50   "Apres 1933, l'entelechie est devenue un *Fuhrer* de l'organisme," Canguilhem, "Aspects du vitalisme," 124.

51 Harrington, *Reenchanted Science*, 190. After Hitler came to power in 1933, "Driesch was one of the first non-Jewish German professors to be forcibly retired" (191).

52 Driesch, *The Science and Philosophy of the Organism*, vol. 2, 72, my emphasis.

53 Terrorists kill because "they hate freedom." White House, "Remarks by President and Mrs. Bush in Interview by Television of Spain." "The more free the Iraqis become, the more electricity is available, the more jobs are available, the more kids that are going to school, the more desperate these killers become, because they can't stand the thought of a free society. They hate freedom. They love terror." White House, "President Bush, Ambassador Bremer Discuss Progress in Iraq."

54 Bakhtin, "Contemporary Vitalism," 92. The fuller quotation reveals Bakhtin's own deterministic materialism: "It obviously goes without saying that at every place and every time, some specific conditions prevail. Therefore it is completely absurd to say [as Driesch does] that any particular possibility of development is really contained in a given blastomere. The potential is contained within it . . . to the same degree that it is part of the complex of its surrounding conditions. What is Driesch doing? He strays from any real conditions, locating abstract blastomere outside of the frames of time and space. . . . Talk of several potentials and possibilities serves only one purpose: it allows for the presupposition that they are all equally possible . . . and that therefore it is possible to choose one of them freely. Freedom of choice, not determinism in organic life, is the ground of all of Driesch's constructions."

55 National Institutes of Health, *Stem Cells*, ES-9, my emphasis.

56 Canguilhem, "Aspects du vitalisme," 121. This is a description evangelical Christians, with their strong sense of an ordered Creation, would most likely reject.

Pheng Cheah

Non-Dialectical Materialism

I gave this essay the tongue-in-cheek title of "non-dialectical materialism" to counterpose what one might call the materialisms of Derrida and Deleuze with that of Marx. Marx himself never used the phrase "dialectical materialism." It was a phrase first used by Plekhanov to distinguish the Marxist approach to the sociohistorical process, which focuses on human needs and the means and methods of their satisfaction, from the teleological view of history in Hegelian idealism.[1] But the concept was already implicit in the distinction Engels drew between the metaphysical mechanical materialism of the eighteenth century and the modern materialism that arose in the wake of the critique of German idealism. "Old materialism looked upon all previous history as a crude heap of irrationality and violence; modern materialism sees in it the process of evolution of humanity, and aims at discovering the laws thereof." Hence, "modern materialism," Engels wrote in "Socialism: Utopian and Scientific," "is essentially dialectic."[2] He further distinguished the materialist dialectic from the Hegelian dialectic in terms of its understanding of history as the history of class struggles, where social classes are the products of economic conditions: "Hegel had freed history from metaphysics — he had made it dialectic; but his conception of history was essentially idealistic. But now idealism was driven from its last refuge, the philosophy of history; now a materialistic treatment of history was propounded, and a method found of explaining man's 'knowing' by his 'being', instead of, as heretofore, his 'being' by his 'knowing.'"[3] Simply put, the two key features of the materialist dialectic are first, the understanding of nature and history as law-governed processes that can be rationally understood instead of immutable metaphysical substances, and, second, the determination of these processes as processes with a *material* existence that can be explained through empirical science.

Regardless of Althusser's qualifications concerning how Marx inverts the Hegelian dialectic, the concept of negation as the source of actualization remains a fundamental principle of Marxist materialism.[4] The decomposition of immediately present reality into social processes and the imminence of the proletarian revolution as the radical transformation of existing social conditions are premised on Marx's understanding of material existence as something created through the purposive mediation of human corporeal activity as this is historically conditioned. Marx suggested that human beings indirectly produce actual material life when we produce our means of subsistence through labor. Material reality is therefore produced by negativity. This is because Marx defined creative labor as a process of actualization whereby given reality or matter is negated through the imposition of a purposive form. As a result of the complex development of forces of production, each immediately given object and also each individual or social subject comes into being only by being constitutively imbricated in a web of social relations that form a system or totality.[5] The template and synecdoche for this system of reciprocally interdependent relations is the vital body of the organism. As I have argued elsewhere, Marxism is irrigated by an ontology of organismic vitalism.[6]

The labor of the negative remains of fundamental importance in the entire tradition of Marxist philosophy even when this power is no longer viewed as primarily manifested in corporeal labor but in the aesthetic sphere, as in the work of the Frankfurt School. Herbert Marcuse expresses this succinctly: "Art contains the rationality of negation. In its advanced positions, it is the Great Refusal — the protest against that which is."[7] This shadow of negativity also animates the accounts of resistance and dynamism in varieties of social constructionism and theories of performativity. In contradistinction, a nondialectical materialism is a materialism that no longer grants primacy to the work of the negative and, indeed, treats negativity as metaphysical in the same way that dialectical materialism characterized mechanistic materialism and idealism as metaphysical. As we will see below, Derrida's delimitation of the metaphysics of presence includes Marxist materialism itself. There are important historical and political reasons for this non-dialectical turn in materialism. What I wish to do in this essay, however, is to elaborate on some of the key features of non-dialectical materialism's break with the concept of negation and some of its implications.

1. Materialism without Substance (Derrida)

In *Specters of Marx* (1994), Derrida spoke in passing of his "obstinate interest in a materialism without substance: a materialism of the *khôra* for a despairing 'messianism.'"[8] Although he did not explicitly elaborate on what this materialism would look like, he had in fact already given some sense of it in a 1971 interview. When pressed insistently by two Marxists to specify his position on Marxism, Derrida made a characteristically enigmatic but suggestive comment that cautioned against the conflation of deconstruction with materialism: "It follows that if, and in the extent to which, *matter* in this general economy designates . . . radical alterity . . . then what I write can be considered 'materialist.'"[9] His reticence in using the word "matter," he added, was not idealist or spiritualist but instead due to the insistent reinvestment of the term with logocentric values, "values associated with those of thing, reality, presence in general, sensible presence, for example, substantial plenitude, content, referent, etc." (64). As long as matter is not defined as "absolute exterior or radical heterogeneity," materialism is complicit with idealism. Both fall back on a transcendental signified.

> Realism or sensualism — "empiricism" — are modifications of logocentrism. . . . [T]he signifier 'matter' appears to me problematical only at the moment when its reinscription cannot avoid making of it a new fundamental principle which, by means of a theoretical regression, would be reconstituted into a "transcendental signified." . . . It can always come to reassure a metaphysical materialism. It then becomes an ultimate referent, according to the classical logic implied by the value of referent, or it becomes an "objective reality" absolutely "ante-

rior" to any work of the mark, the semantic content of a form of presence which guarantees the movement of the text in general from the outside. (65)

In these tantalizing hints of what a deconstructive materialism might involve, Derrida suggests that we might understand matter through the figure of the text in general. This figure depicts the opening up or over-flowing of any form of presence such that it becomes part of a limitless weave of forces or an endless process or movement of referral. In contra-distinction, a metaphysical concept of matter regards materiality either as the endpoint of this movement of referral or as an external presence that sets off and secures this movement. Matter as presence is the arrestation of the text in general. It is important to add here that this movement is not the "free play" of textual indeterminacy, the joyful interpretive anarchy celebrated by deconstructive literary criticism. Paul de Man's definition of the text as an endlessly self-referential object that only offers an allegory of its own reading is well known. Derrida, however, immediately under-mines such auto-referentiality by emphasizing the importance of material-ism as a philosophy of the outside. It is important to understand the text as matter, he emphasizes, so as to prevent us from lapsing into a new idealism of the text as a self-interiority without an outside. For whether it is denigrated as contingent exteriority (as in Hegelian idealism) or cele-brated as the actuality of sensuous corporeal existence (as in Marxist mate-rialism), matter has always been the outside. As Derrida puts it,

> The concept of matter must be marked twice . . . outside the oppo-sitions in which it has been caught (matter/spirit, matter/ideality, matter/form, etc.). . . . [I]n the double writing of which we were just speaking, the insistence on matter as the absolute exterior of opposi-tion, the materialist insistence . . . seems to me necessary. . . . In a very determined field of the most current situation, it seems to me that the materialist insistence can function as a means of having the necessary generalization of the concept of text, its extension with no simple exte-rior limit . . . , not wind up . . . as the definition of a new self-interiority, a new "idealism" . . . of the text. (66)

Yet, Derrida also warns us that this exteriority must not be thought in simple opposition to the inside. A simple outside is complicit with the inside. It is important to remember here that the German word for object is *Gegenstand*, that external thing that stands against the subject. From a dialectical standpoint, the outside qua object is the negation of the inside qua subject. But it can be negated in turn when the outside is recognized by the subject as nothing other than itself, thereby allowing it to return back to itself in a moment of reflective internalization. Or alternatively, the outside can be posited as a reassuring external presence that anchors the subject and arrests its drifting: "The outside can always become again an 'object' in the polarity subject/object, or the reassuring reality of what is outside the text; and there is sometimes an 'inside' that is as troubling as the outside may be reassuring. This is not to be overlooked in the critique of interiority and subjectivity" (67). To think of matter outside the oppositions that have imprisoned it therefore requires us to think of matter outside opposition itself, including the oppositions that most patently denote opposition, the inside/outside and subject/object pairs.

In its interdefinability with text, matter exceeds and confounds the oppositions between the positive and the negative, the immediate and the mediated, presence and its representation. We have conventionally mistaken this materialist understanding of text for a form of linguistic constructionism because we have not framed it through the problem of time. For the implied question here is why is it that matter is text-*ile* or woven? Why is it that any present being always overflows itself and intimates an absolute alterity? Derrida's point is that in order to be present, any being must persist in time. This means that the form of the thing—that which makes it actual—must be identifiable as the same throughout all possible repetitions. But this iterability implies that any presence is in its very constitution always riven by a radical alterity that makes it impossible even as it makes it possible. By definition, this alterity cannot be a form of presence. Because it both gives and destabilizes presence, it subjects presence to a strict law of radical contamination.

Strictly speaking, this force or dynamism, if we can use these words, is inhuman. It is prior to any figure of human consciousness such as the subject, reason, or spirit, and even practical action. Nor does it issue from anthropologistic structures that are commonly viewed as constituting reality through negativity or mediation such as society, culture, or language. In Derrida's view, these are all forms of presence. At the same time, however, "the system of spacing/alterity," he suggests, "[is] an essential and indispensable mechanism of dialectical materialism" (94) even though the dynamism of alterity contravenes the two key terms of dialectical materialism. First, it evades the dialectical moments of negation and position. The non-phenomenality or non-presence of the other is not an absence or negated presence but "'something' . . . that deviates from the opposition presence/absence (negated presence)" (95). A negated presence always holds out the possibility of sublation that returns one to presence. By the same token, the other also cannot be posed or positioned (*setzen*) since this would be to reduce its alterity to the same, to an other that is posited by the subject as *its* other.[10] As Derrida puts it, "The position-of-the-other, in Hegelian dialectics, is always, finally, to pose-oneself by oneself as the other of the Idea, as other — than — oneself in one's finite determination, with the aim of repatriating and reappropriating oneself, of returning close to oneself in the infinite richness of one's determination, etc." (96). Second, the other is also not material in a Marxist sense because within Marxist discourse, body and matter are sensuous forms of presence or existence. Derrida insists that "no more than it is a form of presence, *other* is not a *being* (a determined being, existence, essence, etc.)" (95).

It would not be inappropriate to speak of deconstruction as a materialism of the other, or more precisely, as the thought of the materiality of the reference or relation to the other. This relation to alterity is more material than matter as substance or presence because it is more fundamental or "infrastructural," so to speak, since it constitutes matter as such. Simply put, Derrida's argument is that the very presence of matter — its persistence, endurance, or being in time — is premised on there being such a thing as a true gift of time, or which is the same thing, a pure event. As finite beings, we cannot give ourselves time. Under conditions of radical finitude, where we cannot refer to an infinite presence that can give us time, time can only be thought as the gift of an absolute other that is unpresentable but that leaves a trace in the order of presence even as the phenomenalization, appearance, or presentation of the other is also its violation. Similarly, the very event-ness of an event consists in its not being identified, recognized, or anticipated in advance. Something is not an event if we can tell when and from where it is or will be coming. Hence, the event and the gift can only be if they are entirely other, if they come from the other. They must therefore be understood through the figure of the impossible, that which we cannot imagine or figure within the realm of the possible. They require the thought of an inappropriable other that must necessarily remain unappropriated. For once the other that gives time and the event is appropriated, then it is no longer other, and there is no longer a gift or a pure event.

Although the impossible is not of the order of presence, it is not without relation to concrete actuality since it constitutes it. Indeed, the impossible is curiously more material and real than concrete actuality. In his later writings, Derrida repeatedly insists on the fundamental reality of this impossible relation to or coming of the other.

> The deconstruction of logocentrism, of linguisticism, of economism (of the proper, of the at-home [*chez-soi*], *oikos*, of the same), etc., as well as the affirmation of the impossible are always put forward *in the name of the real*, of the irreducible reality of the real — not of the real as the attribute of the objective, present, perceptible or intelligible *thing* (*res*), but of the real as the coming or event of the other, where the other resists all appropriation, be it ana-onto-phenomenological appropriation. The real is this non-negative impossible, this impossible coming or invention of the event the thinking of which is not an onto-phenomenology. It is a thinking of the event (singularity of the other, in its unanticipatible coming, *hic et nunc*) that resists reappropriation by an ontology or phenomenology of presence as such. . . . Nothing is more "realist," in this sense, than a deconstruction. It is (what-/who-)ever happens [(*ce*) *qui arrive*].[11]

This impossible coming of the other is not utopian. It is a force of precipitation that is experienced as an eruption within the order of presence and that in turn forces the experiencing subject to act. The impossible, Derrida writes, "gives their very movement to desire, action, and decision: it is the very figure of the real. It has its hardness, closeness, and urgency."[12]

For present purposes, the desubstantialization of matter that occurs as a result of the deconstructive inscription of materiality as the impossible relation to the other has at least three practical implications. First, it problematizes the concepts of actuality (*Wirklichkeit*) and actualization (*Verwirklichung*) at the heart of Marxist materialism. Where Marx opposes ghosts and specters such as those of ideology, the commodity, and the money form to the concrete actuality that is actualized by the material corporeal activity of labor, Derrida argues that as instances of presence and objective existence, concrete actuality and the work that effects it or brings it about are only possible because of a certain spectrality. The very form of actuality and the form that material activity seeks to actualize are premised on their iterability and temporalization. But because this iterability can only come from the absolutely other, it breaks apart from within any actuality that is established as a fundamental ground or *arche*. Iterability inscribes "the possibility of the reference to the other, and thus of radical alterity and heterogeneity, of differ*a*nce, of technicity, and of ideality in the very event of presence, in the presence of the present that it dis-joins *a priori* in order to make it possible [thus impossible in its identity or its contemporaneity with itself]."[13]

Second, this movement of desubstantialization — the survival or living-on of the form of a thing — is a paradoxical form of causality that yokes together what have been viewed as diametrical opposites in the history of Western philosophy: automatism and autonomy. We conventionally distinguish the automatism of the machine from free human action on the grounds that the former is a form of mindless mechanical causality and the latter is spontaneous and universal rational-purposive activity. Now, the constitutive dislocation of the living present by iterability is precisely a freeing or independence from presence. But this freedom is inhuman because it is prior to and exceeds the spontaneity of human practical reason. What is broached here, Derrida notes, is "a certain materiality, which is not necessarily a corporeality, a certain technicity, programming, repetition or iterability, a cutting off from or independence from any living subject — the psychological, sociological, transcendental or even human subject."[14] This materiality is a movement of freeing from the spontaneous rational subject. It is thus paradoxically a freedom prior to human freedom. "It is," Derrida writes, "the contradiction of automatic autonomy, mechanical freedom, technical life."[15]

Indeed, this materiality is even inorganic insofar as it is a scarring that threatens the teleological self-return of the organism as a self-organizing proper body or organic totality. Derrida goes as far as to describe it as a "machinistic materiality without materialism and even perhaps without matter."[16] Materiality in this sense has four characteristics. First, as "a very useful generic name for all that resists appropriation, . . . materiality is not . . . the body proper as an organic totality" (154). Second, it is marked by suspended reference, repetition, and the threat of mutilation (156).

Third, it exhibits "a mechanical, machinelike, automatic independence in relation to any subject, any subject of desire and its unconscious" (157). Fourth, it implies the values of the arbitrary, the gratuitous, the contingent, the random, and the fortuitous (158).

In dialectical materialism, the process of actualizing material reality is part of the epigenesis, auto-production, and auto-maintenance of the human corporeal organism as it creates the means of its own subsistence. The proletarian revolution is precisely creative labor's teleological process of appropriative return writ large on a world-historical stage. Deconstructive materialism is a delimitation of organismic vitalism and its teleological understanding of history. By attending to the machinic and spectral effects of iterability, it accounts for the possibility of the supplementation of organic life by *techne* and the contamination of living actuality by commodification, ideology, and so forth.[17] Indeed, Derrida argues that the key concepts of dialectical materialism are no longer adequate for understanding the rhythms and speeds of contemporary technomediated reality because they deconstruct the opposition between the actual and the ideal or virtual. The deconstruction of dialectical materialism is "demonstrated today better than ever by the fantastic, ghostly, 'synthetic,' 'prosthetic,' virtual happenings in the scientific domain and therefore the domain of techno-media and therefore the public or political domain. It is also made more manifest by what inscribes the speed of a virtuality irreducible to the opposition of the act and the potential in the space of the event, in the event-ness of the event."[18]

Yet, despite the scarring, dislocation, and tearing that it inflicts on presence, materiality in the deconstructive sense has a rigorously affirmative and generative character. Because it refers us to the radically other, materiality is also the opening of an unforeseeable future, an *à-venir* (to-come) that cannot be anticipated as a form of presence. Despite his insistence that there was no ethicopolitical turn in his work, Derrida explored the ethicopolitical implications of this messianic dimension of materiality as absolute alterity in his writings from the 1990s onward.[19] Simply put, since the other is that from which time comes, the experience of absolute alterity, however disruptive, must be affirmed because without it, nothing could ever happen. An understanding of materiality in terms of negativity effaces this messianic dimension because, by positing the other as the same, it closes off the experience of radical alterity.

Materiality as the rational subject's experience of alterity puts into question the classical distinction between *dynamis* and *energeia*, the potential and the actual, that underwrites our canonical understanding of power and action. For matter as *dynamis* has always been thought under the concept of possibility. It is potentiality as opposed to the act or *energeia* that actualizes what is merely potential, makes the potential actually existing, by giving it a defining form. In the Aristotelian subordination of potentiality to actuality, *dynamis* is what is *merely* virtual or potential, but it is also power or potency, ability, capacity, and faculty (*Vermögen, Kraft*) and therefore also sheer possibility. In the German philosophical tradition to which Marx belongs, the opposition is sublated in the idea of self-activity or self-actualization, of a power or potentiality that can continually make itself real or actual. This power is deemed to reside in the form of the human subject as the negation of the mere matter that nature gives us, whether negativity is conceived as the capacity of the concept to externalize itself in objective existence or as labor power—the capacity to work and produce the means of subsistence by actualizing ends in matter. In this case, *dynamis* is also the virtuality of the purposive image, what is possible for the subject to actualize through activity as long as it can be imagined or figured as an ideal form or image. What is at stake is possibility as the power of an "I can" or "I am able to." It can have many permutations. For instance, in the vital organic body, living matter is endowed with the capacity of self-organization. Or in the case of performativity, a set of norms or conventions establishes a range of possibilities for the subject that can contest this set of norms even as the power of the subject is secured by this set of norms.

In contradistinction, the deconstructive understanding of materiality indicates a force that is impossible, something not yet and no longer of the order of presence and the possible.

> [The im-possible] announces itself; it precedes me, swoops down upon and seizes me *here and now* in a nonvirtualizable way, in actuality and not potentiality. It comes upon me from on high, in the form of an injunction that does not simply wait on the horizon, that I do not see coming, that never leaves me in peace and never lets me put it off until later. Such an urgency cannot be *idealized* any more than the other as other can. The im-possible is thus not a (regulative) *idea* or *ideal*. It is

what is most undeniably *real*. And sensible. Like the other. Like the irreducible and inappropriable différance of the other.[20]

This weak force can be characterized through three motifs: first, it implies a constitutive heteronomy or finitude that derives from the structural openness of any material being to the gift of time or the pure event. Second, it is a structure of precipitation and urgency that prevents an indefinite deferral of the actualization of the potential. Third, since it comes from outside the capability or power of the subject, it is a fundamental passivity. But this passivity is not opposed to activity because it stimulates the activity of the subject as a response. It forces us to act. "What must be thought here, then, is this inconceivable and unknowable thing, a freedom that would no longer be the power of a subject, a freedom without autonomy, a heteronomy without servitude, in short, something like a passive decision. We would thus have to rethink the philosophemes of decision, of that foundational couple activity and passivity, as well as potentiality and actuality" (152).

In Derrida's view, the experience of absolute alterity is the origin of normativity, imperativity, and responsibility. Such ethicopolitical phenomena arise in situations where we encounter and respond to the inappropriable other who gives us actuality. For example, the undertaking of calculative legal decisions is propelled by our experience of an incalculable justice that escapes all rule. Or a truly responsible decision must break with the order of knowledge and undergo the ordeal of the undecidable because a decision that follows a rule of knowledge is a mere technics and therefore irresponsible. The experience of alterity is essentially the urgent force of any rational decision and action that cannot be reduced to the mastery or sovereignty of the rational subject. It makes every decision originarily passive. Derrida explains it as follows:

The passive decision, condition of the event, is always in me, structurally, another event, a rending decision as the decision of the other. Of the absolute other in me, the other as the absolute that decides on me in me. . . . I decide, I make up my mind in all sovereignty—this would mean: the other than myself, the me as other and other than myself, *he makes or I make* an exception of the same. . . . [K]nowledge is necessary if one is to assume responsibility, but the decisive or deciding moment of responsibility supposes a leap by which an act takes off, ceasing in that instant to follow the consequence of what is — that is, of that which can be determined by science or consciousness — and thereby *frees itself* (this is what is called freedom), by the act of its act, of what is therefore heterogeneous to it, that is, knowledge. *In sum, a decision is unconscious* — insane as that may seem, it involves the unconscious and nevertheless remains responsible. . . . It is this act of the act that we are attempting here to think: "passive," delivered over to the other.[21]

In other words, the force of materiality is nothing other than the constitutive exposure of (the subject of) power to the other. For if the freedom of the rational subject comes in or as its response to the other, then decision is prompted by and also comes from the other. It is therefore in the original instance passive and unconscious, not active and conscious, unlike the sovereign decision of exception (Schmitt) and the deliberation of public reason (Habermas). The force in question is not a counterpower that can be deployed against a given state of power. It is not the dispersal of power into a mobile field of relations between micropowers (Foucault). It is instead the constitutive exposure of power as such, which has been conventionally thought in terms of the circular economy of appropriation or the return-to-self of self-mastery, to what makes it vulnerable and defenseless. As the undoing of the power of the subject, the force of materiality cannot lead to a political program. Indeed, it is what resists and confounds any teleology such as that of Marxism and even any purposive or end-oriented action that is based on rational calculations or the projection of an ideal end. But as that which opens power up unconditionally to the other, this force also has a messianic dimension. It aporetically implies an absolute or incalculable hospitality to the other that demands a response in which we calculate with given conditions in order to act in a responsible manner.

2. Material Forces of Nonorganic Life (Deleuze)

Derrida's understanding of the force of materiality is very close to but also very far from Gilles Deleuze's account of matter as the power of nonorganic life. This concluding section briefly discusses various points of touching and three areas of divergence between their conceptions of materiality. Deleuze's account of matter arises from a trenchant critique of the Hegelian reduction of difference to dialectical negation and contradiction. Deleuze argues that if we understand being and the genesis of the world in terms of negativity, we have fundamentally misunderstood the nature of thought and its relation to being by fettering both within the prison of consciousness. We take consciousness as a starting-point and regard thought as an attribute or power that consciousness deploys in its encounter with what is outside it. The outside is what is different from and opposed to consciousness. By means of propositions, consciousness duplicates, represents, or mediates the outside so that it can resolve this difference. By negating the outside, it can grasp it with apodictic certainty. Deleuze argues that viewing the difference between consciousness and the outside in terms of opposition and negation begs the question of the genesis of both consciousness and the outside by an affirmative power of difference. This affirmative difference cannot be reduced to negation because it is prior to consciousness and the objects and things consciousness confronts. In Deleuze's words,

> Negation is difference, but difference seen from its underside, seen from below. Seen the right way up, from top to bottom, difference is affirmation. . . . It is not the negative which is the motor. . . . Negation results from affirmation: this means that negation arises in the wake of affirmation or beside it, but only as the shadow of the more profound genetic element—of that power or 'will' which engenders the affirmation and the difference in the affirmation. Those who bear the negative know not what they do: they take the shadow for the reality, they encourage phantoms, they uncouple consequences from premises and they give epiphenomena the value of phenomena and essences.[22]

This affirmative power of difference is the key principle of Deleuze's ontology of chance. Being, Deleuze suggests, is a matter of absolute chance because we do not know what it is and why there is being. Being is repeatedly constituted each and every time by events of chance (the fiat of creation) that are projectiles of being, throws of the dice that give rise to different singularities or commencements. These events of chance have the form of questions and imperatives. Ideas or problems arise in response to this clamor of Being. An idea or problem is an infinite field of continuity that is opened up by a specific projectile of being. Hence, instead of being an attribute of a thinking substance, ideas are the neuralgic points where the I is fractured.

> The imperatives of and questions with which we are infused do not emanate from the I: it is not even there to hear them. The imperatives are those of being, while every question is ontological and distributes "that which is" among problems. Ontology is the dice throw, the chaosmos from which the cosmos emerges. If the imperatives of Being have a relation with the I, it is with the fractured I in which, every time, they displace and reconstitute the fracture according to the order of time. . . . Consequently, far from being the properties or attributes of a thinking substance, the Ideas which derive from imperatives enter and leave only by that fracture in the I, which means that another always thinks in me, another who must also be thought. (199–200)

Put another way, ideas do not emanate from us. They are responses to Being. But since Being is absolute chance, it cannot be a simple origin or individuality from which the singularities of being issue through repeated throws. Instead, one must think Being itself as a repetition of singularities, the reprise or recommencement of being. The difference that characterizes being qua singularity would then issue from or be emitted by an originary repetition or difference (200–201). This movement of originary repetition and difference is not (yet) a being or an existent. But this nonbeing is not negative since this would imply something derived from a prior being. Nonbeing corresponds instead to the continuous field of an idea. When we define this nonbeing as a negative, we reduce it to the propositional language of consciousness and obscure the complexity of the problem as a field formed from an imperative of Being. In Deleuze's words, "the negative is an illusion, no more than the shadow of problems. . . . [T]he form of negation appears with propositions which express the problem on which they depend only by distorting it and obscuring its real structure" (202). This originary difference is positive but its positivity is not a simple unity. It is a multiplicity that escapes the opposition between the One and the many because the multiple is not the mere fragmentation of the One into the many.

As we have seen, Derrida also broke away from dialectical negation through the thought of an originary movement of difference (iterability/ *différance*). But whereas for Derrida originary difference intimates a radical alterity that is not of the order of presence and actuality and, thus, is neither negative nor positive, Deleuze characterizes the movement of originary difference as a transcendental field, or which is the same thing, a plane of immanence that generates actuality. An idea denotes a continuous field or plane that contains all ideal distinctions that is the positive "ground" of any actual concrete being. To understand any specific emission of singular being, we must refer first of all to this field of ideal differentiations, "all the varieties of differential relations and all the distributions of singular points coexisting in diverse orders "perplicated" in one another" (206). It is important to emphasize here that these ideal differentiations are not imposed by human rational consciousness. They precede consciousness but also any concrete phenomenon or object of appearance. Actualization is the process by which objects are formed from these differential relations. Here, the differentiations become concretely specified and are "incarnated in distinct species while the singular points which correspond to the values of one variety are incarnated in the distinct parts characteristic of this or that species" (206). In other words, actualization is the cutting up of this continuous field by real relations and concrete settings such that the ideal differentiations are further determined. This *coupure* generates an actual being or given object. As Deleuze puts it, actualization is "the production of finite engendered affirmations which bear upon the actual terms which occupy these places and positions, and upon the real relations which incarnate these relations and these functions" (207). In a strictly Kantian terminology, this plane of originary difference is noumenal insofar as it is the "ground" that generates all appearances or phenomena, all things that are given to us. But unlike noumenality in the Kantian sense, namely the thing-in-itself that is merely possible and thinkable, difference is a structure, a real field of relations. Hence, difference, Deleuze points out, "is that by which the given is given . . . as diverse. Difference is not phenomenon but the noumenon closest to the phenomenon" (222).

This field of differences is transcendental in the sense that it is the ground of genesis and the real "condition of possibility" of the actual. However, this transcendental field, Deleuze argues, cannot be defined in terms of a subject or even a pure stream of immediate consciousness because the intentional subject (and any object it intends) is not foundational. The subject is generated from this transcendental field, which is made up of pre-individual and impersonal singularities. "Singularities," he notes, "are the true transcendental events. . . . Far from being individual or personal, singularities preside over the genesis of individuals and persons; they are distributed in a 'potential' which admits neither Self nor I, but which produces them by actualizing or realizing itself, although the figures of this actualization do not at all resemble the realized potential."[23] Because the transcendental is now no longer connected to the subject or person, or even to a pure stream of an immediate consciousness, it is also a plane of immanence. Deleuze uses this phrase to denote a limitless field that cannot be contained or conditioned by something else. First, the plane of immanence is immanent because it is coextensive with actual existence. But it is not contained within or reducible to actual existence because it generates it. But second, and more important, instead of being an attribute of some other thing that is transcendent, immanence as a plane is *absolute*. It is always implicated in or inheres only in itself. Deleuze notes that it is only when immanence is "no longer immanence to anything other than itself that we can speak of a plane of immanence."[24]

We saw earlier that Derrida characterized materiality as a weak messianic force that exceeds the potentiality/actuality, possible/real oppositions and that renders power defenseless. Deleuze's account of originary difference as a plane of immanence leads to a different account of the virtual/ideal. He distinguishes the virtual/ideal from the merely possible by arguing that the idea as a field of differential relations is real and determined and not merely abstract and potential.[25] The reality of the virtual is that of a completely determined structure that is formed from genetic differential elements and relations and the singular points corresponding to these relations.[26] Every real object has a virtual content. The process of actualization further "differenciates" and determines this virtual content according to actual conditions. "The virtual must be defined as strictly a part of the real object — as though the object had one part of itself in the virtual into which it is plunged as though into an objective dimension" (209). We can understand the virtual as the set of speeds and intensities that generate an actual object. The relation between the actual object and the virtual is therefore twofold. On the one hand, the actual object is the accomplished absorption and destruction of the virtuals that surround it. On the other hand, the actual object also emits or creates virtuals since the process of actualization brings the object back into relation with the field of differential relations in which it can always be dissolved and become actualized otherwise, as something else, by being linked through other differential relations to other particles.[27]

Deleuze's distinction of reality into actual and virtual parts foregrounds the fundamental play of chance and difference in the actualization of an object. In the classical distinctions between the possible and the real, and the ideal and concrete existence, the real or the concretely existing is in a relation of resemblance to the possible or the ideal. The real is a mere duplication of the ideal, and, indeed, a deficient copy. Or the possible is regarded as defective because its actualization requires a leap into existence. In contradistinction, the power of the virtual is not merely that of a preexisting possibility whose actualization is predetermined and limited by the process of duplication or resemblance. The actualization of the virtual is instead a genuine creation of something that corresponds to singularities and differential relations but does not resemble the virtual. As Deleuze puts it, "the actualization of the virtual . . . always takes place by difference, divergence or differenciation. Actualization breaks with resemblance as a process no less than it does with identity as a principle. Actual terms never resemble the singularities they incarnate. . . . [Actualization] creates divergent lines which correspond to — without resembling — a virtual multiplicity."[28]

In actualization, the relation between the actual object and the virtual is that of an immersion or propulsion from a field of differential relations. Deleuze's favorite image for this generative propulsion from the transcendental field or plane of immanence is that of a falling fruit. "The actualization of the virtual is singularity whereas the actual itself is individuality constituted. The actual falls from the plane like a fruit, whilst actualization relates it back to the plane as if to that which turns the object back into a subject."[29] To relate the fruit back to its ground of genesis is to acknowledge that each constituted individuality is composed of multiple singularities and is therefore always subject to a radical movement of becoming deconstituted and reconstituted differently. Otherwise, individuality would become petrified and frozen into a transcendent object that is eternally the same, either a nondynamic thing that is unchanging, or something that only changes according to an internally programmed telos.

For Deleuze, materiality is nothing other than the plane of immanence. In his collaborative work with Guattari, he suggests that we must "try to conceive of this world in which a single fixed plane . . . is traversed by nonformal elements of relative speed that enter this or that individuated assemblage depending on their degrees of speed and slowness. A plane of consistency peopled by anonymous matter, by infinite bits of matter entering into varying connections."[30] Unlike dialectical materialism, the dynamism of matter does not derive from the negativity of human creative labor as it shapes and changes the form of (that is, trans-forms) the inert matter of pregiven objects. It is an inhuman dynamism consisting of speeds and intensities that open up the composition of any individual being, putting it into different connections with other particles, thereby leading to its recomposition.

The radical nature of Deleuze's materialism lies in its overturning of the central principle of dialectical materialism: organization. In dialectical materialism, the dynamism of matter comes from the activity or process of organization, the ordering of things through dialectical relations of mutual interdependence such that they become parts or members of a whole, where each part is an organ with its designated function within an integrated or systemic totality. The template of this kind of causality is the organism, a being that is able to spontaneously generate itself by virtue of its capacity for self-organization. This is why I suggested earlier that Marxism is an organismic vitalism. For Deleuze, however, matter as the plane of immanence is a dynamism of the differentiations, speeds, and flows of particles that are prior to any organized form. Following Hjelmslev, Deleuze and Guattari define matter as "the unformed, unorganized, nonstratified, or destratified body and all its flows: subatomic and submolecular particles, pure intensities, prevital and prephysical free singularities" (43). The *truly* material body is the body that subsists in the plane of immanence. It is not an organized system but "an aggregate whose elements vary according to its connections, its relations of movement and rest, the different individuated assemblages it enters" (256). Hence, the material body is not an organism but a body without organs.

Here, we touch on a third difference between the materialisms of Derrida and Deleuze. Unlike Derrida, what is affirmed is not a form of haunting or afterliving (*sur-vie*) that interrupts and dislocates the organic form of a living being but the pulsing force of a nonorganic and impersonal life that has infinitely greater vitality than any organism. Indeed, Deleuze suggests that organisms do not genuinely embody life but trap and imprison it within an organized form. Organic life is only a form that actualizes the virtual singularities of the plane of immanence by stratifying the flow of forces and constraining singularities in individuals. But organisms can die whereas the plane of immanence in which organized forms are composed is where life itself is liberated from these limited forms. "If everything is alive, it is not because everything is organic or organized but, on the contrary, because the organism is a diversion of life. In short, the life in question is inorganic, germinal, and intensive, a powerful life without organs, a Body that is all the more alive for having no organs, everything that passes *between* organisms" (499).

Inorganic life is the movement at the membrane of the organism, where it begins to quiver with virtuality, decomposes, and is recombined again. It is a life that exceeds the life and death of individual forms: "there is a moment that is only that of a life playing with death. The life of the individual gives way to an impersonal and yet singular life that releases a pure event freed from the accidents of internal and external life, that is, from the subjectivity and objectivity of what happens. . . . A singular essence, a life."[31] The indefinite article of a life indexes virtual singularities prior to their actualization as forms, *and* to the in-between of already actualized forms that are always pulsing with singularity and virtual force. The generative and constitutive relation between inorganic life or the body without organs and the organism always involves force. "The body without organs is . . . a living body all the more alive and teeming once it has blown apart the organism and its organization."[32] But this force is not destructive. Deleuze's privileged figure for inorganic life is the child or the baby. The baby's generative power, he suggests, is emphatically not the destructive force of war. "Combat . . . is a powerful, nonorganic vitality that supplements force with force, and enriches whatever it takes hold of. A baby vividly displays this vitality, this obstinate, stubborn, and indomitable will to live that differs from all organic life."[33]

It is difficult to elaborate on the political implications of Deleuze's understanding of materiality as the power of inorganic life. This is partly because the various figures he employs to characterize this power do not translate easily into our conventional vocabularies of political discourse and institutional practices. Indeed, Deleuze understands institutionalized forms of power as molar forms of organization that stratify and constrain life and counterposes to these forms of organization a micropolitics of becoming that releases the germinal forces or multiple singularities that make up organic forms.

The more general issue that needs to be raised about the materialisms of Derrida and Deleuze is the following: given that their respective views of the force of materiality derive from a radical ontology (in Deleuze's case) and a delimitation of ontology as such (Derrida), what is the bearing of their materialisms on the political sphere, political institutions, and concrete politics? In dialectical materialism, materiality is connected to concrete politics because material life is defined in terms of creative labor qua negativity and labor is embodied in the proletariat as a sociohistorical subject. In contradistinction, because Derrida understands material force as the reference to the impossible other and because Deleuze views materiality in terms of impersonal and preindividual forces, materiality, even if it is not unfigurable as such, is not easily instantiated by concrete figures that are recognizable by political discourse. In political theory, there has been very little productive engagement with Derrida's attempts to delineate ethicopolitical figures of materiality such as hospitality and forgiveness in his final writings. In Deleuze's case, the use of his concept of multiplicity by Michael Hardt and Antonio Negri, who attempt to embody the multiple in the multitude as a sociohistorical subject that replaces the proletariat in contemporary globalization, requires creative appropriation.[34]

But perhaps the better question to ask is not that of the relevance of these new materialisms to political thought and their implications for concrete politics but how they radically put into question the fundamental categories of political theory including the concept of the political itself. For what we consider as concrete political forms, institutions, practices, and activities, and the discourses that irrigate them such as rational choice theory, positivism, empiricism, and dialectical materialism are underwritten by ontologies of matter and life that the materialisms of Derrida and Deleuze put into question. It is important to note here that although their accounts of materiality concern the coming of the new — the advent of the entirely other that disrupts presence or the opening of actuality to multiple becomings — the force of materiality is not "new." It is a (quasi-)transcendental ground that has been obscured by traditional ontologies. The effectivity of these materialisms lies in the urgency of rethinking the ontological bases of current languages and vocabularies of politics and political thought, beginning, for example, with the very idea of political organization. In other words, what is the matter of the political and what is the matter of politics? This may very well open up new domains of the political and lines of political activity that have not been visible before.[35]

Notes

1 See Plekhanov, "The Materialist Conception of History," 20: "By entirely eliminating teleology from social science and explaining the activity of social man by his needs and by the means and methods of satisfying them, prevailing at the given time, dialectical materialism for the first time imparts to this science the 'strictness' of which her sister—the science of nature—would often boast over her. It may be said that the science of society is itself becoming a *natural* science: '*notre doctrine naturaliste d'histoire*', as Labriola justly says."

2 Engels, "Socialism," 698.

3 Ibid., 699.

4 See Althusser, "Contradiction and Overdetermination," 93–94: "If the Marxist dialectic is 'in principle' the opposite of the Hegelian dialectic, if it is rational and not mystical-mystified-mystificatory, this radical distinction must be manifest in its essence, that is, in its characteristic determinations and structures. To be clear, this means that basic structures of the Hegelian dialectic such as negation, the negation of the negation, the identity of opposites, 'supersession', the transformation of quantity into quality, contradiction, etc., *have for Marx . . . a structure different from the structure they have for Hegel.*"

5 On the epigenetic character of labor as it generates an objective dialectical system, see Marx and Engels, *The German Ideology*, ed. C. J. Arthur, 55–56: "Individuals certainly make *one another*, physically and mentally, but they do not make themselves." Compare Marx, *The Eighteenth Brumaire of Louis Bonaparte*, 146: "Men make their own history, but not of their own free will; not under circumstances they themselves have chosen but under the given and inherited circumstances with which they are directly confronted."

6 See Cheah, *Spectral Nationality*, chap. 4.

7 Marcuse, *One-Dimensional Man*, 63.

8 Derrida, *Specters of Marx*, 168–69.

9 Derrida, *Positions*, 64.

10 Derrida, *Positions*, 95–96: "I would even say that the alterity of the other *inscribes* in this relationship that which in no case can be 'posed.' Inscription . . . is not a simple position: it is rather that by means of which every position is *of itself confounded* (*différance*): inscription, mark, text and not only *thesis or theme* — inscription of the *thesis*."

11 Derrida, "As If It Were Possible," 367, translation modified.

12 Derrida, "Not Utopia, the Im-possible," 131.

13 Derrida, *Specters of Marx*, 75.

14 Derrida, "Typewriter Ribbon," 136.

15 Derrida, *Specters of Marx*, 153.

16 Derrida, "Typewriter Ribbon," 75–76.

17 For a fuller discussion of the connections and differences between deconstruction and Althusser's attempt to break away from dialectical materialism in his aleatory materialism or the materialism of the encounter, see Balibar, "Eschatology versus Teleology."

18 Derrida, *Specters of Marx*, 63.

19 Derrida, "As If It Were Possible," 360.

20 Derrida, *Rogues*, 84.

21 Derrida, *Politics of Friendship*, 68–69.

22 Deleuze, *Difference and Repetition*, 55. Deleuze derives this affirmative conception of difference in part from Nietzsche's concept of the eternal return.

23 For Deleuze's account of the transcendental field and his dissociation of the transcendental from consciousness, as well as his critique of the entire tradition of German idealism including Husserlian phenomenology, see *The Logic of Sense*, 98–110, 343–44, n. 5, and "Immanence," 25–28. The quoted passage is from *The Logic of Sense*, 103.

24 Deleuze, "Immanence," 26.

25 Note that in German idealism, the virtual or ideal is seen as synonymous with what is merely possible since ideas are principles of reason rather than objects. The idea is then opposed to the actual, which is synonymous with the real. Deleuze loosens the identification of the actual with the real and expands the real to include the virtual as a power.

26 Deleuze, *Difference and Repetition*, 209.

27 For a fuller elaboration of the relation between the virtual and the actual, see Deleuze, "The Actual and the Virtual."

28 Deleuze, *Difference and Repetition*, 212.

29 Deleuze and Parnet, "The Actual and the Virtual," 149–50.

30 Deleuze and Guattari, *A Thousand Plateaus* (Minneapolis, 1987), 255.

31 Deleuze, "Immanence," 28–29.

32 Deleuze and Guattari, *A Thousand Plateaus* (Minneapolis, 1987), 30.

33 Gilles Deleuze, *Essays Critical and Clinical*, 133.

34 Hardt and Negri, *Empire*.

35 I have attempted a critical assessment of Derrida's idea of democracy to come in "The Untimely Secret of Democracy."

Diana Coole

The Inertia of Matter and the
Generativity of Flesh

The predominant sense of matter in modern Western culture has been that it is essentially passive stuff, set in motion by human agents who use it as a means of survival, modify it as a vehicle of aesthetic expression, and impose subjective meanings upon it. This view of inert matter as inherently devoid of agency or meaning and as heterogeneous to consciousness has an elaborate provenance in classical science and philosophy, but it also seems congruent with, and indeed presupposes, a commonsense, naturalistic attitude which takes for granted a natural world "out there" as an essentially given collection of objects. Yet is it not possible to imagine matter quite differently: as perhaps a lively materiality that is self-transformative and already saturated with the agentic capacities and existential significance that are typically located in a separate, ideal, and subjectivist, realm? If so, what kind of conceptual or metaphorical resources might help us moderns evoke this immanent generativity? Is it possible to understand a process of materialization and the nature of its fecundity, to grasp matter's dynamic and sometimes resistant capacities, without relying upon mysticisms derived from animism, religion, or romanticism?

In this essay I draw on elements of Maurice Merleau-Ponty's pursuit of a new ontology as a way to approach such questions, albeit with some additional help from

Cézanne, Leibniz, and Deleuze. Since Merleau-Ponty did not explicitly pose his research in quite these terms, and his later writings remain very much works in progress, it has been necessary to reconstruct and develop some of the tantalizingly sketchy yet provocative overtures which suggest that the French phenomenologist was envisaging a radically new materialism. This is already implicit in early work on the primacy of perception, and it is this primacy, together with the consequent emphasis on corporeality as productive negativity, that remains at the heart of Merleau-Ponty's account of material existence as folded flesh.[1]

The aim of existential phenomenology as Merleau-Ponty understood it is to return to lived experience before it is written over and objectified by theory. "The first philosophical act would appear to be to return to the world of actual experience which is prior to the objective world" in order to "restore to things their concrete physiognomy" and thereby to undertake a "genealogy of being."[2] For him, this meant suspending our habitual assumptions about the visible realm in order to look afresh at the genesis of the perceptual world. Empiricism, Merleau-Ponty complains, robs sense experience of all mystery by reducing it to physico-chemical processes and causal relationships of stimulus and response. In modernity, only romantics like Herder retained a richer appreciation of a sense experience that yields "not 'dead' qualities, but active ones" (52). The task of a phenomenology of perception is accordingly to rediscover that "vital communication with the world" which precedes yet is taken for granted by the physicist's "freezing of being." "We must rediscover the origin of the object at the very core of our experience; we must describe the emergence of being" and with it, a "certain energy in the pulsation of existence" (71, 80). This is what is achieved by recognizing the body as "the pivot of the world" and nature as a phenomenal field inhabited by bodies as beings-in-the-world. Merleau-Ponty's aim, as I see it, is to explain a generative, self-transformative, and creative materiality without relying on any metaphysical invocation of mysterious, immaterial forces or agencies.

The Death of Nature / Matter

In order to appreciate the novelty of this approach to matter, it is helpful to reconstruct some relevant aspects of the Cartesian view that is Merleau-Ponty's principal target. Descartes had rejected materialist arguments that everything is matter. His approach is that of the rationalist, who deduces the coordinates of materiality rather than constructing it from sensuous experience or empirical observation.[3] Ontologically dualist, he distinguishes between thinking substance, *res cogitans*, and extended substance, *res extensa*, the latter being a single but infinitely modifiable substance of matter in extension. There are local velocities and vortices that individuate matter into particles, here, but its separate parts are simply juxtaposed, *partes extra partes*, like grains of sand. According to this Cartesian account, matter and space are inseparable. Matter occupies space and inversely, whatever occupies space is matter, whose sole irreducible property is extension. Its coordinates yield the kind of grid-like arrangement one finds in many American cities and they render matter a fundamentally quantitative phenomenon, amenable to precise measurement and, in particular, to the sort of calculations facilitated by Euclidian geometry, which for Descartes was the science of matter par excellence. Despite subjecting its existence to methodical doubt, Descartes concluded that matter does exist in the sort of mechanical, mathematical way he describes. This is quite antithetical to the phenomenological understanding of its perceptual emergence, for which "Nature is not in itself geometrical."[4]

Some of the more interesting aspects of the Cartesian understanding of matter are indeed what it excludes. As sheer exteriority, matter is devoid of interiority or ontological depth. It is without qualities like color or smell, which are relegated to secondary qualities and classified as unreliable, unstable sensations that are attributed by thought rather than being intrinsic to matter. Matter's geography is one of straight lines and rectangles rather than a topography of curves or labyrinths. As such, it is laid out before the searchlight of reason, the *lumen naturale*, without dark recesses, crevices, or hollows. Cartesian matter is unaffected by time or negativity, although it does obey laws of cause and effect. It is inert stuff emptied of all immanent vitality: Descartes's work is resolutely antivitalist. On the one hand, his philosophy is radically subjectivist. The thinking subject (*cogito*) is able to understand matter by deploying the correct, deductive method. Because, moreover, matter is without value or internal qualities or significance, it is not forbidden for this subject to control the material domain that is, for Descartes, synonymous with nature (including animals, whose lack of a soul or self-awareness renders them mere automata). Subjectivity is from this rationalist perspective immaterial (disembodied), potentially omniscient, and legitimately omnipotent. On the other hand, although Descartes's account is anthropocentric inasmuch as it depends on deductions made by the thinking subject, it is not humanist because it relies ultimately on God who is, strictly speaking, the only Substance and the One on which all else depends. It is God who guarantees the correspondence between exterior nature and mind and who finally therefore lays to rest the specter of skepticism. Having deduced that God must have created and set in motion the great cosmic machine, however, Descartes concludes that its divine creator thence vacated it, leaving behind a mechanism that is amenable to the calculations and deductions of reason.

In summary, Cartesian matter is as intrinsically empty of metaphysical purposes or ends as it is devoid of animistic or human spirit. This is what sets it free for modernity's secular and technoindustrial projects, thereby granting to Cartesian discourse an efficacy in regard to matter's subsequent adventures that would have been inconceivable in the seventeenth century. It is this apparently postmetaphysical sense of the material realm that would pave the way for Newtonian mechanics and provide the foundation for classical physics until the late nineteenth century, whence it would be modified by a language of fields and forces and, in the twentieth, by theories of relativity and elementary particles. Merleau-Ponty contends that it is impossible to reappraise humanism until the Cartesian perspective that "still overhangs ideas about nature" has been laid to rest since "an ontology which leaves nature in silence shuts itself in the incorporeal and for this very reason gives a fantastic image of man, spirit and history."[5] This is why nature's internal productivity needs to be "understood in some other way."

What Cartesianism most explicitly broke away from was the prevailing Aristotelianism, which had itself understood natural productivity in another way. For Aristotle, nature (*physis*) was not coextensive with matter (*hule*) because, although natural objects are composed of matter, they have an actuality that matter has merely the potential to achieve. As such, matter acquires its full meaning or form only relative to nature, which is in turn characterized by its immanent, formative efficacy. The survival of some of Aristotle's main terms — *physis* (nature; in Latin, *natura*), *morphe* and *eidos* (shape and form), *telos* (end; in Latin, *finis*), *entelexeia* (actuality, completeness), *energeia* (activity) — within subsequent philosophies of nature is testimony to his ideas' enduring legacy. Aristotle's account of nature's generative immanence, as sui generis, serves as a counterpoint to Descartes's unproductive alternative, but it also remains saturated with metaphysical, teleological assumptions.

Rethinking Nature: Beyond Mechanism and Mysticism

Debates about matter and its relationship with consciousness or qualitative meaningfulness are often still conducted in terms of the very oppositions Descartes proposed: between subject and object, or mind and body. Merleau-Ponty's critique, too, is often conducted as a rejection of such *binary* oppositions. He shows how these reify and separate processes that are irreducibly interwoven within the perceptual lifeworld. But in his later writings there sometimes surfaces an intriguing additional challenge to a *triadic* classification whose vestiges he finds still suffusing modern thinking.[6] Planning a return to ontology, he now determines that his project "must be presented without any compromise with humanism, nor moreover with naturalism, nor finally with theology . . . to show that philosophy can no longer think according to the cleavage: God, man, creatures."[7] This is echoed in his lectures on Nature, where he claims that there is "a unique theme of philosophy: the *nexus*, the *vinculum* 'Nature'-'Man'-'God.'"[8] What are we to make of this cryptic assertion? It surely encapsulates his realization that what is at stake in reconceptualizing materiality is how to describe an emergent, internally productive materiality without recourse to mechanistic or mystical assumptions or to the notions of causality and finalism (teleology) that are respectively associated with them. His account of folded, reversible flesh will be his way of finessing this nexus so as to avoid both unwarranted ontological distinctions and the naturalist, humanist, and theological presuppositions associated with them. Nature, Merleau-Ponty suggests, is an ontological leaf "divided into folds, doubled, even tripled. . . . There are no substantial differences between physical Nature, life, and mind" (212). To be faithful to it, one must pursue an ontology that "defines being from within and not from without," where "Nature, life, Man" are understood as manifestations of diverse folds rather than as essentially separate categories (220).

That Merleau-Ponty was considering a return to ontology in these terms has only become clear since the publication of three lecture courses he delivered between 1956 and 1960, collectively entitled *Nature*. One function of these lectures was evidently to help him work through issues he would need to address in the ontology that emerges in the unfinished chapters and working notes of *The Visible and the Invisible* (in process between 1959 and his death in 1961). The lectures offer critical reflections on philosophical and scientific accounts of nature, but they also invoke a primordial, "prehuman" realm of wild Being. If they elicit the theological and rationalist presuppositions that cover over this emergent, existential realm, they also show how entangled these apparently antithetical approaches to nature remain. Far from displacing metaphysics, Merleau-Ponty shows, scientific categories of space, time, matter, causality, and agency are legacies of a theological affirmation of Substance qua God as Unity, and they need to be rethought in their entirety (88, 112). Elsewhere he surmises that modernity's conceptions of acts or states of consciousness, as well as its understanding of form, perception, and matter, all require a fundamental reconfiguration.[9]

Examining philosophies of nature since the ancients, the first lecture course recognizes that these inevitably entail ontological claims about Being. It identifies an enduring tension between accounts of nature's auto-productive genesis and those of its mechanical repetition. Merleau-Ponty addresses this tension by invoking a distinction between *natura naturans* and *natura naturata* that he traces to the twelfth-century Andalusian-Arab philosopher, Averroës.[10] The first term may be literally translated as "nature naturing," that is, as producing itself, while the second may be translated as "nature natured," that is, created forms. The former is thus a verb, intrinsically and internally dynamic; the second, a noun, suggesting greater inertia and heteronomy. Much depends on their relationship, in particular whether the producing and the produced are aspects of a single process that is immanently generative of its own forms or assemblages — as Spinoza (*conatus*), Nietzsche (*will to power*), Bergson (*élan vital*), or Deleuze (*difference*) generally suggest and as Merleau-Ponty's ontology of flesh entails — or whether these are distinct terms whose linkage is more or less contingent: for example, as cause and effect, maker and machine, force and form, subject and object. A good deal also hinges on the kind of agency that is bestowed on the "naturing" force (the *naturans*) regarding its efficacy or pedigree and whether it is internal or external to materialization. What is at issue, then, is whether nature is internally productive of itself—such that there is an immanent and irreducible relationship between creating and created that renders matter a lively process of self-formation—or whether matter is inert stuff that is worked upon by some immaterial force or agency external to it, such as God or the subject. If such concerns seem rather arcane, it is germane to anticipate Merleau-Ponty's demonstration of their continuing salience for postclassical physics and the "new biology."

In pre-Socratic thought, Merleau-Ponty explains, nature had remained enigmatic; it was considered inhuman yet fecund. Already in Aristotelian and Stoic thinking, however, this primordial ground was being covered over and imbued with finalist notions of destiny. But if finalism and causality would subsequently emerge as opposing ways of setting matter in motion, Merleau-Ponty's critique of Descartes suggests that they are not after all entirely antithetical since they share certain metaphysical assumptions. Despite the new understanding of nature that emerged with Descartes and the transition to science, he contends, Descartes and Newton did not reject the idea of finality associated with an end or the perfectibility of nature; they merely sublimated it in an idea of God as infinity, derived from the Judeo-Christian tradition.[11]

Merleau-Ponty argues that, although it was the way Descartes interpreted God's role that paved the way for his sense of nature as infinitely extended matter, this also infused modern science with vestiges of religion. "The concept of Nature is mixed with the concepts of God and human being in Cartesian thinking" (131). Indeed, the scientific conception of nature often, he claims, remains "entirely theological in its infrastructure" because it is still informed by a philosophy of Substance (88). Where Descartes was nevertheless original was in "doubling" or differentiating nature, "as *naturans* and as *naturata*," which had the effect of separating its interiority and exteriority. The productivity that had for the ancients been internal to and of nature was now located in a God whose agency was external to it, with nature persisting as a mechanical system that nevertheless manifests His perfect laws inasmuch as like Him, it is an infinite, homogenous positivity.[12] "*Meaning finds its refuge in the naturans; naturata becomes product, pure exteriority*" (9). This view of nature / matter as self-identical positivity is criticized by Merleau-Ponty because the absence of any temporality, lack, or weakness in its fabric, inherited from theological ideas of God's perfection, means that it is without negativity or difference to set it in motion. It is therefore bereft of contingency or possibility for self-transformation, too: there is no "scope for any difference between actual and possible beings." This is why Cartesian matter is dead and anathema to the phenomenologist: what Descartes describes is a uniform, static world regulated by necessity and devoid of generativity, virtuality, or vitality. Descartes "undoes the unreflected communication with the world" (126) with which phenomenology begins.

Kant, by contrast, humanized the *naturans* by identifying it with human consciousness (the "return to human being appears as the return to a *naturans* that operates in us" [22]). But Merleau-Ponty insists that this destroys the interiority and productive immanence of matter as thoroughly as do mechanistic accounts since it similarly entails a migration of nature's self-transformative powers into an external agency. In both cases, productivity vacates nature and is ascribed to an external, idealized authority. The reproduction of universal laws is a poor substitute for nature's contingent exuberance.

It is because they endeavor to retain this inherent exuberance that Merleau-Ponty is sympathetic to romantic and vitalist efforts that he interprets as trying to reunite *natura naturans* and *natura naturata*. He is nevertheless concerned that in (re)turning to philosophies of immanence, they risk reviving the theological and teleological senses of internal productivity that render such approaches vulnerable to mysticism. Schelling, for example, is accorded an important role in the lectures (although not in Merleau-Ponty's published work) inasmuch as he sought a "phenomenology of prereflexive Being" (41) that anticipates later efforts by Bergson, Husserl, and Merleau-Ponty himself. Schelling is credited with trying to reunite *naturans* and *naturata* by describing a "sort of pure, unmotivated surging-forth" where nature is productivity anterior to reflection: a terrifying and barbaric excess that is the fundamental stuff of life (37). There is no essential difference between organic and inorganic nature in this account; they are merely potencies with different powers of organization such that inanimate matter becomes living being through its internal development. This already anticipates a common thread running through many new vitalisms and materialisms.

In Schelling's romantic version it is because there is no rupture that nature remains intuitively accessible to us through perception or poetry. He had wanted to live and feel this productivity. Yet this is where his romanticism failed him in Merleau-Ponty's opinion. For while he held on to a certain obstinacy of nature as irreducible to reflection and recognized the creativity required to access it, Schelling presented art as an experience of subject-object identity, thereby reestablishing the indivisibility of consciousness and nature broken by reflection. Merleau-Ponty detects an element of mysticism in this desire for unmediated fusion, where according to Schelling we become one with nature in order to think it. The fact that Merleau-Ponty's criticism is largely delivered by way of proxies, that is, via critiques of Hegel and Lukács, suggests that a broader issue is at stake here. Subject-object identity and a romantic or teleological view of non-alienated nature (as origin and telos) portend a violent political legacy, as Merleau-Ponty had shown in his critique of Marxism in the more or less contemporaneous *Adventures of the Dialectic*. The ambition of intuitive coincidence is sheer mysticism, he concludes, just as the illusion of representational correspondence is confused positivism.

Merleau-Ponty's excursus through philosophy's conceptions of nature ends with Husserl, a thinker to whose later work he owed a considerable debt. This is the Husserl who renounced transcendental idealism once he realized that the "role of phenomenology is not so much to break the bond that unites us with the world as to reveal it to us and explicate it" (71), and who had referred to the lifeworld (*Lebenswelt*) as a "new" or "third" dimension of previously unknown phenomena that unfolds between and beneath the oppositions presupposed by common sense, philosophy, and science.[13] In alluding to this third, existential dimension, Merleau-Ponty claims, Husserl glimpsed the enigma of sensible things plus the virtual, thereby suggesting a postdualist ontology of "wild-flowering world and mind"; a "jointing and framing of Being" wherein there is "*a genesis of sense*."[14] From the perspective of the lectures, it is apparent why this phenomenological project of returning to the lifeworld would have commended itself both as a resolution to the separation of *natura naturans* and *natura naturata* and as an account of the productivity of the *naturans* as inherent in corporeal, existential processes that are irreducible to mechanism, subjectivity, or mysticism. It is from this perspective that modernity's untenable triad of naturalism, humanism, and theology is to be overcome.

The Phenomenological Return to the Lifeworld

If for Merleau-Ponty it is corporeality that introduces meaning or structure into matter, this is because the body literally incarnates material capacities for agency. Existence is for him an internally productive, *formative* process wherein meaning and matter are irreducibly interwoven: "the very process whereby the hitherto meaningless takes on meaning."[15] The phenomenological task is to show how consciousness emerges from, yet remains enmeshed in, this material world. To remain faithful to its own insights here, it "must plunge into the world instead of surveying it."[16] Crucially, this does not entail a precritical return to the immediately given or the sort of intuitive coincidence Merleau-Ponty criticizes in Schelling (and Bergson). He never forgets that "our idea of nature is impregnated with artifice."[17] Our apprehending nature/matter entails a raft of bodily accomplishments, linguistic practices, and cultural assumptions that are integral to nature's unfurling and to our own place within it. Reversals, lines of force, and folds ripple across the phenomenal field to render its materiality multidimensional, contingent, and overdetermined. For the phenomenologist there is a critical obligation to interrogate every presupposition, including the one that assumes some pristine material reality awaiting discovery beneath our constructions. When phenomenology strives to describe the presubjective, primordial processes that yield and sustain reflective consciousness, it also participates in a creative disclosing of "*Lebenswelt* as universal Being," whence "all the particular analyses concerning Nature, life, the human body, language will make us progressively enter into the *Lebenswelt* and the 'wild being.'"[18] Making "a philosophy of the *Lebenswelt*" thus proceeds as an interrogative, iterative, creative process. For the "brute or wild Being (= the perceived world)" to which it returns "is at bottom Being in Heidegger's sense, which . . . appears as containing everything that will ever be said, and yet leaving us to create it" (170). This is why Merleau-Ponty maintains that phenomenology's target is not, "like Bergsonian intuition, that of a reality of which we are ignorant and leading to which there is no methodical bridge."[19] The folded, indeterminate field of existence defies all attempts at intuitive coincidence or absolute knowledge. But one can "plunge" into it, watching with wonder as new meanings emerge and striving creatively to express, indeed to emulate, the *form*ative process before it is overwritten by reifying discourses and performances.

For Merleau-Ponty, references to an essential consciousness, subjectivity, or mind are but reifications of contingent, disparate capacities to structure and stylize the world that emerge hazardously through and within corporeal practices. It is therefore corporeality that is privileged as *naturans* in this account, inasmuch as it is here that productive difference and agentic capacity emerge through being-in-the-world. The qualities Descartes designated as secondary and external now lend to objects a sensuous unity that is meaningful for the body because it has existential familiarity as a style of being — "a certain rhythm of existence" — that is recognized as a variant of the body's own and thereby delivered to it "in the flesh" (212, 319, 320). The antithesis between matter and ideality, or between materialism and idealism, is thus overcome at both the corporeal level (by perception) and the philosophical level (by phenomenological interrogation). The body knows the world "laterally, by the *style*."[20] For the phenomenal body "is *not* a mass of matter, it is rather a standard of things," a level around which divergences form, a "measurant of the things" that thereby brings "an ideality that is not alien to the flesh" and which grants it "its axes, its depth, its dimensions."[21] The body is accordingly "a frontier which ordinary spatial relations do not cross."[22] Corporeal space is lived spatiality, oriented to a situation wherein the lived/living/lively body embarks on an architectural dance that actively spatializes (and temporalizes) through its movements, activities, and gestures. The body introduces patterns, intervals, duration, and affects into Cartesian or Euclidian space from within it, and it continuously reconfigures its own corporeal schema in responding to and recomposing its milieu (*Umwelt*).

It becomes clear on reading the *Nature* lectures how important this last term, developed by Jacob von Uexküll, was to Merleau-Ponty's sense of a body enveloped in its environment. Giorgio Agamben will later refer to Uexküll as one of the twentieth-century's greatest zoologists and credit him with the "unreserved abandonment of every anthropocentric perspective."[23] It was partly thanks to Uexküll's work that Merleau-Ponty was able to conclude in the late 1950s that the quarrel between (mechanistic) materialists and vitalists had been resolved through their mutual appreciation of form (*Gestalt*).[24] Uexküll's sense of *Umwelt* as an "intermediary reality" (167), the between, serves here as the animal equivalent to Husserl's

Lebenswelt. Already operative at the organic and embryonic levels, the *Um-welt* is the environment to which behavior is practically oriented through experiencing stimuli as meaningful signs. For lower animals, according to Uexküll, their *Umwelt* operates as a closure that allows entry only to those stimuli that are immediately relevant to their lives. But for higher animals, it operates as an opening wherein behavior and perception "deposit a sur-plus of signification on the surface of objects" and life is understood as "the opening of a field of action" (171, 173). It was on this basis that the new biology understood animal cells and even the human species as particular modes of "concrescence" within the natural process, and the body as a behavioral Gestalt situated within an environment (*Umwelt*). In particu-lar, it rejected the model of the organism as a physical machine animated by consciousness or by some vital spark, describing instead an emergent, future-oriented but open organization that is immanent to the organism ("the spirit is not what descends into the body in order to organize it, but is what emerges from it" [140]). The animal is accordingly conceptualized as a field rather than a machine, its behavior being produced from a system of emergent motor powers. While Merleau-Ponty warns against import-ing finalist assumptions into this process, he applauded this new biological sense of life as a contingent unfurling of possibilities whose development is not predetermined and whose vitality is strictly immanent. "It is not that life is a power of being or a spirit, but rather, that we install ourselves in perceived being/brute being, in the sensible, in the flesh" (210).

Painting "Inhuman Nature"

In trying to glimpse the lifeworld as it unfolds, the phenomenologist "steps back to watch the forms of transcendence fly up like sparks from a fire."[25] Because of a tendency for language to reify meaning, however, Merleau-Ponty suggests that the painter is in some ways more adept at the process of inventive disclosure than the thinker. His exemplar here is Cézanne, whom he credits with being a phenomenologist *avant la lettre*. By suspending our everyday, anthropocentric assumptions about familiar objects, Cézanne's painting draws attention to their precarious perceptual emergence, while his reflections on his experience of painting also reveal something of the creative engagement with the world that effaces any rigid distinction between creator and created. "We live in the midst of man-made objects, among tools, in houses, streets, cities, and most of the time we see them only through the human actions which put them to use. We become used to thinking that all of this exists necessarily and unshakably. Cézanne's painting suspends these habits of thought and reveals the base of inhuman nature upon which man has installed himself."[26] Human artifacts and natural objects are generally just treated as the taken-for-granted material background and paraphernalia of our everyday lives. We rarely pause to consider the contingent processes through which our familiar, visible world comes into being, not only through the hard labor of production and the economic hierarchies that structure it, but also via the creative contingencies of perception. Art can help us suspend these naturalistic and humanistic habits by encouraging us to observe the very "fabric of brute meaning" as it takes shape.[27] Like philosophy or the body, painting is also a fold; it expresses the "reflexivity of the sensible" whereby it becomes "impossible to distinguish between what sees and what is seen, what paints and what is painted."[28] When Merleau-Ponty quotes Cézanne —"The landscape thinks itself in me and I am its consciousness"[29]—it is to draw attention to the way the artist's body poses a question to a world whose vectors seem in response to "emanate from the things themselves, like the patterns of the constellations."[30] This, too, is congruent with a description of folded flesh as immanently generative. "There is no break at all in this circuit; it is impossible to say that nature ends here and that man or expression starts here. It is, therefore, mute Being which itself comes to show forth its own meaning."[31] This is not an act of mastery, but the self-disclosing of matter that is " 'pregnant' with its form" and "that poses itself by its own means."[32]

For the rationalist, depth is deduced from two-dimensional height and length; for the phenomenologist, it is integral to the embodied experience of living among things. When the body moves around in space, it does not perceive things with the relative sizes objective calculation would predict. It does not inhabit a flat, geometrical, fully determinate plane but a milieu, an *Umwelt* that remains ambiguous, indeterminate, and resonant with an expressive significance that affects the body's perception of spatial relations. Merleau-Ponty discerns Cézanne as trying to capture these perspectival distortions as they occur in perception, in order to convey "an emerging order," where the object is "in the act of appearing, organizing itself before our eyes."[33] In his Cubist phase he shattered things' spatial shells as he struggled to convey depth by expressing their "voluminosity," with all perspectives and dimensions coexisting. But later he recognized the inadequacy of pure forms because it was inside them that "the things began to move, color against color; they began to modulate in instability."[34] Color seems to catch this internal generativity of visibility so much better than shape or line because it creates subtle identities and differences that allow a painting to break the "skin of things" and show them emerging into visibility. During his impressionist phase Cézanne thus tried to capture "the very way in which objects strike our eyes and attack our senses. Objects are depicted as they appear to instantaneous perception, without fixed contours, bound together by light and air." He wanted, Merleau-Ponty comments, "to depict matter as it takes form, the birth of order through spontaneous organization."[35]

As opposed to rationalism's objects, petrified in space and time, or its formal calculation of perspective, Cézanne's painting brings the material world alive; it does not measure or represent reality but emulates the way it materializes in perception. A formal focus on contours that define objects or calculation that places them correctly in their relative spatial relations, in order to achieve perspectival depth, is recognized by Merleau-Ponty as the artistic equivalent of the physicists' Euclidian coordinates: the space that is "positive, a network of straight lines" and appropriate to classical ontology. For Descartes in his *Optics*, art was a representation of extension, and perspective was crucial for portraying the right order of things, while color was mere ornamentation.[36] This Cartesian metaphysics in turn informed those classical artists who calculated perspective in the belief that it would allow them to present nature more accurately. For Merleau-Ponty, this ostensible realism is however but one possible artistic style and an impoverished one at that. "I say that Renaissance perspective is a cultural fact, that perception itself is polymorphic and that if it becomes Euclidian, this is because it allows itself to be oriented by the system." The challenge is to suspend this culturally fashioned perception in order to uncover the "vertical" world of "brute" or "wild" perception as it emerges.[37]

This emphasis on perspective has broader ramifications inasmuch as perspective presumes an idealized observer from whom vision emanates. The body-subject must have a perspective because it is situated, enveloped in space and time. This is why Merleau-Ponty rejects the conceit of the bird's-eye view that surveys a material plane laid out before its gaze or understanding. In moving to an antihumanist ontology of flesh, he would therefore need to maintain this sense of perspective yet eschew its subjectivist or anthropocentric implications. He did so, I suggest, by *multiplying* perspectives, a move made feasible by the recognition that bodies and objects are simultaneously seeing and seen, such that the rays or arcs of vision/visibility that crisscross the visual field emanate simultaneously from each profile of every object, all jostling together and intersecting to gestate and agitate the dense tissue of relationships that constitute the flesh and to place the philosopher everywhere and nowhere. This image of coexistence as an intercorporeal field then suggests a pre- or postclassical "topographical space": a "milieu in which are circumscribed relations of proximity, or envelopment."[38]

There are many places, too—such as when he defines the perceptual Gestalt as "a diacritical, oppositional, relative system," or perception as being "structured as a language," or life as "the establishment of a level" around which divergences form, a "system of oppositions"[39]—where the influence of structural linguistics is apparent in helping Merleau-Ponty to conceptualize a productivity that is attributable solely to differentiation and relationality. It is this kind of shifting differentiation that breaks up the positivity of nature to yield its contingent, febrile productivity. But unlike the unhinged, linguistic plays of *différance*, existence has its gravitational points that lend it meaning and direction (*sens*), and these are bodies. They coexist within a relational field that loops and effervesces around and through them, where flesh folds over itself to engender, traverse, and "animate other bodies as well as my own."[40] All are caught in the pell-mell of an anonymous, prepersonal visibility with whose "modulations" and "reliefs" they enjoy existential contact, whence they are caught in the circuitry of a world whose intercorporeal, "intermundane space" they inhabit.[41] Such is the immanent generativity of existence.

Folded Matter

I have suggested that corporeality, painting, and philosophy all exemplify folds within existence. I end this essay by exploring this notion of folded matter a little further, by suggesting Merleau-Ponty's possible indebtedness to Leibniz. In his *Phenomenology of Perception*, Merleau-Ponty writes of the body-subject that "I am not, therefore, in Hegel's phrase, 'a hole in being', but a hollow, a fold, which has been made and which can be unmade."[42] The emergence of living being from physical matter is later described as a surging forth that opens a spatiotemporal field, with life itself now being described as "a fold."[43] Nature's capacity for productive relationality and reflexivity is derived by Merleau-Ponty from Husserl's account of two hands touching: "When I touch my right hand with my left, my right hand, as an object, has the strange property of being able to feel too."[44] In the flesh of my fingers, each digit is both objective and phenomenal: "outside and inside of the finger in reciprocity, in chiasm, activity and passivity, coupled," mutually encroaching, with things touching me as I touch them and myself.[45] This reversibility is nonetheless an "ambiguous set-up" because the reversal between touching and touched "always miscarries at the last moment," such that there is a "shift" or "spread" (écart) between them (9, 138, 147f., 254). Indeed, if this slippage or noncoincidence did not occur there would be only inert repetition rather than the "dehiscence" that "opens my body in two" as a productive "difference between the identicals" (263). Merleau-Ponty is explicit that "*reversibility* is not actual *identity*" but equally that "this divergence is not a *void*, it is filled precisely by the flesh as the emergence of a vision, a passivity that bears an activity — and so also the divergence between the exterior visible and the body which forms the upholstering [*capitonnage*] of the world" (272). It is this chiasm — between touching and touched, activity and passivity, phenomenal and objective being — that grants the body its capacity for "double sensations" and which opens it onto a world or, to express it more ontologically, this is Being, flesh, existence, opening itself to contingency, meaning, and self-transformation; a hollowing out whereby interiority, dimensionality, and productive differentiation occur.

It is in this context that the terminology of the fold proliferates in the later ontological writings. "The only 'place' where the negative would really be is the fold, the application of the inside and the outside to one another, the turning point" (264). It is due to this folding that "the body is not an empirical fact" but the reverse or other dimension of sensible being (255), yielding a body "of two leaves" (137), an agentic thing among things: a "*sensible for itself*" (135), an "exemplar sensible" (135), a "sensible sentient" (136), a "two-dimensional being" (136), "subject-object."[46] Such is the "realization of life as a fold or a singularity of physiochemistry

— or structure."[47] There is no external or mystical power at work here, no subject or God, no new force; there is merely existence and corporeity enfolded along a spatiotemporal shift. Merleau-Ponty is adamant that there is no teleological presumption. Rather, there are folds, deferrals and reversals that render flesh productive and emergent yet contingent. This notion of folding is sometimes used in conjunction with that of envelopment (*Ineinander*), as when Merleau-Ponty refers to "the wrapping of the body-object around itself."[48]

Deleuze will acknowledge that "it was Merleau-Ponty who showed us how a radical, 'vertical' visibility was folded into a self-seeing." He explains that it "is as though there were an 'opening', a 'gap', an ontological 'fold' which relates being and the question to one another. In this relation, being is difference itself."[49] This sense of opening is related by Deleuze to an antihumanist, Heideggerian sense of *Dasein* (being-there) that he thinks Merleau-Ponty appreciated (as distinct from Sartre, who erroneously humanized it as human subjectivity). He also notes Foucault's indebtedness to Merleau-Ponty as Foucault eventually understood subjectivization as a fold, with moving matter replete with an interiority constituted by its folding, such that it "resembles exactly the invagination of a tissue in embryology."[50] The advantage of this imagery of folding is that it allows a sense of matter as pleated, creased, rippled, hollowed, and reflexive without ascribing its interiority to any essentialist notion of consciousness. It is where, following Merleau-Ponty, one can identify immanent agentic capacities in Being's creative effulgence.

Merleau-Ponty was nonetheless still dissatisfied with the language he was deploying to describe the reversibility of flesh. Perhaps this is because it is tempting when one thinks of a fold to imagine a piece of cloth neatly, if not quite perfectly, laid over itself. Although this is suggestive of a certain difference, it surely does not capture the density or hollowing that he wanted to evoke. He urges himself, moreover, to avoid "thinking by planes and perspectives," cognizant no doubt that an imagery of layers, dimensions, vectors, and rays is still reminiscent of the Euclidian geometry he eschews. He therefore considers substituting a more curvilinear terminology, where the body's reversibility might be better described as "two circles, or two vortexes, or two spheres, concentric when I live them naively, and as soon as I question myself, the one slightly decentered with respect to the other."[51] This is surely more congruent with the topographical space he cites as the milieu of envelopment and where there are—as Cézanne had shown—primordial relations of proximity irreducible to matter as extension.[52] It is also more consonant with life understood not as "a hard nucleus of being, but the softness of the flesh" qua an investment, installation, relief, or "watermark" in Being.[53] Inasmuch as the fold is imagined as a two-dimensional folding back or folding over of two planes, it is not therefore quite satisfactory. I would like, however, to suggest that Merleau-Ponty also entertained a rather richer sense of the fold, which is indicated by the references to coiling, labyrinths, hollows, watermarks, soft flesh, and vortices, and for which his inspiration may have been Leibniz.

This connection is not simply fanciful. Although he never wrote in detail about Leibniz, Merleau-Ponty refers to him on enough occasions to show familiarity with his work. In his *Phenomenology*, for example, he associates Leibniz with a way of describing the visual field from the sort of nonanthropocentric, "perspectiveless position" that he will aspire to in his own ontology.[54] Elsewhere he includes Leibniz among those thinkers of the Baroque age who still recognized "beneath the chain of causal relations, another type of being which sustains that chain without breaking it. Being is not completely reduced or flattened out upon the level of external Being. It still has interiority."[55] Sometimes he refers to politics as a labyrinth, which is, as Deleuze explains, a multiplicity of folds.[56] Finally, there are twelve references to Leibniz in the final working notes, with Merleau-Ponty stating that "I clarify my philosophical project by recourse to Descartes and Leibniz" and several times repeating his intention to explore Leibniz's ontology, where he will substitute being-in-the-world for Leibniz's God but will in other respects maintain "entirely" certain of Leibniz's descriptions, only ridding them of their substantialist and ontotheological elaborations in order to apply them to wild Being.[57]

So Merleau-Ponty was certainly intrigued by Leibniz. But if his allusions to folding do incorporate a Leibnizean sense, what might the implications have been for his description of emergent materialization? One advantage would have been the radically anti-Cartesian, anti-Newtonian rhythms of matter it suggests. Thus David Harvey associates Leibniz with a "relational concept of space," which "holds that there is no such thing as space or time outside of the processes that define them." Processes accordingly define their own spatial frame, with an event or object depending on the multiplicity of disparate influences swirling and congealing around it.[58] Deleuze aptly mentions that the exemplary science of the fold is not Euclidian geometry but origami. He notes anticipations of Leibnizean folding among those pre-Socratics whose enigmatic philosophies of nature fascinated Merleau-Ponty, but he also finds it echoing within post-classical physics (as in Merleau-Ponty's *Nature* lectures, the work of A.N. Whitehead plays a significant role here). Although the flows of matter Deleuze invokes resemble the movement of elementary particles rather than Cartesian or Newtonian objects, it is in the folded proteins of microbiology that he finds the most contemporary affinity with Leibniz. Of course, there are significant differences between Merleau-Ponty, Leibniz, and Deleuze, particularly regarding ontology, but I am more interested in this context in the provocative resonances and intersections that emerge from their descriptions of the rhythms and images of Being's immanent unfurling.

If Deleuze is a helpful source for clues that link Merleau-Ponty to Leibniz, it is because he wrote a book about the latter called *The Fold* (*Le Pli*). Earlier I noted his association of Merleau-Ponty's sense of the fold with Heideggerian opening, but Heidegger's sense of folding and unfolding is elaborated here as "a coextensive unveiling and veiling of Being" that is indebted to Leibniz (albeit mistakenly interpreting Leibniz's being-for-the-world as being-in-the-world).[59] Deleuze's account of the Leibnizean fold resonates with Merleau-Ponty's sense of Being as "between." Organic folding is described by Deleuze not as a "fold in two" but as a "fold-of-two," an *entre-deux*; as differentiation of difference, where the "fold is always between two folds" and "the between-two-folds seems to move about everywhere" (11, 14). Heidegger, too, is found subscribing to this Leibnizean sense of "Difference that endlessly unfolds and folds over each of its two sides" (33). In conjunction with the anti-Euclidian geometries it suggests, this sense of folding as an active, extremely lively verb helps to overcome the sometimes more static sense of the fold as passive or as a noun or as two-dimensional in some of Merleau-Ponty's invocations of folded flesh. It is more appropriate for suggesting the volatility and complexity of the immanent, relational field of the visible and invisible. If the organism is conceived here as an "originary folding and creasing," there is no fundamental distinction for Leibniz between organic and inorganic matter, while the Baroque "soul entertains a complex relation with the body" that defies mind-body dualism (8f., 12).

Leibnizean folding would surely, then, have been evocative for the kind of wild being Merleau-Ponty was trying to describe as sensuous, visual/tactile, pluri-dimensional flesh, where matter is a fabric coiled over and over in its more material or ethereal layerings and gatherings. Like this dense flesh, Leibniz's articulated matter is without voids. "Folds replace holes." "Matter thus offers," as Deleuze glosses him, "an infinitely porous, spongy, or cavernous texture without emptiness," with each body being elastic, "pierced with irregular passages" and dependent for its cohesion on the pressure of external forces (5, 30). These Leibnizean modes of expression could surely have helped the phenomenologist to evoke the twisted coils that texture materiality and that challenge the subject-centered formula of perceptual perspective in favor of a dense field traversed by multiple perspectives that subtend and emanate from manifold points. For Deleuze/Leibniz this teeming, turbulent, convoluted world suggests an infinity of folded matter which, like time and space, is continuously folding and unfolding. As matter swirls and metamorphoses, its modulations do yield provisional forms as styles of existing. But these also subdivide into increasingly tiny folds that sustain their internal integrity across a continuous fabric of folds within folds. They are folded, Deleuze suggests, in order to be enveloped and wrapped in something else (23).

It is perhaps in examples of Baroque art that this folding and enveloping seems most redolent of Merleau-Ponty's visual/tactile field, where sensuous images portray matter as a richly pleated cloth, a tactile textile. Deleuze observes that Descartes mistakenly tried to move through this labyrinth along rectilinear tracks and thus failed to grasp the curvature of matter. In place of the latter's physics of light, he invokes the Baroque art of Caravaggio or Tintoretto, for whom contours are effaced by a chiaroscuro where clarity "endlessly plunges into obscurity" (rather like perception for Merleau-Ponty, provided one adds: and vice versa). Sometimes, Deleuze adds, "light vibrates color in the pleats and crannies of matter, sometimes light vibrates in the folds of an immaterial surface" (36, 40). Sometimes, too, Leibnizean matter resists.

Tom Conley's foreword to *The Fold* is helpful in itemizing some of the folded things that populate the Baroque imaginary: draperies, tresses, tessellated fabrics, dermal surfaces of the body, domestic architecture, novels with an "invaginated" narrative, complex harmonics with multiple rhythms and tempos, philosophies that "resolve Cartesian distinctions of mind and matter through physical means . . . grasped as foldings," and painterly styles that hide shapely forms within billowing fabrics or that confuse the viewer through artifice about space, surface, and perspective (xii).[60] Merleau-Ponty's description of the color red (which occurs, significantly, in the only relatively complete chapter of *The Visible and the Invisible*: "The Intertwining—The Chiasm") as a "concretion" of visibility rather than a discrete atom, where any particular shade of red forms a "constellation" with other reds through its real and imaginary relations of similarity and difference with them, surely evokes a congruent materialist imaginary. Color is defined here not as "a chunk of absolutely hard, indivisible being, offered all naked to a vision," but rather as "a sort of straights between exterior horizons and interior horizons ever gaping open"; "an ephemeral modulation of the world" and of that "tissue" of differences and possibilities that lines and nourishes all visible forms.[61]

> The red dress a fortiori holds with all its fibers onto the fabric of the visible, and thereby onto a fabric of invisible being. A punctuation in the field of red things, which includes the tiles of roof tops, the flags of gatekeepers and of the Revolution, certain terrains near Aix or in Madagascar, it is also a punctuation in the field of red garments, which includes, along with the dresses of women, robes of professors, bishops, and advocate generals, and also in the field of adornments and that of uniforms.[62]

Conclusion

Reading Merleau-Ponty's oeuvre overall, it is clear that he envisaged his return to ontology as a detour back to politics. He knew that one must avoid moving too swiftly from ontology to its political implications, but he was also profoundly aware that the way we think about matter and the images we use to do so have far-reaching implications for the way we think about ourselves as human as well as for the way we treat nature and other embodied selves. We accordingly find in his work some timely suggestions as to how an anti- or posthumanist philosophy might proceed by conceptualizing an embodied humanity enveloped in nature, rather than as external to inert stuff it dominates. As a corollary, Merleau-Ponty also helps us to rethink agency: not as an essential characteristic of the rational subject, a deity or some vital force, but as those contingent capacities for reflexivity, creative disclosure, and transformation that emerge hazardously within the folds and reversals of material / meaningful flesh.[63] In conjunction with the imagery of collective life as a complex relational field that emerges in an intercorporeal, intersubjective "between," such an approach to agency has significant implications for the way we interpret the political, as well as for how we go about making sense of the situations we inhabit and engender at any particular time. Merleau-Ponty's abiding image of the political was drawn not from the Baroque but from the Renaissance. It is Machiavelli whom he credits with recognizing the "milieu proper to politics":[64] a politics that is not a transparent realm to be surveyed and controlled by the light of reason or the power of a state external to society, but a politics that is a field of competing forces, strategies, reversals, and subterfuges that have incessantly to be finessed, interpreted, and negotiated from within. Perhaps, nonetheless, it was the imagery of Leibniz's folds that alerted him to the way a world devoid of transcendental mysteries is still nonetheless rippled with hidden recesses, shadows and shade, secrets and anonymity; with an obstinate resistance to the *lumen naturale* whose obscurity or veiling is inseparable from forming and disclosing but which is confused with transcendent forces or certainty at our peril.

Notes

1   I explore Merleau-Ponty's conception of negativity as productive difference in more detail in my *Negativity and Politics* (2000), chap. 4, and in *Merleau-Ponty and Modern Politics after Anti-Humanism* (2007). It is only subsequently that I have, however, come to appreciate the significance of the framework he developed in his lectures on nature.

2   Merleau-Ponty, *Phenomenology of Perception*, 54, 57.

3   See Descartes, *Principles of Philosophy*, book 1.

4   Merleau-Ponty, *Phenomenology of Perception*, 56f.

5   Merleau-Ponty, *In Praise of Philosophy*, 130.

6   Merleau-Ponty, *Nature*.

7   Merleau-Ponty, *The Visible and the Invisible*, 274.

8   Merleau-Ponty, *Nature*, 204.

9   Merleau-Ponty, *The Visible and the Invisible*, 158.

10   Although he does not explicitly discuss its use by Spinoza, it is in the context of Spinoza's pantheistic, radical monism and his "complex, layered materialism" that the terms are currently better known. See Williams, "Thinking the Political in the Wake of Spinoza," 353.

11   Merleau-Ponty, *Nature*, 7f.

12   "The Cartesians see Nature as the manifestation of an infinite being that posits itself" and whose production enjoys the same quality of necessity as the mechanistic laws with which Cartesian nature is more commonly associated (83).

13   Merleau-Ponty, *Signs*, 162; *In Praise of Philosophy*, 183; Husserl, *The Crisis of the European Sciences and Transcendental Phenomenology*, 112, 123.

14   Merleau-Ponty, *Signs*, 165, 172, 181; *Adventures of the Dialectic*, 138n.

15   Merleau-Ponty, *Phenomenology of Perception*, 169.

16   Merleau-Ponty, *The Visible and the Invisible*, 38–39.

17   Merleau-Ponty, *Nature*, 86.

18   Merleau-Ponty, *The Visible and the Invisible*, 167.

19   Merleau-Ponty, *Phenomenology of Perception*, 58.

20   Merleau-Ponty, *The Visible and the Invisible*, 188.

21   Merleau-Ponty, *Nature*, 238; *The Visible and the Invisible*, 152.

22   Merleau-Ponty, *Phenomenology of Perception*, 98.

23   Agamben, *The Open*, 39.

24   Merleau-Ponty, *Nature*, 139.

25   Merleau-Ponty, *Phenomenology of Perception*, xiii.

26   Merleau-Ponty, *Sense and Non-Sense*, 16.

27   Merleau-Ponty, *The Primacy of Perception*, 161.

28   Ibid., 167f.

29   Merleau-Ponty, *Sense and Non-Sense*, 17.

30   Merleau-Ponty, *The Primacy of Perception*, 167.

31   Ibid., 188.

32   Merleau-Ponty, *The Primacy of Perception*, 12, 15; *The Visible and the Invisible*, 208, 216.

33   Merleau-Ponty, *Sense and Non-Sense*, 13ff.

34   Merleau-Ponty, *The Primacy of Perception*, 180

35   Merleau-Ponty, *Sense and Non-Sense*, 11.

36   Merleau-Ponty, *The Primacy of Perception*, 171f; *The Visible and the Invisible*, 210.

37   Merleau-Ponty, *The Visible and the Invisible*, 212f.

38   Ibid., 210f.

39   Merleau-Ponty, *Nature*, 238; *The Visible and the Invisible*, 126, 206.

40   Merleau-Ponty, *The Visible and the Invisible*, 140.

41   Ibid., 143, 269.

42 Merleau-Ponty, *Phenomenology of Perception*, 215.

43 Merleau-Ponty, *Nature*, 157.

44 Merleau-Ponty, *Phenomenology of Perception*, 93.

45 Merleau-Ponty, *The Visible and the Invisible*, 261.

46 Merleau-Ponty, *Signs*, 166. See also *Phenomenology of Perception*, 237; *The Primacy of Perception*, 162; *Nature*, 209f.

47 Merleau-Ponty, *Nature*, 208.

48 Ibid., 209.

49 Deleuze, *Foucault*, 110; Deleuze, *Difference and Repetition*, 64–65.

50 Deleuze, *Foucault*, 96ff. It is to the unpublished fourth volume of *The History of Sexuality*, *Les Aveux de la Chair* (*Confessions of the Flesh*) that Deleuze refers here.

51 Merleau-Ponty, *The Visible and the Invisible*, 138.

52 Ibid., 210f.

53 Merleau-Ponty, *Nature*, 210, 238.

54 Merleau-Ponty, *Phenomenology of Perception*, 67.

55 Merleau-Ponty, *Signs*, 148.

56 Deleuze, *The Fold*, 3.

57 Merleau-Ponty, *The Visible and the Invisible*, 166, 176, 177, 185, 222f.

58 Harvey, *Spaces of Global Capitalism*, 124.

59 Deleuze, *The Fold*, 28, 34.

60 See Panagia, "The Effects of Viewing," for an intriguing account of "haptic vision" as immersion that is more attuned to the mystical experience invoked by the Baroque and developed by Deleuze.

61 Merleau-Ponty, *The Visible and the Invisible*, 132f.

62 Ibid., 132.

63 I develop some of these implications further in "Rethinking Agency."

64 Merleau-Ponty, *Signs*, 214.

Melissa A. Orlie

Impersonal Matter

> Whenever the world is not good
> enough, one has a mind instead.
> ADAM PHILLIPS, *Terrors and Experts*

> We, whose task is wakefulness itself . . .
> NIETZSCHE, *Beyond Good and Evil*

Conventionally, we think of our lives and activities as our own. But can we rightly call our thoughts, words, and deeds our own once we acknowledge the degree to which the material conditions of our social and psychic lives are created neither by nor for us? If all we are is matter, and if the matter of which we are made is neither originated nor controlled by us—as persons or as a species—then what sense can it make to speak of human beings as critical, creative, or free? In this essay, I outline an answer to this question by sketching an impersonal materialism of which I take Nietzsche to be a founding figure.

The Problem of Creative Subjectivity

Let us cast this existential issue in more theoretical terms. It is commonly believed that materialist understandings of subjectivity challenge our presumption that human beings are capable of creative action and critical judgment. Thus, predominant accounts of thinking, judging, and willing remain "idealist" in some measure. Despite some of the most influential thinkers of the nineteenth and twentieth centuries—Marx, Nietzsche, Freud, and Darwin—being avowed materialists or naturalists, reasons for a reluctance to embrace materialism are not difficult to surmise. For, insofar as accounts of human nature and behavior acknowledge that we are formed by material conditions not of our own making, they may struggle to explain how our values and views are not simply determined by forces outside our control. If nature is in accord with neither divine nor human purposes, it seems that creative and critical minds must somehow rise above matter. It is not therefore surprising that predominant accounts of subjectivity should still tend to assume that mental capacities are distinct from physical bodies since it is difficult to make sense of thinking, judging, and acting if they are not somehow distinctly our own, human in a way that differentiates them from the matter that makes up the rest of nature. Even some materialist accounts of subjectivity, such as more ego-oriented modes of psychoanalysis, insist on preserving a sense of personal individuality by emphasizing the irreducibly singular quality of subjective experience. Yet such accounts struggle to explain not only how that experience becomes consciously available to "us" but also how in its idiosyncrasy it can prove to be anything but meaningless to others. An impersonal materialism, I suggest, can circumvent these difficulties by affording a post-Darwinian, naturalist but not reductionist account of creative subjectivity.

Will to Power as Impersonal Matter

Nietzsche's work may seem an unpropitious place to begin searching for an account of critical judgment and creative action that would avoid the problems which have bedeviled materialist accounts of subjectivity. To be sure, Nietzsche's critique of theories predicated on the subject as a "doer behind the deed," like his insistence that the "deed is everything," suggests an impersonal understanding of subjectivity by emphasizing the action rather than the actor.[1] Equally, his insistence that the "soul is only a word for something about the body" exemplifies his materialism.[2] But Nietzsche can also be read as an example of the difficulties inherent in impersonal and materialist accounts of action or judgment and as an example of the performative contradiction to which such approaches may be prone. Consider, then, two apparently countervailing tendencies in his thought. On the one hand, there is Nietzsche's notion of will to power, commonly taken to maintain that every event in the organic world is a subduing and hence that something subdues while something else is subdued. On the other hand, Nietzsche explicitly rejects the philosophy of substances: he denies that there are discrete subjugating or subjugated phenomena.[3] Since it is hard to see how both views can be held simultaneously, interpreters of Nietzsche tend to emphasize one or the other of these doctrines. Some conclude that his insistence on speaking of "genuine activity" and being "truly creative" is wedded to a notion of becoming master over and subduing things, but this then betrays what they take to be his greater insight regarding the absence of discrete, permanent, and definable substances. For others, the apparent recourse to doers behind deeds is evidence that Nietzsche was unable after all to avoid resorting to the notion of discrete personal identity, even as he pronounced the death of the subject. Still others take the presence of two such apparently contradictory ideas as confirmation that Nietzsche was simply an incoherent thinker.

There are undoubtedly many passages in Nietzsche's texts that associate creativity with the image of a sovereign individual who is strong enough to create on her own terms, free from the influence of others.[4] But Nietzsche's better insights offer a rather different understanding of the aim and practice of creativity. Crucial to this alternative account is an understanding of will to power as an impersonal force within our lives rather than as a personal one that is a property of individuals. In other words, there is only a contradiction between Nietzsche's denial of substances and his hypothesis of will to power if the latter is conceived as something that is personally ours rather than as impersonal matter from which we arise. Impersonal matter from this perspective consists of something that is both more and other than that which I think of as me and mine. The relations and causes it implies defy mapping; they are possibly infinite and certainly ever-changing and unmasterable. Inasmuch as will to power refers to these impersonal energies that constitute our lives, then the doctrine of will to power is perfectly consistent with Nietzsche's denial of substances. Indeed, such an impersonal rendering of will to power is a most apt characterization of the denial of discrete substances.

It is tempting, while reading Nietzsche, to imagine this will to power as a single, overriding drive. Nietzsche himself, however, refers to it as a complex of competing drives and passions, consonant with his insight that willing is "above all something complicated" and "a unit only as a word."[5] When he speaks of the body as a "social structure composed of many souls," and refers to the multiple souls within subjects as "under-souls" or "under-wills," he does so as part of his effort at explaining the complexity of willing (sec. 19). It is true that in such passages Nietzsche relies upon more conventional associations of willing with commanding, subduing, and making something obey; with the expression of power and the discharge of strength; with overcoming and, sometimes, destroying that which is not commanding. But when he speaks of the multiplicity which is each person, Nietzsche is clear that there is no one drive but multiple drives. These sometimes compete and sometimes collaborate to produce affective states; in short, they both conflict and cooperate to engender the perceptions and interpretations that arise within individuals at any given moment. Mental activity, whether conscious or not, is an activity of the body and an outcome of the relationships between the "under-wills" and "under-souls" that make up each of us. As Nietzsche says, thinking "is merely a relation of these drives to each other" and the "will to overcome an affect is ultimately only the will of another, or of several other, affects" (secs. 36, 117). For the "will is not only a complex of sensation and thinking, but it is above all an affect, and specifically an affect of a command" (sec. 19).

According to this account, what is conventionally called a self is actually a complex of competing drives, each with its own philosophy and each seeking to become master on its own terms (sec. 6). All such drives are evaluative in the sense that they have a sense of what is good for the body, and they strive to achieve it. This is a more affirmative way of saying that each of the diverse drives seeks to become master; to remake the world according to the needs and health of the body as it interprets them; to overcome resistance from competing forces or interpretations. If a self is the totality of such drives, then who we are at any moment encompasses the order of rank among them (sec. 6). In sum, when I refer to the impersonality of will to power, I mean precisely this: at the heart of who we are there are multiple, conflicting drives that represent different senses of the good and aspirations toward the better.

To say that a particular drive or affect has a sense of the good and strives to achieve its sense of the better is not, of course, to say that this would be the view of other affective states or persons, or even the perspective of what we conventionally call our selves. As both Nietzsche and Freud so vividly convey, our psychic life is a war of competing passions and wishes without a sovereign to bring permanent order or to pass final judgment. It is our abyssal freedom — perhaps our misfortune — to have to achieve some rank order among these drives and the various satisfactions they seek. For Nietzsche, as for Freud, whatever humanity we have achieved or may become capable of involves bringing to awareness some of what has hitherto been unconscious. We do so by subjecting to reflection, yet thereby transfiguring, what had heretofore been accidental, partial, and error-ridden in our psychic life. The practice of understanding that Nietzsche invokes as "wakefulness itself" suggests how we might become disposed to affirm the earth, life, even the self as impersonal yet productive matter.

Before considering the qualities of such wakefulness, we need to consider why, if this sketch of will to power as impersonal matter is plausible, we remain attached to a sovereign conception of subjectivity. Why are we so wedded to this personal perspective on selves and world that precludes our hearing and seeing, let alone digesting, Nietzsche's understanding of will to power as impersonal matter? The answer seems evident: we are positively averse to the experience of impersonality; hostile to the claim that neither the matter of our selves nor that of the world is me or mine, ours or yours. Indeed, most of our mental activity, as well as the content of the dominant ego psychology, is constructed as a defense against experiencing or acknowledging the impersonal forces that compose us. The building of personal and interpersonal bulwarks against the impersonal is the preoccupation and content of most lives, or at least of those lives that lack the quality of wakefulness which Nietzsche summons or the capacity for eliciting unconscious relationships through free association that Freud would have us cultivate. Because we are neither awake in Nietzsche's sense nor open to our uncanniness in Freud's, we remain ignorant of the extent to which our daily lives are composed of endless and ultimately fruitless measures to remain unaware of the body's vulnerability and of the imminent death that portends our return to nature, whence fantasies of personal identity are swallowed up by omnipotent, if purposeless, matter.

A Sovereign Fantasy

To say that the mind is embodied does not adequately convey what Nietzsche means when he says that soul, mind, or ego are different names for aspects of the body. For him, mind *is* body. This is not to say that mind or mindedness can be reduced to some particular physical location or organ, such as the brain; rather, it is to claim that various forms of mental activity are aspects or manifestations of matter. All mental activity, from the so-called highest states of consciousness to what Freudians call primary process and refer to as unconscious, arises, according to this view, from the same basic material elements that compose the physical body. That human beings can think, read, and write, that they can give and receive instruction from one another and sometimes be changed by it, are capacities that are integral to the developmental trajectory of matter. Nietzsche's judgment is indeed that consciousness is the weakest, last, and least developed of our instincts.[6] In his view all of our affects, from the most immediate physical sensations of pleasure and pain to the most refined aesthetic and moral judgments, grow from and change with our *physis*. He does not believe that moral and aesthetic judgments are reducible to basic sensory sensations and reactions — indeed, he designates these more mindful judgments as some of the "subtlest nuances" of *physis* (sec. 39) — but he does insist that critical judgment and creative deeds are born of, and known only by and as, matter.

If this is the case, why do we associate thinking, willing, and acting with something immaterial, with "spirit" rather than matter? How do we arrive at the idea and experience of ourselves as having a mind that is distinct from, indeed master of, the body? From Nietzsche's perspective, when we observe philosophy abandoning the body for the sake of an immaterial soul, we must ask why and how the body despairs of the body.[7] The short answer is that the body despairs of the body when it cannot bear its own experience or digest its suffering. An aspect of the body — what we come to know as mind or call an ego — refuses to accept its limited mastery over what arises within experience as a consequence of events that befall it. This aspect has a fantasy of itself as master of its experience, although ironically such fantasies of sovereignty arise at just those moments when mastery is most foreclosed. What happens to and within a self occurs without its choice or knowledge, a sure sign of its constitutive weakness and symptomatic of the profound impersonality of ourselves. Weakness is constitutive of who we are because our capacity to give shape to the world or to our selves is always limited; we are not sovereign. The stuff of which selves are made is impersonal because the matter of which they are born and made does not begin with us nor is it ever possessed or controlled by us. In sum, each of us is not only matter but impersonal matter; made of stuff over which nothing is master and whose entirety no one is in a position to know. It is precisely when this unpalatable fact is glimpsed that the ego is most likely to submit to delusions of sovereignty.

We begin life rather like the camel in Nietzsche's "Three Metamorphoses": we are made to bear much.[8] It may well be, as he says, that only the "lucky ones" are capable of becoming like children again, able to say yes to life on terms that are made our own. But who are these lucky ones? In the fifth book that was added to the second edition of *The Gay Science*, Nietzsche suggests that they are the ones who suffer an "overfullness of life," whereas the unlucky ones suffer from the "impoverishment of life." If we have faith in substances and subjects, we may be inclined to think that we are born one way or the other: some being abundant and strong, others impoverished and weak. Yet it seems to me more probable that Nietzsche wanted to claim that overfullness of life arises among sufferers who do not flee but experience the full range and depth of the suffering that is the lot of embodied selves. Inversely, the impoverishment of life arises among sufferers who have "a certain warm narrowness that keeps away fear and encloses one in optimistic horizons."[9] In short, we are *strong* to the extent that we undergo the suffering which arises from our basic weakness, while we are *weak* to the extent that we flee from experiencing the impersonal chaos that sustains the self. We are *strong* inasmuch as we are wakeful to the full range of experience, to what is unbidden as well as bidden, but we are *weak* inasmuch as our experience of our selves and of the world is limited by a traumatic fixation of otherwise ceaselessly changing, never fully knowable or graspable experience.

In the first part of *Thus Spoke Zarathustra*, Nietzsche endeavors to describe how, although we are entirely body, we come to experience certain aspects of the body as not-body.

> Your self laughs at your ego and at its bold leaps. "What are these leaps and flights of thought to me?" it says to itself. "A detour to my end. I am the leading strings of the ego and the prompter of its concepts."
>
> The self says to the ego, "Feel pain here!" Then the ego suffers and thinks how it might suffer no more — and that is why it is made to think.

The self says to the ego, "Feel pleasure here!" Then the ego is pleased and thinks how it might often be pleased again—and that is why it is made to think.[10]

In this passage, Nietzsche suggests that in those moments when something happens to the body that challenges its powers, an aspect of the body generates a defensive fantasy of its autonomy from and power over the body. The ego that says "I think" emerges in response to experiences of either pain or pleasure because both are always to some degree beyond its control. The "mind" is the means by which the body imagines itself as master of the conditions of its experience but at exactly those moments when the body actually feels the limits of its strength and suffers under these conditions. This experience of vulnerability and the emergence of "mind" as a response to suffering to which it attests is the very process of the body despairing at and of itself.

To be cut off from life and the range of experience it entails, to lose a visceral sense of the matter that composes us, is our human affliction. The body despairing of itself is our affliction because we become fixated by an image of our experience and a false impression of a self. As a result, our selves and our experience are limited by this image, typically in the form of a perception of the past joined to a projection about the future. In this way, paradoxically, we suffer from our experience and are victims of it precisely because we do not actually undergo or experience our suffering with any intensity. Given the modern Western preoccupation with reducing suffering, such efforts may seem commendable and their achievement no basis for regret. Yet by failing to work through the inevitable suffering of mortal, material beings whose being is in question, Nietzsche maintains that we remove ourselves from the energy needed to affirm life. We are cut off from precisely the resources we need to discern what is worthy of esteem.

Broadly speaking, there are two responses of mindful matter to the experience of impersonality: receptive and reactive. A receptive response is awake to the fullest range of experience, moment by moment, aware of variation and dissonance among perceptions, feelings, thoughts, drives, and their passions. A reactive response to impersonality refuses this variation and dissonance within experience and does so by means of techniques that generate fixated ideas about self and world (hence Freud's sense of repression and of neurotic symptoms such as the compulsion to repeat and, ultimately, the death drive itself). Yet primary among these techniques is the generation of mind as distinct from body. Nietzsche sees promise as well as danger in this reaction to a world that is not deemed good enough. The danger in the birth of an ego that says "I think" is a fixation of self and the loss of a fuller range of experience: the very experiences that are prime sources of energy and resources for critical, creative subjectivity. But the promise in the birth of the ego is that this reactive creation bears witness to, and traces of, another experience of mindful matter. This is why Nietzsche says that our affliction is the way to our selves, through the recovery of an "instinct for freedom" inherent in aspects of will to power "forcibly made latent."[11] This recovery of freedom is not however achieved through the assertion of a fixated, already delimited self; rather, it is gained through receptivity and wakefulness to the fullest range of experience we can muster moment by moment.

Creatures without a Creator

Nietzsche repeatedly associates creativity with strength of will and lack of creativity with weakness. But we do not need to have recourse to the idea of a subject as a doer behind deeds in order to speak of the strength or weakness of willing. Whether willing is strong or weak need not be understood as a question of given character, physiological stature, or unchanging nature. Rather, our capacity to experience the purposeless necessity of impersonal matter as the condition of our creative freedom depends upon the accessibility of our bodily drives and passions. Paradoxically, the degree to which will to power can become what Nietzsche calls an instinct for freedom increases as we acknowledge and experience the impersonality of our selves, as we accept that the conditions of our drives and passions are not of our own making and are not therefore sources for personal merit or blame. Drives and passions are merely effects of the conditions in which we find ourselves. As such, the strength or weakness of our willing is not an index of what is actually "firm and settled" within, qua physiological stature, character, or psychological diagnosis.[12] Instead, the strength or weakness of the ego's willing depends upon the degree to which it can acknowledge and accept that what is firm and settled within it emerges from what is at first perceived as outside or overpowering. That is to say, acknowledging and accepting the impersonality of our selves is a necessary condition for experiencing a full range of drives and passions and, thus, of recovering what Nietzsche calls our creative body. Strength or weakness of willing is not measured by the degree to which we can remake what he says is at "the bottom of us, 'right deep down.'" Rather, willing is strong or weak to the extent that it acknowledges and feels "something unteachable, a granite stratum of spiritual fate, of predetermined decisions and answers to predetermined selected questions" (sec. 231).

This "spiritual fate" is not the essence or the truth of who we are: Nietzsche would rather have us take our spiritual fate as the throw of the dice that poses for us the problem of who we are. Convictions that we feel are deeply embedded in who we are may inspire a strong belief in our own selfhood, its desires, and sense of truth. But Nietzsche would have us use signs of our "spiritual fate" differently: not to discern the truth of who we are but rather as "footsteps to self-knowledge, signposts of the problem which we are" (sec. 231). Such mindful awareness of the impersonal experience that we routinely take personally is captured with brilliant simplicity in Freud's description of Leonardo da Vinci as one who "did not love and hate, but asked himself about the origin and significance of what he was to love and hate."[13] Likewise for Nietzsche, our freedom and creativity are exercised when we "learn more fully" what is "firm and settled" and recognize it as the accidental, meaningless, raw material out of which we can make virtues and values. Only then may we truly come to call these our own, through accepting that they were not our own to begin with nor will they ever fully become so.[14]

By contrast, the personal self and what we are most readily conscious of thinking and feeling are products of fixation and of ideas born of defensive reaction to what makes us suffer, what overpowers or humiliates us. Accordingly, these fixed ideas about ourselves and what we value are always partial rather than fully representative of the experience we are undergoing at any given moment. Self-trust is difficult precisely because what is most readily available to us is what D. W. Winnicott calls a false self. Winnicott's false self feels neither fully alive nor creative or real. Such feelings, for Winnicott as for Nietzsche, are a psychological achievement predicated on the dissolution of the ego and yielding a capacity for spontaneous experience that Winnicott calls unintegration. To become increasingly awake to all that is, is to wake up to the impersonality of matter which is nature; it is to live with a joyousness that arises only when we are able to cease holding the self together without at the same time falling apart.[15]

Wakefulness Itself

Nietzsche's notion of will to power remains for him a working hypothesis rather than an article of faith or uncontestable presumption. How does he arrive at this hypothesis? He suggests that his conjecture arises from what is possibly the only thing "given" to us as real, namely, "our world of desires and passions," what he calls "the reality of our drives."[16] Now clearly, the reality of our drives is available to us only through interpretation since the "human intellect cannot avoid seeing itself in its own perspectives, and only in these."[17] Our "affects" grow from and change with bodily drives and passions, running the gamut from immediate physical sensations of pleasure and pain to aesthetic and moral judgments. We habitually fail to see (even as we may theoretically acknowledge) that a particular affective state fosters specific perceptions and interpretations of events, while another affective state may foster entirely different perceptions and interpretations. When we do acknowledge variation in perspective, it is more commonly thought about as an occurrence *between* persons. But Nietzsche insists that this waxing and waning of affective states and the shifting perceptions and interpretations associated with them operates *within* persons. According to an impersonal understanding of will to power, this often dissonant fluctuation of *physis*, affect, perception, and interpretation is the effect of impersonal energies rather than a matter of personal choice alone, when it is a matter of choice at all. There is a point beyond which it ceases to make sense to speak of the fluctuations of *physis* that occur within the person as belonging to that person. It is more apt to describe an impersonal flow of affective states.[18] In short, what we feel, perceive, and think "comes upon us" as much as, and probably more than, we craft or control it.[19]

Although Nietzsche's readers often highlight agonistic contest among persons,[20] it is self-overcoming rather than overcoming others that he emphasizes. Despite his insistence on the impersonality of selves, he regards agonistic contest within the self as primary. It is quite usual for us to experience a particular affective state as definitive of who we are or to regard the perceptions and interpretations that arise within that state as definitive of the way things are. If we experience a similar fixation during another moment of time, we typically neglect any dissonance within the moments or between them. This is in part why Nietzsche speaks of consciousness as the weakest, last, and least developed of our instincts.[21] We simply are not very aware of our experience, of what is taking place within and about this body, on this earth, at any moment. So, Nietzsche declares us to be asleep, while calling upon us to assume the task of "wakefulness itself."[22] Our stupor begins with the misapprehension of our own experience. We can awaken from this delusion only by transforming our reception of the perceptions and interpretations that arise within that experience.

Understanding, as Nietzsche says, is a certain behavior of drives or instincts toward one another. He contrasts his views with those of Spinoza on this score. Understanding is achieved not when I overcome what makes me laugh, lament, or curse (a view Nietzsche attributes to Spinoza in the quotation below). Rather, we achieve understanding when we come to *feel* what makes us laugh, lament, and curse all at once. In other words, understanding is the conflict among these affects in some measure sustained and brought to awareness rather than resolved and forgotten. This is what Nietzsche means by wakefulness itself. He explains his meaning in the following terms:

> Before knowledge is possible, each of these instincts must first have presented its one-sided view of the thing or event; after this comes the fight of these one-sided views, and occasionally this results in a mean, one grows calm, one finds all three sides right, and there is a kind of justice and a contract; for by virtue of justice and a contract all these instincts can maintain their existence and assert their rights against each other. Since only the last scenes of reconciliation and the final accounting at the end of this long process rise to our consciousness, we suppose that *intelligere* must be something conciliatory, just, and good — something that stands essentially opposed to the instincts, while it is actually nothing but a certain behavior of the instincts toward one another. (sec. 333)

Nietzsche suggests that we begin to understand more truly who we are when we can do justice to all that makes us laugh, lament, and curse. This means sustaining the conflict among all these elements rather than imagining that we can somehow rise above or judge them in a way that is independent of the conflict among them. If there is a hero in our psychic life, it is "certainly nothing divine that eternally rests in itself"; rather, it is a "concealed heroism in our warring depths" (sec. 333). Nietzsche does not bar access to what he calls drives and instincts but only access to anything other than drives and instincts. We are capable of achieving a different, more just relationship among these drives and instincts and their warring conceptions of the good and better. Indeed, this just war could become our experience of self.

Nietzsche maintains that "the greatest part of our spirit's activity remains unconscious and unfelt" (sec. 333). Few have yet achieved this experience of themselves, as a battlefield in a contest over the good. "Believing that they possess consciousness, men have not exerted themselves very much to acquire it; and things haven't changed much in this respect. To this day the task of incorporating knowledge and making it instinctive is only beginning to dawn on the human eye and is not yet clearly discernible; it is a task that is seen only by those who have comprehended that so far we have incorporated only our errors and that all our consciousness relates to errors" (sec. 11). Until now, then, we have mainly incorporated errors rather than knowledge because we have taken a portion of our experience — particular affective states, perceptions, and interpretations — as its entirety. By contrast, Nietzsche advocates incorporating the full range of experience, not only what makes us laugh (for which we would expect praise from the advocate of joyful wisdom) but also what makes us lament and curse. We should not grant our drives and instincts any more than their due, but they all require their due, and it is our freedom and fate to determine what that is.

Why should the conflict among our instincts and their senses of the good and better be internalized and sustained? It seems, at the very least, that we need to do this for pragmatic reasons of health. If the rightful claims of an instinct are not consciously sustained, Nietzsche contends, then its claim may be unfelt, yet its repression is not the end of its effects. Instead, obscure impulses which are not given their due and incorporated into conscious awareness seek to undermine other instincts and diminish the energy of the "social structure composed of many souls" which we conventionally call our self. Although they may remain "unfelt" from the perspective of our conscious mind, these instincts can therefore have decisive and potentially debilitating effects. "But I suppose that these instincts which are here contending with one another understand very well how to make themselves felt by, and how to hurt, one another. This may well be the source of that sudden and violent exhaustion that afflicts all thinkers (it is exhaustion on a battlefield)" (sec. 333). In Nietzsche's view, it seems, each instinct has some rightful claim to be experienced in awareness and, if that claim is denied, it will work efficaciously to undermine the claims of competing drives.

More important, from the perspective of creative subjectivity, when our access to some drives and instincts is barred, we lose aspects of experience as well as energy and resources for creative and critical activity. Each affective state fosters certain perceptions and interpretations and bars others. Nietzsche maintains that we tend to be unconscious regarding the nature of our experience in any particular moment, let alone between moments. His concern is not that the result of such inhibition and exclusion is untruthful: this would hardly be a decisive argument for a thinker for whom untruth is a condition of life.[23] The trouble with the narrowing of our experience is that it blocks energy for evaluation and action and thereby restricts our capacity to judge and act. And sustaining the capacity for judgment and action in the face of nihilism is the main problem Nietzsche sees confronting us. Nietzsche is not as explicit and detailed as Freud in accounting for the effects of repression, but he is clear that the aims of drives of which we are unconscious do have effects. Like Freud, he offers no guarantee of liberation or greater health if we bring the conflict among our instincts and their sense of the good to awareness and allow each to make its case for the rightness of its view in an open conflict. We might yet die of exhaustion or be torn asunder. But the health of all the drives and instincts that make up the social structure which is our soul does depend upon achieving a just rank order among them. This means becoming conscious of what sense of the good animates each instinct; how it strives after what it takes to be better and what effects this has upon the other instincts and the whole (the "whole" of which we are born being the entirety of nature as all of impersonal matter). We must become interpreters of our experience, asking questions of it such as: "What did I really experience?" and "What happened in me and around me at that time?"[24] Becoming interpreters of our experience means that we must learn to see as we do not yet see; we must practice material sensitivity as well as reflective judgment.

> Learning to see–accustoming the eye to calmness, to patience, to letting things come up to it; postponing judgment, learning to go around and grasp each individual case from all sides. That is the first preliminary schooling for spirituality: not to react at once to stimulus, but to gain control of all the inhibiting, excluding instincts. Learning to see, as I understand it, is almost what, unphilosophically speaking, is called a strong will: the essential feature is precisely not to "will" — to be able to suspend decision.[25]

In this and other passages like it, we hear a Nietzsche for whom the way to a freer experience of will to power is achieved by receptivity rather than masterful assertion. Learning to see involves experiencing the impersonality of ourselves rather than affirming who we already believe ourselves to be. It is a condition of creativity that we should learn to appreciate our instincts and their aims as they become manifest in our experience. If Nietzsche's primary concern is self-overcoming, then this requires the cultivation of a receptivity that is aesthetic in the sense of being sensually, viscerally sensitive to flows of generative matter. It depends upon capacities that are alien to the sort of rational cognition that is usually taken to be the sum of reflection. Learning to see in this way is the condition of self-overcoming, but such "seeing" of experience requires control over those drives that would block its full range. It is only by opening the self in this way that we might hope to achieve some just and orderly behavior of the drives in relation to one another.

Creativity and Impersonal Matter

The primary way we make the impersonality of our world and selves socially and psychically manageable is to imagine them being ruled by an order that issues from and is amenable to sovereign commands. Like Jacques Lacan, Nietzsche documents the force of this fantasy of sovereignty even as he seeks to debunk it. Like Lacan, he tries to help us see how we are ruled by our sense that there is something to know and someone who knows it; by our sense that there is something to achieve or prove and someone who judges whether it is achieved or proven.

Before the death of God, Adam Phillips argues, we take what is and what comes to us as if they were commands. After the death of God, what is and what comes to us are more aptly taken to be hints, inasmuch as "hints . . . can be made something of; orders can only be submitted to or rejected." But as Phillips himself acknowledges, declaration of the death of God is no guarantee of the end of our feeling commanded. Indeed, such loss may heighten our inclination to feel commanded since fear of the unknown can most readily be "cured through flight into the intelligible." From the earliest age, we receive and exert pressure upon ourselves "to make something easily shareable, to produce the consensual object — the acceptable phrase, the reassuring drawing — rather than the ambiguous or enigmatic object."[26] And as we feel commanded to make ourselves intelligible to others, so too do we feel compelled to read the order of the social and natural world as if it necessarily issues purposeful and meaningful events and opportunities.

For the tradition of impersonal materialism arising from Nietzsche and Freud, however, both worldly events and ruptures in mental life are ripe with possibility precisely because they are devoid of determined purpose. Jonathan Lear offers a picture of mind functioning with an inherent tendency toward disruption. Mindful matter tends toward disruption simply by virtue of the fact that life is lived under pressure: life is simply "too much." We are helpless and sometimes consciously humbled whenever we catch a glimpse of the impersonal energies that we ordinarily reify into definitive ideas of selves and world. Such disruptive, impersonal energies are at once intimately present but neither identifiable as completely our own nor controllable by us. In response we make every effort to personalize the impersonal, to make it our own by projecting meaning upon it. Yet our efforts are doomed since the excess before which we tremble and waver is quantitative energy with its intensities and flows. The repetition of human helplessness, Lear stresses, is a repetition of something without content. The helplessness that breaks out over and again derives from an experience of too much energy; an irruption of quantity without quality.

If there is actual repetition, then it inheres in our attempts at infusing this breakthrough of energy and disruption into ordinary life with meaning.[27]

Inasmuch as we are deeply influenced by American ego psychology, it is easy to miss Freud's own profoundly impersonal understanding of human psychic life where what is unconscious holds sway. In the opening section of *Civilization and Its Discontents*, Freud writes that "originally the ego includes everything, later it separates off an external world from itself."[28] In the beginning the ego is one with all of matter and experiences its impersonal unity. Freud doubts our capacity to recover this sense of unity or the desirability of doing so. In fact, he associates desire for such unity with the illusions of religion and nonproductive or even dangerous forms of regression. In Hans Loewald's view, however, the aim of sublimation is to achieve *differentiated* unity, which amounts to a reversal with a difference of the ego's developmental trend.[29] More specifically, sublimation in this account involves forms of regression that yield satisfaction through attaining more complex, differentiated unities whose internal tensions are not eliminated but "bound."[30] In the opening arguments of *Civilization and Its Discontents*, Freud seems disinclined to imagine such productive achievements emerging from regressive moments. But for Loewald (following arguments similar to those of Marcuse in his *Eros and Civilization*), it is only open receptivity to regressive energies and experiences that can issue in the truly creative inventions of sublimation. Indeed, Loewald thinks his account is more faithful here to Freud's logic than was Freud's. According to Loewald's nondefensive concept of healthy sublimation, the higher, more differentiated achievements of Eros (invoked favorably by Freud in later passages of *Civilization and Its Discontents*) arise from an open receptivity to unconscious and primary processes, from a return (although not an entire regression) to that sense of unity with nature as all of matter which Freud denigrates in the opening pages and claims himself not to have experienced. My concern here is not to demonstrate that Loewald is right about Freud's deeper understanding, although I think he is, but to draw upon his understanding of sublimation because I believe it illuminates, at least as well as any discussion I have yet found, an impersonal materialist understanding of creativity.

One of the vicissitudes of our development of a fantasy of ourselves as distinct persons is a sense of alienation from all of nature of which we are actually part and parcel. But when *physis* assumes the form of individual mentation, whereby we have the impression that we are each an individual subject confronting a world of objects, the sense of lost union is a prelude to the possibility of higher, more differentiated forms of union: the subtler forms of *physis* that both Nietzsche and Freud desire. "In genuine sublimation," Loewald writes, "this alienating differentiation is being reversed in such a way that a fresh unity is created by an act of uniting. In this reversal—a restoration of unity—there comes into being a differentiated unity (a manifold) that captures separateness in the act of uniting, and unity in the act of separating."[31] This is why for Loewald, sublimation is not a defense against, but a reconciliation of, disjunctures that civilization requires or of renunciations that are required in the first adulthood phases of the false self.[32] Genuine sublimation achieves reconciliation of the conventional divisions of the divine and the sexual, nature and human, subject and object, unconscious and conscious, primary and secondary process thinking. Following Darwin, we are true to Freud's best insights, Loewald concludes, when we refrain from saying higher or lower in selecting among forms of *physis*.[33]

In a more technical language, Loewald's account entails that sublimation arises from a change of object libido into narcissistic libido, that is, from a transformation of object relations into *intra*psychic relations (19). In the terms of this essay, I would describe the process as a double movement. First, what was presumed to be personal or one's own is acknowledged as profoundly impersonal, as neither me nor mine. But this first movement of defamiliarization is then followed by a second task: of achieving a distinct, singular relationship to what is impersonal and thus to what is only conventionally located within one's person but which is actually not yet personal because it is not differentiated by means of awareness. I may feel love or hatred, but as in Freud's understanding of Leonardo, I do not take these expressions of desire as straightforward truths of my self or the world. Rather, seeing that these loves and hates are neither me nor mine, I am finally poised to seek a singular relationship to impersonal matter. A singular relationship to impersonal matter cannot take its loves and hates at face value since this would be to treat accidental necessities to which I have been subject as if they had been freely chosen by me. Our freedom is manifest in the order of rank we are able to achieve among all that drives us, as a result of conditions which may be full of necessity but which nonetheless serve no given purpose or meaning. Our freedom is manifest in actions which bespeak what we value, actions which show whether and how we are creative or mere creatures of the conditions from which we arise.

What does creative subjectivity look like when it is not a defensive maneuver against our experience of impersonal matter? Nondefensive sublimation is simply experiential acknowledgment and symbolic articulation of and by impersonal matter. According to this impersonal materialist understanding, subjectivity is nature's activity: the creative-destructive power of nature itself (78–81). Nietzsche's sense of learning to see, as expansion of moment-by-moment awareness of nature as all of matter, is sublimation in action when it issues in symbolizations that manifest a singular relationship to impersonal matter. What we conventionally call mind is, in short, matter working upon matter. Creative subjectivity is *not*, then, human action *with* or *against* nature. Creative subjectivity is quite literally a manifestation of natural selection, where those subtle forms of *physis* by which Nietzsche designates ethical or aesthetic judgment work through and select among other forms of *physis*. Once we acknowledge that we are nature, that we are only in and of nature, then we see that there is no longer any question of what is natural *or* human. The question for each moment is only for "what parts of nature do we show a preference by our words and deeds?"[34] What "rank order of drives and passions do we select for with our attention?" From this perspective, as Loewald notes, sublimation entails invention rather than discovery of something already given or created ex nihilo. The articulations of subtler nuances of *physis* form combinations which were previously unknown, yet which bring to expression what has always existed but has been absent of consciousness. Nondefensive sublimations are intimations of the all-embracing and all-embraced unity of impersonal matter.[35] The ego development of the initial stages of life, of the false self, requires us to renounce the all-embracing unity of nature as all of impersonal matter. But, if we are among the lucky ones, later stages of ego development may issue in singular, differentiated symbolizations of impersonal matter.[36] We have always existed as impersonal matter. But we come to experience and symbolize this nature only by emerging from *and* toward its more differentiated forms. Perhaps this is why Nietzsche has Zarathustra declare that "this most honest being, the ego, speaks of the body and still wants the body, even when it poetizes and raves and flutters with broken wings. It learns to speak ever more honestly, this ego; and the more it learns, the more words and honors it finds for body and earth."[37]

Notes

1   Nietzsche, *On the Genealogy of Morals*, essay 1, sec. 13.

2   Nietzsche, *Thus Spoke Zarathustra*, part 1, "Despisers of the Body."

3   See a helpful discussion by Bittner, "Masters without Substance."

4   For instance, this sovereign imagination of subjectivity resonates with the most literal interpretations of Nietzsche's distinction between what is noble and what is slavelike. I criticize this reading of the noble and slave as it appears in *On the Genealogy of Morals* and offer an alternative in Orlie, "The Art of Despising Oneself."

5   Nietzsche, *Beyond Good and Evil*, sec. 19.

6   Nietzsche, *The Gay Science*, sec. 11.

7   Nietzsche, *Thus Spoke Zarathustra*, part 1, "Afterworldly."

8   Ibid., preface, "On the Three Metamorphoses."

9   Nietzsche, *The Gay Science*, sec. 370.

10 Nietzsche, *Thus Spoke Zarathustra*, part 1, "Despisers of the Body."

11 Nietzsche, *On the Genealogy of Morals*, essay 2, sec. 18.

12 Nietzsche, *Beyond Good and Evil*, sec. 233.

13 I arrived at the significance of Freud's passage for the first time while reading Loewald, *Sublimation*, 9.

14 Nietzsche, *Beyond Good and Evil*, sec. 231.

15 See Adam Phillips's helpful survey of Winnicott's papers on the false self in *Winnicott*, 98–137. On Winnicott's notion of unintegration, see Phillips, *Winnicott*, 79–97, as well as Epstein, *Going to Pieces without Falling Apart*, 36–48.

16 Nietzsche, *Beyond Good and Evil*, sec. 36.

17 Nietzsche, *The Gay Science*, sec. 374.

18 Compare Brennan, *The Transmission of Affect*.

19 Nietzsche, *Beyond Good and Evil*, sec. 17.

20 For this typical formulation in an otherwise excellent book, see Cox, *Nietzsche*, 229–35.

21 Nietzsche, *The Gay Science*, sec. 11.

22 Ibid., "Preface."

23 Nietzsche, *Beyond Good and Evil*, sec. 4.

24 Nietzsche, *The Gay Science*, sec. 319.

25 Nietzsche, *Twilight of the Idols*, "What the Germans Lack," sec. 6.

26 Phillips, *The Beast in the Nursery*, 111, 101.

27 Lear, *Happiness, Death, and the Remainders of Life*, 108–9.

28   Freud, *The Standard Edition of the Complete Psychological Works*, vol. 21, p. 68.

29   Loewald, *Sublimation*, 24.

30   Loewald, *Sublimation*, 27. On parallels between mystic and analytic experience and the importance of regression as a condition of further differentiation, see Fingarette, "The Ego and Mystic Selflessness." Thanks to George Shulman for the Fingarette reference and for our ongoing conversations about these matters.

31   Loewald, *Sublimation*, 24.

32   For the notions of the first adulthood of the false self and the second adulthood, see Hollis, *The Middle Passage*; and *Swamplands of the Soul*. Thanks to Martin Srajek for introducing me to Hollis's work.

33   Loewald, *Sublimation*, 12–13.

34   Phillips, *Darwin's Worms*, 6. See also pp. 3–63.

35   Loewald, *Sublimation*, 76.

36   See note 32.

37   Nietzsche, *Thus Spoke Zarathustra*, part 1, "Despisers of the Body."

POLITICAL MATTERS

Elizabeth Grosz

Feminism, Materialism, and Freedom

Concepts of autonomy, agency, and freedom — the central terms by which subjectivity has been understood in the twentieth century and beyond — have been central to feminist politics since its theoretical reeruption in the writings of Simone de Beauvoir. While these concepts are continually evoked in feminist theory, however, they have been rarely defined, explained, or analyzed. Instead they have functioned as a kind of mantra of liberation, a given ideal, not only for a politics directed purely to feminist questions but to any politics directed to class, race, or national and ethnic struggles. I propose in this essay to provide an opening up of these terms that are so commonly used to define subjectivity or identity, a problematization of their common usage in feminist and other political discourses, and their recasting in the terms of a philosophical tradition which is rarely used by feminists but which may dynamize and make such concepts ontological conditions rather than moral ideals.

Instead of turning to those philosophical traditions in which the questions of freedom and autonomy are irremediably tied to the functioning and deprivatory power of the (oppressive or dominant) other — that is, the tradition of dialectical phenomenology that dates from Hegel, through Marxism, and influences and inflects existentialism, structuralism, and poststructuralism, which in turn have so heavily influenced most contemporary forms of feminist thought regarding the subject — I want to turn to a more archaic tradition but also a more modernist one that feminists have tended to avoid — the philosophy of life, the philosophy of biology, the philosophy of nature, initiated to some extent by the pre-Socratics, but fully elaborated primarily in the nineteenth century through the texts of Darwin, Nietzsche, and Bergson and flourishing well into the earliest decades of the twentieth century.

I will attempt here to rethink concepts like freedom, autonomy, and even subjectivity in ontological, even metaphysical terms rather than what has been more common over the last century and well before, namely, through the discourses of political philosophy and the debates between liberalism, historical materialism, and postmodernism regarding the sovereignty and rights of subjects and social groups. In doing so, I hope to provide new resources, new concepts, and new questions for feminist thought in reconsidering subjectivity beyond the constraints of the paradigm of recognition that have marked it since Beauvoir. In elaborating the centrality of matter to any understanding of subjectivity or consciousness as free or autonomous, we need to look outside the traditions of thought that have considered subjectivity as the realm of agency and freedom only through the attainment of reason, rights, and recognition: that is, only through the operation of forces — social, cultural, or identificatory — outside the subject.

Thus, instead of linking the question of freedom to the concept of emancipation or to some understanding of liberation from, or removal of, an oppressive or unfair form of constraint or limitation, as is most common in feminist and other antioppressive struggles and discourses, I develop a concept of life, bare life, where freedom is conceived not only or primarily as the elimination of constraint or coercion but more positively as the condition of, or capacity for, action in life. In doing so, I hope to elaborate and explain my understanding of freedom, agency, and autonomy not in terms of a concept of "freedom from," where freedom is conceived negatively, as the elimination of constraint, but in terms of a "freedom to," a positive understanding of freedom as the capacity for action. I do not believe that this is a depoliticization of the concept but rather its reframing in a different context that may provide it with other, different political affiliations and associations and a different understanding of subjectivity.

The difference between "freedom from" and "freedom to" has of course a long and illustrious history. It perhaps finds its most recent expression in the genealogical writings of Michel Foucault, who, in distinguishing the negative or repressive hypothesis of power from the positive understanding of power as that which produces or enables, relies heavily on Nietzsche's distinction between the other-directedness of a reactive herd morality and the self-affirmation of an active or noble morality, unconcerned with the other and its constraints, directed only to its own powers and to the fullest affirmation of its own forces. The distinction between a freedom from and a freedom to is, to a large extent, correlated with a conception of freedom that is bound up with a shared existence with the other and the other's powers over the subject, on the one hand, and a freedom directed only to one's actions and their conditions and consequences, on the other. Is feminist theory best served through its traditional focus on women's attainment of a freedom from patriarchal, racist, colonialist, and heteronormative constraint? Or by exploring what the female—or feminist —subject is and is capable of making and doing? It is this broad and overarching question—one of the imponderable dilemmas facing contemporary politics well beyond feminism—that is at stake here in exploring the subject's freedom through its immersion in materiality.

I have no intention of presenting a critique of the notion of "freedom from," for it clearly has a certain political relevance;[1] but its relevance should not be overstated, and if freedom remains tied to only this negative concept of liberty, it remains tied to the options or alternatives provided by the present and its prevailing and admittedly limiting forces, instead of accessing and opening up the present to the invention of the new. In other words, a "freedom from," while arguably necessary for understanding concepts like subjectivity, agency, and autonomy, is not sufficient for at best it addresses and attempts to redress wrongs of the past without providing any positive direction for action in the future. It entails that once the subject has had restraints and inhibitions, the negative limitations, to freedom removed, a natural or given autonomy is somehow preserved. If external interference can be minimized, the subject can be (or rather become) itself, can be left to itself and as itself, can enact its given freedom. Freedom is attained through rights, laws, and rules that minimize negative interference rather than affirm positive actions.

I want to focus on the tradition of "freedom to" which has tended to be neglected in feminist and other radical political struggles, though it may make more explicit and clear what is at stake in feminist notions of subjectivity, agency, and autonomy. But rather than turning to Nietzsche and Foucault to articulate this network of connections (as I have done elsewhere)[2] — for they are the most obvious and explicit proponents of a positive conception of freedom, freedom as the ability to act and in acting to make oneself even as one is made by external forces — I will look at the work of someone more or less entirely neglected in feminist and much of postmodern literature, Henri Bergson, whose understanding of freedom is remarkably subtle and complex and may provide new ways of understanding both the openness of subjectivity and politics as well as their integration and cohesion with their respective pasts or history.[3] I believe that Bergson may help us to articulate an understanding of subjectivity, agency, and freedom that is more consonant with a feminism of difference than with an egalitarian feminism, which more clearly finds its support in various projects centered around the struggles for rights and recognition. In this sense, although there may be no direct connection between the writings of Irigaray and those of Bergson, nevertheless, some Bergsonian conceptions may serve to explain Irigaray's understanding of what autonomy might be for a subject only in the process of coming into existence, a subject-to-be (a female subject).[4] Bergson might help to rethink how subjectivity and freedom are always and only enacted within and through the materiality that life and the nonliving share, a materiality not adequately addressed in alternative traditions that have until now remained so influential in feminist thought.

Bergson and Freedom

Bergson's understanding of freedom and its links to subjectivity is initially articulated in his first major publication, *Time and Free Will*, which not only outlines his conceptions of duration and space (which will become the centerpiece of his analyses in *Matter and Memory* and *Creative Evolution*) but also embeds his work in the traditional metaphysical opposition between free will and determinism, an ancient debate, still articulating itself with great insistence, ironically, even within contemporary feminism. His understanding of freedom, as with his notions of perception, life, and intuition, lies outside and beyond the traditional binary distinctions that characterize so much of Western thought.

Bergson argues that in traditional debates regarding free will and determinism, both sides share a number of problematic commitments: both presume the separation or discontinuity of the subject from the range of available options or alternatives and from the subject's own ongoing self-identity; a fundamental continuity between present causes and future effects (whether causes are regarded as internal to the subject or as external tends to define the positions of the determinist and the libertarian respectively); and an atomistic separation or logical division between cause and effect. In other words, as in all oppositional or dichotomized divisions, both sides of the free will/determinism debate are problematic and share founding assumptions that enable them to regard themselves as opposites.[5] As with all oppositional structures, we need to find something that articulates what both views, in spite of their contradictions, share in common and what exceeds their terms and functions outside their constraints.

For the hard-core determinist, if one had an adequately detailed knowledge of antecedent events, that is, causes, one could predict with absolute certainty what their effects would be, whether these causes are material and external, or psychical and internal. In its most recent incarnations, determinism has affirmed that causes may lodge themselves within the living organism, as effects of an en masse conditioning of the body and its behavior, or as a consequence of the more microscopic molecular movements and structure of the brain or the even more miniscule chromosomal structure of each cell. (Recent discourses on "the gay brain,"[6] the "gay gene," or the construction of queer through too close a "contamination" by queer lifestyles are merely contemporary versions of this ancient debate.) What lies behind each variation of this position is the belief that, if one could know the brain structure or genetic or behavioral patterns intimately enough, one could predict future behavior, whether criminal, sexual, or cultural.

On the other side is the libertarian or free will position which asserts that even if determinism regulates the material order, in the realm of the human subject, there is an inherent unpredictability of effects from given causes. Given a variety of options or alternatives, it is unpredictable which one will be chosen: it is an open or free act. Freedom is understood, on the antideterminist position, as the performance of an act that could have been done otherwise, even under the same exact conditions. Both libertarians and determinists share the belief that the subject is the same subject, the same entity, before and after the alternatives have been posed and one chosen; the subject, even after choosing a particular course, could review that course and either would make the same choice again in precisely the same way (the determinist position) or could make a different choice, even in the same circumstances (the libertarian position). For both, the choice of one of the options does not annihilate the existence of the others but leaves them intact, capable of being chosen (or not) again.

Bergson's position on the question of freedom is more complex than either the determinist or the libertarian view. For him, it is not so much that subjects are free or not free: rather, it is *acts* that, in expressing a consonance (or not) with their agent, are free (or automatized), have (or lack) the qualitative character of free acts. An act is free to the extent that "the self alone will have been the author of it, and . . . it will express the whole of the self."[7] Bergson's position is both alluringly and nostalgically metaphysical and strikingly simple: free acts are those that spring from the subject alone (and not from any psychical state of the subject or any manipulated behavior around the subject); they not only originate in or through a subject, they express *all* of that subject. In other words, they are integral to who or what the subject is.

In this understanding, the question whether the subject would or would not make the same choice again is ill posed: such a situation is unrealistic and impossible. The precise circumstances cannot be repeated, at the very least, because the subject is not the same: the subject has inevitably changed, grown older, been affected by earlier decisions, is aware of the previous choice, and so on. If the subject were absolutely identical in the replaying of a particular choice, neither the determinist's nor the libertarian's position would be affirmed. All one could say is that the subject is the self-same subject. Yet even in the case of an example favored by the determinist — the subject under hypnosis — there is a measure of freedom insofar as the act performed through suggestion must still be rationalized, integrated in the agent's life history, given a history, qualitatively inserted into all the agent's other acts in order to be performed or undertaken.[8]

With even the most constrained and manipulated of circumstances, when one person's will is imposed on another's without his or her conscious awareness, Bergson argues that there must nevertheless be a retrospective cohesion between the subject's current act and the previous chain of connections that prepared for and made it possible. Even in this case, it is only retroactively, after the act is completed, that we can discern or mark the distinction between a cause and an effect for in psychical life there cannot be the logical separation of cause from effect that characterizes material objects in their external relations to each other. What characterizes psychical life, Bergson insists, is not the capacity to lay parts (in this case, psychical states) side by side for this accomplishes a certain spatial ordering that is not possible for, or lived by, the living being but the inherent immersion and coherence of a being in time. Psychical states are not like objects for they have no parts, cannot be directly compared, and admit of no magnitude or degree.

Psychical states have three relevant characteristics: (*a*) they are always qualitative, and thus incapable of measurement without the imposition of an external grid (this already makes psychical determinism an incoherent position — if causes cannot be measured and precisely calculated, then even if determinism is in principle correct, ironically it remains unable to attain its most explicit goal — prediction);[9] (*b*) they function not through distinction, opposition, categories, or identities but through "fusion or interpenetration,"[10] through an immersion or permeation that generates a continuity between states or processes and makes their juxtaposition impossible (this is the basis of Bergson's critique of associationism);[11] and (*c*) they emerge or can be understood only in duration rather than through the conventional modes of spatialization that generally regulate thought, especially scientific or instrumental thought, that is to say, any mode of analysis or division into parts. Parts, elements, and states are discernible only as spatial categories or terms. While these attributes or divisions may be imposed on the continuity of life and consciousness, they do not arise from them for life is as much becoming as it is being; it is durational as much as it is spatial, though we are less able to see or comprehend the durational flux than the mappable geometries of spatial organization.

For Bergson, then, at least in his earlier works, free acts erupt from the subject insofar as they express the whole of that subject even when they are unexpected and unprepared for: "we are free when our acts spring from our whole personality, when they express it, when they have that indefinable resemblance to it which one sometimes finds between the artist and his work" (172). Acts are free insofar as they express and resemble the subject, not insofar as the subject is always the same, an essence, an identity but insofar as the subject is transformed by and engaged through its acts, becomes through its acts: "Those who ask whether we are free to alter our character lay themselves open to [this] objection. Certainly our character is altering imperceptibly every day, and our freedom would suffer if these new acquisitions were grafted on to our self and not blended with it. But, as soon as this blending takes place, it must be admitted that the change which has supervened in our character belongs to us, that we have appropriated it" (172).

Bergson's point is that free acts come from or even through us (it is not clear if it matters where the impetus of the act originates — what matters is how it is retroactively integrated into the subject's history and continuity). More significantly, if this subject from which acts spring is never the same, never self-identical, always and imperceptibly becoming other than what it once was and is now, then free acts, having been undertaken, are those which transform us, which we can incorporate into our becomings in the very process of their changing us. Free acts are those which both express us and which transform us, which express our transforming.

What both the determinists and the libertarians misunderstand is the very notion of *possibility*: the determinist assumes that there is only one possible act that can occur from given conditions or antecedents for any given subject, whereas the libertarian assumes that there could be several different acts that could ensue from given conditions or antecedents. Given two possible outcomes, X and Y (and fixing the antecedent conditions), the determinist assumes that only one was ever in fact possible; in contrast the libertarian assumes that both were equally possible. Neither understands that the two options were never of equal value because neither exists in itself as an abstract possibility. If we follow Bergson's famous distinction between the possible and the virtual,[12] the possible is at best the retrospective projection of a real that wishes to conceive itself as eternally, always, possible but which becomes actual only through an unpredictable labor and effort of differentiation, an epigenesis that exceeds its preconditions. It is only after a work of art, a concept, formula, or act exists, is real, and has had some actuality that we can say that it must have been possible, that it was one of the available options. Its possibility can be gleaned only from its actuality for the possible never prefigures the real, it simply accompanies it as its post facto shadow. So although we can posit that X and Y are equally possible (or not equally possible), it is only after one of them has been actualized or chosen that we can see the path of reasons, causes, or explanations which made it desirable.[13] Only after one of the options has been chosen can we see that the unchosen option is not preserved there in its possibility but entirely dissolves, becoming simply a reminiscence or projection.

Bergson has provided an understanding of freedom that is not fundamentally linked to the question of choice, to the operations of alternatives, to the selection of options outside the subject and independently available to him or her. It is not a freedom of selection, of consumption, a freedom linked to the acquisition of objects but a freedom of action that is above all connected to an active self, an embodied being, a being who acts in a world of other beings and objects. Acts, having been undertaken, transform their agent so that the paths that the agent took to the act are no longer available to him or her except abstractly or in reconstruction. Indeed, there are no paths to any possible action (that is why an action remains possible but not real) until the action is acted, and then the path exists only in reconstruction not in actuality. The path can be drawn only after the movement is completed. Once the act is performed, we can divide, analyze, assess, and treat as necessary what in the process of its performance remains undivided, unanalyzable, surprising, and utterly contingent. The act, once performed, once actualized, is different from the indeterminacy of its performance.

Moreover, Bergson's understanding of freedom dissolves the intimate connection between freedom and the subject's internal constitution or pregiven right. Freedom is not a quality or property of the human subject, as implied within the phenomenological tradition, but can only characterize a process, an action, a movement that has no particular qualities. Freedom has no given content; it cannot be defined. "Any positive definition of freedom will ensure the victory of determinism."[14] This is in part because it is not an attribute, quality, or capacity that exists independent of its exercise. It is not that subjects are or are not free; rather, actions, those undertaken by living beings, may sometimes express such freedom. Freedom is a matter of degree and characterizes only those acts in which one acts with all of one's being, and in the process those acts become capable of transforming that being. It is rare that our actions express with such intimate intensity the uniqueness of our situation and our own position within it.[15] But it is at these moments that freedom at its most intense is expressed.

Freedom is thus the exception rather than the rule in the sense that it can function only through the "autonomy" of the living being against a background of routinized or habituated activity. It is only insofar as most of everyday life is accommodated through automatism, by a kind of reflex or habit, that free acts have their energetic and aesthetico-moral force and their effects on their author or agent. Associationism and determinism have their relevance in conscious life: they provide an explanation of the automatized substrate of daily behavior that provides a probabilistic guarantee of accomplished action. It is only against this assumed or taken-for-granted background economy of details that free acts may erupt.[16] In place of either a rigid determinism or the pointless and undirected openness of libertarianism, Bergson poses indeterminacy as the defining characteristic of life and the condition for freedom: "It is at the great and solemn crisis, decisive in our reputation with others, and yet more with ourself, that we choose in defiance of what is conventionally called a motive, and this absence of any tangible reason is the more striking the deeper our freedom goes" (170).

Freedom and Materiality

In his later works, Bergson focuses less on freedom as the exclusive attribute of a self, concentrated on only the one, conscious side of the distinction between the organic and the inorganic, as he did in his earlier *Time and Free Will*, and more on the relations between the organic and the inorganic, the internal constitution of freedom through its encounters with the resistance of matter.[17] If freedom is located in acts rather than in subjects, then the capacity to act and the effectivity of action is to a large extent structured by the ability to harness and utilize matter for one's own purposes and interests. Freedom is not a transcendent quality inherent in subjects but is immanent in the relations that the living has with the material world, including other forms of life.

As the correlate of life itself, whose accompaniment is consciousness in a more or less dormant or active state, freedom is not a transcendental property of the human but an immanent and sometimes latent capacity in life in all its complexity. Life is consciousness, though not always an active consciousness. Consciousness is the projection onto materiality of the possibility of a choice, a decision whose outcome is not given in advance, which is to say, a mode of simplifying or skeletalizing matter so that it affords us materials on and with which to act.[18] It is linked to the capacity for choice, for freedom. It is not tied to the emergence of reason, to the capacity for reflection, or to some inherent quality of the human. Life in its evolutionary forms expresses various degrees of freedom, correlated with the extent and range of consciousness, which is itself correlated with the various possibilities of action. The torpor or unconsciousness that characterizes most plant life makes the concept of freedom largely irrelevant or operational only at its most minimal level insofar as "choice" or action is not generally available to vegetal existence.[19]

Yet the most elementary forms of mobile life, animal existence from the protozoa upward, exhibit a kind of incipient freedom in some of their most significant actions. The capacity for "choice"—even if reduced to the choice of when and where to contract or expand, when and what to eat, and so forth—expresses both the particularity of each species and the specificity of individuals within them.[20] Each species, Bergson suggests, has the consciousness precisely appropriate to the range of actions available to it: each species, and here Bergson anticipates the work of some of the theoretical biologists to follow,[21] has a world opened up to it within which its organs have, through natural selection, the capacity to extract for it what it needs for its ongoing existence. Each animal species, whether regulated by instinct as are the social insects or by intelligence as occurs in gradations through the vertebrates, has a world in which it can act, in which it requires a certain consciousness and in which there is for it a "fringe" of freedom, a zone of indetermination that elevates it above mere automated responses to given stimuli.

It is this "zone of indetermination" that for Bergson characterizes both the freedom representative of life and the capacity for being otherwise that life can bestow on (elements or factors of) material organization. Indetermination is the "true principle" of life, the condition for the open-ended action of living beings, the ways in which living bodies are mobilized for action that cannot be specified in advance.[22] The degrees of indetermination are the degrees of freedom. Living bodies act not simply or mainly through deliberation or conscious decision but through indetermination, through the capacity they bring to the material world and objects to make them useful for life in ways that cannot be specified in advance.[23]

Indetermination spreads from the living to the nonliving through the virtuality that the living brings to the inorganic, the potential for the inorganic to be otherwise, to lend itself to incorporation, transformation, and energetic protraction in the life and activities of species and individuals: "At the root of life there is an effort to engraft on to the necessity of physical forces the largest possible amount of *indetermination*."[24] Life opens the universe to becoming more than it is.

But equally, Bergson argues, matter as a whole, the material universe, must contain within itself the very conditions for the indeterminacy of the life which it generated. Those mixtures or compounds may yield memory, history, and the past and make them linger, press on, and remain relevant to the present and future. Matter must contain as its most latent principle, its most virtual recess, the same indeterminacy that life returns to it. This is the common point of binary terms (matter and memory, extension and consciousness, space and duration) and that which exceeds them—the fundamental interimplications of mind and matter, of life and the inorganic, as well as their origins in the indeterminacy of the universe itself, the point of their endosmosis, where matter expands into life and life contracts into matter in pure duration. Life, and its growing complications through the evolutionary elaboration, generates a "reservoir of indetermination" (126) that it returns to the inorganic universe to expand it and make it amenable to, and the resource for, life in its multiple becomings; and matter in turn, while providing the resources and objects of living activity, is also the internal condition of freedom as well as its external limit or constraint. "[The evolution of life] is at the mercy of the materiality which it has had to assume. It is what each of us may experience in himself. Our freedom, in the very movements by which it is affirmed, creates the growing habits that will stifle it if it fails to renew itself by a constant effort: it is dogged by automatism" (127).

Materiality tends to determination; it gives itself up to calculation, precision, and spatialization. But at the same time, it is also the field in and through which free acts are generated through the encounter of life with matter and the capacity of each to yield to the other its forms and forces, both its inertia and its dynamism. Matter, inorganic matter, is both the contracting condition of determination and the dilating expression of indetermination, and these two possibilities characterize both matter in its inorganic forms and those organized material bodies that are living. Immersed in matter and an eruption from it, life is the continuous negotiation with matter that creates the conditions for its own expansion and the opening up of matter to its own virtualities: "[Life] was to create with matter, which is necessity itself, an instrument of freedom, to make a machine which should triumph over mechanism, and to use the determinism of nature to pass through the meshes of the net which this very determinism had spread" (264).

As isolatable systems, fixed entities, objects with extrinsic relations to each other, the material universe is the very source of regularity, predictability, and determination that enables a perceiving being to perform habitual actions with a measure of some guarantee of efficacy. Yet as an interconnected whole, the universe itself exhibits hesitation, uncertainty, and the openness to evolutionary emergence, that is, the very indetermination that characterizes life. At its most contracted, the material universe is regular, reborn at each moment, fully actual and in the present. But at its most expansive, it is part of the flow of pure duration, carrying along the past with the present, the virtual with the actual, and enabling them to give way to a future they do not contain. The universe has this expansive possibility, the possibility of being otherwise not because life recognizes it as such but because life can exist only because of the simultaneity of the past with the present that matter affords it.[25]

Feminism and Freedom

Feminists have long assumed that, as a coercive form of constraint, it is patriarchy and patriarchal power relations that have limited women's freedom by not making available to women the full range of options for action that it affords men. And it is certainly true that the range of "choices" available to women as a group is smaller and more restricted than that available to men as a group. But the question of freedom for women, or for any oppressed social group, is never simply a question of expanding the range of available options so much as it is about transforming the quality and activity of the subjects who choose and who make themselves through how and what they do. Freedom is not so much linked to choice (a selection from pregiven options or commodities) as it is to autonomy, and autonomy is linked to the ability to make (or refuse to make) activities (including language and systems of representation and value) one's own, that is, to integrate the activities one undertakes into one's history, one's becoming. It is my claim that something like a Bergsonian understanding of freedom coheres more readily with an Irigarayan conception of sexual autonomy than with a feminist egalitarianism that is necessarily rooted in sexual indifference. Although of course Bergson was not interested in and predates the paradigm of sexual difference posed by Irigaray, his conception of freedom links actions to a process of self-making that closely anticipates Irigaray's understanding of sexual difference, the autonomy and dual symmetry of the two sexes, as that which is virtual and that which is in the process of becoming.[26]

Bergson has elucidated a concept of freedom that links it not to choice but to innovation and invention. Freedom pertains to the realm of actions, processes, and events that are not contained within, or predictable from, the present; it is that which emerges, surprises, and cannot be entirely anticipated in advance. It is not a state one is in or a quality that one has, but it resides in the activities one undertakes that transform oneself and (a part of) the world. It is not a property or right bestowed on, or removed from, individuals by others but a capacity or potentiality to act both in accordance with one's past as well as "out of character," in a manner that surprises.

Freedom is thus not primarily a capacity of mind but of body: it is linked to the body's capacity for movement, and thus its multiple possibilities of action. Freedom is not an accomplishment granted by the grace or good will of the other but is attained only through the struggle with matter, the struggle of bodies to become more than they are, a struggle that occurs not only on the level of the individual but also of the species.

Freedom is the consequence of indetermination, the very indetermination that characterizes both consciousness and perception. It is this indetermination — the discriminations of the real based on perception, the discriminations of interest that consciousness performs on material objects, including other bodies — that liberates life from the immediacy and givenness of objects but also from the immediacy and givenness of the past. Life is not the coincidence of the present with its past, its history, it is also the forward thrust of a direction whose path is clear only in retrospect. Indetermination liberates life from the constraints of the present. Life is the protraction of the past into the present, the suffusing of matter with memory, which is the capacity to contract matter into what is useful for future action and to make matter function differently in the future than in the past. The spark of indetermination that made life possible spreads through matter by means of the activities that life performs on matter. As a result, the world itself comes to vibrate with its possibilities for being otherwise.

So what does Bergsonism, or the philosophy of life, offer to feminist theory over and above the liberal and Marxist, empiricist or phenomeno-logical conceptions of freedom? If we rely on a conception of freedom that is linked to the controlling power of the other, the socially dominant others, whether a class, a sex, a race, or groups and individuals — a view which all these conceptions in some way share — we abandon in advance the concept of autonomy. If freedom is that which is bestowed on us by others, it cannot be lodged in autonomy, in the individual's inner cohe-sion and historical continuity: it comes from outside, from rights granted to us rather than capacities inherent in us. Freedom becomes transcenden-tal rather than immanent, other oriented rather than autonomous, linked to being rather than to doing. Such an understanding of freedom, at least from the point of view of a philosophy of life, is reactive, secondary, peripheral, outside of life instead of being seen as the very (inalienable) condition of life. Freedom is a question of degree rather than an absolute right. It is attained rather than bestowed, and it functions through activity rather than waiting passively for its moment. Being gay or straight, for example, is not a question of choice (of options already given in their independent neutrality — men or women as sexual objects, or masculine or feminine as modes of identification) but an expression of who one is and what one enjoys doing, of one's being. It is an expression of freedom without necessarily constraining itself to options already laid out. Gayness (or straightness) is neither produced from causes — whether physiologi-cal, genetic, neurological, or sociological — nor is it the consequence of a free choice among equally appealing given alternatives. It is the enactment of a freedom that can refuse to constrain sexuality and sexual partners to any given function, purpose, or activity and that makes sexuality an open invention even as it carries the burden of biological, cultural, and individ-ual construction.

The problem of feminism is not the problem of women's lack of freedom, or simply the constraints that patriarchal power relations impose on women and their identities. If women are not, in some sense, free, feminism could not be possible. The problem, rather, is how to expand the variety of activities, including the activities of knowledge-production,[27] so that women and men may be able to act differently and open up activities to new interests, perspectives, and frameworks hitherto not adequately explored or invented. The problem is not how to give women more adequate recognition (who is it that women require recognition from?), more rights, or more of a voice but how to enable more action, more making and doing, more difference. That is, the challenge facing feminism today is no longer only how to give women a more equal place within existing social networks and relations but how to enable women to partake in the creation of a future unlike the present.

Notes

1 It is perfectly obvious that a freedom to create, to make, or to produce is a luxury that can be attained only with a certain level of the absence of constraint. However, even in the most extreme cases of slavery and in situations of political or natural catastrophe of the kinds globally experienced in recent years, there is always a small space for innovation and not simply reaction. What remains remarkable about genocidal struggles, the horrors of long-term incarceration, concentration camps, prisoner of war camps, and the prospects of long-term social coexistence in situations of natural and social catastrophe is the inventiveness of the activities of the constrained — the flourishing of minor and hidden arts and literature, technologies and instruments, networks of communication, and the transmission of information. What is most striking about the extreme situations of constraint, those which require a "freedom from," is that they do not eliminate a "freedom to" but only complicate it.

2 In *The Nick of Time* (2004) as well as in *Volatile Bodies* (1994).

3 There have been some, a few, feminist texts on Bergson. See, in particular, Olkowski, "The End of Phenomenology"; and Hill, "Interval, Sexual Difference."

4 Irigaray articulates her objections to, and her differences from, the feminist egalitarian project in "Equal to Whom?"

5 At bottom, Bergson argues, both the libertarian and the determinist are committed to a tautology, in fact to complementary tautologies: "The argument of the determinists assumes this puerile form: 'The act, once performed, is

performed,' and . . . their opponents reply: 'The act, before being performed, was not yet performed.' In other words, the question of freedom remains after this discussion exactly where it was to begin with; nor must we be surprised at it, since freedom must be sought in a certain shade or quality of the action itself and not in the relation of this act to what it is not or to what it might have been." Bergson, *Time and Free Will*, 182.

6   See LeVay, *Queer Science*.

7   Bergson, *Time and Free Will*, 165–66.

8   "For it is by no means the case that all conscious states blend with one another as raindrops with the water of a lake. The self, in so far as it has to do with a homogeneous space, develops on a kind of surface, and on this surface independent growths may form and float. Thus a suggestion received in the hypnotic state is not incorporated in the mass of conscious states, but, endowed with a life of its own, it will usurp the whole personality when its time comes. A violent anger roused by some accidental circumstance, a hereditary vice suddenly emerged from the obscure depths of the organism to the surface of consciousness, will act almost like a hypnotic suggestion." Ibid., 166.

9   "The causes here, unique in their kind, are part of the effect, have come into existence with it and are determined by it as much as they determine it." Bergson, *Creative Evolution*, 164.

10 Bergson, *Time and Free Will*, 163.

11 "In proportion as we dig below the surface and get to the real self, do its states of consciousness cease to stand in juxtaposition and begin to permeate and melt into one another, and each to be tinged with the colouring of the others. Thus each of us has his own way of loving and hating; and this love or hatred reflects his whole personality." Ibid., 164.

12 See Bergson, *The Creative Mind*, "The Possible and the Real."

13 "As reality is created as something unforeseeable and new, its image is reflected behind into the indefinite past; thus it finds that it has from all time been possible, but it is at this precise moment that it begins to have been always possible, and that is why I said that it's possible, but it is at this precise moment that it begins to have been always possible, and that is why I said that its possibility, which does not precede its reality, will have preceded it once the reality has appeared. The possible is therefore the mirage of the present in the past." Bergson, *The Creative Mind*, 119.

14 Bergson, *Time and Free Will*, 220.

15 "It is the whole soul, in fact, which gives rise to the free decision: and the act will be so much the freer the more the dynamic series with which it is connected tends to be the fundamental self. Thus understood, free acts are exceptional, even on the part of those who are most given to controlling and reasoning out what they do." Ibid., 167.

16 "It is to this these acts, which are very numerous but for the most part

insignificant, that the associationist theory is applicable. They are, taken all together, the substratum of our free activity, and with respect to this activity they play the same part as our organic functions in relation to the whole of our conscious life. Moreover we will grant to determinism that we often resign our freedom in more serious circumstances, and that, by sluggishness or indolence, we allow this same local process to run its course when our whole personality ought, so to speak, to vibrate." Ibid., 169.

17   Most notably in, *Matter and Memory*; *The Creative Mind*; *Mind-Energy*; and *Creative Evolution*.

18   "Theoretically, then, everything living must be conscious. *In principle*, consciousness is co-extensive with life." Bergson, *Mind-Energy*, 8.

19   "Even in the vegetable world, where the organism is generally fixed to the soil, the faculty of movement is dormant rather than absent: it awakens when it can be of use. . . . It appears to me therefore extremely likely that consciousness, originally immanent in all that lives, is dormant where there is no longer spontaneous movement." Ibid., 10–11.

20   "The amoeba . . . when in the presence of a substance which can be made food, pushes out towards it filaments able to seize and enfold foreign bodies. These pseudopodia are real organs and therefore mechanisms; but they are only temporary organs created for the particular purpose, and it seems they still show the rudiments of a choice. From top to bottom, therefore, of the scale of animal life we see being exercised, though the form is ever vaguer as we descend, the faculty of choice, that is, the responding to a definite stimulus of movements more or less unforeseen." Ibid., 9–10.

21   See in particular Uexküll, *Theoretical Biology*; Uexküll, *Instinctive Behavior*; Raymond Ruyer, *Néo-finalisme*; and Simondon, "The Genesis of the Individual."

22   Bergson, *Matter and Memory*, 31.

23   "Matter is inertia, geometry, necessity. But with life there appears free, predictable, movement. The living being chooses or tends to choose. Its role is to create. In a world where everything else is determined, a zone of indetermination surrounds it. To create the future requires preparatory action in the present, to prepare what will be is to utilize what has been; life therefore is employed from its start in conserving the past and anticipating the future in a duration in which past, present and future tread one on another, forming an indivisible continuity. Such memory, such anticipation, are consciousness itself. This is why, in right if not in fact, consciousness is coextensive with life." Bergson, *Mind-Energy*, 13.

24   Bergson, *Creative Evolution*, 114.

25   "This is precisely what life is, — freedom inserting itself into necessity, turning it to its profit. Life would be an impossibility were the determinism of matter so absolute as to admit no relaxation. Suppose, however, that at particular points matter shows a certain elasticity, then and there will be opportunity for

consciousness to install itself. It will have to humble itself at first; yet, once installed, it will dilate, it will spread from its point of entry and not rest till it has conquered the whole, for time is at its disposal and the slightest quantity of indetermination, by continually adding to itself, will make up as much freedom as you like." Bergson, *Mind-Energy*, 13–14.

26   It is primarily Irigaray's earlier works — *Speculum of the Other Woman*; *This Sex Which is Not One*; *Marine Lover*; and *An Ethics of Sexual Difference* that outline her understanding of autonomy and identity and a project of becoming, a project of the future that overcomes the sexual indifference of the past and present.

27   See in particular, Irigaray, "Is the Subject of Science Sexed?"

Samantha Frost

Fear and the Illusion of Autonomy

Thomas Hobbes is notorious for his conjunction of fear and politics. Yet, despite this notoriety, we do not often give him credit for having a sophisticated and well-thought-out account of just what fear is. The accounts of fear that are often attributed to Hobbes mirror more common understandings of fear: Fear is the screaming physical response to the threat of injury or to threats to survival. Fear is a response to the limits of epistemology, which is to say that it is a response to the obscurity of the unknown.[1] Or, fear is an ideological formation, an affect we learn in response to cultural and political prompts.[2] Although each of these renditions differs in its presumptions about the roots of fear, in each it is figured as a powerful motivator for action. Indeed, the common textbook version of Hobbes's politics combines all three accounts of fear to foreground Hobbes's statement that, in politics, "the Passion to be reckoned upon, is Fear."[3] According to this tale, fear arises organically and inevitably from the competitiveness and contentiousness of individuals' pursuits of their desires. Although fear is primal—a kind of animal instinct for survival—its imperatives nevertheless can coincide with the demands of reason, which is to say that fear compels us to see the wisdom of leaving the uncertainties and violence of the natural condition by setting up a sovereign to rule over us.[4] Through the mechanism of the covenant, we leave the "warre of every one against every one,"[5] in which each fears every other, and we install a supremely powerful sovereign our common fear of whom impels us to obedience and orderliness. Here, then, fear is conceived as the catalyst and precipitate of social antagonism as well as the foundation for political order.

In reconsidering Hobbes's account of fear, I do not want to discount altogether such treatments for each captures important elements of the passions we group under the rubric of fear. But through his materialist metaphysics — and its account of the subject — Hobbes gives us a way to think about fear that is not purely animalistic, is not fundamentally epistemological, and does not position us as so completely saturated by culture that we cannot but be the dupes of political manipulation. If we trace Hobbes's materialist account of the profound complexity of causation along with his analysis of the way in which fear orients the subject in time, we see that fear is both a response to, and a disavowal of, the impossibility of self-sovereignty. That is, the movements of memory and anticipation that Hobbes depicts as central to the passion of fear transform a complicated causal field for the subject in such a way as to give her a sense of possible mastery both over herself and over the world around her. In showing us how fear fosters an illusion of autonomous agency in individuals, Hobbes points to the possibility that the immense and fearsome power attributed to the sovereign is not simply a response to the need to quell unruliness and disorder but is also the condition for each individual's sense of her own self-sovereignty.

Heteronomy

Hobbes's arguments about the impossibility of self-sovereignty rest on the account of complex causation that is at the center of his materialist metaphysics. In Hobbes's view, everything is matter or material. As he puts it, "The Universe, that is, the whole masse of all things that are" is "Corporeall, that is to say, Body."[6] What is particularly interesting in Hobbes's materialism is his conception of matter itself. As the philosopher who penned the Third Set of Objections to René Descartes's *Meditations*, Hobbes vehemently rejected not only the latter's dualist configuration of the subject but also the conception of matter that is integral to the Cartesian dualist framework. Against Descartes's conception of matter as in itself and essentially incapable of thinking, Hobbes forwarded what I call a "varie-gated materialism," in which some forms of matter are conceived as alive or thoughtful without the liveliness or capacity for thought somehow "added" onto an inert substrate.[7] That is to say, for Hobbes, some matter is simply alive or capable of thought as such. Accordingly, he proposes that we conceive of people as "thinking-bodies."[8]

Of course, to figure people as thinking-bodies—as bodies with the capacity to think—is to raise a host of questions about the nature of self-consciousness, cognition, freedom, and determinism that I cannot ad-dress fully in this context. But a brief sketch of some of the concerns raised by materialist understandings of the self runs as follows. To portray people as wholly embodied—and to refuse philosophically to preserve some non-physical or nonbodily element that can serve as the agent or mechanism that sets the body apart from its physical environment—is to risk dissolv-ing the self into the world. That is, the figure of a wholly embodied subject elicits the concern that such a body could do nothing but reproduce mechanically the causal movements and trajectories at play in the context in which it exists. In evoking the specter of a subject that is not much more than a vehicle for the causal forces around it, Hobbes's materialism seem-ingly presents itself as the antithesis of a theory of autonomous agency: his materialism seems to promise nothing more than a reductive mecha-nistic determinism. Hobbes's materialist account of causation does indeed call into question the possibility of autonomous agency—autonomy here conceived not in the strict Kantian sense of the will adhering to naught but rational principle but rather in the more general sense of independent, self-conscious self-determination. But his denial of the individual's self-sovereignty as an actor does not amount to the denial of human agency altogether. In addition to proposing that our interdependence is the con-dition for our effective actions, Hobbes also suggests that in spite of the fact of heteronomy—or perhaps in the need to deny it—we actively foster an illusion of autonomy so that we can *feel* effective when we act.[9] Indeed, in this essay, I want to argue that fear is a passion among whose effects is the illusion of individual autonomous agency.

According to Hobbes, all events and actions are caused, and each has a broad array of causal antecedents that are related to one another in a complex, nonlinear fashion. As he explains it, each event or act is pro-duced or determined by not just one or two causal factors but rather by "the sum of all things."[10] Hobbes even grants that astrological factors may have some (impossible to calculate) causal weight (246). However, the immense range of causal factors that contribute to determining an act are not connected in a unilinear fashion, as if one thing leads to the next which leads to the next. Rejecting a unilinear and cumulative conception of causality, Hobbes explains that the "sum of all things" is not "one simple *chain* or concatenation, but an innumerable number of chains, joined together . . . and consequently the whole cause of an event, doth not always depend on one single chain, but on many together" (246–47).

Importantly, Hobbes's sense of the complexity of the causal determination of events and actions is not captured in toto by the image of a network of bodies whose motile forces move inexorably in a particular direction to produce an inevitable effect. For in addition to pointing to the manifold causes whose trajectories coincide to produce an event, Hobbes reminds us that the fields or contexts in which events and actions occur are equally causes of the events and actions. In his discussion of cause and effect in *De Corpore*, he analytically resolves events or acts into two distinguishable elements. On the one hand, there is the body whose movement "generates motion" in another body.[11] This "generative" body is what Hobbes calls the agent of an act; its motion is "action." On the other hand, there is the body in which the movement is generated. This moved body is what Hobbes calls the patient; its motion is "passion." For any act to occur, there must be both agent and patient. Or to say the same thing in terms of the movement involved: every act requires both action and passion. Of course, we are well accustomed to thinking about acts in terms of agents and action. We are not so used to thinking about the patient of, and the passion in, an act, that which is moved and the being-moved movement that is a constitutive part of every act. But in Hobbes's analysis, without passion, that is, without a patient, an act might be initiated but it will not occur. So, in considering the causes that coalesce to produce an act, we must think of the complex of contextual passive causes as well as the complex of active causes.

To make matters even more complicated, Hobbes argues that the causes of specifically human actions are likewise determined. In other words, he extends his account of complex causation to our thoughts and passions to claim that we must conceive of our actions as produced by the coalescence of numerous causes, internal and external, that are related to one another in a complex, nonlinear fashion. To put the point succinctly, Hobbes's materialist claim that "nothing taketh beginning from *itself*" entails that human actions must be considered heteronomous.[12]

For Hobbes, neither our thoughts nor our passions have their origin in us. According to his materialism, our thoughts are caused rather than being the intuited product of our self-conscious effort and rational direction.[13] Each thought or "imagination" is a composite of sensory percepts and memories that arise and resound as the body ages, moves, and encounters and responds to the context of its action.[14] Likewise, Hobbes claims, our passions are not born with us but rather are constituted through a variable configuration and confluence of bodily constitution, experience, cultural norms, material opportunity, and dumb luck.[15] Since we cannot direct ourselves to feel any particular one or other of the passions, we are not the original and singular source of the will that is the motive force in our actions.[16] In short, the thoughts and desires that propel and occasion our actions have as complex a causal history as any event.[17] As a result, Hobbes claims, the subject cannot be taken to be the *single origin* of an act.[18]

Importantly, however, the claim that an individual is not the single origin of her act is not the claim that her actions are simply the result of her passive absorption and transmission of the extant ambient causal forces. Hobbes contends that thinking-bodies can and do in fact act in contradistinction to the determinations of the contexts of their actions. In his analysis, distinctive or innovative actions are possible because there is a temporal disjuncture between the determination of the subject's imagination and desires and the determinants of the causal context which provokes and is the condition of the subject's actions.

According to Hobbes, "the Imagination is the first *internall* beginning of all Voluntary motion."[19] The imagination can be conceived as the first internal beginning of action because the thoughts that constitute the imagination are not a simple and direct imprint of the perceptual objects immediately before the subject. Rather, as noted above, the imagination is a form of memory that comprises past perceptual experience, past affective responses, as well as current perceptual and physiological stimuli. In other words, each thinking-body carries its own history as memory and that ever-changing collection of memories is the basis of both perception and imagination. Accordingly, the mutual transfiguration of memory, affect, and percept that together constitute particular thoughts and passions is unique to the singular history that is each individual's life. So, while thoughts and passions are indeed caused, the chains of their causation are nonsynchronous and noncontemporaneous with the causal determinations of the context. That is, because of what Hobbes describes as the internal causal history of the imagination, the causes of the imagination and the passions do not coincide with, and are not comprehended by, the environmental stimuli that provoke them.

As is no doubt clear in even this brief excursus into his philosophy of causation, Hobbes's materialism calls into question our status as masterful, self-sovereign subjects. Although we are not mere puppets of the causal forces in the field of our action, neither are we completely self-determining agents. Likewise, many among the vast and complicated range of contextual causes that coalesce to produce an event are beyond our ken and control, which is to say that we cannot unfailingly regulate or direct the future course of events. Yet, while the complexity of causation makes it close to impossible definitively to single out a particular patchwork of causes and effects and from within that to identify one cause as decisive for a particular act or event, Hobbes says we isolate causes in this way all the time. In fact, we are driven to do so.

As Hobbes explains, "Anxiety for the future time, disposeth men to enquire into the causes of things: because the knowledge of them, maketh men the better able to order the present to their best advantage."[20] In other words, because we want to be more rather than less happy and successful, we try to discern why good and bad things happen to us and, following that, what we should do. But of course, for all our researches into causes and consequences, what we can come up with is just "conjecture" whose insights are often "very fallacious" (chap. 3, 97). In the best of circumstances, those with a lot of experience can act with some certainty of what consequences will come "but not with certainty enough" (97). Hobbes points out that even when "the Event answereth our Expectation," even when a prediction turns out to be correct, the foresight is "in its own nature . . . but Presumption" (97), which is to say that it is good guesswork. And in situations in which we cannot find "the true causes of things," we are compelled to "suppose causes," fabricating them "either such as [our] own fancy suggesteth; or trusteth to the Authority of other men" (chap. 12, 168–69). And in fact, the propensity to select and identify causes is especially pronounced in the experience of fear. As we shall see, below, according to Hobbes's analysis, the identification of causes in fear can be seen as an effort to produce the illusion of autonomy under conditions of heteronomy.

Fear

As mentioned above, for Hobbes, the passions have a temporal depth that makes them more than an immediate reaction to stimulation. As their name might suggest, the passions are a form of "being-moved" provoked by stimuli. Yet, the provocation is not the only causal force at play: the various textures and gravity of the passions derive from the play of memory, evaluation, and anticipation that is a part of perception itself. Indeed, in Hobbes's elaboration of the passions, each has its own peculiar temporality. I am interested in the temporality of fear in particular not simply because Hobbes says that fear is the most compelling of the passions in politics. I want to focus on Hobbes's account of fear because there is a recursive temporal movement in fear that simplifies the causal field and that, in so simplifying, grants to the subject the possibility of effective agency. The fact that fear is implicated in the aspiration to autonomy means that its place and significance in politics is more complicated and productive than its figuration as a motivation has led us to believe.

To be clear, to say that fear has a temporality to it is not the same as to say it has a history. Certainly, Hobbes's materialist account of the subject does entail that fear has a history. Contrary to the common view that for Hobbes individuals' desires and fears are "intrinsic" to each person, he claims in *Leviathan* that the passions "proceed from Experience, and triall of their effects upon themselves, or other men" (chap. 6, 120).[21] In fact, in *De Homine* he gives a broader account of the extrinsic or cultural factors that constitute the passions. He writes there that "men's inclinations toward certain things, arise from a six-fold source: namely from the constitution of the body, from experience, from habit, from the goods of fortune, from the opinion one hath of oneself, and from authorities" (chap. 13, 63). In other words, rather than being original to ourselves, our dispositions and desires arise through the complex interaction of physiology, personal history, and historical, cultural, and political context, and they change as these factors change over time (63). If we take Hobbes's notion of inclinations to include *dis*inclinations—just as he includes fears and aversions as well as desires and appetites in his account of the passions—we can see him pointing here to as complex a history for individuals' fears as there is for their desires. To insist, as Hobbes does, that fear has a history is to give it a richness and texture that is both socially and historically recognizable as well as specific to the particular individual experiencing it. But this anchoring of the subject's particularity in his or her historical context is not what I am after in specifying fear's temporality. By "temporality," I mean to highlight the way in which the feeling of fear orients the subject in time: forward-looking, backward-looking, or some combination of these.[22] Of course, as we shall see, the temporality of fear is intimately linked to its historicity. But what I am particularly interested in is how the movements of memory and anticipation in fear place the subject in relationship to time in such a way as to give her a sense of possible mastery over the field of her actions and (therefore) over the future.

In order to get at the temporality of fear as Hobbes understands it, we need to be rather technical in distinguishing the passion of fear from other aversive passions. First, then, to the passions more generally. According to Hobbes, each perceptual object an individual encounters has an effect upon the equilibrium of the person's vital life activity—or what he calls "vitall motion."[23] As he tells it, the motions that "presseth the organ proper to each Sense" are translated "by the Mediation of Nerves, and other strings, and membranes of the body" to the brain and heart where they "causeth . . . a resistance, or counter-pressure, or endeavour of the heart, to deliver itself" (chap. 1, 85). In other words, in the process of perception, a person is not simply acted upon but also resists the motions precipitated by a perceptual encounter. The perceiver is not passively impressed upon by stimuli but rather actively responds in the very process of perceiving. The event of perception, then, is as much a rejoinder or a resistance to transformation as it is a stimulation. And if we recall that for Hobbes memory quite simply comprises the residual motions triggered by perception lingering in the thinking-body over time (chap. 2, 88–89), we can see that both forms of perceptual effect—the stimulation and the resistance—become constituent elements of the perception cum memory of what the perceptual object is. In other words, each thought or memory has an evaluative or affective dimension.

In Hobbes's analysis, the passions as a group constitute different kinds of responses or rejoinders that a person might have to a stimulating object. A positive effect on vital motion compels the organism to draw closer, an impetus Hobbes calls appetite. A negative effect on vital motion repulses the organism, a movement he calls aversion (chap. 6, 119). Appetite and aversion, then, are the imperceptible movements or "endeavours" in a thinking-body toward or away from a stimulating object "before [these movements] appear in walking, speaking, striking, and other visible actions" (119). And importantly, while the motions instigated by a perceptual encounter are "nothing else but motion in some of the internal parts of the organs of the sentient,"[24] they are experienced as something else. As Hobbes explains, when the body's equilibrium is enhanced or disrupted in the course of perception, "the reall effect there is nothing but Motion, or Endeavour; which consisteth in Appetite, or Aversion, to, or from the object moving."[25] Yet, while the "reall effect" of perception is naught but the motion of the body toward or away from the stimulating object, "the apparence or sense of that motion, is that wee either call Delight, or Trouble of Mind" (121). In other words, the experience or "apparence" of those effects for the person is the feeling of pleasure or displeasure at the presence of a particular object (122). The passions are various kinds of this experience or "apparence" of being-moved.

Not too surprisingly, passions take different forms depending upon the presence or absence of an object. Anticipating the Freudian understanding of desire as constituted through loss, Hobbes states that desire signals "the Absence of the Object" and love "the Presence of the same" (119).[26] Similarly, aversion signals "the Absence; . . . and . . . Hate, the Presence of the Object" (119). In other words, hate is the repulsion felt by a subject in response to an object currently before her. And aversion is the repulsion felt by a subject as part of her memory of an object. Aversion, then, is constituted through absence and must be seen as the subject's felt experience of her on-going movement away from an absent object of memory.

Just as we can distinguish between passions that arise in the presence or the absence of a particular stimulating object, so for Hobbes can we distinguish between those that are *"Pleasures of Sense"* (or *"sensuall"*) and those that are *"Pleasures of the Mind"* (122). Superficially, it might seem difficult to square such a distinction with Hobbes's refusal of Cartesian dualism. However, he means by "sensuall" pleasures those that are felt

immediately in the flesh either in the presence of, or in the physical encounter with, an object: "Of this kind are all Onerations and Exonerations
of the body; as also all that is pleasant, in the *Sight*, *Hearing*, *Smell*, *Tast*, or
Touch" (122). By contrast, he says, the pleasures of the mind are tied
up with the imagination and can be said to "arise from the Expectation,
that proceeds from the foresight of the End, or Consequences of things"
(122). In other words, the pleasures and the displeasures of the mind are a
kind of anticipation. And while such anticipation certainly consists in
"Motions in the body" — as do all thoughts and passions for Hobbes — the
imagination that is the basis of anticipation involves residual motions
rather than the relatively fresh motions of sensual pleasure.

Now, importantly, for Hobbes, any anticipation of, or expectation
about, the future must draw on memories of the past. As he points out,
the future is not something that actually exists. Rather, it is "but a fiction
of the mind, applying the sequels of actions Past, to the actions that are
Present" (chap. 3, 97). What this means is that we can conceive of the
future, and hence generate expectations, only by extrapolating imaginatively from memories. We could say, speaking loosely, that to look forward
we must first look backward: any future we imagine will be drawn from a
configuration or reconfiguration of our memories of the past. Accordingly, the passions that arise from "the Expectation of consequences"
(chap. 6, 122) are characterized by an imaginative projection of the past
forward through time.

It is once we apprehend both the backward-looking and the forward-
looking dimensions of the passions that we can begin to appreciate
Hobbes's account of fear. Fear, he says, is "Aversion, with opinion of Hurt
from the object" (122). Since aversion involves an absent object and
"opinion of hurt" involves an expectation about the future, we can try to
be very precise and say that fear is the feeling of the repulsive movement
at play in the imaginative expectation of a future experience of pain from
an absent offensive object. Put less awkwardly, fear is the displeasure felt
either toward an object whose resemblance to a remembered object is
taken as an indication of a noxious experience to come or toward the
memory of an object whose threatened return heralds a repeat of what
came before. Fear, then, entails a figurative movement from the present
back toward a remembered past and then from the past toward an anticipated future. This recursive temporal movement of fear is important for

it recasts the causal field and so provides for the possibility of the subject's agency.[27]

Implicit in the recursivity of fear is a presumption that "like events will follow like actions."[28] That is, the recall and then the projection of the subject's past into an imagined future rests on the supposition that prospective experiences will resemble those of the past. On the face of it, the relationships between events implicit in this assumption that the past repeats itself are merely correlations: as an antecedent of this consequence, this object is a sign of this coming experience.[29] But in Hobbes's discussions of prudence and science, he suggests that, over time and with the aid of experience and language, the conditional form that such anticipation takes slips from the observation of correlation to a presumption about causation. He says that in addition to seeking out the causes, consequences, and effects of various things, "Man . . . can by words reduce the consequences he findes to generall Rules, called *Theorems*, or *Aphorisms*" (chap. 5, 113). That is, we can summarize our observations by formulating conditional statements that can be taken as rules of thumb about what happens when. What is so useful about such collections of rules — about science, as he calls this knowledge of consequences — is that together they tell us the "dependance of one fact upon another" (115). In other words, we take such rules to specify causal relations.

Indeed, it is in this assumption of regularity of movement — of repetition — that we can imagine how to intervene in a causal chain and make things happen as we will. As Hobbes puts the point, "when we see how anything comes about, upon what causes, and by what manner; when the like causes come into our power, wee see how to make it produce the like effects" (115). Of course, like the observations that come from experience, the insights of science are often uncertain: "onely some particular events answer to [the] pretence [of science], and upon many occasions prove so as [one] sayes they must" (117).[30] That is, only some events regularly transpire in the manner that scientific knowledge specifies. Yet, Hobbes says, despite uncertainty about the accuracy of our observations or the applicability of the rules we formulate about causation, we use them as the basis for our own actions. That is, our knowledge about causation — stipulative and uncertain as it is — makes us feel like effective agents: if I do this, then that will happen. To put the point briefly, then, the theory of causation that is the corollary of the presumption that the past repeats itself enables the subject to take the self as a cause of action.

This centering of the subject as a cause of action in a simple causal field is precisely what occurs in the passion of fear. In fear, a subject's perception of a threat is anchored to, and made possible by, a memory of an unpleasant but absent object. Indeed, it is the memory around which the feeling of fear pivots that is so important, for in the figurative movement back to the aversive memory, the causal horizon is narrowed: there was the object and there was me. More specifically, the aversive object recalled in fear is remembered as the cause of displeasure: *that* object, or its past arrival, caused *me* pain. In other words, the narrowing of the causal horizon that is the corollary of the aversive memory is also a simplification of the causal chain. When such a memory and its conjectured and simplified causal baggage are projected forward in time, they serve as a forecast of what might happen in the future: this object caused me pain in the past, so this (other) object will cause me pain soon.

Hobbes's analysis suggests, then, that the object of memory around which fear forms presents the subject with what Adam Phillips has called "a repertoire of possibilities from the past."[31] The consequences of the events and actions related to the aversive object past are projected forward as examples of what happens in such situations. If we recall Hobbes's contention that to stipulate a rule of causation is to generate a sense of agency, then we can see that the repertoire of possibilities provided by fear's aversive object grants to the subject the sense that there *are* possibilities for action: there is something she can do.[32] In other words, the temporal movements in fear enable the subject to imagine herself as an effective agent. More than this, they allow the subject to take herself as the origin of her own actions.

Now, among the passions Hobbes discusses in *Leviathan* is one he identifies as "Panique Terror" (chap. 6, 124). His initial elaboration of this passion depicts it as "Fear, without apprehension of why, or what" (124). In other words, it is a fear without an identifiable cause or object. Importantly, to have an objectless fear is not simply to not know what one is scared of. If fear has no object, then no recursive movement around memory is possible, no simplification of causality can take place, and no anticipatory projection can occur. Without a remembered object to project into the future, the movement of the imagination stalls; the subject can conjure no imaginative possibilities for the future, possibilities around whose consequences the passions might otherwise do their deliberative work. Where there is no deliberation, there is no willing: no willing, no action. Or, perhaps it is better to say that there is no voluntary action. Hobbes explains that when panic terror takes place in a crowd, there is always someone who has "some apprehension of the cause," an apprehension that, as we have seen, might well be a fabrication. However, "the rest run away by Example; everyone supposing his fellow to know why" (124). In other words, in panic terror, the actions performed by the subject take place through a kind of mimesis. When fear has no object, the subject is bereft of the "repertoire of possibilities" generally provided by fear's object and so cannot imaginatively compose a simple field of action in which she might act as an voluntary agent. Without the all-important work of the imagination, the subject becomes not much more than a conduit for ambient causal forces, responding reflexively, mimetically, to other people's reactions. So, an objectless fear rips the illusion of agency from the subject and thereby deprives her of the ability to initiate actions. This is not simply a kind of disorientation born of disillusionment: I thought I was an agent, but I'm not; what now? Rather, having lost the future, the subject becomes lost to herself.

For Hobbes, then, if we are not to be hurled into blind terror by our inability to map with certainty the complex causes that roil the world around us, we must give our fear an object: our fear "must needs have for object something" (chap. 12, 169–70). That is, we must conjure an object, excavate a memory — any memory — so that our imagination can do its temporal do-si-do and render the field available for our active intervention. The recursive temporal movement around fear's object enables the subject to confront a field that is impossible to master and yet act as if she were nonetheless a masterful agent. That is, the recursive movement that pivots around fear's object furnishes the subject with a sense, if only a semblance, of agency. According to Hobbes's arguments, then, the compulsion in fear to suppose causes, to secure fear's object, is annexed to an insight into our impotence — our lack of sovereignty over ourselves, our actions, and the world. Indeed, in fear we can see the subject's disavowal of that lack of sovereignty.

The Politics in and of Fear

Hobbes's insight that fear produces in individuals a semblance of self-sovereignty is reflected in his discussions of the political sovereign authorized and instituted via covenant. Indeed, a reading of his politics through the framework of the analysis of fear elaborated above suggests that the infamously large and concentrated power of the sovereign functions to formalize the dynamic through which individuals gain a sense of themselves as autonomous agents. That is to say, the inflated sovereignty of the sovereign serves as a locus for each individual's imagination of herself as self-sovereign.

Such a reading runs roughly thus: In the chaos of civil war, the "miseries, and horrible calamities" that attend the "dissolute condition of masterlesse men" (chap. 18, 238) make individual lives insecure and the outcomes of individual actions and work uncertain (chap. 13, 186). In such a tumultuous context, replete with a myriad of possible obstacles, accidents, and injurious encounters, individuals cannot imagine and sustain a sense of their own effectiveness at securing a future. That is, without a comprehensibly stable and linear perception of causality from which to infer the possibility of their own agency, they are unable to engage in "Industry, . . . Culture of the Earth; Navigation . . . Building, . . . Arts, . . . Letters" and so forth (186). In such a complex and indomitable causal field, Hobbes says, individuals face a "continuall feare, and danger of violent death," which is to say that the object of their fears is a future that is no future (186). In these circumstances, Hobbes says, people need an alternative object for their fear, an object of fear that enables them to map and thence to intervene in a causal field. The sovereign functions as just such an object: a common object of fear.

According to Hobbes, the sovereign does not simply impose order through the threat of punishment (the familiar fear-as-motivation story). The sovereign also reduces and narrows the causal field within which people act. That is, the sovereign power serves both as the object around which each individual's fear turns and as the reference point in a simplified causal field. Hobbes elucidates this point in his discussion of laws and punishment. He contends, for example, that "he that foresees what wil become of a Criminal, re-cons what he has seen follow on the like

Crime before; having this order of thoughts, The Crime, the Officer, the Prison, the Judge, and the Gallowes" (chap. 3, 97). As we can see here in Hobbes's presentation of what he supposes will be an individual's tracing of the causes and consequences of a particular action, the sovereign-as-fearsome object reduces the causal field by giving it a focus: this action caused this punishment. In regularizing actions and their consequences, the sovereign's laws serve as the material for an imagined future that itself gives the subject a basis for choosing and acting.[33] It is with an eye to the imagined (and delimited) consequences possible in this reduced field of action that the individual makes a decision to act (97). But in addition to mapping a field of consequences, the threat of punishment also modifies people's behavior such that it regularizes or makes more predictable the threats and dangers within the field of action. When the causal field is simplified and rendered more manageable in this way, individuals are able to insert themselves into now-comprehensible causal chains and take themselves to be effective agents. So, the sovereign is not simply a common object of fear around which individuals orient their actions as if to avoid punishment. The sovereign also functions as the ground for each subject's presumption of her own status as an autonomous actor. That is, as a consequence of its simplification of the causal field, the sovereignty of the sovereign constitutes the condition for each individual's construction of the illusion of her own sovereignty as an individual agent.[34]

And crucially, the masterful unitary appearance of the sovereign conceals the heteronomous causes of its actions. Not only is the sovereign a fictive person whose singular authority is created through a broadly held agreement (chap. 17, 227–28) but the sovereign's actions depend for their success upon the subjects' passions—in both the philosophical causal sense as well as in the affective sense.[35] For Hobbes, individuals' activities and more specifically their obedience are the passions that are the necessary complement to the sovereign's actions. In other words, the subjects of the sovereign are the moved-movers who actuate the sovereign's initiatives. So, the sovereign is not in fact a masterful agent whose will is a singular, self-originating, and efficacious cause and whose actions have a circumscribed and pointed effect. Yet, it must appear to be so if it is to function to simplify the causal field in such a way as to enable individuals to imagine themselves as effective, autonomous actors. In Hobbes's analysis, then, out of a complicated field of causation, individuals produce the sovereign as the simplifying object of fear that serves as the guarantor of their agency as individuals.

It is important to emphasize the insight here — the fact that individuals actively produce the sovereign whose fearsome and singular effectiveness is the condition for their sense of themselves as autonomous agents. As suggested above, for individuals the comfort to be had in the illusion of autonomy rests upon the apparent autogenesis of the fearsome sovereign's actions. In other words, in order to work as an object of fear, the sovereign must appear to be a singular and self-contained entity whose actions are easy to map in and as a causal field. However, to make the sovereign appear as a simple and simplifying unity, the individuals who collectively produce it must disavow the complex causes of the sovereign's acts. In other words, to give the heteronomous sovereign the dressing of autonomy it must have if it is to be an effective object of fear, individuals must distance themselves from the sovereign power and efface their contributions to, and their facilitation of, its actions. To put the point differently, for individuals, the fantasy of self-sovereign autonomy is parasitic on the illusion of the sovereign's simple unity. Accordingly, their pursuit of that fantasy entails the enhancement and centralization of the sovereign power and the differentiation of its actions from those of its subjects.[36] Paradoxically, then, individuals' efforts to generate a sense of themselves as effective autonomous actors results in an inflated sovereign power whose efficaciousness is seemingly disconnected from, as well as set against, the daily activities of the populace. Not only are individuals thereby alienated from the ways in which they are in fact effective, that is, from the complex interdependencies through which all actions take place but they also invest themselves in a fantasy of autonomy whose inevitable fragility demands recurrent efforts to produce the sovereign as the object of fear that can make their illusory and elusive self-sovereignty feel more real.

Conclusion

When fear is figured as a motivation, the individuals who are fearful are portrayed as not wanting fearsome things in their lives: fear and the things that inspire it are phenomena of which we strive to rid ourselves. As such, fear can be a reliable instrument in the effort to institute law and order — and also a tool in an arsenal gathered for the purpose of political manipulation. Yet, Hobbes's analysis suggests that because the dynamics of fear simplify the world in such a way that we can imagine how to act — because fear gives a focus to our perception and apprehension of causality — individuals might actually seek out a measure of fear in order to shore up their self-image as autonomous self-sovereign agents. As we have seen, Hobbes suggests that in moments in which our ontological condition becomes distressingly obvious to us, that is, when the complexity of causation and the heteronomy of our actions becomes more conspicuous in our daily lives, we will evince a tendency to increase the power of the sovereign. In other words, because the recursive temporal movements in fear efface the indeterminacy of all actions by centering subjects as autonomous individual agents, individuals might bolster the fearsome power of the state. At issue here is not the matter of identification, as if the sovereign's effectiveness serves as a proxy for individuals' effectiveness in a time of crisis. Rather, Hobbes suggests, even in situations of noncrisis, the endeavor to generate a sense of individual effectiveness in the form of autonomy proceeds by way of the selection — and even the production — of an object to fear.

Notes

1   See, for example, Blits, "Hobbesian Fear." Blits claims that, for Hobbes, fear is fear of the unknown, a fear that arises out of the epistemological limits that Blits argues are the corollary of Hobbes's solipsistic account of perception. Although I cannot dispute the argument about solipsism in full here, I do present contrary arguments in "Hobbes and the Matter of Self-Consciousness."

2   Corey Robin argues that, for Hobbes, fear is not a natural emotion but rather the fabrication of a political machinery, a necessary tool for the production of order. In his reading, Hobbes suggests that fear must be cultivated for the purposes of politics: "Fear had to be created. . . . It was a rational, moral emotion, taught by influential men in churches and universities." See Robin, *Fear*, 33. In essays that provide something akin to combined versions of the fabrication and the epistemological arguments, William Sokoloff and Chad Lavin point to the need for a strong and fearsome sovereign given the uncertainties produced by the unknown. See Sokoloff, "Politics and Anxiety in Thomas Hobbes's *Leviathan*"; Lavin, "Fear, Radical Democracy, and Ontological Methadone."

3   Hobbes, *Leviathan*, chap. 14, 200.

4   For an example of such an argument, see Leo Strauss's now-classic account in *The Political Philosophy of Thomas Hobbes*.

5   Hobbes, *Leviathan*, chap. 14, 189.

6   Ibid., chap. 46, 689.

7   For a full elaboration of Hobbes's materialism and its ethical and political implications, see Frost, *Lessons from a Materialist Thinker*.

8   Hobbes, *De Corpore*, chap. 3, 34.

9   Thanks to James Martell for pushing me to articulate this point.

10 Although it is too cumbersome to include in the text, the full quote is: "That which I say necessitateth and determinateth every action . . . is the sum of all things, which being now existent, conduce and concur to the production of that action hereafter, whereof if any one thing now were wanting, the effect could not be produced." Hobbes, *Of Liberty and Necessity*, 246.

11 Hobbes, *De Corpore*, chap. 9, 120.

12 Hobbes, *Of Liberty and Necessity*, 274.

13 Hobbes notes our lack of mastery over our own thoughts in *Human Nature*, pointing out that "one conception followeth not another, according to our election, but as it chanceth us to hear or see such things as shall bring them to our mind." Hobbes, *Human Nature*, chap. 5, 35.

14 Hobbes contends that imagination is nothing but "decaying sense" and that "when we would express the *decay*, and signifie that the Sense is fading, old, and past, it is called *Memory*. So that *Imagination* and *Memory*, are but one thing, which for divers considerations hath divers names." Hobbes, *Leviathan*, chap. 2, 89.

15 Hobbes, *De Homine*, chap. 13, 63. The text referred to here is actually included in the present essay, 164.

16 In a remark whose very articulation questions the presumption that a subject might be sovereign over his or her own actions, Hobbes denounces the idea that the will has anything to do with self-mastery. He rejects the claim that "to will is to have dominion over his own action, and actually to determine his own will," declaring to the contrary that "no man can determine his own will, for the will is appetite; nor can man more determine his will than any other appetite, that is, more than he can determine when he shall be hungry and when not." Hobbes, *The Questions Concerning Liberty, Necessity, and Chance*, 34.

17 As is the case with the complex causal chains that determine worldly events, we may not be aware of all the memories and experiences that shape our imagination and passions, or of all the movements of passion and memory that cause us to choose to do this act rather than that. Indeed, our inability to recall or trace them all makes it seem as if we and our actions are "free" in some existential sense. But, Hobbes says, "to him that could see the connexion of those causes, the *necessity* of all mens voluntary actions, would appeare manifest." Hobbes, *Leviathan*, chap. 21, 263.

18 See Hobbes, *De Corpore*, "Of Cause and Effect," 120. See also, Hobbes, *Of Liberty and Necessity*, 270–74.

19   Hobbes, *Leviathan*, chap. 6, 118, emphasis added.

20   Ibid., chap. 11, 167. Each of us, Hobbes remarks, is "curious in the search of the causes of their own good and evill fortune" (chap. 12, 168).

21   This particular claim is Jean Hampton's, although the presumption that desires and fears originate within the subject is a feature of many interpretations of Hobbes. See Hampton, *Hobbes and the Social Contract Tradition*, 6.

22   Patchen Markell uses the notion of temporality to capture how something "links an agent's past and present to her future." See Markell, *Bound by Recognition*, 10. In a very interesting argument about aesthetic experiences of fear, Philip Fisher periodizes what he identifies as two different temporal movements of fear. In his analysis, the "classic" model of fear involves a temporal movement akin to the movement of the future anterior–the imagination of this single moment soon to be past from the perspective of an imagined future. The other model is distinctively modern, he argues, and involves a temporal movement that is more straightforwardly an open serial into an unpredictable and uncertain future. See Fisher, "The Aesthetics of Fear." Let me note here that while Fisher claims that Hobbes provides us with the prototype of this modern temporal movement of fear, the temporality that I identify in Hobbes's account of fear is quite different.

23   Hobbes, *Leviathan*, chap. 6, 118.

24   Hobbes, *De Corpore*, chap. 25, 390.

25   Hobbes, *Leviathan*, chap. 6, 121.

26   Of course, given the crucial role that memory plays in the process of perception, we must acknowledge that a memory of an absent object is necessarily nested in the perception of a present object. See my "Hobbes and the Matter of Self-Consciousness." However, for the present purposes, the simpler distinction between absent and present objects will suffice.

27   In a provocative analysis, Brian Massumi uses the notion of recursivity in relation to the temporality of perception. See *Parables of the Virtual*, 15.

28   Hobbes, *Leviathan*, chap. 3, 97.

29   Hobbes says that "A *Signe*, is the Event Antecedent, of the Consequent; and contrarily, the Consequent of the Antecedent, when the like Consequences have been observed, before: And the oftner they have been observed, the lesse uncertain is the Signe." Ibid., chap. 3, 98.

30   Hobbes observes that "this is certain: by how much one man has more experience of things past, than another; by so much also he is more Prudent, and his expectations the seldomer fail him" (chap. 3, 97). Yet, he notes, "Signes of prudence are all uncertain; because to observe by experience, and remember all circumstances that may alter the successe, is impossible" (chap. 5, 117).

31   Phillips, *Terrors and Experts*, 53.

32   It is important to point out that the expectation in the feeling of fear does not

in itself include the subject's sense of his or her capacity or incapacity to act to evade or repel the object of fear. If it encompassed the subject's feelings of competence or incompetence, the fearful feeling would instead be the feeling of courage or the feeling of despair, respectively. Hobbes, *Leviathan*, chap. 6, 123. As "a certain foresight of future evil," fear is about the possibilities rather than the capacities for agency. The latter quote comes from Hobbes, *De Cive*, chap. 1, 6.

33   Hobbes himself claims that the laws promulgated by the sovereign are aimed at guiding or mapping the possibilities for action. He writes that the purpose of the laws is "not to bind the People from all Voluntary actions; but to direct and keep them from such a motion, as not to hurt themselves by their own impetuous desires, rashnesse, or indiscretion, as Hedges are set, not to stop Travellers, but to keep them in the way." Hobbes, *Leviathan*, chap. 30, 388.

34   In fact, Hobbes points out that it is not until there is a sovereign articulation of law that an individual can be considered a person whose will is ascriptively taken as the cause of his or her actions (chap. 16, 217–20).

35   Hobbes specifies in numerous places in his work that the power of the sovereign is effective in action only insofar as the opinions and actions of subjects and the sovereign's deputies make it so. For example, in *Behemoth*, Hobbes claims that the power of the sovereign rests on nothing "but . . . the opinion and belief of the people." See Hobbes, *Behemoth, or the Long Parliament*, chap. 1, 16. Likewise, he claims in *Leviathan* that the "Actions of men proceed from their Opinions, and in the wel governing of Opinions, consisteth the wel governing of men's Actions, in order to their Peace, and Concord" (chap. 18, 233). One might also consider book 2 of *Leviathan*, in which Hobbes specifies the different ways in which the sovereign's power is constituted through reputation and the opinion held by the many people over whom it must rule.

36   For an analysis of a contemporary instance of this dynamic, see Nelson, "The President and Presidentialism."

William E. Connolly

Materialities of Experience

the materiality of perception

I seek to come to terms with the materiality of perception by placing Maurice Merleau-Ponty, Michel Foucault, and Gilles Deleuze into conversations with each other and all of them with recent work in neuroscience. The first conversation has been obstructed by the judgment that Merleau-Ponty is a phenomenologist while the latter two are opposed to phenomenology. My sense, however, is that there is a phenomenological moment in both Foucault and Deleuze. Moreover, the conception of the subject they criticize is one from which Merleau-Ponty progressively departed. He also moved toward a conception of nonhuman nature which, he thought, was needed to redeem themes in the *Phenomenology of Perception*. This double movement — revising the idea of the subject and articulating a conception of nature compatible with it — draws Merleau-Ponty closer to what I will call a philosophy of immanence. Whether that migration was completed or punctuated by a moment of transcendence is a question I will not answer here.

the phenomenology of perception

By immanence I mean a philosophy of becoming in which the universe is not dependent on a higher power. It is reducible to neither mechanistic materialism, dualism, theo-teleology nor the absent God of minimal theology. It concurs with the last three philosophies that there is more to reality than actuality. But that "more" is not given by a

immanence: a philosophy of becoming in which the universe is not dependent on a higher power.

robust or minimal God. We bear no debts or primordial guilt for being, even if there are features of the human condition that tempt many to act as if we do.[1] Rather, there are uncertain exchanges between stabilized formations and mobile forces that subsist within and below them. Biological evolution, the evolution of the universe, radical changes in politics, and the significant conversion experiences of individuals attest to the periodic amplification of such circuits of exchange.

Gilles Deleuze and Félix Guattari state the idea this way. First, they challenge the idea of transcendence lodged "in the mind of a god, or in the unconscious of life, of the soul, or of language, . . . always inferred." Second, they affirm historically shifting "relations of movement and rest, speed and slowness between unformed elements, or at last between elements that are relatively unformed, molecules and particles of all kinds."[2] Such a philosophy of "movement and rest" does not imply that everything is always in flux, though its detractors often reduce it to that view.[3] It means that though any species, thing, system, or civilization may last for a long time, nothing lasts forever. Each force field (set in the chrono-time appropriate to it) oscillates between periods of relative arrest and periods of heightened imbalance and change, followed again by new stabilizations. The universe does not consist of long cycles of repetition, exhibit linear causality, or have an intrinsic purpose in being, but, as the Nobel prize–winning chemist Ilya Prigogine puts it, "our universe is far from equilibrium, nonlinear and full of irreversible processes."[4]

There is no denying that we humans — while often differing from one another — *judge* the new outcomes to which we are exposed or that we have helped usher into being. What is denied is that the judgments express an eternal law or bring us into attunement with an intrinsic purpose of being. For immanent materialists deny there is such a law or intrinsic purpose. We anchor our ethics elsewhere and in a different way.

there is no intrinsic purpose

Immanent materialism is defined in contrast to mechanistic materialism, too. Many causal relations are not susceptible to either efficient or mechanical modes of analysis. There are efficient causes, as when, to take a classic example, one billiard ball moves another in a specific direction. But *emergent causality* — the dicey process by which new entities and processes periodically surge into being — is irreducible to efficient causality. It is a mode in which new forces can trigger novel patterns of *self-organization* in a thing, species, system, or being, sometimes allowing something new to emerge from the swirl back and forth between them: a new species, state of the universe, weather system, ecological balance, or political formation.

Merleau-Ponty traveled from his early work on perception to an image that draws humanity closer to the rest of nature than the dominant philosophies of the past had proposed. A certain pressure to pursue that journey was always there: a layered theory of human embodiment faces pressure to identify selective *affinities* between the capacities of humans and other living beings and physical systems.

Consider some statements from *Nature,* a collection of lectures given by Merleau-Ponty just before his untimely death: "Thus, for instance, the Nature in us must have some relation to Nature outside of us; moreover, Nature outside of us must be unveiled to us by the Nature that we are. . . . We are part of some Nature, and reciprocally, it is from ourselves that living beings and even space speak to us."[5] Here Merleau-Ponty solicits affinities between human and nonhuman nature. Does he also suggest that, once preliminary affinities have been disclosed, it is possible to organize experimental investigations to uncover dimensions of human and nonhuman nature previously outside the range of that experience? And that these findings might then be folded into an enlarged experience of ourselves and the world?[6] If so, when the neuroscientist V. S. Ramachandran, using magnetic imaging and other technologies of observation, exposes body-brain processes in the production of phantom pain exceeding those assumed in Merleau-Ponty's experiential account of it,[7] those findings could be folded into the latter's account along with the techniques Ramachandran invented to relieve such pain. Here *experimental* and *experiential* perspectives circulate back and forth, with each sometimes triggering a surprising change in the other. Consider another formulation: "All these ideas (vitalism, entelechy) suppose preformation, yet modern embryology defines the thesis of epigenesis. . . . The future must not be contained in the present. . . . It would be arbitrary to understand this history as the epiphenomenon of a mechanical causality. Mechanistic thinking rests upon a causality which traverses and never stops in something."[8]

"The future must not be contained in the present." Just as the future of human culture is not sufficiently determined by efficient causes from the past, in nonhuman nature, too—when the chrono-periods identified are appropriate to the field in question—the future is not sufficiently contained in the present. Now mechanical causality, vitalism, and entelechy, on Merleau-Ponty's reading of them at least, bite the dust together.

But if the future is not sufficiently contained in the present, what enables change over short and long periods? Here Merleau-Ponty approaches an orientation now familiar in the work of scientists such as Ilya Prigogine in chemistry, Brian Goodwin and Lynn Margulis in biology, Antonio Damasio and Ramachandran in neuroscience, and Stephen Gould in evolutionary biology:[9] "The outlines of the organism in the embryo constitute a factor of imbalance. It is not because humans consider them as outlines that they are such but because they break the current balance and fix the conditions for a future balance."[10] The "imbalance" noted by Merleau-Ponty is close to what Deleuze calls the "asymmetry of nature," an energized asymmetry that periodically sets the stage, when other conditions are in place, for old formations to disintegrate and new ones to surge into being. It bears a family resemblance to Prigogine's account of systems that enter a period of "disequilibrium" and to the behavior "on the edge of chaos" that Brian Goodwin studies when a species either evolves into a new, unpredictable one or faces extinction. Merleau-Ponty, in alliance with these thinkers, does not shift from a mechanical conception of natural order to a world of chaos. He suggests that in each object domain periods of imbalance alternate with those of new and imperfect stabilizations. I take these formulations to support the adventure pursued here.

The Complexity of Perception

Visual perception involves a complex mixing—during the half-second delay between the reception of sensory experience and the formation of an image—of language, affect, feeling, touch, and anticipation.[11] This mixing is set in the memory-infused life of human beings whose experience is conditioned by the previous discipline of the chemical-electrical *network* in which perception is set and by the characteristic *shape* of human embodiment and motility. Human mobility is enabled by our two-leggedness and the position of the head at the top of the body, with two eyes pointed forward. This mode of embodiment, for instance, encourages the production of widespread analogies between a future "in front of us" and the past "behind us." Most importantly, the act of perception is permeated by implicit reference to the position and mood of one's own body in relation to the phenomenal field.[12] Experience is grasped, says Merleau-Ponty, "first in its meaning for us, for that heavy mass which is our body, whence it comes about that it always involves reference to the body."[13] My "body appears to me as an attitude directed towards a certain existing or possible task. And indeed its spatiality is not . . . a *spatiality of position* but a *spatiality of situation*."[14]

We also need to come to terms with how perception is *intersensory*, never fully divisible into separate sense experiences.[15] For example, visual experience is saturated with the tactile history of the experiencing agent. The tactile and the visual are interwoven, in that my history of touching objects similar to the one in question is woven into my current vision of it. A poignant example of this is offered by Laura Marks, as she elucidates a film scene in which the composition of voice and the grainy visual image convey the daughter's tactile memory of her deceased mother's skin.[16] Similarly, language and sense experience are neither entirely separate nor reducible to one another. They are imbricated in a way that allows each to exceed the other in experience: "the sense being held within the word, and the word being the external existence of the sense."[17]

Continuing down this path, Merleau-Ponty indicates how the color of an object triggers an affective charge. People with specific motor disturbances make jerky movements if the color field is blue and more smooth ones if it is red or yellow. And in "normal" subjects, too, the visual field of color is interwoven with an experience of warmth or coldness that precedes and infuses specific awareness of it, depending upon whether the field is red or blue (209, 211). This field of inter-involvement, in turn, flows into that between color and sound, in which specific types of sound infect the experience of color, intensifying or dampening it (228). Words participate in this process, too, as when the "word 'hard' produces a stiffening of the back or neck." Even "before becoming the indication of a concept the word is first an event which grips my body, and this grip circumscribes the area of significance to which it has reference" (235). The "before" in this sentence does not refer to an uncultured body but to a preliminary tendency in encultured beings. To put the point another way, the imbrications between embodiment, language, disposition, perception, and mood are always in operation. A philosophy of language that ignores these essential connections may appear precise and rigorous, but it does so by missing circuits of inter-involvement through which perception is organized.

These preliminary experiences vary across individuals and cultures, and those variations are important to an appreciation of cultural diversity. The key point, however, is that some series of inter-involvements is always encoded into the preliminary character of experience, flowing into the tone and color of perception. Phenomenologists, Buddhist monks, corporate advertisers, cultural anthropologists, neuroscientists, TV dramatists, Catholic priests, filmmakers, and evangelical preachers are attuned to such memory-soaked patterns of inter-involvement. Too many social scientists, analytic philosophers, rational choice theorists, deliberative democrats, and "intellectualists" of various sorts are less so. An intellectualist, to Merleau-Ponty, is one who overstates the autonomy of conceptual life, the independence of vision, the self-sufficiency of reason, the power of pure deliberation, or the self-sufficiency of argument.

Here is a juncture at which the phenomenology of Merleau-Ponty meets the recent discovery of mirror neurons by the neuroscientist Giacomo Rizzolatti. To both, social experience is not merely mediated by the web of language, it is also infused by the ability humans and monkeys have to read and mimic the intentions of others before and below language. Thus Rizzolatti explores how culturally coded mirror neurons allow us both to read the intentions of others immediately and to rehearse their behavior enough to install some of those tendencies into our own body schemas. Here is one way Rizzolatti makes the point: "the sight of acts performed by others produces an immediate activation of the motor areas deputed to the organization and execution of those acts . . . ; through this activation it is possible to decipher the meaning of the 'motor events' observed, i.e., to understand them in terms of goal centred movements. This understanding is completely devoid of any reflexive, conceptual and or linguistic mediation, as it is based on the vocabulary of acts and the motor knowledge on which our capacity to act depends."[18] It is important to emphasize that the mirror neurons doing the work do not simply express a fixed genetic inheritance. They themselves become culturally coded through the give and take of experience. Language-mediated experience without this background of less mediated interpretation would be reduced to a perception "purely cognitive in form, pale, colorless, destitute of emotional warmth."[19] I take Merleau-Ponty to agree in advance with these points, even though his own tendency is to emphasize (correctly I think) how the two modes of experience readily become mixed together once a sophisticated use of language is accomplished.

Perception not only has multiple layers of intersensory *memory* folded into it, it is suffused with *anticipation*. This does not mean merely that you anticipate a result and then test it against the effect of experience. It means that perception expresses a set of anticipatory expectations that help to constitute what it actually becomes. The case of the word "hardness" already suggests this. A more recent experiment by neuroscientists dramatizes the point. The body-brain patterns of the respondents were observed through various imaging techniques as the subjects were asked to follow a series of pictures moving from left to right. The images at first glance look the same, but upon closer inspection your experience shifts abruptly from that of the bare head of a man to the nude body of a woman as you proceed down the line of images. People vary at which point the gestalt switch occurs. More compellingly, when asked to view the series a second time from right to left, almost everyone identifies the shift from the nude woman to the man's face farther down the line than they had in moving from left to right. The authors contend that the body-brain processes catalyzed by this series engender dicey transitions between two embodied attractors. The first attractor retains its hold as long as possible; the second, triggered as you move from right to left, is retained until pressed to give way to another. The suddenness of the shift in experience correlates with dramatic shifts in observable body/brain patterns. "By placing electrodes on the appropriate muscles to measure their electromagnetic activity, [neurobiologist Scott] Kelso could clearly measure the sudden shift from one pattern to another. The underlying idea in Kelso's studies was that the brain is a self-organizing, pattern-forming system that operates close to instability points, thereby allowing it to switch flexibly and spontaneously from one coherent state to another."[20] The "imbalance" that Merleau-Ponty identifies in embryos also operates in the perception of mobile human beings who must respond to rapidly shifting contexts.[21] Perception, to be flexible, is organized through multiple points of "instability" through which one set of memory-infused attractors gives way to another when the pressure of the encounter becomes intense enough. Each attractor helps to structure the actuality of perception.

Perception could not function without a rich history of inter-involvements between embodiment, movement, body image, touch, sight, smell, language, affect, and color. The anticipatory structure of perception enables it to carry out its functions in the rapidly changing contexts of everyday life; it also opens it to subliminal influence by mystics, priests, lovers, politicians, parents, military leaders, filmmakers, teachers, talk show hosts, and TV advertisers.

Another way of putting the point is to say that the actuality of perception is "normative," where that word now means the application of a culturally organized attractor to a situation roughly responsive to it. A visual percept, for instance, contains the norm of a well-rounded object, compensating for the limitations of the particular position from which it starts. As Merleau-Ponty puts it, "The unity of either the subject or the object is not a real unity, *but a presumptive unity on the horizon of experience. We must rediscover, as anterior to the ideas of subject and object, that primordial layer at which both things and ideas come into being.*"[22] The import of this presumptive unity becomes more clear through the discussions of depth and discipline.

Visibility and Depth

Merleau-Ponty concludes that we make a singular contribution to the experience of spatial depth, even though, as Diana Coole says, "the depth and perspective that permit visual clarity belong to neither seer nor seen [alone], but unfold where they meet."[23] The experience of depth, you might say, incorporates different possible perspectives upon the object *into* the angle of vision from which it is now engaged. The experience is ubiquitous. If you draw a Necker cube on a flat piece of paper, depth will be immediately projected into it. Upon viewing the image for a few seconds, the image becomes inverted, so that a figure in which depth had moved from left to right now flips in the other direction. Upon learning how to produce the flips — by focusing your eye first on the bottom right angle and then the top left angle — it becomes clear how difficult it is to purge experience of depth. The short interval between the switch of gaze and the flip of the angle also testifies to the half-second delay between the reception of sensory experience and cultural participation in the organization of perception. It teaches us that perception must be disciplined to be and draws attention to the fugitive interval during which that organization occurs. Perception depends upon projection into experience of multiple perspectives you do not now have. This automatic projection into experience also makes it seem that objects see you as you see them. Merleau-Ponty puts it this way: In this "strange adhesion of the seer and the visible, . . . *I feel myself looked at by the things,* my activity is equally a passivity."[24] To have the experience of depth is to feel things looking at you, to feel yourself as object. This self-awareness is usually subliminal, but it becomes more apparent when you shift from the process of action-oriented perception to dwell in experience itself. The result is uncanny: to see is to experience yourself as an object of visibility, not simply in that you realize someone *could* look at you because you are composed of opaque materiality, but also because the very structure of vision incorporates into itself the projection of what it would be like to be seen from a variety of angles. This experience codifies, in the anticipatory structure of perception, potential angles of vision upon yourself and what it would be like to touch, hold, or move the object from different angles. The codification of operational angles of possible action and the background sense of being seen combine to produce depth.

That codification, however, cannot be reduced to the sum of all angles, to a view from *nowhere*, because each potential angle of vision fades into a diffuse background against which it is set. The codification, then, is closer to a view from *everywhere*, a view projected as a norm into an experience that depends upon implicit reference to it. In an essay on Merleau-Ponty, Sean Dorrance Kelly pulls these themes of anticipation and perspective together. First, the experience of a particular light or color is normative in the sense that "each presentation of the color in a given lighting context necessarily makes an implicit reference to a more completely presented *real* color, the color as it would be revealed if the lighting context were changed in the direction of the norm. This real color, implicitly referred to in every experience, is the constant color I see the color *to be*." Second, "the view from everywhere" built into the experience of depth is not a view you could ever actually have, separate from these memory-soaked projections, because there is no potential perspective that could add up the angles and backgrounds appropriate to all perspectives. Backgrounds are not additive in this way. The experience of depth is, rather, "a view . . . from which my own perspective is felt to deviate."[25] The perception of depth anticipates a perspective from which my actual angle of vision is felt to deviate. Perception thus closes into itself *as* actuality, a norm it cannot in fact instantiate. Perception *is* anticipatory and normative. The only thing Kelly omits is how the perception of depth is also one in which "I feel myself looked at by things," in which my activity of perception "is equally a passivity." That theme has consequences for contemporary politics.

Perception and Discipline

It might still seem that the gap between Michel Foucault and Merleau-Ponty remains too large to enable either to illuminate the other. Did not the early Foucault argue that because of the opacity of "life, labor and language" the structure of experience cannot provide a solid base from which to redeem a theory of the subject? Did he not say that the transcendental arguments that phenomenologists seek — whereby you first locate something indubitable in experience and then show what conception of the subject is necessarily presupposed by that experience — cannot be stabilized when the "doubles" of life, labor, and language fade into obscurity? Yes. But those strictures may be more applicable to Husserl than to Merleau-Ponty, particularly regarding the latter's later work.

Foucault speaks of "discipline" as a political anatomy of detail that molds the posture, demeanor, and sensibilities of the constituencies subjected to it, "in which power relations have an immediate hold on [the body]; they invest it, mark it, train it, torture it, force it to carry out tasks, to perform ceremonies, to enact signs."[26] We note already a difference in rhythm between the sentences of Foucault and those of Merleau-Ponty. Merleau-Ponty's sentences convey an implicit sense of belonging to the world, while Foucault's often identify or mobilize elements of resistance and disaffection circulating within modern modalities of experience. The initial connection between these two thinkers across their differences is that both see how perception requires a prior *disciplining* of the senses in which a rich history of inter-involvement sets the stage for experience. The critical relation between corporeo-cultural discipline and the shape of experience is emphasized by the fact that adults who have the neural machinery of vision repaired after having been blind from birth remain operationally blind unless and until a new history of inter-involvements between movement, touch, and object manipulation is synthesized into the synapses of the visual system. Only about ten percent of the synaptic connections for vision are wired in at birth. The rest emerge from the interplay between body/brain pluripotentiality and the history of intersensory experience.[27]

Let's return to Merleau-Ponty's finding that to perceive depth is implicitly to feel yourself as an object of vision. In a disciplinary society this implicit sense morphs into a more intensive experience of being an actual or potential object of *surveillance* in a national security state. That latter experience was amplified in the United States after the Al Qaeda attack of 9/11, the event in which Osama bin Laden invited George W. Bush to organize the world through the prism of security against a pervasive, nonstate enemy, an invitation that the cowboy eagerly accepted. The indubitable experience of self-visibility now swells into that of being an object of surveillance. Everyday awareness of that possibility recoils back upon the shape and emotional tone of experience. Methods and devices for tracking and surveilling people now include airport-screening devices, the circulation of social security numbers, credit profiles, medical records, electric identification bracelets, telephone caller ID services, product surveys, NSA sweeps, telephone records, license plates, internet use profiles, IRS audits, driver's licenses, police phone calls for "contributions," credit card numbers, DNA records, fingerprints, smellprints, eyeprints, promotion and hiring profiles, drug tests, and traffic, street, and building surveillance cameras. These are used, for example, at work, in schools, on the streets, and for voter solicitations, job interviews, police scrutiny, prison observations, political paybacks, racial profiling, e-mail solicitations, church judgments, divorce proceedings, and the publication of sexual proclivities. As such methods and devices proliferate, the experience of *potential* observability becomes an active element in everyday experience.[28]

> A whole problematic then develops: that of an architecture that is no longer built simply to be seen, . . . or to observe the external space, . . . but to permit an internal, articulated and detailed control — to render visible those who are inside it . . . an architecture that would operate to transform individuals: to act on those it shelters, to provide a hold on their conduct, to carry the effects of power right to them, to make it possible to know them, to alter them.[29]

True, Foucault's description of disciplinary society does not deal adequately with differences in age, class, and race. There is today an urban underclass that is subjected to general strategies of urban *containment* and impersonal modes of *surveillance* in stores, streets, public facilities, reform schools, prisons, and schools. There is also a suburban, upper-middle, career-oriented class enmeshed in detailed disciplines in several domains, anticipating the day it rises above them. And there are several other subject positions too, including those who rise more or less above generalized surveillance.

Watch out. Are you a war dissenter? Gay? Interested in drugs? An atheist who talks about it? A critic of the war on terrorism, drug policies, or government corruption? Sexually active? Be careful. You may want a new job someday or to protect yourself against this or that charge. Protect yourself now in anticipation of uncertain possibilities in the future. Discipline yourself in response to future threats. In advanced capitalism, where the affluent organize life around the prospect of a long career, many others look for jobs without security or benefits, and yet others find themselves stuck in illegal, informal, and underground economies, the implicit message of the surveillance society is to remain unobtrusive and politically quiescent by appearing more devout, regular, and patriotic than the next guy. The implicit sense of belonging to the world that Merleau-Ponty found folded into the fiber of experience now begins to ripple and scatter.

Neither Foucault nor Merleau-Ponty, understandably, was as alert to the electronic media as we must be today. This ubiquitous force flows into the circuits of discipline, perception, self-awareness, and conduct. It is not enough to survey the pattern of media ownership. It is equally pertinent to examine the methods through which it becomes insinuated into the shape and tone of perception.

Here I note one dimension of a larger topic. To decode electoral campaigns it is useful to see how media advertising works. According to Robert Heath, a successful ad executive and follower of recent work in neuroscience, the most effective product ads target viewers who are distracted from them. The ad solicits "implicit learning" below the level of refined intellectual attention. It plants "triggers" that insinuate a mood or an association into perception, which are called into action the next time the product is seen, mentioned, smelled, heard, or touched. Implicit learning is key because, unlike the refined intellectual activity into which it flows, "it is on all the time." It is "automatic, almost inexhaustible, in its capacity and more durable" in retention.[30]

The link to Foucault and Merleau-Ponty is that they too attend to the preconscious, affective dimensions of discipline and experience without focusing upon the media. Today, programs such as *Hannity & Colmes*, *Crossfire*, and *The O'Reilly Factor* infiltrate the tonalities of political perception. As viewers focus on points made by guests and hosts, the program is laced with interruptions, people talking over one another, sharp accusations, and yelling. The endless reiteration of those intensities secretes a simple standard of objectivity as the gold standard of perception while insinuating the corollary suspicion that no one actually measures up to it. As a result resentment and cynicism now become coded into the very color of perception. The cumulative result of the process itself favors a neoconservative agenda. For cynics typically ridicule the legacy of big government in employment, services, and welfare while yearning for a figure to reassert the unquestionable authority of "the nation." A cynic is an authoritarian who rejects the current regime of authority. Cynical realists experience the fragility and uncertainty that help to constitute perception. But they join to that experience an overweening demand for authority, and they accuse everyone else of failing to conform to the model of simple objectivity they claim to meet. Justification of this model is not sustained by showing how they meet it but by repeated accusations that others regularly fail to do so.

Cynical realism is one response to the complexity of perception. Another, in a world of surveillance, is self-depoliticization. You avert your gaze from disturbing events to curtail dangerous temptations to action. The goal is to avoid close attention or intimidation in the venues of work, family, school, church, electoral politics, and neighborhood life. But, of course, such a retreat can also amplify a feeling of resentment against the organization of life itself, opening up some of these same constituencies for recruitment by the forces of ressentiment. Such responses can be mixed in several ways. What is undeniable is that the circuits between discipline, media, layered memories, and self-awareness find expression in the color of perception itself. Power is coded into perception.

The Micropolitics of Perception

Sensory inter-involvement, disciplinary processes, detailed modes of surveillance, media infiltration, congealed attractors, affective dispositions, self-regulation in response to future susceptibility—these elements participate in perpetual circuits of exchange, feedback, and reentry, with each loop folding another variation and degree into its predecessor. The imbrications are so close that it is impossible to sort out each element from the other once they have merged into a larger complex. The circuits fold, bend, and blend into each other, inflecting the shape of political experience. Even as they are ubiquitous, however, there are numerous points of dissonance, variation, hesitation, and disturbance in them. These interruptions provide potential triggers to the pursuit of other spiritual possibilities, where the term "spirit" means a refined state of the body in an individual *and* those existential dispositions that are embedded in institutional practices.

What are the dissonances? In the following formulations the "you form" can be taken in both its singular and plural forms. A past replete with religious ritual clashes with an alternative representation of God in a film, church, or school; an emergent practice of heterodox sexuality encourages you to question established habits in other domains; the interruption of a heretofore smooth career path solicits doubts previously submerged in habits of anticipation; a trip abroad exposes you to disturbing news items and attitudes seldom allowed expression in your own country; neurotherapy fosters a modest shift in your sensibility; a stock market crash disrupts assumptions about the future; a new religious experience shakes you; a terrorist attack folds an implacable desire for revenge into you; a devastating natural event shakes your faith in providence.

The anticipatory habits of perception are not self-contained. Rather, dominant tendencies of the day periodically bump into minor dispositions, submerged tendencies, and wavering incipiencies. The instability of the attractors and conjunctions that make perception possible thus also make it a ubiquitous medium of power and politics.

What might be done today to open the anticipatory habits and sedimented dispositions of more constituencies during a time when media politics diverts attention from the most urgent dilemmas of the day?

Television could be a site upon which to run such experiments. A few dramas do so. I would place *Six Feet Under* on that list, as it disrupts conventional habits of perception and occasionally works to recast them. But the closer a program is to a "news program" or a "talk show," the more it either enacts virulent partisanship, adopts the hackneyed voice of simple objectivity, or purports to do the one while doing the other. What is needed are subtle media experiments, news and talk shows that expose and address the complexity of experience in a media-saturated society. *The Daily Show* and *The Colbert Report* take a couple of steps in the right direction, calling into question the voice of simple objectivity through exaggeration and satirization of it. Their stills and close-ups of public figures in action reveal how passions infiltrate our perceptual experience below the level of conscious attention. But because we live in a media-saturated society much more is needed.

Mark Hansen, in *New Philosophy for New Media*, pursues this issue. In chapter 6, he reviews Skulls, an exhibit presented by Robert Lazzarini at the Whitney Museum in 2000. Lazzarini's sculptures are uncanny. They seem like skulls, but you soon find that, however you tilt your head or change your position, it is impossible to vindicate the anticipation of them. Lazzarini has in fact laser-scanned an actual human skull, reformatted it into several images, and constructed a few statues from the reformatted images. These three-dimensional images cannot be brought into alignment with the anticipations triggered by their appearances. "At each effort to align your point of view with the perspective of one of these weird sculptural objects, you experience a gradually mounting feeling of incredible strangeness. *It is as though these skulls refuse to return your gaze.*"[31]

The anticipation of being seen by the objects you see is shattered by these deformed images that refuse to support that sense. You now feel "the space around you begin to ripple, to bubble, to infold, as if it were becoming unstuck from the fixed coordinates of its three dimensional extension."[32] The exhibit Skulls, when joined to Merleau-Ponty's phenomenology of perception, heightens awareness of the fugitive role we play in perception by making it impossible to find an attractor to which it corresponds. These sculptures also dramatize the role that *affect* plays in perception, as they jolt the tacit feeling of belonging to the world that Merleau-Ponty imports into the depth grammar of experience. The implicit sense of belonging to the world is transfigured into a feeling of vertigo. Do such experiments dramatize a sense of disruption already lurking within experience in a world marked by the acceleration of tempo, the exacerbation of surveillance, and the disturbance of traditional images of time? At a minimum, in conjunction with the work of Merleau-Ponty and Foucault, they sharpen our awareness of the multiple inter-involvements between affect, memory, and tactility in the organization of perception. You now more readily call into question simple models of vision and better appreciate how a disciplinary society inflects affect-imbued perception.

You might even become attracted to experimental strategies to deepen visceral attachment to the complexity of existence itself during a time when the automatic sense of belonging to this world is often stretched and disrupted. None of the above responses is automatic. An opportunity merely opens. Pursuing it requires moving back and forth between perceptual experimentation and reflection on changes in the larger circumstances of life that enter into affect-imbued judgments and perceptions.

As a preliminary to the latter, consider some processes and conditions that disrupt the tacit sense of belonging to the world that Merleau-Ponty found sedimented in the pores of experience itself. They include: the acceleration of speed and expansion of scope in many domains of life, including military deployment, global communication systems, air travel, tourism, population migrations, fashion, financial transactions, and cultural exchanges; a flood of popular films that complicate visual experience and sometimes call the linear image of time into question; publicity about new discoveries in neuroscience, which include attention to that half-second delay between multisensory reception and the organization of perception; greater awareness of work in the sciences of complexity that transduct the Newtonian model of linear cause into the ideas of resonance and emergent causality; scientific speculations that extend the creative element already discernible in biological evolution to the unfolding of the universe itself; increased media attention to events that periodically shock habitual assumptions coded into perception; media attention to the devastation occasioned here or there by earthquakes, hurricanes, volcanic eruptions, and tsunamis; and a vague but urgent sense that the world's fragile ecological balance is careening into radical imbalance.

The signs that these disruptive experiences have taken a toll are also diverse. They include, on the revenge or aggressive side of life, the extreme levels of violence and superhuman heroism in "action" films, as they strive to redeem simple models of objectivism and mastery under unfavorable circumstances; the intensification of accusatory voices in the media in conjunction with the righteous self-assertion by talking heads of simple objectivism; new intensities of apocalyptic prophecy in several religious movements; the heightened virulence of electoral campaigns; and a popular desire for abstract revenge that finds ample expression in preemptive wars, state regimes of torture, massacres, collective rapes, and the like.

The obverse side of those responses is discernible as well in other practices and constituencies. Today more people in a variety of social positions — including those of class, age, formal religious faith, gender, and ethnicity — are less convinced than heretofore of the simple model of perception. They seek to consolidate attachment to a world populated by sensory inter-involvements, resonance, attractors, the complexity of duration, time as becoming, and an uncertain future. Take, as merely one sign of these developments, the receptive responses of many to minor films such as *Far from Heaven, I ♥ Huckabees, Time Code, Blow-Up, Eternal Sunshine of the Spotless Mind, Memento, Waking Life, Run Lola Run*, and *Synecdoche.*

These films focus on the role of duration in perception, scramble old habits in this way or that, highlight sensory inter-involvements, challenge simple objectivism, and call into question self-confidence in the linear image of time. Some take another turn as well. Going through and beyond the anxiety fomented by Skulls, they encourage a spiritual awakening — either theistic or nontheistic in form — that is most apt to emerge *after* such anxieties have been tapped. To take one example, *Waking Life* is a long cartoon consisting of wavy, undulating figures. It charts the layering of memory into the existential orientations in a man whose brain, it turns out, is alive and active for six minutes after he has died in other respects. He is filled with a muddle of affect-imbued memories, some profound and others silly, about the point of existence. He is compelled to let these diverse memories speak to each other in this instance because the link between perception and action has been severed. He thus dwells in action-suspended experience because he is unable to do anything else. Here a high-tech cartoon, composed of uncertain and indistinct figures, poses issues about what it takes to be attached to a fast-paced world in which the connecting strings have become stretched. This film invites us to probe and renew attachment to a world increasingly disjoined from the pace of life tacitly assumed by Merleau-Ponty. We are moved to cultivate further strains of attachment to this world and to fend off the seed of abstract resentment that so readily rises up in and around us. And we are invited to ponder how embers of existential resentment, once sown, can be inflamed by disruptive events, media frenzies, and political campaigns, and how it then becomes infused into institutional practices such as investment, consumption, church assemblies, media reporting, voting patterns, and state priorities. An incipient sense of care for this world is tapped and amplified, a sense that can either be ignored or worked upon further by tactical means and micropolitics.[33]

This is the juncture at which to address the engagements by Deleuze in *Cinema II* with those features of late-modern life that disrupt belief in this world as well as his accentuation of other, more subtle strategies which reactivate it. The stage is set by explorations of flashbacks that expose strange moments of bifurcation in experience, comedic figures who enact exquisite sensitivity to "aberrant" movements of world, irrational cuts that scramble the action image, crystals of time that enact the complexity of duration, and engagements with "powers of the false" that open up dissonant traces of experience typically superseded by resolute calls to action. The suggestion is that most of us have already been infected by such experiences both in the vicissitudes of daily life I listed earlier and by films that dramatize and extend them. Several of them dramatize seeds of attachment to this world that can then be amplified further.

Such dramatizations can, of course, themselves trigger existential resentment, magnetize drives to reassert the simple model of objectivity, or encourage retreats from public engagement. Especially if you are occupied by a prior sense that we humans are somehow entitled to a world of simple objectivity. But Deleuze challenges these responses at the nodal points of their reception because they incite revenge against the world as such. He encourages tactics to deepen attachment to the complexity of "this world," so as to challenge bellicose mastery, passive skepticism, and authoritarian cynicism at their nodal points of formation. He contends that commitment to radical political agendas that go beyond negative critique require expansive surges of positive existential attachment.

By "belief in this world" Deleuze certainly does not mean the established distribution of power and political priorities. Those are the things to resist and overcome with positive alternatives. He means, in the first instance, affirmation of the largest compass of being in which human beings are set as opposed to existential resentment of it or resignation about it. He means, in the second instance, acceptance without resentment of the fact that in a mobile world composed of minorities of multiple types, *numerous constituencies we encounter on a regular basis increasingly bring different final conceptions of the world to experience as such.* The agenda is to connect positive attachment to this world as we interpret it to presumptive acceptance of the fact that, during an age when minoritization of the world is proceeding at a faster pace, we increasingly bump into people who adopt different final interpretations of the largest compass of being as such. As he puts it in one instance, "Whether we are Christians or atheists, in our universal schizophrenia, we need reasons to believe in this world."[34] The idea seems to be, again, to consolidate attachment to this world as we ourselves interpret it to be and to overcome the tendency to resent the veritable minoritization of the world that is taking place at a faster pace today.

In his usage the term "belief" functions on more than one register. There are epistemic beliefs, some of which can be altered relatively easily by recourse to new evidence and argument. And there are more intense, vague existential dispositions in which creed and affect mix together below the ready reach of change by reflective considerations alone. This is the zone that prophets tap. It is one the media engages too through the interplay of rhythm, image, music, and sound. "Belief" at this level touches, for instance, the tightening of the gut, coldness of the skin, contraction of the pupils, and hunching of the back that occur when a judgment or faith in which you are deeply invested is contested, ridiculed, ruled illegal, or punished more severely yet. It also touches those feelings of abundance and joy that emerge whenever we sense the surplus of life over the structure of our identities. That is the surplus Deleuze seeks to mobilize and to attach to positive political movements that embrace minoritization of the world. It may be surprising to some to hear an immanent naturalist embrace the spiritual dimension of life. But it is not surprising to those of us who at once contest faith in transcendence in the strongest sense of that word and appreciate the profound role that the quality of spirituality plays in public life.

It may be important to follow Deleuze's lead in part because the mode of belonging embraced by Merleau-Ponty has been shaken by the acceleration of pace in many zones of culture and the pervasive role of the media in everyday life.[35] And in part because various efforts to ground care for difference only in the experience of the negative or vulnerability are not apt to succeed unless they are themselves situated in a prior experience of the vitality of being. At the very least they do not have that much to show for themselves to date.

Wider negotiation of attachment to the most fundamental terms of existence would not sanction existing injustices, nor would it *suffice* to generate the critical politics needed today—though some will predictably project both assumptions into this essay. Such energies, rather, must simultaneously be cultivated by individuals, mobilized in various institutions of associational life, and inserted into larger circuits of political action. For we no longer inhabit a world where a sense of belonging is securely installed in the infrastructure of experience, if we ever did. Nor is a single religious faith apt to repair the deficit on its terms alone, at least without introducing massive repression during a time when minorities of many types inhabit the same territorial space. The issue is fundamental.

Let's tarry on the question of existential ethos a bit. My experience is that many on the democratic left who point correctly to the *insufficiency* of such awakenings move quickly from that point to assert its *irrelevance* or to announce its *foolishness*. They do not want to seem soft or feminine. They fear that the nerve of critique will be severed if ontological affirmation is pursued. Indeed, some seem to assume that a healthy *resentment* of suffering, inequality, and closure cannot be advanced if you also affirm a positive existential spirituality. Sometimes they assume as well that to drop theism in favor of any version of materialism *means* to forfeit or go beyond spirituality. Those are the judgments I seek to contest. I suggest that Friedrich Nietzsche, Maurice Merleau-Ponty, Michel Foucault, and Gilles Deleuze are with me on this point, each showing how a spirituality of some sort or other is always infused into experience, interpretation, and action and all seeking to draw sustenance from positive attachment to this world. Today, work on the infrastructure of perception is linked to the possibility of positive politics. To ignore the first is to give too much ground to prophets of revenge or despair as they work to insert a spirituality of existential revenge into the pores of experience and as they identify vulnerable targets upon whom to vent the intensities they mobilize. Ontological affirmation, the democratic left, and political militancy belong together in the late-modern era. It takes all three in tandem—in their theistic and nontheistic forms—to press for pluralism, equality, and ecological sensitivity.

In this essay I have begun to chart reverberations between existential seeds, the subtle organization of perception, social practices of surveillance, the acceleration of pace in several zones of life, the expansion of minorities of multiple types, the critical role of the media in the politics of perception, the place of spirituality in perception and other aspects of institutional life, and the pertinence of all of these to a militant politics of the democratic left. Each site and dimension demands more reflection and experimentation in relation to the others.

Notes

1   You could speak, as Merleau-Ponty occasionally does, of transcendence without the Transcendent. But such a formulation may blur a contestation between alternative faiths or philosophies that needs to be kept alive.

2   Deleuze and Guattari, *A Thousand Plateaus* (Minneapolis, 1987), 266.

3   In their introduction to *Problems and Methods in The Study of Politics*, the editors, Ian Shapiro, Rogers M. Smith, and Tarek E. Masoud, report me as saying that "the world is in a state of constant and unpredictable flux" (11). That signifies to me that awareness of one side of my position has been blocked by the shock of meeting the other.

4   Prigogine, *Is the Future Given?*, 65.

5   Merleau-Ponty, *Nature*, 206.

6   The formulation in fact suggests the doctrine of parallelism introduced by Spinoza in the seventeenth century. For a fine study in neuroscience that draws upon both Spinoza's philosophy of parallelism and his idea that affect always accompanies perception, belief, and thinking, see Damasio, *Looking for Spinoza*.

7   See Ramachandran, *Phantoms in the Brain*. Some implications of this research for cultural theory are explored in Connolly, *Neuropolitics*, chap. 1.

8   Merleau-Ponty, *Nature*, 152.

9   See, besides the references to works by Damasio, Prigogine, and Ramachandran above, Goodwin, *How the Leopard Changed Its Spots*. In *The Structure of Evolutionary Theory*, Stephen Jay Gould emphasizes how close his revision of Darwinian theory is to the notion of genealogy developed by Nietzsche.

10 Merleau-Ponty, *Nature*, 156.

11 The phrase, "the half-second delay" comes out of work in neuroscience pioneered by Benjamin Libet. Merleau-Ponty was certainly aware of a time lag, however. An excellent discussion of the delay and its significance can be found in Massumi, *Parables for the Virtual*.

12 Merleau-Ponty, *Nature*, 100.

13 Merleau-Ponty, *Phenomenology of Perception*, 52.

14 Ibid., 100.

15   This theme is increasingly accepted in neuroscience today. See Durie, "Doors of Perception." Durie agrees, too, that the senses are interinvolved.

16   Marks, *The Skin of the Film*, chap. 3, "The Memory of Touch."

17   Merleau-Ponty, *Phenomenology of Perception*, 183. Such a pattern of inter-involvement will seem impossible only to those who are captured by the analytic-synthetic dichotomy, in which every connection is reducible either to a definitional or an empirical (causal) relation. Once you break that di-chotomy, you can come to terms with the series of memory-infused inter-involvements through which perception is organized. You are also able to consider models of causality that transcend efficient causality.

18   Rizzolatti and Sinigaglia, *Mirrors in the Brain*, 125. Rizzolatti and Sinigaglia think that language would not have developed without this base of pre-linguistic experience enabled by the cultural coding of mirror neurons. (I am aware that the word "linguistic" can be stretched to include such processes, but the value in not doing so is to help us understand how language evolved out of cultural experience rather than popping up all at once and to appreci-ate more closely the multilayered character of experience.) Rizzolatti and Sinigaglia also sprinkle their book with quotations from Merleau-Ponty, ap-preciating numerous points at which his observational experiments support their phenomenological work. One point at which Merleau-Ponty's work suggests a modest revision to me, however, is that it points to the way that tactics of the self and media micropolitics help to code seeds of cultural experience by means of multimedia that exceed the ready reach of intellectual self-consciousness. He draws us, then, into political territory mapped by Foucault and Deleuze.

19   Ibid., 189.

20   Soló and Goodwin, *Signs of Life*, 142–43.

21   In fact, Henri Bergson is better than Merleau-Ponty at focusing attention on the role that the imperative to make perceptual judgments rapidly as one runs through the numerous encounters of everyday life plays in creating the sub-tractions and simplifications of operational perception. It is beyond the scope of this essay to explore the comparative advantages and weaknesses of each perspective. But if I were to do so, the above limitation in Merleau-Ponty would be balanced against his reflective appreciation of the numerous sensory "inter-involvements" that make perception possible. The starting point to engage Bergson on these issues is *Matter and Memory*.

22   Merleau-Ponty, *Phenomenology of Perception*, 219, my italics.

23   Coole, *Negativity and Politics*, 132. This book prompted me to take another look at Merleau-Ponty in relation to Foucault and Deleuze. Some will protest her assertion, saying that priority must be given either to the subject or to the object. But they then have to come to terms with the multiple inter-involvements elucidated by Merleau-Ponty and his judgment that you can't

unsort entirely—once these mixings and remixings have occurred—exactly what contribution is made by one "side" or "the other." Even the painter, alert to his powers of perception, is not "able to say (since the distinction has no meaning) what comes from him and what comes from things, what the new work adds to the old ones, or what it has taken from the others." "Indirect Language and the Voices of Silence," 58–59.

24 Merleau-Ponty, *The Visible and Invisible*, 13, my italics. That text also deepens our experience of "the flesh" in ways which extend all the points made about the sensorium discussed above. But we cannot pursue that pregnant topic here.

25 Kelly, "Seeing Things in Merleau-Ponty," 86 and 92.

26 Foucault, *Discipline and Punish*, 25.

27 For a review of the neuroscience literature on bodily and cultural elements in the formation of sight, see Zeman, *Consciousness*, chaps. 5 and 6.

28 In April of 2005, *The Johns Hopkins Gazette* released the following bulletin: "Continuing its efforts to enhance the security of students, faculty and staff, the university has installed a state of the art closed-circuit TV system. The system can be programmed to look for as many as 16 behavior patterns and to assign them a priority score for operator follow-up. . . . The cameras are helping us to make the transition to a more fully integrated 'virtual policing' system."

29 Foucault, *Discipline and Punish*, 172.

30 Heath, *The Hidden Power of Advertising*, 67. Heath is not speaking of subliminal inserts here; he is talking about advertisements that distract attention from themselves and encourage viewers to be distracted too as the advertisements insert connections between affect, words, and images.

31 Hansen, *New Philosophy for New Media*, 198.

32 Ibid.

33 It is pertinent to emphasize that the "attachment to this world" spoken of here is not to existing injustices, class suffering, dogmatism, repression of diversity, and the like but to the human existential condition itself as it finds expression in a world in which some zones of life proceed at a more rapid tempo. The wager is that the enhancement of attachment to this world increases the energy and will to oppose the dangers and injustices built into it.

34 Deleuze, *Cinema II, The Time Image*, 172.

35 I review specific strategies, both individual and collective, to rework tacit dispositions to perception and sensibility in chapters 4, 5, and 6 of *Neuropolitics* and in "Experience and Experiment."

Rosi Braidotti

The Politics of "Life Itself" and New Ways of Dying

This essay focuses on contemporary debates on the politics of life itself, with special emphasis on the shifting boundaries between life and death. As a starting assumption, I want to suggest here that we understand biopower not only in the sense of the government of the living but also with relation to practices of dying. By extension, this means that our relationship to pain, loss, and practices of mourning needs to be reconsidered in the light of biopolitical concerns.

Generally speaking, "the politics of life itself" refers to the extent to which the notion of biopower has emerged as an organizing principle for the proliferating discourses and practices that make technologically mediated "life" into a self-constituting entity.[1] Living matter itself becomes the subject and not the object of inquiry, and this shift toward a biocentered perspective affects the very fiber and structure of social subjects.[2] One of the manifestations of this materialist shift toward what could be called a genetic social imaginary is the changing roles and representations of the human body.[3] As a result of information and biogenetic technologies, bodily materialism is being revised in ways that challenge accepted social constructivist notions. The matter of the body and the specific materiality of bodies have come to the fore with more prominence, for example, in stem-cell research and in everyday media-driven dissemination of "gene-centric" images and rep-resentations. Contemporary social and cultural examples of this shift are practices linked to genetic citizenship as a form of spectatorship, for in-stance, the visualizations of the life of genes in medical practices, popular culture, cinema, and advertising. Another social aspect to this trend con-cerns the uses of genetics in political debates on race, ethnicity, and immi-gration. Yet another example is the rhetoric of "life" or living matter in public debates from abortion and stem-cell research to new kinship and family structures. This development pertains to a trend that is becoming known as neovitalism and vital politics.[4] Considering the problematic nature of vitalism in European thought and modern history, in view of its link with the organicist philosophies of fascism, I shall not pursue it fur-ther in this essay.

The Current Situation

These social discourses about "life" are often taken as indicating the return of "real bodies" and real materiality: an ontology of presence after so much postmodernist deconstruction. I refer to this return of a neorealist practice of bodily materialism as *matter-ialism*, or radical neomaterialism. This trend has caused both the neoliberal[5] and the neo-Kantian thinkers to be struck by high levels of anxiety about the sheer thinkability of the human future.[6] Technology is central to this matter-ialistic debate.

Claudia Springer argues, for instance, that this discourse celebrating the union of humans and electronic technology is currently circulating with equal success among the scientific community and in popular cul-ture.[7] It can therefore be seen and, to a certain extent, dismissed today as a dominant mode of representation. The work of Donna Haraway is of seminal importance here. The cyborg as a technologically enhanced body-machine is the dominant social and discursive figuration for the inter-action between the human and the technological in postindustrial so-cieties. It is also a living or active, materially embedded cartography of the kind of power-relations that are operative in the postindustrial social sphere. Scott Bukatman argues that this projection of the physical self into an artificial environment feeds into a dream of terminal identity outside the body, a sort of "cybersubject" that feeds into the New Age fantasies of cosmic redemption through technology.[8] New Age spirituality or techno-mysticism form part of this trend.

This affects the question of death and makes possible new ways of dying. A rather complex relationship has emerged in the cyber universe we inhabit: one in which the link between the flesh and the machine is symbiotic and therefore can best be described as a bond of mutual dependence. This engenders some significant paradoxes when it comes to the human body. The corporeal site of subjectivity is simultaneously denied, in a fantasy of escape, and strengthened or reinforced. Anne Balsamo stresses the paradoxical concomitance of effects surrounding the new posthuman bodies as enabling a fantastic dream of immortality and control over life and death. "And yet, such beliefs about the technological future "life" of the body are complemented by a palpable fear of death and annihilation from uncontrollable and spectacular body-threats: antibiotic-resistant viruses, random contamination, flesh-eating bacteria."[9]

In other words, the new practices of "life" mobilize not only generative forces but also new and subtler degrees of extinction. This type of vitality, unconcerned by clear-cut distinctions between living and dying, composes the notion of *zoē* as a nonhuman yet affirmative life-force. This vitalist materialism has nothing in common with the postmodern emphasis on the inorganic and the aesthetics of fake, pastiche, and camp simulation. It also moves beyond "high" cyber studies, into post-cyber-materialism.

Through these practices, the traditional humanistic unity of the embodied human is dislocated by a number of social forces, driven by the convergence of information, communication, and biotechnologies.[10] This engenders a variety of social practices of extended, fragmented, enhanced, or prosthetically empowered embodiment. In my previous work on nomadic political and feminist theory, I have extensively analyzed this phenomenon, which I do not assess necessarily in a negative mode. In this essay, I want to test the hypothesis that the emphasis on life itself has some positive sides because it focuses with greater accuracy on the complexities of contemporary technologically mediated bodies and on social practices of human embodiment.

This marks a shift away from anthropocentrism, in favor of a new emphasis on the mutual interdependence of material, biocultural, and symbolic forces in the making of social and political practices. The focus on life itself may encourage a sort of biocentered egalitarianism,[11] forcing a reconsideration of the concept of subjectivity in terms of "life-forces." It dislocates but also redefines the relationship between self and other by shifting the axes of genderization, racialization, and naturalization away from a binary opposition into a more complex and less oppositional mode of interaction. Biopolitics thus opens up an ecophilosophical dimension of reflection and inaugurates alternative ecologies of belonging both in kinship systems and in forms of social and political participation. I would like to explore the possibility that these "hybrid" social identities and the new modes of multiple belonging they enact may constitute the starting point for mutual and respective accountability and pave the way for an ethical regrounding of social participation and community building.

I would like, in other words, to defend the politics of "life itself" as a form of active ethical citizenship. Social examples of biocitizenship as a technology of the self are the emphasis currently placed on the responsibility for the self-management of one's health and one's own lifestyle in the case of medical insurance, or the social drive toward eternal youth, which is linked to the suspension of time in globally mediated societies and can be juxtaposed to euthanasia and other social practices of assisted death. Also relevant to this discussion are contemporary embodied social practices that are often pathologized: addictions, eating disorders, and melancholia, ranging from burnout to states of apathy or disaffection. I want to approach these phenomena in a nonnormative manner as social manifestations of the shifting relation between living and dying in the era of the politics of "life itself."

Biopower Revisited

Issues of power and power relations are central to this project. The notion of "life itself" lies at the heart of biogenetic capitalism as a site of financial investments and potential profit.[12] Technological interventions neither suspend nor automatically improve the social relations of exclusion and inclusion that historically had been predicated along the axes of class and socioeconomics, as well as along the sexualized and racialized lines of demarcation of "otherness." Also denounced as "biopiracy," the ongoing technological revolution often intensifies patterns of traditional discrimination and exploitation.[13] We have all become the subjects of biopower, but we differ considerably in the degrees and modes of actualization of that very power.

This has three major consequences: the first is conceptual and, as I anticipated earlier, focuses on the more negative aspects of the politics of "life itself," namely, the new practices of dying in contemporary society. "Life" can be a threatening force, which engenders new epidemics and environmental catastrophes, blurring the distinction between the natural and the cultural dimensions. Another obvious example of the politics of death is the new forms of warfare and specifically terrorists' use of suicide bombers. Equally significant are the changes that have occurred in the political practice of bearing witness to the dead as a form of activism, from the Mothers of the Plaza de Mayo to the Chechnya war widows. From a posthuman perspective, there is also the proliferation of viruses that travel back and forth between humans and animals — and between computers and other digital devices through the internet. Relevant cultural practices that reflect this changing status of death can be traced in the success of forensic detectives in contemporary popular culture. The corpse is a daily presence in global media and journalistic news, while it is also an object of entertainment. The dislocation of gender roles in relation to death and killing is reflected in the image of women who kill, from recent stage productions of *Medea* and *Hecuba* to the character of Lara Croft. It might also be interesting to analyze the currency granted to both legal and illegal drugs in contemporary culture, which blurs the boundaries between self-destruction and fashionable behavior and forces a reconsideration of what is the value of "life itself."

The second consequence concerns the status of social and political theory itself. It is urgent to assess the state of the theoretical debates on biopower after Foucault, especially in terms of its legal, political, and ethical implications. Several positions have emerged in recent biopower research. Some thinkers stress the role of moral accountability as a form of biopolitical citizenship, thus inscribing the notion of "life" as "*bios*," that is to say, an instance of governmentality that is as empowering as it is confining.[14] This school of thought locates the political moment in the relational and self-regulating accountability of a bioethical subject and results in the radicalization of the project of modernity.

The second grouping takes its lead from Heidegger and is best exemplified by Giorgio Agamben.[15] It defines *"bios"* as the result of the intervention of sovereign power as that which is capable of reducing the subject to "bare life," that is to say *"zoē."* The being-aliveness of the subject (*zoē*) is identified with its perishability, its propensity and vulnerability to death and extinction. Biopower here means Thanatos-politics and results, among others, in the indictment of the project of modernity.

A third important group is formed by feminist, environmentalist, and race theorists who have addressed the shifting status of "difference" in advanced capitalism in a manner that respects the complexity of social relations and critiques liberalism, while highlighting the specificity of a gender and race approach.[16] These critical thinkers approach biopolitical analyses from the angle of the greed and ruthless exploitation that marks contemporary globalized capitalism. The notion of biopiracy is significant in this respect.[17]

A fourth significant community of scholars works within a Spinozist framework and includes Gilles Deleuze, Félix Guattari, Edouard Glissant, Moira Gatens and Genevieve Lloyd, Etienne Balibar, Michael Hardt and Antonio Negri, and myself.[18] The emphasis falls on the politics of life itself as a relentlessly generative force. This requires an interrogation of the shifting interrelations between human and nonhuman forces. The latter are defined both as inhuman and posthuman.[19]

The third consequence is methodological. If it is indeed the case that all technologies have a strong "biopower" effect, in that they affect bodies and immerse them in social and legal relations of power, then a higher degree of interdisciplinary effort is needed in social and political thought to come to terms with our historical predicament. This challenge requires a methodology that focuses on processes and interconnections. Moreover, the speed of transformations induced by technology displaces established conventions of thought and moral certainties. In culture at large, technological changes are received with a mixture of fascination and horror, euphoria and anxiety.[20] This raises serious ethical issues. I would like to assess the hypothesis that, far from being merely a "crisis" of values, this historical situation presents us with new opportunities. Renewed conceptual creativity and a leap of the social imaginary may be needed in order to meet the challenge. I want to explore accordingly a postanthropocentric approach to the analysis of "life itself" as a way of broadening the sense of community. Examples of this are the new global environmentalism, which assesses allegedly "natural" catastrophes as an interesting hybrid mix of cultural and political forces. Also significant to this discussion is the return of evolutionary discourses in contemporary social theory, as is the revival of a vitalist Spinozist political theory. The state of the debates on these issues in fields as diverse as political, legal, social, environmental, feminist, and technology theories, to name just a few, shows a range of positions that need to be assessed critically. This essay aims to elaborate sets of criteria for a new social and political theory that steers a course between humanistic nostalgia and neoliberal euphoria about biocapitalism. Social and political practices that take life itself as the point of reference need not aim at the restoration of unitary norms or the celebration of the master-narrative of global profit, but rather at social cohesion, the respect for diversity, and sustainable growth. At the heart of this project lies an ethics that respects vulnerability while actively constructing social horizons of hope.

The Emergence of *Zoē*

Life is half animal, *zoē* (*zoology*, *zoophilic*, *zoo*) and half discursive, *bios* (*biology*). *Zoē*, of course, is the poor half of a couple that foregrounds *bios* defined as intelligent life. Centuries of Christian indoctrination have left a deep mark here. The relationship to animal life, to *zoē* rather than *bios*, constitutes one of those qualitative distinctions upon which Western reason erected its empire. *Bios* is almost holy, *zoē* is certainly gritty. That they intersect in the human body turns the physical self into a contested space and into a political arena. The mind-body dualism has historically functioned as a shortcut through the complexities of this in-between contested zone. One of the most persistent and helpful fictions that is told about human life is its alleged self-evidence, its implicit worth. *Zoē* is always second best, and the idea of life carrying on independent of, even regardless of, and at times in spite of rational control is the dubious privilege attributed to the nonhumans. These cover all of the animal kingdoms as well as the classical "others" of metaphysically based visions of the subject, namely the sexual other (woman) and the ethnic other (the native). In the old regime this used to be called "Nature."

Traditionally, the self-reflexive control over life is reserved for the humans, whereas the mere unfolding of biological sequences is for the nonhumans. Given that this concept of "the human" was colonized by phallogocentrism, it has come to be identified with male, white, heterosexual, Christian, property-owning, standard-language-speaking citizens. *Zoē* marks the outside of this vision of the subject, in spite of the efforts of evolutionary theory to strike a new relationship to the nonhuman. Contemporary scientific practices have forced us to touch the bottom of some inhumanity that connects to the human precisely in the immanence of its bodily materialism. With the genetic revolution, we can speak of a generalized "becoming infrahuman" of *bios*. The category of "*bios*" has cracked under the strain and has splintered into a web of interconnected "bits-of-life" effects.

With the postmodern collapse of the qualitative divide between the human and his (the gender is no coincidence) others, the deep vitality of the embodied self has resurfaced from under the crust of the old metaphysical vision of the subject. *Zoē*, this obscenity, this life in me, is intrinsic to my being and yet so much "itself" that it is independent of the will, the demands and expectations of the sovereign consciousness. This *zoē* makes me tick and yet escapes the control of the supervision of the self. *Zoē* carries on relentlessly and gets cast out of the holy precinct of the "me" that demands control and fails to obtain it. It thus ends up being experienced as an alien other. Life is experienced as inhuman because it is all too human, obscene because it lives on mindlessly. Are we not baffled by this scandal, this wonder, this *zoē*, that is to say, by an idea of life that exuberantly exceeds *bios* and supremely ignores logos? Are we not in awe of this piece of flesh called our "body," of this aching meat called our "self" expressing the abject and simultaneously divine potency of life?

Classical philosophy is resolutely on the side of a dialogue with the biological. Nomadic subjectivity is, in contrast, in love with *zoē*. It's about the posthuman as becoming animal, becoming other, becoming insect — trespassing all metaphysical boundaries. Ultimately, it leads to becoming imperceptible and fading — death being just another time sequence. Some of these "bits-of-life" effects are therefore very closely related to that aspect of life that goes by the name of death, but is nonetheless an integral part of the *bios*/*zoē* process. The *bios*/*zoē* compound refers to what was previously known as life by introducing a differentiation internal to this category. By making the notion of life more complex, this distinction implies the notion of multiplicity. This allows for a nonbinary way of positing the relationship between same and other, between different categories of living beings, and ultimately between life and death. The emphasis and hence the mark of "difference" now falls on the "other" of the living body following its humanistic definition: *thanatos* — the dead body, the corpse or spectral other.

Of Limits as Thresholds

One other concern that prompts this essay is the awareness of the vulnerability of many humans, including those who are committed to pursuing change and making a difference. Progressive thinkers are just as human as others, only considerably more mortal. The issue of suffering, pain, and loss raises its disturbing head.

We lost so many of its specimens to dead-end experimentations of the existential, political, sexual, narcotic, or technological kind. Although it is true that we lost as many if not more of our members to the stultifying inertia of the status quo — a sort of generalized "Stepford wives" syndrome — it is nonetheless the case that I have developed an acute awareness of how difficult changes are. This is not meant as a deterrent against them, on the contrary: I think that the current political climate has placed undue emphasis on the risks involved in pursuing social changes, playing ad nauseam the refrain about the death of ideologies. Such a conservative reaction aims at disciplining the citizens and reducing their desire for the "new" to docile and compulsive forms of consumerism. Nothing could be further removed from my project than this approach. I simply want to issue a cautionary note: processes of change and transformation are so important and ever so vital and necessary that they have to be handled with care. The concept of ethical sustainability addresses these complex issues. We have to take pain into account as a major incentive for, and not only an obstacle to, an ethics of changes and transformations. We also need to rethink the knowing subject in terms of affectivity, interrelationality, territories, ecophilosophical resources, locations, and forces. The nomadic ethico-political project focuses on becomings as a pragmatic philosophy that stresses the need to act, to experiment with different modes of constituting subjectivity and different ways of inhabiting our corporeality. Accordingly, nomadic ethics is not about a master theory but rather about multiple micropolitical modes of daily activism. It is essential to put the "active" back into activism.

Zoē, or life as absolute vitality, however, is not above negativity, and it can hurt. It is always too much for the specific slab of enfleshed existence that single subjects actualize. It is a constant challenge for us to rise to the occasion, to catch the wave of life's intensities and ride it, exposing the boundaries or limits as we transgress them. We often crack in the process and just cannot take it anymore. The sheer activity of thinking about such intensity is painful: it causes intense strain, psychic unrest, and nervous tension. If thinking were pleasurable, more humans might be tempted to engage in this activity. Accelerations or increased intensities, however, are that which most humans prefer to avoid.

Crucial to this ethics of affirmation or affirmative compassion (as opposed to moral pity) is the concept of limit. For Spinoza-Deleuze the limit is built into the affective definition of subjectivity. Affectivity in fact is what activates an embodied subject, empowering him or her to interact with others. This acceleration of one's existential speed, or increase of one's affective temperature, is the dynamic process of becoming. It follows that a subject can think/understand/do/become no more than what he or she can take or sustain within his or her embodied, spatiotemporal coordinates. This deeply positive understanding of the human subject posits built-in, bioorganic limitations.

Thus the ethical challenge, as Nietzsche had recommended, consists in cultivating joyful modes of confronting the overwhelming intensity of *bios-zoē*. This implies approaching the world through affectivity and not cognition: as singularity, force, movement, through assemblages or webs of interconnections with all that lives. The subject is an autopoietic machine, fuelled by targeted perceptions, and it functions as the echoing chamber of *zoē*. This nonanthropocentric view expresses both a profound love for Life as a cosmic force and the desire to depersonalize subjective life-and-death. This is just one life, not *my* life. The life in "me" does not answer to my name: "I" is just passing.

To live intensely and be alive to the nth degree pushes us to the extreme edge of mortality. This has implications for the question of the limits, which are built-in to the very embodied and embedded structure of the subject. The limits are those of one's endurance — in the double sense of lasting in time and bearing the pain of confronting "Life" as *zoē*. The ethical subject is one that can bear this confrontation, cracking up a bit but without having its physical or affective intensity destroyed by it. Ethics consists in reworking the pain into a threshold of sustainability, when and if possible: cracking, but holding it, still.

Bios/Zoē Ethics and Thanatos

My understanding of "life" as the *bios-zoē* ethics of sustainable transformations differs considerably from what Giorgio Agamben (1998) calls "bare life" or "the rest" after the humanized "bio-logical" wrapping is taken over.[21] "Bare life" is that in you which sovereign power can kill: it is the body as disposable matter in the hands of the despotic force of power (*potestas*). Included as necessarily excluded, "bare life" inscribes fluid vitality at the heart of the mechanisms of capture of the state system. Agamben stresses that this vitality, or "aliveness," however, is all the more mortal for it. This is linked to Heidegger's theory of Being as deriving its force from the annihilation of animal life.

The position of *zoē* in Agamben's system is analogous to the role and the location of language in psychoanalytic theory: it is the site of constitution or "capture" of the subject. This "capture" functions by positing—as an a posteriori construction—a prelinguistic dimension of subjectivity which is apprehended as "always already" lost and out of reach. *Zoē*—like the prediscursive in Lacan, the *chora* of Kristeva, and the maternal feminine of Irigaray—becomes for Agamben the ever-receding horizon of an alterity which has to be included as necessarily excluded in order to sustain the framing of the subject in the first place. This introduces finitude as a constitutive element within the framework of subjectivity, which also fuels an affective political economy of loss and melancholia at the heart of the subject.[22]

In his important work on the totalitarian edge of regimes of "biopower," Agamben perpetuates the philosophical habit, which consists in taking mortality or finitude as the transhistorical horizon for discussions of "life." This fixation on Thanatos—which Nietzsche criticized over a century ago—is still very present in critical debates today. It often produces a gloomy and pessimistic vision not only of power but also of the technological developments that propel the regimes of biopower. I beg to differ from the habit that favors the deployment of the problem of *bios-zoē* on the horizon of death or of a liminal state of not-life or in the spectral economy of the never-dead. Instead, I prefer to stress the generative powers of *zoē* and to turn to the Spinozist political ontology defended by Deleuze and Guattari.[23] I propose to extend this positive approach to the discussion of death as well.

Speaking from the position of an embodied and embedded female subject, I find the metaphysics of finitude to be a myopic way of putting the question of the limits of what we call "life." It is not because Thanatos always wins out in the end that it should enjoy such conceptual high status. Death is overrated. The ultimate subtraction is after all only another phase in a generative process. Too bad that the relentless generative powers of death require the suppression of that which is the nearest and dearest to me, namely myself, my own vital being-there. For the narcissistic human subject, as psychoanalysis teaches us, it is unthinkable that Life should go on without my being there. The process of confronting the thinkability of a Life that may not have "me" or any "human" at the center is actually a sobering and instructive process. I see this postanthropocentric shift as the start for an ethics of sustainability that aims at shifting the focus toward the positivity of *zoē*. As Hardt and Negri suggest, Agamben fails to identify the materialist and productive dimension of this concept, making it in fact indifferent.[24]

The Question of Limits

I want to end this section with the suggestion that one of the reasons why the negative associations linked to pain, especially in relation to political processes of change, are ideologically laden is that it fits in with the logic of claims and compensations which is central to advanced capitalism. This is a form of institutionalized management of the negative that has become quite common also in gender and antiracism politics.

Two more problematic aspects need to be raised as a consequence. The first is that our culture tends to glorify pain by equating it with suffering, and it thus promotes an ideology of compensation. Contemporary culture has encouraged and rewarded a public morality based on the twin principles of claims and compensation. As if legal and financial settlements could constitute the answer to the injury suffered, the pain endured, and the long-lasting effects of the injustice. Cases that exemplify this trend are the compensation for the Shoah in the sense of restitution of stolen property, artworks, bank deposits; similar claims have been made by the descendants of slaves forcefully removed from Africa to North America,[25] and more recently there have been claims for compensation for damages caused by Soviet communism, notably the confiscation of properties across eastern Europe, both from Jewish and other former citizens. A great deal of contemporary mainstream feminism has also moved in the direction of claims and compensation. This makes affirmative ethics of transformation into a struggle against the mainstream. It also makes it appear more counterintuitive than it actually is.

The second problem is the force of habit. Starting from the assumption that a subject is a sedimentation of established habits, these can be seen as patterns of repetitions that consolidate modes of relation and forces of interaction. Habits are the frame within which nonunitary or complex subjects get reterritorialized, albeit temporarily. One of the established habits in our culture is to frame "pain" within a discourse and social practice of suffering which requires rightful compensation.

Equally strong is the urge to understand and empathize with pain. People go to great lengths in order to ease all pain. Great distress follows from not knowing or not being able to articulate the source of one's suffering, or from knowing it all too well, all the time. The yearning for solace, closure, and justice is understandable and worthy of respect.

This ethical dilemma was already posed by J. F. Lyotard and, much earlier, by Primo Levi about the survivors of Nazi concentration camps,[26] namely, that the kind of vulnerability we humans experience in the face of events on the scale of small or high horror is something for which no adequate compensation is even thinkable. It is just incommensurable: a hurt, or wound, beyond repair. This means that the notion of justice in the sense of a logic of rights and reparation is not applicable. For the poststructuralist Lyotard, ethics consists in accepting the impossibility of adequate compensation — and living with the open wound.

This is the road to an ethics of affirmation, which respects the pain but suspends the quest for both claims and compensation and resists the logic of retribution or rights. This is achieved through a sort of depersonalization of the event, which is the ultimate ethical challenge. The displacement of the "zoē"-indexed reaction reveals the fundamental meaninglessness of the hurt, the injustice, or injury one has suffered. "Why me?" is the refrain most commonly heard in situations of extreme distress. This expresses rage as well as anguish at one's ill fate. The answer is plain: actually, for no reason at all. Examples of this are the banality of evil in large-scale genocides like the Holocaust and the randomness of surviving them.[27] There is something intrinsically senseless about the pain, hurt, or injustice: lives are lost or saved for all and no reason at all. Why did some go to work in the World Trade Center on 9/11 while others missed the train? Why did Frida Kahlo take that tram which crashed so that she was impaled by a metal rod, and not the next one? For no reason at all. Reason has nothing to do with it. That's precisely the point. We need to delink pain from the quest for meaning and move beyond, to the next stage. That is the transformation of negative into positive passions.

This is not fatalism, and even less resignation, but rather a Nietzschean ethics of overturning the negative. Let us call it: *amor fati*: we have to be worthy of what happens to us and rework it within an ethics of relation. Of course repugnant and unbearable events do happen. Ethics consists, however, in reworking these events in the direction of positive relations. This is not carelessness or lack of compassion but rather a form of lucidity that acknowledges the meaninglessness of pain and the futility of compensation. It also reasserts that the ethical instance is not that of retaliation or compensation, but rather it rests on active transformation of the negative.

This requires a double shift. First, the affect itself moves from the frozen or reactive effect of pain to the proactive affirmation of its generative potential. Second, the line of questioning also shifts from the quest for the origin or source to a process of elaboration of the questions that express and enhance a subject's capacity to achieve freedom through the understanding of its limits. Biocentered egalitarianism breaks the expectation of mutual reciprocity that is central not only to liberal individualism but also to a poststructuralist ethics of otherness. Accepting the impossibility of mutual recognition and replacing it with one of mutual specification and mutual codependence is what is at stake in postsecular affirmative ethics. The ethical process of transforming negative into positive passions introduces time and motion into the frozen enclosure of seething pain. It is a postsecularist gesture of affirmation of hope, in the sense of creating the conditions for endurance and hence for a sustainable future.

What is an adequate ethical question? One that is capable of sustaining the subject in his or her quest for more interrelations with others, that is, more "Life," motion, change, and transformation. The adequate ethical question provides the subject with a frame for interaction and change, growth and movement. It affirms life as difference-at-work. An ethical question has to be adequate in relation to how much a body can take. How much can an embodied entity take in the mode of interrelations and connections, that is, how much freedom of action can we endure? Affirmative ethics assumes, following Nietzsche, that humanity does not stem from freedom but rather freedom is extracted from the awareness of limitations. Postsecular ethics is about freedom from the burden of negativity, freedom through the understanding of our bondage.

The Case of Intergenerational Justice

The last aspect of the postsecular ethics of affirmation I want to spell out is the generational time-lines — in the sense of the construction of social horizons of hope, that is, sustainable futures.

Modernity, as an ideology of progress, postulated boundless faith in the future as the ultimate destination of the human. Zygmunt Bauman quotes one of my favorite writers, Diderot, who stated that modern man is in love with posterity. Postmodernity, on the other hand, is death-bound and sets as its horizon the globalization process in terms of technological and economic interdependence. Capitalism has no built-in teleological purpose, historical logic, or structure but rather is a self-imploding system that will not stop at anything in order to fulfil its aim: profit. This inherently self-destructive system feeds on and thus destroys the very conditions of its survival: it is omnivorous, and what it ultimately eats is the future itself.

Being nothing more than this all-consuming entropic energy, capitalism lacks the ability to create anything new: it can merely promote the recycling of spent hopes, repackaged in the rhetorical frame of the " next generation of gadgets." Affirmative ethics expresses the desire to endure in time and thus clashes with the deadly spin of the present.

The future today is no longer the self-projection of the modernist subject: Eve and the New Jerusalem. It is a basic and rather humble act of faith in the possibility of endurance, as duration or continuity, which honors our obligation to the generations to come. It involves the virtual unfolding of the affirmative aspect of what we manage to actualize here and now. Virtual futures grow out of sustainable presents and vice-versa. This is how qualitative transformations can be actualized and transmitted along the genetic or time line. Transformative postsecular ethics takes on the future affirmatively, as the shared collective imagining that goes on becoming, to effect multiple modes of interaction with heterogeneous others. Futurity is made of this. Nonlinear evolution: an ethics that moves away from the paradigm of reciprocity and the logic of recognition and installs a rhizomic relation of mutual affirmation.

By targeting those who come after us as the rightful ethical interlocutors and assessors of our own actions, we are taking seriously the implications of our own situated position. This form of intergenerational justice is crucial. This point about intergenerational fairness need not, however, be expressed or conceptualized in the social imaginary as an Oedipal narrative. To be concerned about the future need not result in linearity, that is, in restating the unity of space and time as the horizon of subjectivity. On the contrary, nonlinear genealogical models of intergenerational decency are a way of displacing the Oedipal hierarchy.

These models of intergenerational decency involve a becoming-minoritarian of the elderly, the senior, and the parental figures, but also the de-Oedipalization of the bond of the young to those who preceded them. The process also calls for new ways of addressing and solving intergenerational conflicts — other than envy and rivalry — for joining forces across the generational divide by working together toward sustainable futures and practicing an ethics of nonreciprocity in the pursuit of affirmation.

An example: the older feminists may feel the cruel pinch of aging, but some of the young ones suffer from envy of the time period of the 1970s. The middle-aged survivors of the second wave may feel like war veterans or survivors but some of generation Y, as Iris van der Tuin taught me, call themselves "born-again baby boomers!"

So who's envying whom?

We are in *this* together, indeed. Those who go through life under the sign of the desire for change need accelerations that jolt them out of set habits; political thinkers of the postsecular era need to be visionary, prophetic, and upbeat — insofar as they are passionately committed to writing the prehistory of the future, which is to say, to introducing change in the present so as to affect multiple modes of belonging through complex and heterogeneous relations. This is the horizon of sustainable futures.

Hope is a sort of "dreaming forward," it is an anticipatory virtue that permeates our lives and activates them. It is a powerful motivating force grounded in our collective imaginings indeed. These collective imaginings express very grounded concerns for the multitude of "anybodies" (*homo tantum*) that compose the human community lest our greed and selfishness destroy or diminish it for generations to come. Given that posterity per definition can never pay us back, this gesture is perfectly gratuitous.

Against the general lethargy, the rhetoric of selfish genes and possessive individualism on the one hand, and the dominant ideology of the melancholic lament on the other, hope rests with an affirmative ethics of sustainable futures, a deep and careless generosity, the ethics of nonprofit at an ontological level.

Why should one pursue this project?

For no reason at all. Reason has nothing to do with this. Let's just do it for the hell of it and for love of the world.

Notes

1 Rose, "The Politics of Life Itself."
2 Fraser, Kember, and Lury, eds., *Inventive Life*.
3 Franklin, Lury, and Stacey, *Global Nature, Global Culture*.
4 For "neovitalism," see Fraser, Kember, and Lury, eds., *Inventive Life*, and for "vital politics," see Rose, "The Politics of Life Itself."
5 Fukuyama, *Our Posthuman Future*.
6 Habermas, *The Future of Human Nature*.
7 Springer, *Electronic Eros*.
8 Bukatman, *Terminal Identity*, 187.
9 Balsamo, *Technologies of the Gendered Body*, 1–2.
10 Castells, *The Rise of the Network Society*.
11 Ansell-Pearson, *Viroid Life*.
12 Parisi, "For a Schizogenesis of Sexual Difference."
13 Shiva, *Biopiracy*.
14 Rabinow, *Anthropos Today*; Esposito, *Bios*.
15 Agamben, *Homo Sacer*.
16 Haraway, *Modest_Witness@second_Millennium*; Gilroy, *Against Race*; Ben-

habib, *The Claims of Culture*; Butler, *Precarious Life*; Braidotti, *Metamorphoses*; Grosz, *The Nick of Time*.

17   Shiva, *Biopiracy*.

18   Deleuze, *Spinoza et le problème de l'expression*; Deleuze, *Logique du sens*; Deleuze, "L'immanence"; Guattari, *Chaosmosis*; Glissant, *Poétique de la relation*; Gatens and Lloyd, *Collective Imaginings*; Balibar, *Politics and the Other Scene*; Hardt and Negri, *Empire*.

19   Hayles, *How We Became Posthuman*.

20   Braidotti, *Metamorphoses*.

21   Agamben, *Homo Sacer*.

22   Braidotti, *Metamorphoses*.

23   Deleuze and Guattari, "Capitalisme énurgumène"; Deleuze and Guattari, *Mille plateaux*.

24   Hardt and Negri, *Empire*.

25   Gilroy, *Against Race*.

26   Lyotard, *Le Différend*.

27   Arendt, *Eichmann in Jerusalem*.

ECONOMIES OF DISRUPTION

Rey Chow

The Elusive Material,
What the Dog Doesn't Understand

> Take your dog with you to the butcher and
> watch how much he understands of the goings
> on when you purchase your meat. It is a great
> deal and even includes a keen sense of prop-
> erty which will make him snap at a stranger's
> hand daring to come near the meat his master
> has obtained and which he will be allowed to
> carry home in his mouth. But when you have
> to tell him, "Wait, doggy, I haven't paid yet!"
> his understanding is at an end.
>
> ALFRED SOHN-RETHEL

The Problematic of the Material

In a study of the centrality of commodity exchange in modern times, *Intellectual and Manual Labour: A Critique of Epistemology*, the German Marxist scholar Alfred Sohn-Rethel
suggests the above experiment of taking a dog to the
butcher as a way to discover the specifically human quality
of the exchange practice.[1] Offering an erudite account
of the historical knowledge about human labor (in what
evolved to become political economy) and its gradual division from the sphere of "science," Sohn-Rethel's book is a
perceptive response to Marx's famous statement: "It is not
the consciousness of men that determines their being, but,
on the contrary, their social being that determines their
consciousness."[2] As the narrative of "Wait, doggy, I haven't
paid yet!" demonstrates, this "social being" may be best
identified in what Sohn-Rethel calls the exchange abstrac-

tion, which originated in ancient times and reached its completion under capitalism. Sohn-Rethel goes on:

> The pieces of metal or paper which he [the dog] watches you hand over, and which carry your scent, he knows, of course; he has seen them before. But their function as money lies outside the animal range. *It is not related to our natural or physical being, but comprehensible only in our interrelations as human beings.* It has reality in time and space, has the quality of a real occurrence taking place between me and the butcher and requiring a means of payment of material reality. *The meaning of this action registers exclusively in our human minds and yet has definite reality outside it — a social reality, though, sharply contrasting with the natural realities accessible to my dog.*[3]

As Sohn-Rethel argues throughout his book, this social being, unique to humans, exists as a kind of paradox: although it arises in the spatio-temporal sphere of human interrelations, its reality is typically outside the actors' conscious comprehension at the moment of the exchange. (In other words, human beings participate in this exchange spontaneously and unconsciously, without knowing or thinking much about it: as the French historian Paul Veyne puts it in another context, "The role of consciousness is not to make us notice the world but to allow us to move within it."[4]) In order to underscore this significance of the exchange abstraction as what happens *outside* the historicality of human consciousness, Sohn-Rethel goes so far as to state, "The exchange abstraction excludes everything that makes up history, human and even natural history. The entire empirical reality of facts, events and description by which one moment and locality of time and space is distinguishable from another is wiped out."[5]

By foregrounding the formal, or structural, specificity of commodity exchange in this dramatic manner, Sohn-Rethel is pointing to a problematic that reverberates as well throughout contemporary theoretical debates: what exactly do we mean when we invoke terms such as "materialism" and "materiality"?

On the one hand, of course, is the traditional philosophical understanding of materialism/materiality as matter and content, as it appears, for instance, even in the classic Marxist vocabulary of sensuousness (traceable to the essentialist humanism of Feuerbach), manual labor, and raw materials. Materialism/materiality in this instance stands as the dialectic opposite of idealism, for which all things originate in the form of ideas, perhaps in the mind of some higher being. On the other hand, as Sohn-Rethel writes, Marx's painstaking analysis of commodity fetishism at the beginning of *Capital* has drawn attention to a process, a type of relation, that is not physically or sensorially perceptible and that nonetheless underlies and regulates interpersonal transactions of property ownership. This abstract or "mystical" process, in which, as Marx repeatedly reminds us, *things are other than what they seem*, constitutes nothing less than a radicalized epistemic frame and medium of signification in which the meanings of human activities unfold not only according to apparently rational, numerically calculable expenditures, profits, and balances but also according to an ongoing situation of inequity, a struggle between labor and capital. Understood in this sense, materialism/materiality is no longer simply inert matter, content, or essence but rather a long-standing series of interpersonal transactions of conflicting interests, bearing significances of cunning, manipulation, and exploitation that lie considerably beyond the dog's world. Needless to say, by amplifying the exchange abstraction and dramatizing it as definitively exclusive of "history," the "entire empirical reality of facts, events," and so forth, Sohn-Rethel has not exactly resolved the large, messy question of social inequity behind Marx's analysis. However, by underscoring the specifically human character of such exchange, he has helped crystallize and delimit the conceptual issues at stake.

Remembering another of Marx's famous remarks, in the eleventh and last of his *Theses on Feuerbach*, that "the philosophers have only *interpreted* the world in various ways; the point however is to *change* it,"[6] it would be logical to conclude that this problematic of materialism and materiality — reformulated by subsequent generations of scholars such as Sohn-Rethel as a second-order nature, unique to human undertakings and irreducible to nonhuman or animal nature — is implicitly linked to the ethical imperative of bringing about improved human (and perhaps nonhuman) conditions. In this linkage, the material is conceived of as, or analogized with, agency — more precisely, an agency of motion and transformation, an agency aimed at an increasingly *better* (that is, more advanced, more enlightened, and more democratic) world.[7]

In what follows, I would like to explore, in reference to a number of contemporary theorists, the extent to which this implied and often presumed mutual linkage among these key terms — materialism/materiality (understood as human activity), change (understood as progress), and agency — is ineluctable. As Paul Veyne puts it succinctly, "How can one do better than a philosophy of consciousness and still avoid falling into the aporias of Marxism?"[8] In other words, what if we were to adopt Marxism's focus on materialism/materiality (as a way to critique the philosophy of consciousness), yet without defining it (as Marxism tends to) as an agency of change-as-improvement? Or what if we argued that change-as-improvement is not necessarily the most crucial aspect of materialism/materiality? Would delinking these terms be at all conceivable — and what would be some of the consequences?

Poststructuralist Interventions

The long-standing popular tendency to equate materialism with matter — and thus with what is thought to be fundamental and concrete — has led, in the case of classic Marxist thinking, to the privileging of the so-called infrastructure or economic base, often at the expense of a proper investigation of the so-called superstructure. This was in part what led the French Marxist philosopher Louis Althusser to advance his rereading of ideology in terms of the critical role it plays in constituting the human subject. In his influential essay "Ideology and Ideological State Apparatuses (Notes towards an Investigation)," written in the 1960s, Althusser goes against the custom in classic Marxism of associating ideology with "false consciousness" by arguing, instead, that ideology has a "material existence" in an apparatus and its practice or practices. Rather than a matter of false consciousness, he holds, ideology is the representation of an imaginary relationship between people and the social structure in which they live their lives on a daily basis. "What is represented in ideology," Althusser writes, "is . . . not the system of real relations which govern the existence of individuals, but the imaginary relation of these individuals to the real relations in which they live."[9] By emphasizing the notion of the imaginary, what Althusser intended was not (simply) that ideology resides in people's heads but, more important, that its functioning is inextricable from the intangible yet nondismissible, and therefore material, *psychosomatic mediation* involved in subject formation. Ideology works because, in the process of coming to terms with it, people become "interpellated" — are hailed, constituted, and affirmed — as socially viable and coherent subjects, as who they (need to) think or believe they are. This process of interpellation, a process in which body and soul imbricate each other inseparably, lies at the heart of Althusser's formulation of materialism / materiality-as-practice.

As is well known, Althusser's recasting of ideology in these terms was indebted to Jacques Lacan's poststructuralist psychoanalysis of the subject,[10] but what is equally remarkable is that he also drew his rationale from Blaise Pascal's provocative (and to some blasphemous) ruminations on traditional religious worship, thus enabling an articulation of materialism / materiality to action, practice, ritual, and apparatus:

> [We] are indebted to Pascal's defensive "dialectic" for the wonderful formula which will enable us to invert the order of the notional schema of ideology. Pascal says more or less: "Kneel down, move your lips in prayer, and you will believe." He thus scandalously inverts the order of things. . . .
>
> . . . where only a single subject (such and such an individual) is concerned, the existence of the ideas of his belief is material in that *his ideas are his material actions inserted into material practices governed by material rituals which are themselves defined by the material ideological apparatus from which derive the ideas of that subject.*[11]

Through Pascal, Althusser inverts the conventionally assumed relationship between consciousness and actions. It is, he argues, actions (such as the human routines of worship) that produce consciousness (such as belief in God) rather than the other way around, and it is this inverted process that leads to the production — and successful interpellation — of the so-called human subject.

Whereas Althusser traces ideology's function of interpellation back to the Christian church, the Slovenian theorist Slavoj Žižek identifies such a function in the operations of the secular, totalitarian state, as he demonstrates with characteristic good humor in *The Sublime Object of Ideology* and numerous other works since the early 1990s. As Žižek understands it, totalitarianism is a superb instance of how ideology works in an atheist universe, with a logic that resembles Pascal's and that may be paraphrased as follows: Even if I cannot prove that there is a God or Great Party Leader, my (material) acting *as if* there were one would give me great practical benefits. I pray, then I believe; I support the Great Party Leader, then he exists. In other words, just as the prayers and practices of the churchgoers authenticate God, so also do the loyal and submissive acts of the people in a totalitarian regime substantiate the reality of the Great Party Leader. Žižek refers to this logic as the Pascalian-Marxian argument, "It is as if the totalitarian Leader is addressing his subjects and legitimizing his power precisely by referring to the . . . Pascalian-Marxian argument— that is, revealing to them the secret of the classical Master; basically, he is saying to them: 'I'm your Master because you treat me as your Master; it is you, with your activity, who make me your Master!' "[12]

The signature intervention made by poststructuralist theory in this instance is thus a transformation of the classic Marxist opposition between "head" and "hand" (or superstructure and base, or thoughts and actions) into what may be called the determinacy of the signifier—whether that signifier be in the form of language, practice, or ritual—in the fundamental constitution of subjectivity.[13] Accordingly, any evaluation of the legacy of Marxism and its particular claim to materialism/materiality would need, in my view, to come to terms with this paradigm shift from the (time-honored and still prevalent) conflation of materialism with economism to a revamped materialism defined primarily as signification and subjectivity-in-process.[14] A major outcome of this revamped materialism/ materiality—or, more precisely, this alternative appropriation of, or claim to, the material—is the dethronement—and reconceptualization—of what used to be called consciousness. Rather than a unified "being" with a rational "mind" or "consciousness," the human subject is now drastically repositioned as the never-quite-complete product of an ongoing structuring process, a process that may be imperceptible and yet is materially evident and undeniable as effect. As a form of agency, therefore, the status of materialism/materiality has, with such poststructuralist interventions, moved from being a preexisting concrete ground (for example, "economic base") to being a destabilizable chain of signification, the certitude of which is at best provisional and subject to slippage.

The Question of Iteration

In so far as they unanimously displace the phenomenon of consciousness (what used to be considered as an inner or prior mental condition) onto material practices, the accounts by Sohn-Rethel, Althusser, and Žižek share important epistemic insights. As Žižek remarks of Sohn-Rethel's argument: "The abstraction appertaining to the act of exchange is in an irreducible way external, decentered."[15] Pretty much the same can be said of religious belief and panjandrum worship. However, a crucial dimension to these theorists' reconceptualization of consciousness remains to be explored in its full intricacy.

In these theorists' depictions of commodity exchange, religion, and totalitarianism, readers should have noticed that, although materialism/materiality is no longer understood as inert matter or content, it is not exactly equated with "mind" either. What these theorists call for is not a simple swapping of places between materialism and idealism. Instead, something else is revealed in the process, complicating the picture of this revamped materialism that is, in the final analysis, neither inert matter nor pure mentation. In his work, Žižek defines this something else by the term "sublime object." Using money as his primary example, he alludes to the sublime object in a manner that reminds us of Ferdinand de Saussure's description of language: "We have touched a problem unsolved by Marx, that of the *material* character of money: not of the empirical, material stuff money is made of, but of the *sublime* material, of that other 'indestructible and immutable' body which persists beyond the corruption of the body physical. . . . This immaterial corporeality of the 'body within the body' gives us a precise definition of the sublime object."[16] Going a step further, we may ask: how does this sublimity, this "immaterial corporeality" that is at once absent and present, occur? How does it come into being in the first place?

Well, what do the exchanges of commodities, the prayers and rituals in church, and the submissive acts (including speech acts) toward the Great Party Leader have in common? However little noticed, is it not a certain *iterative behavior*? Are not the *mindless repetitions* — repetitions that escape, that do not require "consciousness," as it were — precisely what make the realities of interpersonal monetary transactions, God, and the Great Party Leader *materialize*, even as they then become misrecognized as the originating "causes"?

Although they are seldom discussed in conjunction with each other, Žižek's proposal of the sublime object of ideology calls to mind the French literary and cultural critic René Girard's well-known argument about the mimetic basis of human social interaction. For Girard, some readers may recall, mimesis, the act of imitation, is not simply a (temporally subsequent) response to something that exists beforehand; it is, instead, the originating impulse, the primary event that engenders its own momentum and power of contagion. In close parallel to the aforementioned theorists' radicalization of consciousness, Girard reconceptualizes "desire" by showing how, rather than residing in a repressed manner inside individual human beings, desire may be seen as the outcome of social or group relations: we desire something, he suggests, not because that something is intrinsically desirable but because we notice that someone else desires it. Desire (like consciousness) is thus mimetic, to be located in the interstices of interactions between people. In the context of our present discussion, it might be appropriate to recast mimesis as a variety of iterative behavior and to see Girard's paradigm as another demonstration of how, to cite Žižek again, "the abstraction appertaining to the act of exchange is in an irreducible way external, decentered."

Precisely because it is blind—the classic case being a mob in which people echo, mimic, and repeat each other without thinking—mimetic behavior for Girard always contains the potential for violence and destruction, which must be forestalled by temporary remedies (such as sacrifice and scapegoating, which Girard identifies in myth, religion, art, and other age-old cultural practices).[17] Although Sohn-Rethel, Althusser, and Žižek do not seem to view iterative behavior with the same pessimistic sense of a catastrophe in the making, their narratives—especially of the Christian church (Althusser) and the totalitarian state (Žižek)—amount to an unambiguous recognition of mimetic behavior's alarming manifestation as spontaneous (that is, "unthinking") surrender to authoritarianism, religious or secular. Even in the case of the commodified exchange abstraction, as Sohn-Rethel presents it, what is clearly foregrounded is a kind of automatized habit or reflex action—a "doing" that proceeds matter-of-factly without the actors' "knowing" or "reflecting." In short, notwithstanding the destabilizable nature of signification, these theorists' writings register in various forms of iterative behavior an unmistakable sense of the potential of terror.

Iteration as the Agency of Change
toward a Better World?

In this light, an account that draws on iteration for a sense of hope, however qualified, such as the argument of gender as performance by the American theorist Judith Butler, is particularly thought provoking. In the essay "Imitation and Gender Insubordination" and other renowned works such as *Gender Trouble* and *Bodies That Matter*,[18] Butler advances the compelling point that all gendered identities may be considered as impersonation and approximation of an original that does not exist. Taking as her point of departure the conventional homophobic assumption that lesbianism (or gayness) is a derivative identity, secondary and inferior to the norm of heterosexuality, Butler argues that such derivativeness can — and should — instead be redeployed in the service of displacing hegemonic heterosexual norms. If lesbianism is dismissed as a mere imitation, a bad copy, she writes, "the political problem is not to establish the specificity of lesbian sexuality over and against its derivativeness, but to turn the homophobic construction of the bad copy against the framework that privileges heterosexuality as origin."[19]

If, for some of our other theorists, repetitive group behavior often constitutes the basis for ideological and political terror, for Butler, repetitive behavior rather constitutes the basis for psychic and social subversion. Taking her hint, among other things, from Jacques Derrida's inversion and displacement of mimesis in "The Double Session," Butler contends that "*imitation* does not copy that which is prior, but produces and *inverts* the very terms of priority and derivativeness."[20] Her logic may be glimpsed in the following, nuanced fleshing-out of her general argument about identity politics:

> It is through the repeated play of this sexuality that the "I" is insistently reconstituted as a lesbian "I"; paradoxically, it is precisely the *repetition* of that play that establishes as well the *instability* of the very category that it constitutes. For if the "I" is a site of repetition, that is, if the "I" only achieves the semblance of identity through a certain repetition of itself, then the I is always displaced by the very repetition that sustains it. In other words, does or can the "I" ever repeat itself, cite itself, faithfully, or is there always a displacement from its former moment

that establishes the permanently non-self-identical status of that "I" or its "being lesbian"? *What "performs" does not exhaust the "I"; it does not lay out in visible terms the comprehensive content of that "I," for if the performance is "repeated," there is always the question of what differentiates from each other the moments of identity that are repeated.*[21]

Or, as she similarly formulates it in another context:

I would suggest that performativity cannot be understood outside of a process of iterability, a regularized and constrained repetition of norms. And this repetition is not performed *by* a subject; this repetition is what enables a subject and constitutes the temporal condition for the subject. This iterability implies that "performance" is not a singular "act" or event, but a ritualized production, a ritual reiterated under and through constraint, under and through the force of prohibition and taboo, with the threat of ostracism and even death controlling and compelling the shape of the production, *but not, I will insist, determining it fully in advance.*[22]

Whereas the very contingency of iteration — its inherent instability — represents for Althusser, Žižek, and Girard a potential for instrumentalization by institutions of power such as the church or the state, institutions which typically capitalize on such contingency for purposes of domination and indoctrination, for Butler, precisely the same contingency lends itself to the chance of differentiation — "What 'performs' does not exhaust the 'I'" or "[determine] it fully in advance" — and thus to the possibility of subversion. In this way, even the oppressive conformity inscribed in the speeches, actions, and rituals of, say, compulsory heterosexual normativity becomes, paradoxically, a kind of still-malleable material, a porous "ground" on which alternative performances (of seemingly fixed identities) may be reiterated, played out, and reinvented. As Butler writes: "if there is *agency*, it is to be found, paradoxically, in the possibilities opened up in and by that constrained appropriation of the regulatory law, by the materialization of that law, the compulsory appropriation and identification with those normative demands."[23]

Interestingly, then, although she begins with a comparable poststructuralist reconceptualization of consciousness, whereby the primacy of consciousness is overthrown and displaced onto repeated material processes (including speech acts and embodied performances), Butler seems to arrive at a very different kind of conclusion as to the potentiality of the fundamentally changed relationship between — to recall Marx's words — "consciousness" and "social being." Where the other theorists emphasize or imply probable scenarios of horror, disaster, and sacrifice (scenarios that may be ideologically inscribed without the use of physical violence, politically instituted with physical violence, or both), Butler, in a utopian gesture that categorically refutes the likelihood of complete self-identity (that is, closure) in any type of signification, holds onto a hope for freedom,[24] for a *possible* disruption of that "process of materialization that stabilizes over time to produce the effect of boundary, fixity, and surface we call matter."[25]

In this confrontation between terror and freedom, has materialism/ materiality arrived at a crossroads, or an inevitable impasse, marked as it seems to be by ultimately incommensurable analytic intentions, leanings, and passions? Might such a confrontation signal that the time is ripe for a realignment of the conceptual stakes involved — as is suggested, for instance, by the questions I pose near the beginning?

That is to say, if, after poststructuralism, attempts to lay claim to materialism/materiality are irrevocably traversed by an insistence on the determinacy of the signifier (understood broadly as language, action, practice, ritual, or gendered orientation and behavior) and if, by the same theoretical orientation, the signifier is recognized as what works by iteration, would iteration henceforth have to become the only viable way to imagine agency? (Can there be other ways?) And yet, all too clearly, as much as a potentiality for radical social transformation ("progress"; "freedom"), such agency also embeds in it the potentiality for sustaining and reinforcing relations of subordination, subjugation, and social unevenness. How, then, should we rethink the hitherto presumed mutual — and arguably circular — linkages among materialism, agency, and change-as-improvement? What forms of disarticulation and rearticulation would be possible — indeed, would be necessary?

Whatever it is about the material that the dog doesn't understand, we too are far from puzzling out . . .

Notes

1   Sohn-Rethel, *Intellectual and Manual Labour*, 45.

2   Marx, preface (1859) to *A Contribution to the Critique of Political Economy*, 356.

3   Sohn-Rethel, *Intellectual and Manual Labour*, 45; my emphases.

4   Veyne, "Foucault Revolutionizes History," 157.

5   Sohn-Rethel, *Intellectual and Manual Labour*, 48–49.

6   Marx, *Theses on Feuerbach*, 3.

7   Civilization, as it is understood by Western historians such as Hegel, a major influence on Marx, has always stood for *progress* in time. For an interesting critique of this predominant notion of history, see Guha, *History at the Limit of World-History*, in particular chap. 2, "Historicality and the Prose of the World."

8   Veyne, "Foucault Revolutionizes History," 179.

9   Althusser, *Lenin and Philosophy and Other Essays*, 125–26, 155.

10 For an informative discussion, see Coward and Ellis, *Language and Materialism*, in particular chaps. 5 and 6.

11 Althusser, *Lenin and Philosophy and Other Essays*, 168–69; emphasis his.

12 Žižek, *The Sublime Object of Ideology*, 146.

13 I have discussed other figures associated with poststructuralism elsewhere and will not repeat myself here. See, for instance, "Poststructuralism" and *The Age of the World Target*, introduction and chap. 2.

14 See the helpful discussions in Coward and Ellis, *Language and Materialism*.

15 Žižek, *The Sublime Object of Ideology*, 19.

16 Ibid., 18; emphases his. Interestingly, when he made his point about language, Saussure also used money as an analogy: "It is impossible for sound alone, a material element, to belong to language. . . . All our conventional values have the characteristic of not being confused with the tangible element which supports them. For instance, it is not the metal in a piece of money that fixes its value. A coin nominally worth five francs may contain less than half its worth of silver. Its value will vary according to the amount stamped upon it and according to its use inside or outside a political boundary. This is even more true of the linguistic signifier, which is not phonic but incorporeal — constituted not by its material substance but by the differences that separate its sound-image from all others." Saussure, *Course in General Linguistics*, 118–19.

17 For a more detailed discussion of the implications of Girard's work, see my "Sacrifice, Mimesis, and the Theorizing of Victimhood."

18 See Butler, "Imitation and Gender Insubordination"; *Gender Trouble*, in particular chap. 3; *Bodies That Matter*, in particular the introduction and part 1.

19 Butler, "Imitation and Gender Insubordination," 304.

20 Ibid., 307; emphases hers. See also Derrida, "The Double Session," 173–286.

21 Butler, "Imitation and Gender Insubordination," 304; first two emphases hers, last emphasis mine.

22 Butler, *Bodies That Matter*, 95; first emphasis hers, second emphasis mine.

23 Ibid., 12; emphasis hers.

24 This sense of freedom is, admittedly, qualified because agency can only be inscribed in reiterative practice: "The paradox of subjectivation (*assujetisse-ment*) is precisely that the subject who would resist such norms is itself enabled, if not produced, by such norms. Although this constitutive constraint does not foreclose the possibility of agency, it does locate agency as a reiterative or rearticulatory practice, immanent to power, and not a relation of external opposition to power." Ibid., 15.

25 This is the definition of matter that Butler proposes for thinking about gendered subjectivity in place of "conceptions of construction"; see ibid., 9.

Sara Ahmed

Orientations Matter

This essay attempts to show why and how orientations matter. To say orientations matter affects how we think "matter." Orientations might shape how matter "matters." If matter is affected by orientations, by the ways in which bodies are directed toward things, it follows that matter is dynamic, unstable, and contingent. What matters is itself an effect of proximities: we are touched by what comes near, just as what comes near is affected by directions we have already taken. Orientations are how the world acquires a certain shape through contact between bodies that are not in a relation of exteriority. In thinking the dynamism of matter, this essay joins a body of scholarship that has been called by the editors of this volume a "critical materialism." I would nonetheless resist calling my own contribution a "new" materialism inasmuch as my own work draws on, and is indebted to, earlier feminist engagements with phenomenology that were undertaken during the period of "the cultural turn." These phenomenological engagements belie the claim made by some recent materialist critics to the effect that, during this period, matter was the only thing that did not matter.[1]

Orientations matter. Let's say I am oriented toward writing. This means writing would be something that mattered, as well as something I do. To sustain such an orientation would mean certain objects must be available to me (tables, computers, pens, paper). Orientations shape how the world coheres around me. Orientations affect what is near or proximate to the body, those objects that we do things with.

Orientations thus "matter" in both senses of the word "matter." First, orientations matter in the simple sense that orientations are significant and important. To be oriented in a certain way is how certain things come to be significant, come to be objects *for me*. Such orientations are not only personal. Spaces too are oriented in the sense that certain bodies are "in place" in this or that place. The study might be oriented around the writer, who is then "in place" in the study. To say spaces are oriented around certain bodies is to show how some bodies will be more "in place" than others.

Orientations also matter in the second sense of being about physical or corporeal substance. Orientations shape the corporeal substance of bodies and whatever occupies space. Orientations affect how subjects and objects materialize or come to take shape in the way that they do. The writer writes, and the labor of writing shapes the surface of the writer's body. The objects used for writing are shaped by the intention to write; they are assembled around the support they give. Orientations are about how matter surfaces by being directed in one way or another.

In this essay, I take "the table" as my primary object for thinking about how orientations matter. Why tables? Tables matter, you could say, as objects we do things on. We could describe the table as an "on" device; the table provides a surface on which we place things as well as do things. If we do things on tables, then tables are effects of what we do. To explore how tables function as orientation devices, I will bring together Marxism and phenomenology. My aim is to consider how the materialization of bodies involves forms of labor that disappear in the familiarity or "given-ness" of objects such as tables. My analysis of how orientations matter will thus combine historical materialism with a materialism of the body.

Starting Points

If we start with the point of orientations, we find that orientations are about starting points. As Husserl describes in the second volume of *Ideas*: "If we consider the characteristic way in which the Body presents itself and do the same for things, then we find the following situation: each Ego has its own domain of perceptual things and necessarily perceives the things in a certain orientation. The things that appear do so from this or that side, and in this mode of appearing is included irrevocably a relation to a here and its basic directions."[2] Orientations are about how we begin, how we proceed from "here." Husserl relates the questions of "this or that side" to the point of "here," which he also describes as the zero-point of orientation, the point from which the world unfolds and which makes what is "there" over "there." It is also given that we are "here" only at this point, that near and far are lived as relative markers of distance. Alfred Schutz and Thomas Luckmann also describe orientation as a question of one's starting point: "The place in which I find myself, my actual 'here', is the starting point for my orientation in space."[3] The starting point for orientation is the point from which the world unfolds: the "here" of the body and the "where" of its dwelling.

At what point does the world unfold? Or at what point does Husserl's world unfold? Let's start where he starts, in his first volume of *Ideas*, which is with the world as it is given "from the natural standpoint." Such a world is the world that we are "in" as the world that takes place around me: "I am aware of a world, spread out in space endlessly."[4] This world is not simply spread out; it has already taken certain shapes, which are the very form of what is "more and less" familiar:

> For me real objects are there, definite, more or less familiar, agreeing with what is actually perceived without being themselves perceived or even intuitively present. I can let my attention wander from the writing-table I have just seen or observed, through the unseen portions of the room behind my back to the veranda into the garden, to the children in the summer house, and so forth, to all the objects concerning which I precisely "know" that they are there and yonder in my immediate co-perceived surroundings.[5]

The familiar world begins with the writing table, which is in the room: we can name this room as Husserl's study, as the room in which he writes. *It is from here that the world unfolds*. He begins with the writing table, and then turns to other parts of the room, those which are, as it were, behind him. We are reminded that what we can see in the first place depends on which way we are facing. Having begun here, with what is in front of his front and behind his back, Husserl then turns to other spaces, which he describes as rooms, and which he knows are there insofar as they are already given to him as places by memory. These other rooms are coperceived: they are not singled out; and they do not have his attention.

By noticing the objects that appear in Husserl's writing, we get a sense of how being directed toward some objects and not others involves a more general orientation toward the world. The philosopher is oriented toward the writing table, as the object on which writing happens, which means keeping other things and rooms relegated to the background. After all, it is not surprising that philosophy is full of tables. As Ann Banfield observes in her wonderful book *The Phantom Table*: "Tables and chairs, things nearest to hand for the sedentary philosopher, who comes to occupy chairs of philosophy, are the furniture of that 'room of one's own' from which the real world is observed."[6] Tables are "near to hand" along with chairs as the furniture that secures the very "place" of philosophy. The use of tables shows us the very orientation of philosophy in part by showing us what is proximate to the body of the philosopher or what the philosopher comes into contact with.

Even if Husserl's writing table first appears as being in front of him, it does not necessarily keep its place. For Husserl suggests that phenomenology must "bracket" or put aside what is given, what is made available by ordinary perception. If phenomenology is to see the table, he suggests, it must see "without" the natural attitude, which keeps us within the familiar, and indeed, within the space already "decided" as "being" the family home. Phenomenology, in Husserl's formulation, can come into being as a first philosophy only if it suspends all that gathers together as a natural attitude, not through Cartesian doubt but through a way of perceiving the world "as if" one did not assume its existence as taking some forms rather than others.[7]

So Husserl begins again by taking the table as an object that matters in a different way. How does the object appear when it is no longer familiar? As he describes: "We start by taking an example. Keeping this table steadily in view as I go round it, changing my position in space all the time, I have continually the consciousness of the bodily presence out there of this one and the self-same table, which in itself remains unchanged throughout" (vol. 1, 130). We can see here how Husserl turns to "the table" as an object by looking at it rather than over it. The bracketing means "this table" becomes "the table." By beginning with the table, on its own, as it were, the object appears self-same. It is not that the object's self-sameness is available at first sight. Husserl moves around the table, changing his position. For such movement to be possible, consciousness must flow: we must not be interrupted by other matters. As Husserl elaborates:

> I close my eyes. The other senses are inactive in relation to the table. I have now no perception of it. I open my eyes and the perception returns. The perception? Let us be more accurate. Under no circumstances does it return to me individually the same. *Only the table is the same*, known as identical through the synthetic consciousness, which connects the new experience with the recollection. The perceived thing can be, without being perceived, without my being aware of it even as a potential only (in the way, actuality, as previously described) and perhaps even without itself changing at all. But the perception itself is what it is within the steady flow of consciousness, and is itself constantly in flux; the perceptual now is ever passing over into the adjacent consciousness of the just-past, a new now simultaneously gleams forth, and so on. (vol. 1, 130, emphasis added)

This argument suggests the table as object is given, as "the same," as a givenness which "holds" or is shaped by the "flow" of perception. This is precisely Husserl's point: the object is intended through perception. As Robert Sokolowski puts it, "When we perceive an object, we do not just have a flow of profiles, a series of impressions; in and through them all, we have one and the same object given to us, and the identity of the object is intended and given."[8] Each new impression is connected with what has gone before, in the very form of an active "re-collection." Significantly, the object becomes an object of perception only given this work of recollection, such that the "new" exists in relation to what is already gathered by consciousness: each impression is linked to the other, so that the object becomes more than the profile that is available in any moment.

Given this, the sameness of the object involves the specter of absence and nonpresence. I do not see it as itself. I cannot view the table from all points of view at once. Given that the table's sameness can only be intended, Husserl makes what is an extraordinary claim: *Only the table remains the same*. The table is the only thing that keeps its place in the flow of perception. The sameness of the table is hence spectral. If the table is the same, it is only because we have conjured its missing sides. Or, we can even say that we have conjured its behind. I want to relate what is "missed" when we "miss" the table to the spectrality of history, what we miss may be behind the table in another sense: what is behind the table is what must have already taken place for the table to arrive.

Backgrounds and Arrivals

As we have seen, phenomenology, for Husserl, means apprehending the object as if it was unfamiliar, so that we can attend to the flow of perception itself. What this flow of perception tells is the partiality of absence as well as presence: what we do not see (say, the back or side of the object) is hidden from view and can only be intended. We single out this object only by pushing other objects to the edges or "fringes" of vision.

Husserl suggests that inhabiting the familiar makes "things" into backgrounds for action: they are there, but they are there in such a way that I don't see them. The background is a *"dimly apprehended depth or fringe of indeterminate reality."*[9] So although Husserl faces his writing table, it does not mean the table is singled out as an object. Even though the table is before him, it might also be in the background. My argument in the previous section needs some qualification: even when Husserl faces the writing table, it does not necessarily follow that the table is "in front" of him. What we face can also be part of the background, suggesting that the background may include more and less proximate objects. It is not accidental that when Husserl brings "the table" to the front, the writing table disappears. Being orientated toward the writing table might even provide the condition of possibility for its disappearance.

Husserl's approach to the background as what is "unseen" in its "thereness" or "familiarity" allows us to consider how the familiar takes shape by being unnoticed. I want to extend his model by thinking about the "background" of the writing table in another sense. Husserl considers how this table might be *in* the background as well as the background that is *around* the table, when "it" comes into view. I want us to consider how the table itself may *have* a background. The background would be understood as that which must take place in order for something to arrive. We can recall the different meanings of the word "background." A background can refer to the ground or parts situated in the rear, or to the portions of the picture represented at a distance, which in turn allows what is "in" the foreground to acquire the shape that it does. Both of these meanings point to the spatiality of the background. We can also think of the background as having a temporal dimension.[10] When we tell a story about someone, for instance, we might give their background: this meaning of "background" would be about "what is behind," where "what is behind" refers to what is in the past or what happened before. We might also speak of "family background," which would refer not just to the past of an individual but to other kinds of histories which shape an individual's arrival into the world and through which the family itself becomes a social given.

At least two entities have to arrive for there to be an encounter, a "bringing forth" in the sense of an occupation. So, this table and Husserl have to "co-incide" for him to write his philosophy about "the table." We must remember not to forget the dash in "co-incidence," as such a forgetting would turn shared arrival into a matter of chance. To "co-incide" suggests how different things happen at the same moment, a happening which brings things near to other things, whereby the nearness shapes the shape of each thing. If being near to this or that object is not a matter of chance, what happens in the "now" of this nearness remains open, in the sense that we do not always know how things will affect each other, or how we will be affected by things.[11]

So, if phenomenology is to attend to the background, it might do so by giving an account of the conditions of emergence for something, which would not necessarily be available in how that thing presents itself to consciousness. If we do not see (but intend) the behind of the object, we might also not see (but intend) its background in this temporal sense. We need to face the background of an object, redefined as the conditions for the emergence of not only the object (we might ask: how did it arrive?) but also the act of perceiving the object, which depends on the arrival of the body that perceives. The background to perception might involve such intertwining histories of arrival, which would explain how Husserl got near enough to his table, as the object that secures the very place of philosophy.

Marxism allows us to rethink the object as not only in history but as an effect of historical processes. The Marxian critique of German Idealism begins after all with a critique of the idea that the object is "in the present" or that the object is "before me." As Marx and Engels describe, in their critique of Feuerbach:

He does not see how the sensuous world around him is, not a thing given direct from all eternity, remaining ever the same, but the product of industry, and of the state of society; and indeed, in the sense that it is a historical product, and the result of the activity of a whole succession of generations, each standing on the shoulders of the preceding one, developing its industry and its intercourse, modifying its social system, according to its changed needs. Even the objects of the simplest "sensuous certainty" are only given to him through social demands, industry and commercial intercourse. The cherry-tree, like almost all fruit trees, was, as is well known, only in a few centuries, transplanted by commerce into our zone, and therefore only by the action of a definite society in a definite age has it become "sensuous certainty" for Feuerbach.[12]

If we were simply to "look at" the object we face, then we would be erasing the "signs" of history. We would apprehend the object as simply there, as given in its sensuous certainty, rather than as "having got here," an arrival which is how objects are binding and how they assume a social form. So objects (such as the cherry tree) are "transplanted." They take shape through social action, through "the activity of a whole succession of generations," which is forgotten when the object is apprehended as simply given.

What passes through history is not only the work done by generations but the "sedimentation" of that work as the condition of arrival for future generations. History cannot simply be perceived on the surface of the object, even if how objects surface or take shape is an effect of such histories. In other words, history cannot simply be turned into something that is given in its sensuous certainty, as if it were a property of an object.

If idealism takes the object as given, then it fails to account for its conditions of arrival, which are not simply given. Idealism is the philosophical counterpart to what Marx would later describe as commodity fetishism. In *Capital*, he suggests that commodities are made up of two elements, "matter and labour."[13] Labor is understood as "changing the form of matter" (50). The commodity is assumed to have value or a life of its own only if we forget this labor: "It becomes value only in its congealed state, when embodied in the form of some object" (57).

Marx uses the example of "the table" to suggest that the table is made from wood (which provides, as it were, the matter) and that the work of the table, the work that it takes to "make the table," changes the form of the wood, even though the table "is" still made out of wood. As he describes: "It is as clear as noon-day that man, by his industry, changes the forms of the material furnished by nature in such a way as to make them useful to him. The form of wood, for instance, is altered by making a table out of it, for all that, the table continues to be that common every-day thing, wood. But, as soon as it steps forth as a commodity, it is changed into something transcendent" (76). Noticeably, the Marxian critique of commodity fetishism relies here on a distinction between matter and form, between the wood and the table. The becoming-table of the wood is not the same as its commodification. The table has use-value, even after it has transformed the "form" of the wood. The table can be used, and in being used, the value of the table is not exchanged and made abstract. The table has use-value until it is exchanged. One problem with this model is that the dynamism of "making form" is located in the transformation of nature into use-value: we could also suggest that the "wood" (nature / matter) has acquired its form over time. Nature then would not be simply "there" waiting to be formed or to take form. Marx's and Engel's earlier critique of idealism involves a more dynamic view of the "facts of matter": even the trees, which provide the wood, are themselves "brought forth" as effects of generational action. The wood is itself "formed matter" insofar as trees are not simply given, but take shape as an effect of labor (trans / plantation).[14] The table is given only through these multiple histories of labor, redefined as matter taking form.[15]

It is not surprising that Jacques Derrida offers a critique of the Marxian distinction between use-value and exchange-value by turning toward the table. He suggests: "The table is familiar, too familiar."[16] For Derrida, the table is not simply something we use: "The table has been worn down, exploited, overexploited, or else set aside and beside itself, no longer in use, in antique shops or auction rooms" (149). He hence suggests that "the table in use" is as metaphysical as "table as commodity": use-value as well as exchange-value involves fetishism (162). While I agree with this argument, we might note that for Marx the table in use is not simply inert or simply matter: it involves the "trans-formation" of matter into form. Use-value is hence not a simple matter for Marx even if he locates the transcendental in the commodity.

What a Marxist approach could allow us to do if we extend his critique of the commodity to the very matter of wood, as well as to the form of the table, is to consider the history of "what appears" as a dynamic history of things being moved around. The table certainly moves around. I buy the table (for this or that amount of money) as a table intended for writing. I have to bring it to the space where it will reside (the study or the space marked out in the corner of a room). Well, others bring it for me. I wince as the edge of the table hits the wall, leaving a mark on the wall, as well as a mark on the table, which shows what it came into contact with in the time of its arrival. The table, having arrived, is nestled in the corner of the room. I use it as a writing desk. And yet, I am not sure what will happen in the future. I could put this table to a different use (I could use it as a dining table if it is big enough "to support" this kind of action) or could even forget about the table if I ceased to write. Then, the table might be put aside or put to one side. The object is not reducible to the commodity, even when it is bought and sold. The object is not reducible to itself, which means it does not "have" an "itself" that is apart from its contact with others.

This table was made by somebody, and there is a history to its arrival, a history of transportation, which could be redescribed as a history of *changing hands*. As Igor Kopytoff puts it, we can have a cultural biography of things "as they move through different hands, contexts and uses."[17] This table, you might say, has a story. What a story it could tell. What we need to recall is how the "thisness" of this table does not, as it were, belong to it: what is particular about this table, what we can tell through its biography, is also what allows us to tell a larger story: a story not only of "things" changing hands but of how things come to matter by taking shape through and in the labor of others.

Such histories are not simply available *on* the surface of the object, apart from the scratches that might be left behind, which could also be thought of as what's left of the behind. Histories are hence spectral, just like Husserl's "missing sides." We do not know, of course, the story of Husserl's table, how it arrived or what happened to the table after Husserl stopped writing. But having arrived, we can follow what the table allowed him to do by reading his philosophy as a philosophy that turns to the table. So even if the "thisness" of the table disappears in his work, we could allow its "thisness" to reappear by making this table matter in our reading.

Bodies Doing Things

The object has arrived. And, having arrived, what then does it do? I want to suggest that objects not only are shaped by work, but they also take the shape of the work they do. We can consider how objects are occupied, how we are busy with them. An occupation is what makes an object busy.

Heidegger poses this question of occupation by turning to the table. In *Ontology — The Hermeneutics of Facticity*, Heidegger contrasts two ways of describing tables.[18] In the first model, the table is encountered as "a thing in space — as a spatial thing."[19] As Heidegger describes it: "Aspects show themselves and open up in ever new ways as we walk around the thing" (68). He suggests that the description of the table as a spatial thing is inaccurate not because it is false (the table might after all appear in this way) but because it fails to describe how the significance of the thing is not simply "in" it, but is rather a "characteristic of being" (67–68). For Heidegger what makes "the table" what it is and not something else is what the table allows us to do.

What follows is a rich phenomenological description of the table as it is experienced from the points of view of those who share the space of its dwelling:

> What is there in *the* room there at home is *the* table (not "a" table among many other tables in other rooms and houses) at which one sits *in order to* write, have a meal, sew, or play. Everyone sees this right away, e.g. during a visit: it is a writing table, a dining table, a sewing table — such is the primary way in which it is being encountered in itself. This characteristic of "in order to do something" is not merely imposed on the table by relating and assimilating it to something else which it is not. (69)

In other words, what we do with the table or what the table allows us to do is essential to the table. The table provides a surface around which the family gathers. Heidegger describes his wife sitting at the table and reading and "the boys" busying themselves at the table. The table is assembled around the support it gives. The "in order to" structure of the table, in other words, means that those who are "at" the table are also part of what makes the table itself. Doing things "at" the table is what makes the table what it is and not some other thing. So while bodies do things, things might also "do bodies."

How do bodies "matter" in what objects do? Let's consider Husserl's table. It does not seem that Husserl is touched by his table. When Husserl "grasps" his table from the series of impressions as being more than what he sees at any point in time, it is his "eyes" that are doing the work. He "closes his eyes" and "opens his eyes."[20] The object's partiality is seen, even if the object is unavailable in a single sight.

In the second volume of *Ideas*, Husserl attends to the lived body (*Leib*) and to the intimacy of touch. The table returns, as one would expect. And yet, what a different table we find if we reach for it differently. Here, it is the hands rather than the eyes that reach the table: "My hand is lying on the table. I experience the table as something solid, cold, smooth" (vol. 2, 153). Husserl conveys the proximity between bodies and objects as things that matter insofar as they make and leave an impression. Bodies are "something touching which is touched" (vol. 2, 155). We touch things and are touched by things. In approaching the table, we are approached by the table. As Husserl shows, the table might be cold and smooth, but the quality of its surface can be felt only when I cease to stand apart from it. Bodies as well as objects take shape through being orientated toward each other, an orientation that may be experienced as the cohabitation or sharing of space.

We might think that we reach for all that simply comes into view. And yet, what "comes into" view or what is within our horizon is not simply a matter of what we find here or there, or even where we find ourselves, as we move here or there. What is reachable is determined precisely by orientations we have already taken. Some objects do not even become objects of perception since the body does not move toward them: they are "beyond the horizon" of the body, out of reach. Orientations are about the direction we take that puts some things and not others in our reach. So the object, which is apprehended only by exceeding my gaze, can be apprehended only insofar as it has come to be available to me: its reachability is not simply a matter of its place or location (the white paper on the table, for instance) but is shaped by the orientations I have taken that mean I face some ways more than others (toward this kind of table, which marks out the space I tend to inhabit).

Phenomenology helps us to explore how bodies are shaped by histories, which they perform in their comportment, their posture, and their gestures. Both Husserl and Merleau-Ponty, after all, describe bodily horizons as "sedimented histories."[21] This model of history as bodily sedimentation has been taken up by social theorists as well as philosophers. For Pierre Bourdieu, such histories are described as the habitus, "systems of durable, transposable, dispositions" which integrate past experiences through the very *"matrix of perceptions, appreciations and actions"* that are necessary to accomplish "infinitely diversified tasks."[22] For Judith Butler, it is precisely how phenomenology exposes the "sedimentation" of history in the repetition of bodily action that makes it a useful resource for feminism.[23]

We could say that history "happens" in the very repetition of gestures, which is what gives bodies their dispositions or tendencies. We might note here that the labor of such repetition disappears through labor: if we work hard at something, then it seems "effortless." This paradox — with effort it becomes effortless — is precisely what makes history disappear in the moment of its enactment. The repetition of work is what makes the signs of work disappear. It is important that we think not only about *what* is repeated but also about how the repetition of actions takes us in certain directions: we are also orientating ourselves toward some objects more than others, including not only physical objects (the different kinds of tables) but also objects of thought, feeling, and judgment, or objects in the sense of aims, aspirations, and objectives. I might orient myself around writing, for instance, not simply as a certain kind of work (although it is that, and it requires certain objects for it to be possible) but also as a goal: writing becomes something that I aspire to, even as an identity (becoming a writer). So the object we aim for, *which we have in our view*, also comes into our view through being held in place as that which we seek to be: the action searches for identity as the mark of attainment (the writer "becomes" a writer through writing).

I too am working on a table, though for me, the kitchen table as much as the writing table provides the setting for action: for cooking, eating, as well as writing. I have a study space, and I work on a table in that space. I type this now, using a keyboard placed on a computer table, which resides in the study, as a space that has been set aside for this kind of work. As I type, I face the table, and it is what I am working on. I am touching the object as well as the keyboard and am aware of it as a sensuous given that is available for me. In repeating the work of typing, my body comes to feel a certain way. My neck gets sore, and I stretch to ease the discomfort. I pull my shoulders back every now and then as the posture I assume (a bad posture I am sure) is a huddle: I huddle over the table as I repeat the action (the banging of keys with the tips of my fingers); the action shapes me, and it leaves its impression through bodily sensations, prickly feelings on the skin surface, and the more intense experience of discomfort. I write, and, in performing this work, I might yet become my object and become a writer, with a writer's body and a writer's tendencies (the sore neck and shoulders are sure signs of having done this kind of work).

Repetitive strain injury (RSI) can be understood as the effect of such repetition: we repeat some actions, sometimes over and over again, and this is partly about the nature of the work we might do. Our body takes the shape of this repetition; *we get stuck in certain alignments as an effect of this work*. For instance, my right ring finger has acquired the shape of its own work: the constant use of a pen, in writing, has created a lump, which is the shape that is shaped by the work of this repetition; my finger almost looks "as if" it has the shape of a pen as an impression upon it. The object leaves its impression: the action, as an intending as well as a tending toward the object, shapes my body in this way and that. The work of repetition is not neutral work; *it orients the body in some ways rather than others*. The lump on my finger is a sure sign of an orientation I have taken not just toward the pen-object or the keyboard but also to the world, as someone who does a certain kind of work for a living.

Bodies hence acquire orientation through the repetitions of some actions over others, as actions that have certain "objects" in view, whether they are physical objects required to do the work (the writing table, the pen, the keyboard) or the ideal objects that one identifies with. The nearness of such objects, their availability within my bodily horizon, is not casual: *it is not just that I find them there, like that*. Bodies tend toward some objects more than others given their tendencies. These tendencies are not originary but are effects of the repetition of the "tending toward."

Over time, we acquire our tendencies, as the acquisition of what is given. Bodies could be described as "becoming given." Orientations thus take time. If orientations are an effect of what we tend toward, then they point to the future, to what is not yet present. And yet, orientations are shaped by what is behind us, creating a loop between what is toward and behind. In other words, we are directed by our background. Your point of arrival is your family background, and the family itself provides a background in which things happen and happen in a certain way. Doing things, as we have seen, is what gives objects a certain place. It is no accident that "the table" is an object around which the family gathers, doing the work of the family or even bringing the family into existence as an object that can be shared. In being given a place at the table, the family takes its place.

The table can thus be described as a kinship object.[24] The shared orientation toward the table allows the family to cohere as a group, even when we do different things "at" the table. So if our arrival is already an inheritance (which is what we mean when we speak so easily of the family background, which is what puts the family into the background), then we inherit the proximity of certain objects, as those things that are given to us within the family home. These objects are not only material: they may be values, capital, aspirations, projects, and styles. We inherit proximities. We inherit the nearness of some objects more than others; the background is what keeps certain things within reach. So the child tends toward that which is near enough, whereby nearness or proximity is what already "resides" at home. Having tended toward what is within reach, the child acquires its tendencies.

The background then *is not simply behind the child*: it is what the child is asked to aspire *toward*. The background, given in this way, can orient us toward the future: it is where the child is asked to direct his or her desire by accepting the family line as his or her own inheritance. There is pressure to inherit this line, a pressure that can speak the language of love, happiness, and care. We do not know what we could become without these points of pressure which insist that happiness will follow if we do this or we do that. And yet, these places where we are under pressure do not always mean we stay on line; at certain points, we can refuse the inheritance, points that are often lived as "breaking points." We do not always know what breaks at these points.

Feminist Tables

I have suggested that bodies materialize; they acquire certain tendencies through proximity to objects whose nearness we have already inherited (the family background). The materialization of subjects is hence inseparable from objects, which circulate as things to do things with. Let's return to Husserl's writing table. Recall that Husserl attends to the writing table, which becomes "the table" by keeping the domestic world behind him. This domestic world, which surrounds the philosopher, must be "put aside" or even "put to one side" in his turn toward objects *as* objects of perception. This disappearance of familiar objects might make more than the object disappear. The writer who does the work of philosophy might disappear if we were to erase the signs of "where" it is that he works. Feminist philosophers have shown us how the masculinity of philosophy is evidenced in the disappearance of the subject under the sign of the universal.[25] The masculinity might also be evident in the disappearance of the materiality of objects, in the bracketing of the materials out of which, as well as upon which, philosophy writes itself, as a way of apprehending the world.

We could call this the fantasy of a "paperless" philosophy, a philosophy that is not dependent on the materials upon which it is written. As Audre Lorde reflects, "A room of one's own may be necessary for writing prose, but so are reams of paper, a typewriter and plenty of time."[26] The fantasy of a paperless philosophy involves the disappearance of political economy, the "materials" of philosophy, as well as its dependence on forms of labor, both domestic and otherwise. In other words, the labor of writing might disappear along with the paper.

Being oriented toward the writing table not only relegates other rooms in the house to the background but might also depend *on the work done to keep the desk clear*. The desk that is clear is one that is ready for writing. One might even consider the domestic work that must have taken place for the philosopher to turn to the writing table, to be writing on the table, and to keep that table as the object of his attention. We can recall here the long history of feminist scholarship and activism on the politics of housework: about the ways in which women, as wives and servants, do the work required to keep such spaces available for men and the work they do. To sustain an orientation toward the writing table might depend on such work, while it erases the signs of that work as signs of its dependence. Such work is often experienced as "the lack of spare time,"[27] for example, the lack of time for oneself or for contemplation. Philosophy might even depend on the concealment of domestic labor and of the labor time that it takes to reproduce the very "materials" of home.

We can pose a simple question: who faces the writing table? Does the writing table have a face, which points it toward some bodies rather than others? Let's consider Adrienne Rich's account of writing a letter:

> From the fifties and early sixties, I remember a cycle. It began when I had picked up a book or began trying to write a letter. . . . The child (or children) might be absorbed in busyness, in his own dream world; but as soon as he felt me gliding into a world which did not include him, he would come to pull at my hand, ask for help, punch at the typewriter keys. And I would feel his wants at such a moment as fraudulent, as an attempt moreover to defraud me of living even for fifteen minutes as myself.[28]

We can see from the point of view of the mother, who is also a writer, poet, and philosopher, that giving attention to the objects of writing, facing those objects, becomes impossible: the children, even if they are behind you, literally pull you away. This loss of time for writing feels like a loss of your own time, as you are returned to the work of giving your attention to the children. One does not need to posit any essential difference to note that there is a political economy of attention: there is an uneven distribution of attention time among those who arrive at the writing table, which affects what they can do once they arrive (and of course, many do not even make it). For some, having time for writing, which means time to face the table upon which writing happens, becomes an orientation that is not available given the ongoing labor of other attachments, which literally pull them away. So whether we can sustain our orientation toward the writing table depends on other orientations, which affect what we can face at any given moment in time.

If orientations affect what bodies do, then they also affect how spaces take shape around certain bodies. The world takes shape by presuming certain bodies as given. If spaces extend bodies, then we could say that spaces extend the bodies that "tend" to inhabit them. So, for instance, if the action of writing is associated with the masculine body, then it is this body that tends to inhabit the space for writing. The space for writing, say, the study, then tends to extend such bodies and may even take their shape. Gender becomes naturalized as a property of bodies, objects, and spaces partly through the loop of this repetition, which leads bodies in some directions more than others as if that direction came from within the body and explains which way it turns.

In a way, the writing table waits for the body of the writer. In waiting for the writer, the table waits for some bodies more than others. This waiting orients the table to a specific kind of body, the body that would "take up" writing. I have already described such a body as a masculine body, by evoking the gendered form of its occupation. Now clearly, gender is not "in" the table, or necessarily "in" the body that turns to the table. Gender is an effect of how bodies take objects up, which involves how they occupy space by being occupied in one way or another. We might note for instance in Heidegger's *Ontology* that the table as a thing on which we do things allows for different ways of being occupied. So Heidegger writes on the table, his wife sews, and his children play. What we do on the table is also about being given a place within a familiar order. Bodies are shaped by the work they do on the table, where work involves gendered forms of occupation.

Consider Charlotte Perkins Gilman's early work on home, where she speaks of the shaping of women's bodies through the way they inhabit domestic interiors. As she puts it:

> See it in furnishing. A stone or block of wood to sit on, a hide to lie on, a shelf to put your food on. See that block of wood change under your eyes and crawl up history on its forthcoming legs — a stool, a chair, a sofa, a settee, and now the endless ranks of sittable furniture wherewith we fill the home to keep ourselves from the floor withal. . . . If you are confined at home you cannot walk much — therefore you must sit — especially if your task is a stationary one. So, to the home-bound woman came much sitting, and much sitting called for ever softer seats.[29]

Gilman is writing here specifically about furnishings in the Orient, and she contrasts the soft bodies and chairs of this imagined interior with the domestic interiors in the West, which give women more mobility. Gilman shows us how orientations involve inhabiting certain bodily positions: sitting, walking, lying down, and so on. Such forms of occupation or of being occupied shape the furniture: the chairs becomes soft, to provide seating for the body that sits. In turn, the body becomes soft, as it occupies the soft seat, taking up the space made available by the seat. Such positions become habitual: they are repeated, and in being repeated, they shape the body and what it can do. The more the body sits, the more it tends to be seated.

What a simple point: what we "do do" affects what we "can do." This is not to argue that "doing" simply restricts capacities. In contrast, what we "do do" opens up and expands some capacities, although an "expansion" in certain directions might in turn restrict what we can do in others. The more we work certain parts of the body, the more work they can do. At the same time, the less we work other parts, the less they can do. So if gender shapes what we "do do," then it shapes what we can do.

It is worth noting that Iris Marion Young's phenomenological model of female embodiment places a key emphasis on the role of orientation. Indeed, Young argues that gender differences *are* differences in orientation. As she suggests, "Even in the most simple body orientations of men and women as they sit, stand, and walk, we can observe a typical difference in body style and extension."[30] This is not to say that orientations are themselves simply given, or that they "cause" such differences. Rather orientations are an effect of differences as well as a mechanism for their reproduction. Young suggests that women have an "inhibited intentionality" in part because they do not get behind their bodies since women see their bodies as "objects" as well as "capacities" (35). Women may throw objects and are thrown by objects in such a way that they take up less space. To put it simply, we acquire the shape of how we throw as well as what we do. Spaces in turn are shaped by the bodies that tend to inhabit them given their tendencies.

And yet, it is not always decided which bodies inhabit which spaces, even when spaces extend the form of some bodies and not others. Women "do things" by claiming spaces that have not historically belonged to them, including the spaces marked out for writing. As Virginia Woolf shows us in *A Room of One's Own*, for women to claim a space to write is a political act. Of course, there are women who write. We know this. Women have taken up spaces orientated toward writing. And yet, the woman writer remains just that: the woman writer, deviating from the somatic norm of "the writer" as such. So what happens when the woman writer takes up her pen? What happens when the study is not reproduced as a masculine domain by the collective repetition of such moments of deviation?

Tables might even appear differently if we follow such moments of deviation and the lines they create. For Virginia Woolf, the tables appears with her writing on it, as a feminist message inscribed on paper: "I must ask you to imagine a room, like many thousands, with a window looking across people's hats and vans and motor-cars to other windows, and on the table inside the room a blank sheet of paper on which was written in large letters Women and Fiction and no more."[31] The table is not simply what she faces but is the "site" upon which she makes her feminist point: that we cannot address the question of women and fiction without asking the prior question of whether women have space to write.

If making feminist points returns us to the table, then the terms of its appearance will be different. In Young's *On Female Body Experience*, the table arrives into her writing in the following way: "The nick on the table here happened during that argument with my daughter" (159). Here the table records the intimacy of the relationship between mother and daughter; such intimacies are not "put to one side." Tables for feminist writers might not bracket or put aside the intimacy of familial attachments. Such intimacies are at the front; they are "on the table" rather than behind it. We might even say that feminist tables are shaped by attachments, which affect the surfaces of tables and how tables surface in feminist writing.

Of course, feminist tables do not simply make gender the point of significance. Just recall the women of color press, The Kitchen Table. Such a press certainly uses the table to make a feminist point. The kitchen table provides the surface on which women tend to work. To use the table that supports domestic work to do political work (including the work that makes explicit the politics of domestic work) is a reorientation device. But such a description misses the point of this table.[32] As a women of color press, The Kitchen Table reminds us that the work of the table involves racial and class-based divisions of labor. Middle-class white women could access the writing table, could turn their attention to this table, by relying on the domestic labor of black and working-class women. A feminist politics of the table cannot afford to lose sight of the political divisions between women who work. The Kitchen Table press, which Audre Lorde referred to as "The Table,"[33] was about generating a space for woman of color within feminism. The politics of the table turns us to the political necessity of clearing spaces in order that some bodies can work at the table. To arrive at the table takes time and requires painstaking labor for those whose backgrounds mean that they do not inherit its place. It is through the labor of Black feminism that women of color can claim "the table" as their own.

So, yes, orientations matter. Those who are "out of place" have to secure a place that is not already given. Such work makes "the table" reappear as an object. The table becomes a disorientation device, making things lose their place, which means the loss of coherence of a certain world. Political work hence reshapes the very surfaces of bodies and worlds. Or we could say that bodies resurface when they turn the tables on the world that keeps things in place.

Notes

This essay is drawn from the first chapter of Ahmed, *Queer Phenomenology*, and has been revised and adapted for this volume.

1 For an articulation of this idea, see Barad, "Posthumanist Performativity." I have elsewhere questioned the way articulations of so-called new materialism have relied on a foundational gesture whereby they constitute earlier work (especially other feminist work) written during the "cultural turn" as against matter, and opposed to related tropes of materiality such as biology or the real. See Ahmed, "Imaginary Prohibitions."

2 Husserl, *Ideas Pertaining to a Pure Phenomenology and to a Phenomenological Philosophy, Second Book*, 165–66.

3 Schutz and Luckmann, *The Structure of the Lifeworld*, 36.

4 Husserl, *Ideas*, 101.

5 Ibid.

6 Banfield, *The Phantom Table*, 66.

7 Husserl, *Ideas*, vol. 1, 107.

8 Sokolowski, *Introduction to Phenomenology*, 20.

9 Husserl, *Ideas*, vol. 1, 102.

10 Husserl attends to the temporality of the background via the notion of the "internal horizon," which he develops throughout the corpus of his work. So the "now" of perception involves retention: it involves the "just past," which is "before" the "now" but evoked as "before" only in the "now." This reminds us that intentionality (to be directed toward something that does not reveal itself "at once") involves a complex temporality, in which the present already exceeds itself: "Even if I stop at perception, I still have the full consciousness of the thing, just as I already have it at the first glance when I see it as this thing. In seeing I always 'mean' it with all the sides which are no way given to me, even in the form of the intuitive, anticipatory presentifications. Thus

every perception has, 'for consciousness' a horizon belonging to its object." Husserl, *The Crisis of the European Sciences and Transcendental Phenomenology*, 158. Phenomenology in its turn to the present of what we perceive does return us to what is "behind" in a temporal as well as spatial sense. For Husserl this is primarily described as "time consciousness," but we can see an important connection between a phenomenology of perception and a more materialist conception of histories that are "behind" or even at the "back" of what is "presented" or in the present.

11 As Gilles Deleuze puts it, following Spinoza, "You do not know beforehand what a mind or body can do, in a given encounter, a given arrangement, a given combination." See Deleuze, "Ethnology," 627. We can add: we do not yet know what a writer can do, let alone the table, once they get near enough to each other. Yes, writing might happen. Or it might not. We don't always know what will happen if writing does not happen: whether the "not" feels like a block, or whether it provides an empty space that appears as an invitation to fill with other things. You might doodle, creating some rather odd kind of impressions. And if writing is what happens, then we don't know what lines will be created on the paper, which lies on the surface of the table, between skin and wood, or on whatever materials happen to come into contact. In due course, I will return to the "can do" and suggest that what bodies "do do" restricts capacities in the present even if it does not "decide" exactly what happens.

12 Marx and Engels, *The German Ideology*, *The Marx-Engels Reader*, 170.

13 Marx, *Capital* (Moscow, 1887), 50.

14 This is not to say that matter comes to matter only given the work of human labor. Such an argument would make the human *into the center of things,* as the absent presence around which all things were centered. Other kinds of labor shape how objects might come to surface in this way or that. Merleau-Ponty uses the example of a pebble and what makes a pebble a pebble. As he puts it, "Beyond a certain range of their changes, they would cease to be this pebble or this shell, they would even cease to be a pebble or a shell." See Merleau-Ponty, *The Visible and the Invisible*, 161. I have often been struck by pebble beaches, for instance, when I imagine how they are becoming sand but a becoming that is not available to consciousness or that has not arrived, in the present. The pebble becomes sand as an effect of time. The pebble could be seen as "becoming sand," but we could not see this becoming simply on the surface of the pebble. We could even see sand as a "having been pebble," but that would also point us beyond what is available in the present. What does time do, if not make available the possibility of seeing that which is not in view? Time is also occupied not only in the sense that we do something with it but also in how it is available to us through what we do. In time, the pebble may become sand; it ceases to have the characteristics that make it recogniz-

able as a pebble. But the pebble acquires its shape through contact; and it is this contact which reshapes the pebble such that it is becoming something "other" than what it is. Time "gives form," which suggests that "matter" is not inert or given but is always in a process of "materializing." The pebble is shaped by its contact with water, and the waves that pound it, which made it "it" (and not a rock), also shape its becoming something other than what it is in the present. The object assumes the form of contact, as a contact that takes place in time, but is also an effect of time. The arrival of the object takes time and involves contact with other objects, which keeps the future open to that which has yet to emerge.

15   It is important that we contest the matter/form hierarchy, which locates what is dynamic in form and leaves matter "for dead." As feminist philosophers have shown us, this binary is gendered: women have been associated with matter and men with form, such that masculinity becomes the gift of life by giving form to matter. See Irigaray, *Speculum of the Other Woman*, 172; Butler, *Bodies That Matter*; and Grosz, *Space, Time and Perversion*, 121.

16   Derrida, *Specters of Marx*, 149.

17   Kopytoff, "The Cultural Biography of Things," 34.

18   I am very grateful to Paul Harrison who directed me towards *Ontology* and Heidegger's table during a seminar I gave at Durham University in October 2005, "Lines, Points and Other Impressions." In the first version of my chapter on phenomenology and tables in *Queer Phenomenology*, I relied on the example of the hammer offered in *Being and Time* and made my own connections between the hammer and the table. It was uncanny to discover that the example of the hammer in *Being and Time* was a substitute for the table in *Ontology*. As John Van Buren suggests in his translator's notes: "What had also dropped out was Heidegger's powerful fifteen-page phenomenological example of 'tarrying for a while' in his home, 'being-in-a-room' there, and the 'sewing of his wife', the 'playing of his children', his own 'writing', and their daily meals at the table in this room. This central example was replaced by 'the hammer', and what survived of it was a cursory mention of a 'table' in a 'room' with 'sewing' and 'writing' equipment on it." See Van Buren, "Translator's Notes" to Heidegger, *Ontology—The Hermeneutics of Facticity*, 92. How fitting that when I was writing about a hammer I was "really" writing about a table.

19   Heidegger, *Ontology*, 20.

20   Husserl, *Ideas*, vol. 1, 130.

21   For a discussion of this idea, see Steinbock, *Home and Beyond*, 36.

22   Bourdieu, *Outline of a Theory of Practice*, 72, 83.

23   Butler, "Performative Acts and Gender Constitutions," 406.

24   For a good discussion of house memories focusing on the kitchen table, see Carsten, *After Kinship*, 31.

25 See, for example, Bordo, *Flight to Objectivity*; and Braidotti, *Patterns of Dissonance*.

26 Lorde, *Sister Outsider*, 116.

27 Davies, "Responsibilities and Daily Life," 141.

28 Rich, *Of Woman Born*, 23.

29 Gilman, *The Home*, 27–28.

30 Young, *On Female Body Experience*, 32.

31 Woolf, *A Room of One's Own*, 24.

32 Here, I am critiquing my own reading of The Kitchen Table in *Queer Phenomenology*, which uses this description and hence misses the importance of this press as a women of color press. See Ahmed, *Queer Phenomenology*, 61.

33 De Veaux, *Warrior Poet*, 277.

Sonia Kruks

Simone de Beauvoir:
Engaging Discrepant Materialisms

"Materialism" is today an essentially contested concept, and its usage in a variety of neo-Marxist, feminist, and gender theories is radically discrepant. Similarly its cognates, such as material, materiality, or materialization, carry diverse and often apparently incommensurate meanings. In what follows I bring into engagement, through a discussion of the work of Simone de Beauvoir, several genres of theory that focus with radical political intent on materialism and its cognates. One is a set of Marxist-inflected, structuralist discourses in which "materialism" refers to the production of social structures (widely conceived to include large-scale social institutions, norms, and so forth, as well as those structures that organize economic production) as effects of human practices. These discourses are "realist" in approach, insofar as they posit both the material world and human beings qua material organisms as real existents, as having import irrespective of the conceptual lenses through which we describe them; but they are also "social constructionist" insofar as consciousness is, in varying degrees, seen as the effect of the organization of practices to meet material needs.[1]

Another genre of "materialist" theory, one broadly informed by poststructuralism, focuses on the production of "material" bodies, or their "materialization," through discourse and discursively constituted performance. In a more nominalist vein, it accounts for subjective experience and identity above all as effects of such discursive production.[2] What both of these genres have in common, however, is that they proceed (to borrow the terms from Elizabeth Grosz) "from the outside in" rather than "from the inside out."[3] That is, they emphasize the ways in which subjectivity arises as the reflex or expression of social practices, or as the effect of discourses. Although thinkers within both of these genres acknowledge that "outside" and "inside" remain mutually implicated, still for the most part these approaches privilege the power of social structures and practices (whether they be based in economic or discourse "production") as constitutive of the "interior" domains of subjectivity, intentionality, and meaning. Thus, their many profound disagreements (notably over the status of the "real") not withstanding, these neo-Marxist and poststructuralist theoretical approaches have in common a constructivist account of subjectivity.

In this they stand broadly in contrast to another genre of "materialist" discourse, one that emerges from within the phenomenological tradition. Phenomenology tends to proceed in the opposite direction. It privileges the "inside," or the experiential, and it often attends to the phenomena of consciousness without regard to their possible "outside" constitutive sources. However, such phenomena do not arise for disembodied consciousnesses, and so some phenomenologies also engage with questions of their own about "materiality." Critically engaging claims (for example, those of sociobiology) that biological differences are not only "real" but also causally explanatory of differences in social roles, these phenomenological approaches seek to move beyond mind-body dualism and explore the paradoxes and ambiguities of human experience as "embodied subjectivity": as at once organic or "factic" body and consciousness.[4] In its more "existential" versions, phenomenology also considers how we may theorize human freedom in the face of the facticity (the apparently "outside" or "objective" aspects) of both bodily and socially structured dimensions of experience.

Recently, feminist and queer theory have been among the key sites for a series of often contentious encounters among proponents of such diverse genres of materialist theory. Debates about "biological essentialism" versus "social constructionism," about "sex" versus "gender," or about whether to "displace" one of these terms by the other or to "destabilize" both have waxed furious. In this essay I propose, through returning to the work of Simone de Beauvoir, that these discrepant genres of materialist theorizing may be brought into a more fruitful relationship than their respective proponents are apt to pursue. Rather than reductively privileging one genre of materiality, I seek to explicate the interconstituent qualities of diverse "materialities" that shape human practices, selves, and social formations. For only such an approach may adequately capture the complexities of human life and account for the phenomena of social oppression with which feminist and other radical social practices are concerned.

Locating Beauvoir

Simone de Beauvoir is most often read as working in the last of the genres of materialist theory mentioned above: phenomenology, and particularly existential phenomenology. Indeed, this is where she explicitly locates herself in *The Second Sex*,[5] and her project, especially in the second volume, is to present a phenomenology of the "lived experience" through which, as she famously puts it, "one is not born but becomes a woman."[6] Furthermore, qua existentialist, she is concerned with exploring the constraints on and possibilities for freedom that accompany such a "becoming." However, I argue, Beauvoir does not work exclusively in this tradition. Rather, she works in and across the interstices between phenomenology and a Marxist-inflected and also a culturally oriented structuralist materialism.

Although she rejects a determinist "historical materialism," such as she critically presents through her reading of Engels,[7] Beauvoir's work is also profoundly attuned to the sensibilities of the "early" Marx: the Marx of the "Economic and Philosophical Manuscripts." Few commentators have remarked upon the fact that at the very end of *The Second Sex* Beauvoir approvingly quotes from this Marx — a Marx whose vision radically historicizes nature and naturalizes history — as precisely summing up her own position. "One could not state it better," she declares after citing him.[8] Beauvoir's self-proclaimed affinity with Marx should make us pause. It should remind us that volume 1 of *The Second Sex* ("Facts and Myths") focuses on the "production" of woman as man's inferiorized other. It explores the social production of woman's otherness across the history of human practices and institutions, as well as in more discursive arenas such as myth and literature.

Beauvoir's attention to Marx also invites a reading of *The Second Sex* as a precursor to the *Critique of Dialectical Reason* (1960), the neo-Marxist magnum opus of Sartre's later years[9] — a reading I develop below. In the *Critique*, Sartre attempts explicitly to conjoin his earlier existential phenomenology (as set out, above all, in *Being and Nothingness* [1943]) with a Marxist-inspired neostructuralism. He sets out to show how what he calls "practico-inert" entities, the products of our own individual and collective production, come to impinge on freedom and to alter our actions and — indeed — our very being as practical subjects. All human activities are mediated by, and in the process are altered by, a world of material things, he argues. They cannot but take place within a world of practico-inert entities which we create from the resources of nature through a multitude of practices, through what Marx had called praxis.

"Reification," that is, the materialization of human activity, of praxis, in tangible objects, is an essential characteristic of the human world, yet it also represents a fundamental alienation of our activity. For the objects we create through praxis always act back against us coercively: "Man has to struggle not only against nature, and against the social environment which has produced him, and against other men, but also against his own action as it becomes other. . . . a permanent anti-praxis is a new and necessary moment of praxis."[10] Practico-inert entities, the products of our praxis, produce their own demands or "exigencies." They drain our freedom from us, reinscribing in us the inertia and passivity of matter, as they constrain and compel our future activity. For example, for a house to remain habitable and meet our need for shelter, we are compelled endlessly to meet the demands that it, itself a product of prior human praxis, now imposes upon us. It must be "heated, swept, repainted, etc; otherwise it deteriorates. This *vampire object* [my emphasis] constantly absorbs human action, lives on blood taken from man and finally lives in symbiosis with him" (169).

Practico-inert entities may be very diverse. They range from commodities and artifacts to the built environment, to the reified and reifying social institutions we (unintentionally) create, and to the language and forms of discourse in which we find our meanings alienated.[11] They also include "series." These are the social ensembles in which we passively participate with others, and in which each unwittingly becomes, through others, his or her own other. Thus we most often encounter the praxis of others above all as the "alteration" of our own, as draining away our freedom and as distorting or "deviating" our intentions: human relations are also invested by alienation.

Ten years after Sartre published *Critique of Dialectical Reason*, Beauvoir published *Old Age* (1970).[12] The book is in many ways an analogue to *The Second Sex*, but it also breaks important new theoretical ground. For now the Marxist-inspired materialist aspects of Beauvoir's thinking, already present in *The Second Sex*, are deepened as she incorporates Sartre's fuller elaborations of her own earlier insights.[13] By rearticulating Sartre's analyses for her own distinctive ends, Beauvoir now more fully addresses the overarching structural social relations of modern Western society through which forms of oppression (here of the aged, but also of other categories of people) are perpetuated. But in both works Beauvoir focuses our attention on the confluences, mutual mediations, and interconstituencies of diverse forms of materiality—on bodies, the structures of worked matter in which we live and act, and the cultural and discursive media we produce —and she thus suggests a route beyond the discrepant and frequently reductionist genres of materialist theory that are pervasive today.

The Second Sex

Although early second-wave feminist interpretations of Beauvoir tended —usually critically—to read *The Second Sex* as simply applying the framework of Sartre's existential phenomenology to women, more recent scholarship on Beauvoir, including my own, has established the important ways in which her thought is distinct from that of the early Sartre.[14] These include her greater attention to the lived body and how it inflects particular lives, to the interdependence of human freedoms, and to the ways in which concrete situations of oppression, born of large-scale structures, institutions, and dominant discourses, may impinge on, or even suppress, the human potentiality for freedom. Thus Beauvoir has increasingly become a resource within feminist theory, especially for those who seek to defend feminism from the reductive excesses that often accompany the poststructuralist "death of the subject" without thereby reverting to forms of biological essentialism. As Toril Moi has recently put it, "to find a third way for feminist theory, one that steers a course between the Scylla of traditional essentialism and biologism and the Charybdis of idealist obsession with 'discourse' and 'construction' . . . Simone de Beauvoir's philoso-phy of feminism is an obvious cornerstone."[15]

As Moi and others argue, Beauvoir's account of the body "as a situa-tion" enables feminist theory to move beyond the antinomies of sex and gender, biology and social construction, nature and culture. For Beauvoir eschews the determinism that may implicitly pervade radical discourse-constructionism as much as biological reductionism. Against reduction-isms of any kind, Beauvoir also enables us to restore the significance of freedom to feminism. Beauvoir shows, as Moi puts it, that "just as the world constantly makes me, I constantly make my self the woman I am . . . a situation is not an 'external' structure that imposes itself on the individ-ual subject, but rather an irreducible amalgam of the freedom (projects) of that subject and the conditions in which freedom finds itself. The body as a situation is the concrete body experienced as meaningful, and socially and historically situated."[16]

However, we may also experience our bodies as sites of profound alien-ation, and Moi attends less fully to this aspect of embodiment in her retrieval of Beauvoir. We may experience several modalities of such alien-ation. We may experience our bodies as physically limiting our abilities to carry out our projects, as the origin of an "I cannot." Or, in their uncon-trollable functions and demands, we may experience them as sources of an "alien vitality"[17] or as sources of an "alien" suffering. In addition, we may also experience them as sites of our social objectification. Such objectifica-tion may emerge in two ways: in interpersonal interactions with particular individuals or through our location in large-scale social structures and practices, including discursive practices, which function as a generalized "other." Most often, especially for socially inferiorized groups such as women, it is phenomenologically impossible to separate out these various modalities of alienation: the body is lived as a failure, or a problem, in which physical and social qualities blend. "Physiological facts," Beauvoir insists, have significance only within specific social contexts so that, for example, the relative "weakness" of women's muscles "is revealed as such only in the light of the ends man proposes, the instruments he has avail-able, and the laws he establishes."[18] Similarly, Beauvoir argues, menstrua-tion is an involuntary bodily function (an "alien vitality") to which most women must attend in one way or another, but the disgust and shame that generally accompany its onset in young girls is integral to their realization of their subordinate social status (315).

For Beauvoir, the particular problem of "becoming a woman" is that one is always engaged in a project in which one's potentialities as a free, agentic human being can never escape the facticities of one's organic body and other life-attributes, including a discursive and social regime through which one is subjected to systematically inferiorized otherness. It is this last (variants of which are, of course, also experienced by those men who do not conform to the predominant — white, middle-class, young, healthy, heterosexual — Western norms of manhood) which makes woman the "second" or subordinate sex, man's "other." Thus Beauvoir's concern is not only phenomenologically to disclose such experiences of inferiorization but also to give an account of their social genesis and means of perpetuation.

In an appreciative but critical engagement with Toril Moi, Iris Young argued, shortly before her death, that feminism — and indeed critical social theory more broadly — should move beyond its current concerns with "issues of experience, identity, and subjectivity" because these have tended problematically to narrow its political focus and efficacy.[19] It needs also to identify and explain the institutions, social relations, and large-scale, or "macro" social structures that produce injustices and other harms to groups such as women (or, as I will discuss later, the aged). Young agrees with Moi that "the concept of the lived body offers more refined tools for theorizing sexed subjectivity, and the experiences of differently situated men and women, than does the more blunt category of gender" (19). However, working from a perspective more inflected by Marxism than is Moi's, Young argues that we need to think more systematically about the "structures of constraint" that operate independently of the individual intentions of either men or women (21). Without attending to such structural realities as the sexual division of labor, normative heterosexuality, and gendered hierarchies of power, we truncate the possibility of a politics of radical transformation (22). If we fail to take account of these realities, we cannot adequately articulate "how persons live out their positioning in social structures along with the opportunities and constraints they produce," for example, how "each person takes up the constrained possibilities that gender structures offer in their own way, forming their own habits as variations on those possibilities, or actively trying to resist or refigure them" (25–26). I read Young's appeal here as one to investigate the possible confluences among the diverse genres of materialist theory that I have briefly sketched and to explore interconstituencies among forms of materiality that are usually considered only singly and reductively. However, if we return to Beauvoir herself and examine her entire text, I want to propose, we find her engaged — by 1949! — in exactly the kind of synthetic project that Young urges.

In an earlier paper, "Gender as Seriality," Young herself explicitly draws on Sartre's notions of seriality and the practico-inert (which Sartre developed primarily to investigate social class relations) in order to explicate gender as a set of oppressive structures in which women find themselves located irrespective of their subjective stances or experiences.[20] In this paper Young persuasively argues that, by using Sartre's theoretical framework, it is possible to avoid difference-erasing forms of essentialism that often attend generalizing about "women" and yet still retain "women" as a significant social and political category. The Sartrean notion of seriality enables one to explain how, as members of the series "women," certain individuals are unintentionally linked such that they will alter each other's actions, each one becoming an other to herself, irrespective of whether or not they share an "inner" subjective sense of identity. Rather, they are, as Sartre puts it, unified "in exteriority." Whether or not they realize it, they are unified by virtue of their shared location in certain practico-inert structures of gender, for example a particular division of labor, or the institutions that enforce the norms of heterosexuality. Thus, says Young, at this level, saying "I am a woman" is to state an anonymous fact that locates me in a series of others. "It means that I check one box rather than another on my driver's license application. . . . As I utter the phrase, I experience a serial interchangeability between myself and others" (30). Thus we should not conceive gender structures as defining attributes of individuals, as fundamental to their identity, but rather as "the material and social facts that each individual must deal with and relate to." Similarly other structures, like class, race, or age, "do not primarily name attributes of individuals, but practico-inert necessities that condition their lives": they are "forms of seriality . . . material structures arising from people's historically congealed, institutionalized actions and expectations that position and limit individuals in determinate ways with which they must deal" (31).

Although in *The Second Sex* Beauvoir does not yet use the conceptual framework of the "practico-inert" and "seriality," this is presaged in her account of the familial, economic, legal, political, and other frameworks through which one "becomes a woman." *The Second Sex* is not only a phenomenology of the lived experience of women's oppression, for Beauvoir is also concerned with questions about how that oppression is perpetuated through social structures, institutions, and practices that women must engage with as the "givens" of their lives. "Yes," she writes, "women on the whole are today inferior to men, that is, their situation affords them fewer possibilities."[21] Indeed, right from the introduction, Beauvoir introduces her claim that "exterior" social realities ineluctably suffuse individual women's lives.

Reflecting on her opening question, "What is a woman?" Beauvoir firmly rejects nominalism: women are not, she insists, "merely the human beings arbitrarily designated by the word woman" (xx). To say there are only human beings, irrespective of sex or race, is "a flight from reality," for "to go for a walk with one's eyes open is enough to demonstrate that humanity is divided into two categories of individuals whose clothes, faces, bodies, smiles, gaits, interests, and occupations are manifestly different. Perhaps these differences are superficial, perhaps they are destined to disappear. What is certain is that right now they do most strikingly exist"(xx–xxi; TA). That is, they have phenomenological reality. They exist as experienced phenomena, as those life-structuring realities within which certain human beings discover themselves to be located, and from which they cannot extricate themselves by an individual act of will. But how to explain these phenomena? Beyond the antinomies of a realist essentialism and a constructionist nominalism another account is necessary. Thus, in her discussion of Freudian psychoanalysis, for example, Beauvoir criticizes Freud for taking for granted what needs to be explained. Freud, she asserts, wrongly essentializes sexuality by taking it as "an irreducible datum" (46), whereas it is only in light of social practices and values and through the individual existential choices that "assume" these that sexuality takes on its meanings.[22] How we experience ourselves as sexual beings, what values we affirm in our sexuality, will be at once idiosyncratic and socially structured. She writes,

> Across the separation of existents, existence is all one: it reveals itself in
> similar bodies, thus there will be constants in the relations between the

ontological and the sexual. At a given epoch, the technologies, the economic and social structure of a collectivity [*collectivité*], will reveal to all its members an identical world. There will also be a relation of sexuality to social forms; individuals, located in similar conditions, will grasp similar significations from what is given. This similarity does not ground a rigorous universality, but it does enable us to rediscover general types within individual histories. (46–47; TA)

Sexuality, then, is at once general and particular. Epoch-wide "technologies and economic and social structures" will permeate particular experiences. Thus, without asserting universal claims, we may still delineate general descriptions. For example, the prohibition of abortion and contraception in France in the 1940s profoundly suffused the sexual experiences of most women, as well as the meanings of motherhood (484). Thus Beauvoir infamously begins the chapter of *The Second Sex* on "The Mother" with a discussion of abortion, the prohibition of which made a free choice of maternity virtually impossible. Although there are "individual histories," and women's lives and experiences are each particular, we see here how women are also a "collectivity." That is, they are members of a series, who, embedded within the same social structures (legal, religious, medical, familial, and so forth), will discover themselves to belong to — and be constrained by — an "identical world."

In her use of the term "collectivity" (*collectivité*) in this passage, Beauvoir already anticipates what, in the *Critique*, Sartre will refer to as a "collective" (*collectif*). By a "collective," Sartre refers to a "series" of individuals who are unified passively, externally to their own intentions and practices, or sometimes even to their knowledge, through their involuntary location in one and the same practico-inert field of structural constraints. Such a "collective" (in contradistinction to what Sartre will call a "group") does not produce shared internal and intentional bonds among its members. Instead, through their insertion in the series, each member alters the significance of the action of the others and so, through them, of his or her own action: "each is something other than himself and behaves like someone else, who in turn is other than himself."[23] Thus women, as Beauvoir characterizes them (anticipating Young by many years), are a series. Each woman, having to accommodate to the "identical world" in which she is situated, becomes, through others, other than herself in a relation of passive, "exterior" unification. As Beauvoir observes, women "do not say 'we' . . . they live dispersed among the males, attached through residence, housework, economic conditions, and social standing to certain men — fathers or husbands — more firmly than they are to other women."[24]

Although Beauvoir underestimates the degree to which women have historically formed bonded groups, her point remains broadly valid: to "become a woman" is to be involuntarily located in various social structures and, through their mediations, to be implicated in serial relations that one has not chosen and yet which one still participates in perpetuating. Thus, already in *The Second Sex*, Beauvoir clearly anticipates Sartre's later project, in the *Critique*, of integrating existential phenomenology (with its emphasis on individual lived experience, freedom, and responsibility) with a Marxist-inflected structural analysis of the material sources of alienation and social oppression.

That Beauvoir views women's inferiorization as emerging through the interconstituencies of social structure and lived, embodied experience is also evident in the organization of *The Second Sex*. Its two volumes should not be read as merely sequential but rather as dialectical. Each sets out, from the opposite pole, to show how socially and discursively produced identities will strongly suffuse subjectivity while never being entirely constitutive of it. To "become a woman" is to "assume" an inferiorized social identity that is not of one's own making and yet with which one does not wholly coincide, to which one is not reducible. Book 1, "Facts and Myths," describes the power-freighted construction of women from "without," that is, in masculinist discourses, practices, and beliefs: "I shall discuss first of all the points of view taken on woman by biology, psychoanalysis, and historical materialism. Next I shall try to show exactly how 'feminine reality' has been constituted, why woman has been defined as the Other — and what have been the consequences from man's point of view" (xxxv; TA). Book 2, "from woman's point of view" (xxxv), next develops a phenomenology of the "lived experience" of "becoming" a woman, an inferiorized Other, within the institutions, practices, and personal relationships that structure and support male dominance. The final section of the book, "Toward Liberation," discusses the "independent woman." Her struggles serve, however, to reveal yet more starkly the weight of domination since it is when it is most resisted that oppression becomes the most apparent.

But although Beauvoir attends at length to the structural dimensions of women's subordination in *The Second Sex*, she still lacks a sufficiently developed conceptual framework to explicate their effects. By contrast, in *Old Age* Beauvoir now possesses, drawing from Sartre's *Critique*, more fully honed tools with which to deepen her own earlier insights about practico-inert structures, serial social relations, and the ways in which they both constrain and are assumed by the self. Moreover, as she reflects on the processes of physical decline that accompany old age, Beauvoir explores in greater depth than in *The Second Sex* the experiences of the body as a limit, as an "I cannot." The brute facticity of a body that is crippled or paralyzed, for example, raises especially pressing questions both about the limits to the discursive materialization of bodies and about the extent to which seriality and material structures of constraint are constitutive of the alienating experiences of the aged and others.

Old Age

The treatment of the aged in modern society is "barbarous"; it is a "scandal," so Beauvoir declares at the beginning of *Old Age*.[25] Moreover, the situation of the aged is subject to a "conspiracy of silence." Indeed (replicating the nominalist assertion that there is no such thing as "woman") many assert: "old age, it doesn't exist! It's just that some people are less young than others."[26] But just as Beauvoir insists, in the opening paragraphs of *The Second Sex*, on the phenomenological "fact" that women do exist, so also do the aged. But the questions, "what is old age?" and "what is an aged person?" will prove to be as complex to answer as the question posed at the very beginning of *The Second Sex*: "what is a woman?" They also provoke the further questions: how far is society at large responsible for the degradations of old age, and what is and is not "ineluctable" in the condition of the aged (10, 541)? How far, she asks, is old age attributable to the organic body's decline; how far to such "existential" factors as the impingement of the weight of one's past on one's projects and one's shrinking horizon for future action; how far to the multiple social practices, structures, institutions, and discursive regimes that constitute the series of "the aged" as inferior others?

Far more than in her treatment of women, Beauvoir frames the oppressive situation of the aged (by whom she means for the most part aged men) as structured also by capitalist society.[27] In a for-profit economy those who are no longer economically productive cease to be valued, and a prior life of alienated labor produces old people who have no existential resources to enjoy the enforced "leisure" of retirement. Indeed, with strong echoes of Marx's notion of the proletariat as a universal class, Beauvoir ends *Old Age* by suggesting that the treatment of the aged "exposes the failure of our entire civilization." More generous pensions and so forth — although she demands them — would not be sufficient to make old age meaningful for most: "It is the whole system that is at issue and our claim cannot be otherwise than radical — change life itself" (543).

But although many of the vicissitudes of old age are structurally produced, they are also "assumed," or interiorized, by those with physically aging bodies and for whom the temporal horizon for actions is increasingly truncated. The aged bear exceptionally heavily the interconstituent facticities of their organic decline and their social inferiorization. Beauvoir talks of the "circularity" of their situation, in which organic, social, and existential elements merge and reinforce each other. Invoking the need for a dialectical investigation, she insists: "An analytical description of the various aspects of old age is therefore not enough: each reacts upon the others and is at the same time affected by them, and it is in the indeterminate movement of this circularity that old age must be grasped" (9; TA).

Old Age is similarly organized to *The Second Sex*, except for the significant absence of an equivalent to the latter's final treatment of the "Liberated Woman." Part 1, "Le point de vue de l'extériorité" (The Viewpoint of Exteriority),[28] covers the "data" on aging offered by various academic disciplines. Part 2, "L'être-dans-le-monde" (Being-in-the-World), offers "from within," (*en intériorité*), a phenomenology of the experience of becoming aged, drawing extensively on memoirs and letters, surveys, and contemporary interview-based research.[29] In the preface Beauvoir writes as follows:

> Every human situation can be viewed from without [*en extériorité*] — as seen from the point of view of an outsider — or from within [*en intériorité*], in so far as the subject assumes and at the same time transcends it. For another, the aged man is an object of knowledge; for himself, he has a lived experience of his condition. In the first part of the book I shall adopt the first view point: I shall examine what biology, anthro-

pology, history and contemporary sociology have to tell us about old age. In the second I shall do my best to describe the way in which the aged man interiorizes his relationship with his body, with time, and with others."[30]

As with *The Second Sex*, the two parts of the book should be read conjointly, rather than sequentially, since they constitute two poles of a dialectical investigation. But Beauvoir now has the resources to better flesh out her earlier methods, having absorbed from Sartre's *Critique* a fuller account of how the "practico-inert" and "seriality" are produced. However, unlike the later Sartre, Beauvoir still integrates into her account a persistent attention to the lived body.[31]

In Beauvoir's investigation of old age, the demands of the body in its organic decline, its objectification in the series of "the aged," and the effect on the individual of large-scale practico-inert institutions such as the market economy, family structure, law, or the system of medical care are revealed as interconstituent. Old age appears to come to us "in exteriority" in several ways: through other individuals and, more generally, from others through our instantiation in the series of "the aged"; from the "alien" facticities of our own bodies; and from our relationship to time and the ways our own past practices and styles of action now weigh on us as forms of the practico-inert. I will discuss each aspect in turn, although Beauvoir's' point is, of course, that they are inseparably "interiorized" or assumed. They give rise to an embodied, lived experience of old age that is generally one of alienation, pervaded by misery, anxiety, and a declining capacity for meaningful action.

Old age comes to us through others from the discovery that, without having chosen such an identity, we belong to the "social category" of old persons. That is, we discover we are both constituted within, and are ourselves a constituting element of, the series of those whom, no longer having a useful social function, modern society designates as "pure objects" — useless, ugly, not worthy of respect.[32] We initially realize we are becoming "old" (just as a young girl discovers she is becoming "a woman") through the words and actions of others, for we do not feel old "inside." Thus even if our bodies begin to suffer from various disabilities of age, such as rheumatism, we will not see these as symptoms of "old age" until we have, through others, interiorized and assumed that condition. Until the intervention of others, "we fail to see that [such symptoms] represent a new status. We remain what we were, with the rheumatism as something additional" (285).

Old age comes to us, then, "as the point of view of the other," as "the other within us" (286). It is always a shock to find oneself so designated, and we do not accept it willingly (288). "We are obliged," however, "to assume a reality which is indubitably our own even though it comes to us from without and remains ungraspable. There is an irresolvable contradiction between the private evidence that assures our unchanging quality and the objective certainty of our transformation. We can only oscillate between them" (290; TA). Although the "onset" of old age — the time when we come to realize we are "old" — may occur suddenly, through a particular encounter, or more gradually through multiple experiences, either way it takes place within the structuring power of the practico-inert field: the social practices, institutions, and discourses that shape old age. "In our society the elderly person is marked as such by custom, by the behaviour of others and by vocabulary itself: he must take up this reality. There is an infinite number of ways of doing so, but not one of them will allow me to coincide with the reality that I assume" (291; TA).

The aged — like women — are not only the "other," they are the inferiorized other. Why? In all societies, Beauvoir suggests, younger adults seek to distinguish themselves from the aged because they fear their own old age. But in modern Western society, where productivity, profit, and the cult of novelty (380–82) are the most prevalent values, once retired (or "redundant"), the elderly are (with the exception of the very wealthy) consistently treated as subhuman. The aged do not become "unproductive" only, or necessarily, through physical or intellectual decline. For it is by current criteria of efficiency that their speed of performance is deemed inadequate or their skills outdated. Retirement is often an enforced and brutally abrupt passage into old age, and for many retirement presents a profound existential crisis. Since in modern society "a man defines his identity by his calling and his pay" (266), retirement constitutes a sudden destruction of prior identity, and it offers very few opportunities to redefine oneself other than through assuming one's membership in the despised series of "the aged." Retirement means "losing one's place in society, one's dignity and almost one's reality" (266). The fall into acute poverty that so often accompanies retirement compounds these tendencies, making it harder to go out and participate in other kinds of social activities even when one still has the physical capacity and desire to do so. Thus, poverty contributes profoundly to the isolation that is one of the greatest scourges of old age (270).

Each isolated and each "the same," the elderly are passively unified by the social institutions and practices that serialize them in the collective of "the aged." Powerlessness is thus their common hallmark. Apart from a small elite (partly cushioned by their wealth), powerlessness and its correlatives—a despised social status and a demeaning dependency—are both the objective condition and the pervasive lived experience of the aged. Dispersed and serialized, excluded from public activities and spaces, they have no capacity for organized resistance. Individually, in their isolation, they may also become vulnerable to exploitation and abuse at the hands of those on whom they must depend, for these macrolevel structural realities will also suffuse their particular relationships with their children or care-givers.

But age does not come to us from "without," through seriality, alone. In approaching old age, we may also make the startling discovery that our bodies, in their brute physical facticity, are "other." "I am my body," yet in old age my lived body becomes, paradoxically, "other" than myself. This is not only, as for women, because of its meaning for others.[33] For I increasingly encounter it more immediately as the source of an unambiguous "I cannot," or as a source of pain and suffering that impinges on my intentions and colors my experience of the world. Although its particular significances will depend on the social context, the aged are "subject to a biological fate," Beauvoir writes.[34] The aging body undergoes a process of "biological decay" (443) that must eventually bring about a decline in activity and reduce the possibility of enacting one's projects. Even without the presence of illness there develops "a 'fatigability' that spares none" (28). "The coefficient of adversity in things rises: stairs are harder to climb, distances longer to travel, streets more dangerous to cross, parcels heavier to carry" (304; TA). Thus, the body is increasingly encountered as an alien presence, as an "I cannot," as an "object" that blocks my projects. We find that instead of being an instrument "the body becomes an obstacle" (317; TA). In *The Second Sex* Beauvoir can conceive of a hypothetical society in which having a female or a male body would not make a very significant difference to one's given life-possibilities and where neither privilege nor oppression would follow from one's sex, and we can conceive of societies in which such attributes as one's skin color, religion, or language would not oppressively delimit a life at all. But we cannot generally conceive of old age without its accompanying inexorable decline of organic bodies.

Beauvoir begins the first part of *Old Age*, "The Viewpoint of Exteriority," with a chapter on the biology of aging. Drawing on extensive medical literatures of the time, in which aging is presented as an objective process, she concurs that real biological changes mark the aging process: cellular regeneration slows, hair whitens, skin wrinkles, teeth fall out, muscular strength declines, and for women, menopause ends reproductive capacity (25–28). Such phenomena are not primarily "materialized" by discourse. Beauvoir would have objected strongly to Donna Haraway's appropriation of her famous statement that "one is not born a woman, one becomes one" to legitimize the alleged "co-text": "One is not born an organism. Organisms are made."[35] For, contra Haraway's discourse-reductionism, Beauvoir insists that organic bodies do have indubitable facticities that may impinge on our ability to act. Even if we could isolate such facticities from their social context, we would still have to say that in old age one's relationship to one's body becomes more and more one of alienation: "my body" is "me," yet "it" constrains me, "it" dominates me, "it" pains me. Beauvoir quotes extensively from memoirs and other sources to show how pervasive the lived experience of the body as an impediment to freedom rather than as "the instrument" of one's projects becomes for the aged. But, of course, such facticities of the body are never lived in a "pure" form, and there are always social processes and discursive forms that imbue bodily experience and shape its meaning. For example, muscular weakness may be a real, objective barrier to certain kinds of actions we wish to undertake, but a contempt for muscular weakness (including our own self-contempt) comes to us from elsewhere. Thus, Beauvoir insists, "for mankind not even the body itself is pure nature."[36]

But if, paradoxically, there are ways that old age comes to us from "without" from "within" our own bodies, in an equally paradoxical manner, it comes to us from our own life-activity: for our past actions continue to bear on our present, and as our past extends and our future is truncated, their weight grows ever greater. All action creates its own inertia: past activity congeals in ways that mold present and future action. Beauvoir (following Sartre here) now calls these congealings forms of the "practico-inert." In old age, the inertia of our own past actions presses ever more heavily on us. Future possibilities become increasingly delimited by how we have already acted over a lifetime. "From the past I carry all the mechanisms of my body, the cultural tools I use, my knowledge and my ignorances, my relationship with others, my activities and my obligations. Everything that I have ever done has been taken back by the past and it has there become reified under the form of the practico-inert. . . . By his praxis every man achieves his objectification in the world and becomes possessed by it" (372–73; TA). Thus, for example, the scientist rarely publishes highly original work when he is old because he has already built up "his being outside himself" (*son être hors de lui*) through his previous work, and this in turn now "possesses" him. His extant work is "an ensemble of inert significations" in which he is presently alienated. He develops what Beauvoir (again using Sartre's term) calls "ideological interests" in continuing along his previous tracks, while habits of mind, earlier laid down, prevent him from thinking in fresh ways (391; TA).[37]

For the aged, rigid habits of mind and fixed routines often shape daily life. These offer a promise (usually unmet) of protection from a threatening and alien world. But habits also preclude new experiences; "inveterate habits . . . create impossibilities." Possessions may also become particularly important sites of alienation, for "the things that belong to us are as it were solidified habits." Indeed, "my objects are myself" and "since the old person no longer makes himself exist by doing, he wants to *have* in order to be."[38] This alienation is particularly strong with regard to money, and the character of the elderly miser may be explained as a "magical" identification of the self with its power. Through his possessions the old miser attempts magically "to assure himself of his identity against those who claim to see him as nothing but an object" (469–70; TA).

Engaging Discrepant Materialisms

But here we have come full circle! In the personage of the old miser, we see exemplified how the individual "existential" crisis of old age is imbued with meaning by the macrolevel structures of society. For it is, as Marx had pointed out, within our particular socioeconomic formation that money promises to be "an omnipotent being" that may turn our attributes and qualities into their opposites.[39] It is within the wider social structures of the practico-inert that our personal habits and prior ways of acting attain their own forms of practical inertia. Even as old age comes to us from "ourselves" — from our own histories and our own bodies — it comes to us also from "elsewhere," from the material mediations of the practico-inert and the serial social relations in which we cannot but act.

Let us return to Simone de Beauvoir's opening questions: How far is society at large responsible for the degradations of old age? What is, and is not, "ineluctable" in the condition of the aged?[40] We can now see why she insists on the dialectical "circularity" of their situation. We can also see why a theoretical approach that focuses on how a multiplicity of materialities constitutes the lived experience of age is necessary. The facticities of the individual body's decline, the large-scale structures of the practico-inert (including discursive formations), the practico-inert weight of our own past actions, all of these mediate the self to itself in ways that both give rise to alienation and are conducive to oppression. Thus theoretical approaches that reductively privilege one aspect of materiality over others will not be adequate to the tasks of social critique — be they of age, gender, or other forms of oppression.

In Beauvoir's descriptions of the "circular flow" of elements that give rise to the lived experience of old age, in her appreciation of the brute facticities of the aging body, and in her simultaneous demonstration that old age is socially and discursively constituted, we find exemplified a method that nonreductively attends to diverse genres of materiality, to their confluences, mutual mediations, and interconstitutive effects. The facticities of organic bodies play a greater role in aging than in many other situations of oppression, but Beauvoir's method has far-reaching potential for critical social theory. Working at once "from the inside out," through phenomenological approaches that illuminate embodied lived experience, and "from the outside in," through analyses of how seriality and practico-inert "macro" structures produce alienation and oppression, Beauvoir suggests why we need to move beyond discrepant materialisms — and how we may begin to do so.

Notes

1   Some work in this genre is informed by Roy Bhaskar's "critical realism." See, for example, Brown, Fleetwood, and Roberts, eds., *Critical Realism and Marxism*. Other works proceed from a feminist perspective, for example, Ebert, *Ludic Feminism and After*; and Hennessy, *Profit and Pleasure*.

2   Paradigmatic for this genre of "materialism" are Butler, *Gender Trouble*, and *Bodies That Matter*.

3   Grosz, *Volatile Bodies*.

4   Recent key works in this vein include Sheets-Johnstone, *The Roots of Power*; and Catalano, *Thinking Matter*.

5   Beauvoir, *The Second Sex*, 34. In citations from this work, and others, I frequently amend the published English translations. Such changes are indicated in the text with the notation "TA" (translation altered) after the page reference.

6   In French the second volume is entitled *L'expérience vécue* — lived experience. Unfortunately it is mistranslated in the English edition as "Woman's Life Today."

7   See chap. 3 of *The Second Sex*, "The Point of View of Historical Materialism," 53–60.

8   The passage she quotes reads: "The immediate, natural and necessary relation of human being to human being is also the relation of man to woman. . . . From this relationship man's whole level of development can be assessed. It follows from the character of this relationship how far man has become, and has understood himself as, a species-being, a human being. The relation of man to woman is the most natural relation of human being to human being. It indicates, therefore, how far man's natural behaviour has become human, and how far his human essence has become a natural essence for him, how far his human nature has become nature for him." *The Second Sex*, 731–32. I cite the Marx passage from "Economic and Philosophical Manuscripts," as given in the English translation by Thomas Bottomore, 154.

9   Sartre, *Critique of Dialectical Reason*.

10   Ibid., 124–25.

11   "Each vocable brings along with it the profound signification which the whole epoch has given to it. As soon as the ideologist speaks, he says more and something different from what he wants to say; the period steals his thought from him. He constantly veers about, and the idea finally expressed is a profound deviation." Sartre, *Search for a Method*, 113. This essay, translated and published as a separate volume in English, is the preface to *Critique of Dialectical Reason*. See also Sartre's response to poststructural discourse theory in "Jean-Paul Sartre répond."

12   Beauvoir, *Old Age*. The U.S. edition is entitled *The Coming of Age* (New York:

Putnam, 1972). Pagination is the same in the 1972 British and U.S. editions. The book was originally published as *La Vieillesse* (Paris: Gallimard, 1970).

13   There has been much debate about the Beauvoir-Sartre relationship and about who influenced whom, with regards to their earlier works. However, very little has been written about the question of influence in the later works. I am suggesting here that profound mutual influences were at play, but I avoid addressing issues of whether they flowed more in one direction than the other.

14   See Kruks, "Simone de Beauvoir." For a wider survey of the topic, see also Kruks, "Beauvoir's Time/Our Time."

15   Moi, *What Is a Woman?*, vii. This work constitutes a tacit autocritique, I believe, because Moi was one of the first enthusiastically to introduce post-structuralism into Anglo-American feminist theory in the highly influential volume *Sexual/Textual Politics*.

16   Moi, *What Is a Woman?*, 74.

17   The phrase is Sara Heinämaa's in *Toward a Phenomenology of Sexual Difference*, 70.

18   Beauvoir, *The Second Sex*, 34.

19   Young, "Lived Body vs. Gender," 19.

20   Young, "Gender as Seriality."

21   Beauvoir, *The Second Sex*, xxx.

22   Beauvoir's use of the verb *assumer* — to assume, or to take up — is complex. Such legalistic English phrases as "assuming a debt" or "assuming responsibility for somebody" gesture toward her meaning. However, she uses the term to imply the existential taking up and making one's own of the factic "givens" of one's situation. One "assumes" one's sex, for example, insofar as one integrates one's sexual being into one's existence. Such an assumption is not "voluntary" in the sense of being a conscious, rational choice but rather is affirmed in action, through one's projects, through one's embodied being-in-the-world.

23   Sartre, *Critique of Dialectical Reason*, 166.

24   Beauvoir, *The Second Sex*, xxv.

25   Beauvoir's focus is mainly on France in the 1950s and 1960s; she also offers some discussion of the United States and other parts of Europe, and an appendix on old age in socialist countries. Attitudes toward old age and treatment of the aged today are not greatly different from what they were in the times that Beauvoir describes. Indeed, the emphasis on "youth culture" that began in the 1960s may have made the condition of the aged worse. Basic state pensions are still not at all adequate in either Britain or the United States; and the aged still mostly live isolated or ghettoized as she describes.

26   Beauvoir, *Old Age*, 1; TA.

27   Although some data on old women is provided, and there is a discussion of sexual desire among the elderly of each sex, the main focus of the book is

explicitly on men. Since, says Beauvoir, men are the workers and are those who are active in public and make history, they suffer the losses of old age far more acutely than women. See especially 89, 217, 261–62. In contrast, Beauvoir suggests that the transition to old age is less difficult for women because they are already in the domestic or private sphere. This argument, made in 1970, is highly problematic because women by this time had much more fully left the domestic sphere than in 1949 and because, as Beauvoir had argued in *The Second Sex*, the decline in sexual attractiveness that accompanies old age presents more of a crisis for women than men, with menopause marking a definitive turning point in the aging process. There is a troubling disjuncture between Beauvoir's treatment of women's aging in *The Second Sex* and her very scant consideration of the specificities of women's aging in *Old Age*.

28   The English translation renders this as "Old Age Seen from Without," a formulation that misses Beauvoir's appropriation of the concept of "exteriority" from the *Critique*. Because the English translation of *Old Age* preceded that of the *Critique* by several years, English conventions for translating Sartre's neologisms were not yet in place. I have frequently altered the translation of *Old Age* to make Beauvoir's use of Sartre's terminology more visible.

29   There is also a tacit autobiographical element to "Being-in-the World," as Beauvoir was sixty-two when *Old Age* was published. Anne Strasser explores some of the similarities between Beauvoir's autobiographical account of her own aging and the account offered in *Old Age* in "La vieillesse comme mutilation."

30   Beauvoir, *Old Age*, 10; TA.

31   In the *Critique*, the body is methodologically important as the origin of the basic "organic" need that necessitates praxis. However, it is not explicitly considered as the site of lived experience, be it of either free action or seriality. Indeed, embodied experience is yet more absent in the *Critique* than it was earlier in *Being and Nothingness*!

32   Beauvoir, *Old Age*, 88.

33   "Woman, like man, is her body," Beauvoir had written, referencing Merleau-Ponty. However, she immediately added, "but her body is something other than herself." Beauvoir, *The Second Sex*, 29. This observation is made as Beauvoir is discussing menstruation, but it is clear from her later remarks that it is the social meaning of menstruation that makes it so alienating for women.

34   Beauvoir, *Old Age*, 86.

35   "One is not born a woman, Simone de Beauvoir correctly insisted. It took the political-epistemological terrain of postmodernism to be able to insist on a co-text to de Beauvoir's: one is not born an organism. Organisms are made; they are constructs of a world-changing kind. The constructions of an organism's boundaries . . . are the job of discourses." Haraway, "The Biopolitics of Postmodern Bodies," 207.

36   Beauvoir, *Old Age*, 12; TA.

37   "Interest is being-wholly-outside-oneself-in-a-thing in so far as it conditions *praxis* as a categorical imperative." Sartre, *Critique of Dialectical Reason*, 197.

38   Beauvoir, *Old Age*, 469–70; TA.

39   "The power to confuse and invert all human and natural qualities, to bring about fraternization of incompatibles, the *divine* power of money, resides in its *character* as the alienated and self-alienating species life of man. . . . What I as a *man* am unable to do, and thus what all my individual faculties are unable to do, is made possible for me by money." Marx, "Economic and Philosophical Manuscripts," 192.

40   Beauvoir, *Old Age*, 10; TA.

Jason Edwards

The Materialism of Historical Materialism

There are innumerable and seemingly interminable interpretations and debates concerning what constitutes the
materialism of historical materialism. Most of these are
only of interest if one buys into the premise that social
and political analysis must proceed from a given ontology.
Now, this is not to say that work on an ontology of human social life is not of interest or value. Part of what such
an ontology has to deal with is the notion of "materialism" as a philosophical doctrine that concerns the nature
and multiform manifestations of matter. But I would argue that such considerations of matter and the doctrine of
materialism have — or should have — little to do with historical materialism as an approach to social and political
analysis. Attempts to import into Marxism philosophical
conceptions of materialism, whether in the form of classical Enlightenment materialism, biological naturalism or,
in more recent times, critical realism,[1] have historically
proven wanting for those who continue to see historical
materialism as a theory of the social and political institutions, practices, and trajectories of contemporary capitalist societies.

It does not follow that historical materialism should be
considered as a set of standard axioms that are picked up
by the social or political theorist and mechanically applied. The materialism of historical materialism should be

seen as more of a heuristic for social and political study rather than a set of explanatory theses. Yet the power of this heuristic seems to have been overlooked by many of the very people who did such service to social theory by dismantling the notion of historical materialism as a positivist science based on metaphysical conceptions of history and the subject. Nebulous as it is, we might identify poststructuralism as cohering around the decentering of the subject and the rejection of historical teleology. Poststructuralism, in this respect, posed a powerful and ongoing challenge to a Marxism founded on the combination of a humanist philosophical anthropology and some form of economic or technological determinism. There are still, of course, people who wish to defend historical materialism as a theory of human nature and of the successive development of modes of production. But I will assume for the purposes of this essay that such an understanding of historical materialism is not defensible and that if the latter is still to be defended, it is by adopting some conception of theoretical antihumanism and antihistoricism. What then remains at the heart of historical materialism is an ongoing analysis of the current social and political conditions of contemporary capitalist societies in light of their historical development, their embedded institutions and practices, and the contingent circumstances that serve to reproduce them — or that threaten their reproduction — over time.

Now, there is nothing "new" in this understanding of historical materialism. But many poststructuralist critics of humanist and determinist Marxism forget this conception of historical materialism precisely at the moment when they need to remember it. Much of the political analysis that appears in poststructuralist literature effectively resorts to a form of liberal multicultural and identity politics that seems blind or indifferent to the major problems faced by all humans today: climate change, global inequality, forced migration and new forms of slavery, and the proliferation of military technology and warfare. I argue in this essay that we will need to remember the materialism of historical materialism in the requisite sense if we are to understand how these problems are the systemic product of the reproduction of modern capitalist societies and the international system of states. The life of social production and consumption continues to be the central feature of human societies and in the absence of either natural or mechanically created super-abundance, it will continue to be so. Struggles for land and resources as global warming continues apace, economic competition between states and the continued inequality between North and South, the "War on Terror" and the modern revolution in military affairs, all have obvious and far-reaching consequences in the present for how material life is organized, disrupted, and transformed. We need to return, then, to a kind of historical materialism that focuses on the reproduction of capitalist societies and the system of states, both in everyday practices of production and consumption and in the ideological and coercive power of states and the international system.

In this essay I elaborate on the features of such a historical materialism in three sections. First, I explore the notion of material practices in Marxism. Here I argue that material practices should not be understood as limited to activities involved in the immediate process of production but must be more broadly conceived as all those practices involving material bodies — organic and nonorganic — that, from the point of view of historical materialism, can be seen as a totality of practices that reproduce the relations of production over time. The second section focuses on the importance of the material practices of everyday life and the organization of lived space for the reproduction of capitalism, which is undertaken primarily through an engagement with the work of Henri Lefebvre. In the final section, I argue that it remains crucial for a credible historical materialism that it should involve a political theory of the way everyday life and space are mediated by the state and the international system in sustaining — and providing challenges to — the currently constituted social and economic order. In this regard, the kind of ontological materialist approach developed in the most prominent work of Marxist theory in recent times, namely Michael Hardt's and Antonio Negri's *Empire*, falls short. Nonetheless, there are important Marxian analyses that can illuminate this relationship between the material practices of everyday life and lived space on the one hand and the global organization of economic and political power on the other.

Marxism and Material Practices

In *Capital*, Marx explored the conditions necessary for the reproduction of capitalist relations of production. The abstract conceptual analysis of the commodity, capital, production and circulation, surplus-value, and so on, set out in part 1 of the first volume, gives way to a survey of the laws, institutions, and practices that are necessary for the extraction of surplus-value to take place in the process of production. The famous chapter on "The Working Day" charts the various quotidian procedures, routines, and prohibitions that workers in different industries were subjected to in mid-nineteenth-century England, whether it be children working in cotton mills, steel founders, bread bakers, or dress makers.[2] What is clear from this analysis is the complex nature of the relations that are required to reproduce the capitalist system of production. In these pages, Marx's approach departs from the programmatic and deterministic summary of historical materialism provided in his preface of 1859.[3] Rather, it is in these more open-ended analyses that we grasp the sense of the materialism in Marx's historical materialism; that is, the totality of the material practices that are required to reproduce the relations of production over time. The character of these practices in any given setting is not easily or neatly drawn out on a conceptual tableau in which the economic has primacy and is a straightforward synonym of the material. The material relations of production are those that are instantiated in specific kinds of practices that in any given setting appear as having various characteristics: legal, political, economic, ideological, and so on. While Marx locates the immediate space of production as central to the modern system of industrial capitalism, historical materialism — understood as a broad analysis of diverse social formations — recognizes the diversity of the forms of practice that are necessary for sustaining the relations of production in very different kinds of societies. This kind of materialist analysis draws our attention to the way in which specific social institutions and relations, whether historical or contemporary, are instantiated in multiple forms of material practices.

Accordingly, it is important to recognize that material practices should not be conceived of simply as those involved in the immediate process of production. It has been argued that Marx's historical materialism maintains a distinction between the material and the social properties of human activity, where material activities are considered to be those that involve the use of productive forces in the immediate process of production and social activities are those that do not.[4] But the problem with this claim is twofold. First, an object does not become a material productive force unless it is selected for use in production by human beings within a social context. Material objects, in this sense, are always socially mediated. Second, a given "material" object — in the sense that it is physical and tangible

— at any given time may be employed in the immediate process of production, in the immediate support of production, or in a way that has little to do with the immediate process of production at all. A gun, for example, is a productive force when it is used to shoot rabbits that are to be consumed; it is not a productive force, although it can be a condition for the immediate process of production, when it is used to coerce or protect the immediate producers; and it has little to do with the immediate process of production when it is used in sport, although here it might support the kind of ideological practice that sustains social order. All such activities concerning human use of guns constitute material practices in the sense that they involve human bodies actively engaging with and transforming the material world and in that they are, at the same time, social activities.

We cannot understand the reproduction of capitalist relations of production in the present except as an expression of manifold and various material practices. I will turn presently to this conception of practice, or material practice, in more detail, but what should be recognized here is that historical materialism is not inconsistent with an approach that emphasizes the significance of nonproductive practices, or at least of practices that are not directly involved in the productive process. It is not fatal to historical materialism that the immediate space of production plays a lesser role in the reproduction of the relations of production than it might have done in the heyday of mass industrial capitalism. Various attempts have been made over the last thirty years or so to establish that transformations in the character of production and consumption have rendered historical materialism obsolete. But this is the case only on the basis of two erroneous assumptions: first, that class analysis — and in particular a certain kind of class analysis in which the existence of a Fordist industrial working class is seen in itself as a necessary condition of capitalist relations of production — lies at the heart of historical materialism and second, that unquestioned primacy is granted in the reproduction of the relations of production to material practices in the immediate sphere of production. Neither assumption operates in the more illuminating texts written by Marx nor in those of authors in the Western Marxist tradition such as Gramsci, Adorno, and Althusser.

It was Althusser who, in rejecting the notion of the Hegelian expressive totality, most prominently made the case for a Marxism in which "from the first moment to the last, the lonely instance of the 'last hour' never comes."[5]

In other words, jettisoning the idea of the expressive totality, which Althusser identified in the work of Hegelian Marxists such as Lukács, involves a recognition of the complex nature of any given social formation. Its various "levels," "moments" or—the expression that Althusser employs most fruitfully, "practices"—appear as relatively autonomous, occupying distinct spaces as well as times. In this respect, different practices have different locations and histories that will determine their relationship. While there is a good deal to be critical of in Althusser's conception of historical materialism—including his assertion of a structure in dominance as well as his attempt to provide a criterion of scientificity for historical materialism in the shape of the theory of theoretical practice[6]—we should not be too hasty in dismissing this notion of a complex totality. The concept of "totality" has exercised poststructuralist thinkers, particularly with respect to deconstruction, where the notion of totality in the human sciences was for a long time associated with the structuralist attempt to discern a structural center. This latter strategy was brilliantly exposed and opposed by Jacques Derrida in the 1960s.[7] And indeed, it was the case that in *For Marx* and *Reading Capital*, Althusser and his collaborators were searching for the key to unlock the totality, something they believed was to be provided by resorting to the epistemological fiat of the theory of theoretical practice. But on the other hand, it is perfectly coherent to speak of a totality without a center, as in effect Althusser was doing despite his (largely rhetorical) nod to the notions of structure in dominance and determination by the economic in the last instance. What deconstructionism points out is that the meaning of the totality is never closed off by its constitutive elements: in Derrida's approach to the reading of texts, meaning is constantly deferred. This is not the place to enter into a discussion of whether texts and societies can both be treated in this deconstructionist fashion, but it is timely to point out that rejecting the idea of a centered totality, as an abstraction of the character of social relations, does not entail a rejection of the notion of a totality of social relations without a center. Indeed, as I show in the final section, this is how more recent Marxian contributions approach the question of totality with respect to the character of the international economic and political system.

A conception of a complex totality of material practices that are constitutive of capitalist relations of production is, then, salvageable out of the work of Marx and Althusser. Material practices, in this regard, should be seen as regular forms of behavior that are norm-governed, and that involve one's relation to one's body and to other bodies, as well as to objects of experience. If we designate such practices "political," "ideological," or "economic," then we do so only insofar as such practices attend to what we generally understand as political, ideological, or economic phenomena: the government of social conflict and cooperation, the production and propagation of systems of belief, and processes of production and consumption. If we talk, however, of a totality of these practices that are constitutive of capitalist relations of production, there is a sense in which this is merely a work of description. As long as we define capitalist relations of production as those in which there are private property rights, legally protected exchange through markets, and a market for labor, then we may talk of the sum of material practices that are required for such relations of production to be reproduced. But it should be clear that we have to go beyond this if we are to demonstrate how this complex totality is instantiated in the everyday life of people and how the material practices of everyday life are implicated in the political and economic power of the state and the international system.

Everyday Life, Space, and Capitalism

So far we have seen how Marx set out in *Capital* to analyze the everyday conditions of production that were necessary for the reproduction of capitalist relations of production. Indeed, Marx was not the first to do this: before he turned to political economy, Engels had already performed this kind of investigation, and there are also earlier passages where the Scottish theorists of commercial society, particularly Adam Smith in his discussion of the division of labor, were doing something similar.[8] Until around the 1920s, when considerations of everyday life did take place, they were undertaken from a primarily Marxian perspective that recognized the space of work as crucial for the analysis. The life of the industrial worker was subject to the rigid and repetitive experience of producing uniform commodities in a system of mass production. Such considerations tended to see the experiences of the worker as relatively passive responses to the quotidian demands of the workplace. Combined with ideological justifications for capitalism, this presented a picture of everyday life as overwhelmingly negative and repressive. As a consequence it was believed that escape from the exploitation and oppression of work under capitalism could be achieved only through revolution, whether that was to come about through the spontaneous development of working-class political consciousness or through the actions of the revolutionary vanguard party.

Accordingly, the analysis of everyday experience from the "classical" Marxist perspective tended to view such experience, structured as it was primarily by the organization of the sphere of production, as a functional consequence of the reproduction of the relations of industrial and financial capitalism. In this regard, the constitution of experience through the manifold forms of material practice outside the immediate space of production, which each individual engages with on a daily basis, was overlooked. The growth in the twentieth century of a sociology that was concerned with exactly such experiences, as expressed in somatic and linguistic conventions and rituals involved in the conduct of everyday life, thus posed a challenge to the kind of Marxism that limited significant experience to the immediate site of production.[9] Subsequently, the Foucauldian analysis of power relations in modern societies would emphasize how the experience of workers in the sphere of production was shaped by the same kind of disciplinary norms that applied to a large variety of institutions and material practices outside the immediate production process.[10] In the Marxist tradition, the lessons of a sociology that focused on the sphere of material culture as a mechanism for the reproduction of capitalism were first taken up by Walter Benjamin and members of the Frankfurt School, most prominently Theodor Adorno and Max Horkheimer.[11] To some extent the latter two anticipated the Foucault of *Discipline and Punish*, especially in their account of how normalizing pacification operates in those areas of modern everyday life that are conceived by liberalism as the domain of the private individual freed from the encroachment of power.

Perhaps the most influential account of how capitalism is reproduced in social spaces outside of the immediate sphere of production was, however, that provided by Henri Lefebvre in his work on everyday life. When Lefebvre published the first volume of his *Critique of Everyday Life* in 1947, the notion of *la vie quotidienne* was intended to convey a meaning that, as Stuart Eldon points out, is not quite captured by the English term "everyday life."[12] The notion of the quotidian, in this respect, is meant to convey the importance of ordinary everyday experience in modernity. Furthermore, it explains how such experience has become uniform, routine, and repetitive. In this regard everyday life outside the immediate space of production has the same kind of routine and repetitive character as in the Taylorist work process. Yet at the same time, the everyday life of consumption and leisure had by the late twentieth century taken on greater significance in the industrial capitalist West, with family and private life absorbing more of the individual's time as working hours declined and leisure time increased, as the production of consumer goods multiplied and diversified, and as an ideology of personal freedom and self-improvement became pervasive. Consumption and leisure now came to be seen as life's goal and work as a necessary means toward that end. In this respect the everyday life of work and the everyday life of consumption came to be widely regarded as two separate forms of experience, the first usually seen as a necessary bind and the second as the domain of freedom and self-improvement. Lefebvre argues throughout his work that this separation is nonetheless merely apparent, for

> daily life, like language, contains manifest forms and deep structures that are implicit in its operations yet concealed in and through them. . . . Everyday acts are repeated. . . . They are simultaneously individual, "group," . . . and social. In ways that are poorly understood, the everyday is thus closely related to the modes of organization and existence of a (particular) society, which imposes relations between forms of work, leisure, "private life," transport, public life. A constraining influence, the everyday imposes itself on all members of the relevant society, who, with some exceptions, have only minor variations on the norms at their disposal.[13]

What Lefebvre points to is the importance of considering the everyday life of consumption and leisure as it features in the totality of material practices — including those of production — that are involved in the reproduction of economic and political life. In this regard we might see practices of individual freedom and self-improvement as effects of social relations that constitute the conditions for the reproduction of capitalist relations of production in the context of the power of the state and the international system.

Lefebvre's emphasis on the importance of everyday life outside the immediate sphere of production is the spur for his extensive analysis of the way in which the production of space in the modern world is tied to the experience of the quotidian.[14] Lefebvre's focus on the manner in which material space is produced in diverse times and places—but particularly in the modern city—marks an important turn in social theory away from the valorization of the historical event or process to a deeper reflection on the manner in which the organization of the material spaces in which human beings live and work both constrain them and provide resources for social action. The analysis of space in this fashion has been continued by contemporary sociologists and geographers interested in the connections between urban space, capitalist production, the state, and the international system.[15] I touch on some of the contributions to this literature in the final section, but here it suffices to note the indebtedness of this more recent work to Lefebvre's conceptualization of space. Space, in this sense, does not denote an empty void or the given physical environment in which human beings live. Space is rather the social space produced by the material practices of human beings. For Lefebvre, the analysis of the social production of space rests on three related concepts. First, the concept of spatial practices: that is, the general practice of the organization of space in a particular social setting, given a society's productive technology, its relations of production, its religious beliefs, cultural conventions, and so on. The spatial practice of the ancient city-state, for example, is very different to that of the medieval or modern city. Second, representations of space: that is, space as it is technically conceptualized in the knowledge and practices of scientists, architects, planners, and so on. Again, the form of these representations will vary in different kinds of social formation. Third, representational spaces: the lived space that people experience in their daily lives, a space that in the main is "passively experienced" and that "tend[s] towards more or less coherent systems of non-verbal symbols and signs."[16]

Lefebvre's work on the experience of everyday life and the production of space through manifold and interdependent material and representational practices is crucial for the operation of a meaningful historical materialism today. While some Marxists have attempted to revive Marxism by searching for new philosophical criteria for its scientific standing, reducing it thereby to a set of discrete explanatory hypotheses, or by transforming it into a purely normative theory of distributive justice, Lefebvre's emphasis on everyday life and space provides for a perspective from which the central problem of historical materialism—how the relations of production sustain and reproduce certain historically determinate forms of production and consumption — can be best explored. Historical materialism in this guise is not a metatheory of the successive development of modes of production but rather points us toward that dense but open totality of material practices that constitute and reproduce a given social formation.

This is not to deny that aspects of Lefebvre's historical materialism are deeply problematic. It is no exaggeration to say that his intellectual nemesis was Althusser. Lefebvre's central objection to the kind of "structural" Marxism that Althusser and his collaborators developed was that it subordinates the individual — or subject — to the structure, such that subjects appear as little more than bearers of social structure. Lefebvre's rejection of this kind of straightforward subordination of subjects to social structure is important to his argument insofar as subjective experience is a central category for understanding the character of everyday life. In some of his work, he accordingly attempted to steer a course between the two major philosophical currents that dominated the postwar French intellectual scene: structuralism and phenomenology. Much of his analysis here sought to demonstrate how the norms and representations of everyday life operate within the experience of individuals.[17] At the same time, however, Lefebvre maintained that "alienation" is "the central notion of philosophy."[18] Despite his explicit rejection of the presumption that a concept of alienation depends on a philosophical anthropology which posits a substantive, presocial human nature, his constant return to the notion is problematic. For it underpins an analysis of everyday life and the contemporary organization of space that is largely negative in character. The implication is that individuals are alienated in the combined processes of production and everyday life and that alienation can be overcome only through their transformation. What such a view still presupposes is a utopian view of nonalienating forms of production and cultural life against which current forms are measured. It simultaneously gives rise to the politically recondite idea that changes to production and everyday life must be brought about from the outside, by external acts of transgression and rejection. This explains the attraction of Lefebvre's work for the situationist revolutionaries.[19]

So far I have endorsed the idea that a materialist analysis of the organization of everyday life and space in capitalist societies can and should proceed on the basis of an understanding of the totality of material practices that are necessary for the reproduction of capitalist relations of production. But it must avoid the reductionist trap of thinking either that the practices of everyday life and the structuring of space are all functionally beneficial for the reproduction of capitalism or that individual experiences of everyday life and space are uniform (or simply passive) in character. To do so would be to paint the kind of unremittingly bleak view of modernity set out in Adorno's and Horkheimer's *Dialectic of Enlightenment*. What such a picture fails to recognize is that the material practices constitutive of modern life are the only grounds from which we could hope and expect to bring about important political and social transformations. Indeed, in his last published book, *Rhythmananlysis*, Lefebvre himself pursues this point through a reflection on the rhythms of everyday life, particularly in the context of urban space. "Rhythm," in this respect, denotes the repetitive character of everyday life, but there can be "no identical absolute repetition indefinitely: Whence the relation between repetition and difference. When it concerns the everyday, rites, ceremonies, fetes, rules and laws, there is always something new and unforeseen that introduces itself into the repetitive: difference."[20] Accordingly, even within contemporary urban practices that appear highly repetitive in character — whether that be travelling into work by the same route every day, going to the same kind of bars, restaurants, or clubs with friends, surfing the internet to expand one's network of contacts, or playing video games that involve some kind of virtual interaction with the space of urban life — there is difference and the potential for such practices to become sites of political resistance and transformation. While historical materialism has traditionally tended to ignore these last kinds of practice, their analysis is central both for understanding the reproduction of capitalist societies over time and for considering how social relations may be transformed. However, important as such an approach toward everyday life and the organization of lived space may be, it must be connected to an analysis of the relationship between economic production, the state, and the international system.

A Materialist Geopolitics

The last decade has seen a remarkable (at least from the perspective of the early 1990s) revival of Marxian analyses of the international economic and political system. Perhaps the most prominent of these is Michael Hardt's and Antonio Negri's work on Empire.[21] Hardt's and Negri's thesis concerning the decline of the nation-state and a new form of sovereignty based on a "network power" of dominant states, supranational organizations, and capitalist corporations—or Empire—is by now well known. But as substantively problematic as this thesis is, what is most striking about the work is the extent to which it turns on the concepts of biopolitics and deterritorialization, as these are taken from the work of Foucault and of Gilles Deleuze and Félix Guattari, respectively.[22] Clearly, both of these concepts are materialist in the sense that they are concerned, in the first instance, with the governing of human bodies and populations, and in the second, with the organization of physical space. But in fact what *Empire* presents to us is not, as one might expect, an uncovering of how biopolitics and the process of deterritorialization work through and transform everyday life and the ordering of lived space but rather a highly conceptual and abstract argument that starts off from the assumption of these concepts and then derives Empire from them.

Influential as Hardt's and Negri's work has been, then, it is difficult to see in what sense it counts as a materialist analysis other than that it points toward the general importance of the organization of bodies and space for the operation of political and economic power in the contemporary world. Their argument provides little in the way of analysis of the specific kinds of material practices—whether they be economic, cultural, or political—that sustain international capitalism. It is only when one turns to Hardt's and Negri's second book that the clear motivation behind the first can be seen. For here we see a developed account of the potential alternative to Empire in the world today: the "multitude," a body that while remaining "multiple and internally different, is able to act in common and thus rule itself" and that is *living flesh* that rules itself"; "the multitude is the only social subject capable of realizing democracy, that is the rule of everyone by everyone."[23] The lens through which Hardt and Negri view this multitude is one that is shaped by their engagement with Spinoza as the author of a philosophy of absolute freedom, and it is this "faculty for freedom and the propensity to refuse authority [that] have become the most healthy and most noble human instincts, the real signs of eternity." This conception of freedom gives shape to an "ontological" multitude, without which "we could not conceive our social being."[24]

For all intents and purposes then, *Empire* and *Multitude* are books built less on the analysis of material practices and more on the attempt to provide an ontological foundation, on a certain reading of Spinoza, for contemporary Marxism.[25] In effect, Hardt and Negri are interested in the revival of a philosophical discourse of materialism that seeks to find unity in the multiplicity of "singularities" that characterize a world they take to have been increasingly rendered fluid and "networked" through the process of economic globalization and the emergence of Empire. But what this analysis skips over is the deeply contestable nature of the processes that they claim to have shaped the world of postmodern imperialism and the multitude. "Globalization" refers to any number of processes whose precise character and consequences vary quite widely. At the very least, the notion of the death of the sovereign state is much overhyped. While the growing internationalization of the economy may have given more leverage to supranational organizations and multinational corporations over the course of the past twenty years, it remains the case that such institutions continue to be highly dependent on the ability of the sovereign state to police populations and borders, provide for internal security and economic regulation, and, where necessary, use military power to eliminate real and perceived threats to international markets and order. Political power and economic production continue to be organized within distinct territories — principally the nation and the region — and to be governed by hierarchies whose authority is derived from the legally recognized sovereign state.

Fortunately, Hardt's and Negri's approach does not exhaust the possibilities for a historical materialist analysis of capitalism in the context of the modern state and international system today. Other authors have attempted to chart the links between the material practices involved in everyday life and the experience of space, and the wider organization of economic and political power. Geographers concerned with how neoliberalism has restructured the form of capital accumulation have charted the way in which, for example, policies of structural adjustment have affected the character of urban growth in recent times. As Mike Davis claims, neoliberalism in Latin America, Asia, and Africa has had the effect of creating megacities that are significantly composed of slum dwellings. The conditions imposed on countries for IMF loans from the late 1970s, including trade liberalization and a reduction in deficit spending, destroyed the livelihood of many small rural producers, forcing them into cities alongside the most marginal of the urban population who were the principal victims of reduction in state expenditure on public services. Responses to living in the slums of the megacities, however, vary and are dependent on contingent circumstances: "Even within a single city, slum populations can support a bewildering variety of responses to structural neglect and deprivation, ranging from charismatic churches and prophetic cults to ethnic militias, street gangs, neoliberal NGOs, and revolutionary social movements."[26]

David Harvey has also charted the effects on urban life of the neoliberal policies pursued by the major states and international economic organizations since the 1980s. In contrast to "Third World" cities, many of the large metropolitan centers in the rich West, starting with New York, underwent a transformation from the late 1970s onward that represents a reclaiming of urban space by an economic and cultural elite.[27] In Harvey's account, neoliberalism largely appears as a tool of a financial elite that wished to reestablish its political, economic, and cultural preeminence after decades of retreat in the face of social democratic reforms that had reduced inequalities in the distribution of wealth. Accordingly, there is a strong element of class analysis in this argument. But in the sense that class remains important in historical materialist analysis, it cannot be conceived of purely in the sense of an abstract relation to the means of production. The notion of a "class in itself" has to be jettisoned, for a social class is always a form of collective identity that can be realized only through shared practices and experiences. In this regard, the view that the "multitude" could ever be an agent of social and political transformation is a fantasy. What binds a group together as a "class," and thus provides it with the capacity for transformative agency, is a set of material practices involved in everyday life and the experience of lived space. It is at least feasible, in this respect, to talk of a revival of a "capitalist class" in recent times, if by that is meant a group of people who work in large financial and business corporations in metropolitan centers such as New York, London, Frankfurt, and Tokyo, have clear links to policy makers, are advocates of neoliberal ideology, and have materially benefited from neoliberal reforms.

The promotion of neoliberal economic policies by the major states and supranational financial organizations is only one feature of the way in which the geopolitical system has transformed the character of everyday life and lived space in recent times. Any developed analysis should of course also focus on other features of this system today, not least the effects of the revolution in military affairs, the Bush doctrine, and the War on Terror. An approach that looks at the broad character of geopolitical organization and processes is necessary if we are to understand the character of everyday life and the structuring of space in the contemporary world and these serve to reproduce and provide challenges to capitalist societies. To be sure, there are a significant number of scholars working in the areas of the international political and economic system and the production and reproduction of space and everyday life who adopt such an approach, some of whom explicitly acknowledge an affiliation to Marxism while others are more critically distant. There remains an important sense in which this approach is a totalizing one, seeking to link up seemingly contingent and local phenomena with large-scale social and political transformations. But in their critique of the notion of "totality" as a hierarchy, many poststructuralist and postmodernist authors arguably moved far too quickly to a model of the world as networked and flowing.[28] For most people, everyday life continues to be experienced in the shape of interactions with a hierarchical ordering of material practices in a given, lived space that is governed by the state and the geopolitical system.

Conclusion

In this essay I have tried to address the question of what does or should constitute the materialism of historical materialism. This is an important question since the powerful criticisms made by poststructuralism of the concepts of the subject and of historical teleology provided an unanswerable challenge to the humanist and historicist Marxism that tended also toward economic determinism. But if we consider historical materialism rather as a theory of the totality of material practices implicated in the reproduction of contemporary capitalist societies, then I would argue that it is not only possible but entirely necessary to save this theory. Poststructuralist and postmodernist attempts to understand the character of the contemporary geopolitical and international economic system have largely resulted in an unrealistic privileging of global networks and flows. Work by influential globalization theorists such as Manuel Castells and Anthony Giddens[29] has effectively resulted in a politics of personal life and self-improvement that often seems blind or indifferent to the structures that constrain peoples' lives. But even authors who are critical of the tendencies of globalization, such as Hardt and Negri, often end up embracing idealist solutions — such as the ontological myth of the multitude — that simply fail to grasp the character of contemporary capitalist societies and the system of states. It is only a historical materialism that concentrates on the multiplicity of material practices in their particular historical and spatial dimensions — by focusing on the character of everyday life and lived space (as set out by Lefebvre) and by attending to its relationship to the ordering of the city, region, state, and international system (as in the recent work of critical geographers and social theorists) — that can aid us in a realistic assessment of solutions to the major problems of climate change, global inequality, and warfare that face the world today.

Notes

1   See Lenin, *Materialism and Empirio-Criticism*; Kolakowski, vol. 2 of *Main Currents of Marxism*, chap. 17; Timpanaro, *On Materialism*; Brown, Fleetwood, and Roberts, eds., *Critical Realism and Marxism*.

2   Marx, *Capital*, vol. 1 (Harmondsworth: Penguin, 1990).

3   Marx, preface to *An Introduction to the Critique of Political Economy*.

4   Cohen, *Karl Marx's Theory of History*.

5   Althusser, *For Marx*, 113; Althusser and Balibar, *Reading Capital*, part 2, chap. 4.

6   See Hindess and Hirst, *Mode of Production and Social Formation*; Glucksmann, "A Ventriloquist Structuralism."

7   Derrida, "Structure, Sign and Play in the Human Sciences."

8   Engels, *The Condition of the Working Class in England*; Smith, *The Wealth of Nations*, books 1–3.

9   Mead, *Mind, Self and Society*; Goffman, *The Presentation of Self in Everyday Life*.

10 Foucault, *Discipline and Punish: The Birth of the Prison*.

11 Benjamin, *The Arcades Project*; Adorno and Horkheimer, *Dialectic of Enlightenment*; Adorno, *The Culture Industry*.

12 Lefebvre, *Critique of Everyday Life*, vol. 1; Eldon, *Understanding Henri Lefebvre*, 112.

13 Lefebvre, *Critique of Everyday Life*, vol. 3, 4–5.

14 Lefebvre, *The Production of Space*.

15 See for example: Jameson, *Postmodernism, or, The Cultural Logic of Late Capitalism*; Harvey, *Spaces of Capital*; Davis, *Planet of Slums*; Massey, *For Space*; Hirst, *Space and Power*.

16   Lefebvre, *The Production of Space*, 31–38, 39.

17   Eldon, *Understanding Henri Lefebvre*, 113.

18   Lefebvre, *Critique of Everyday Life*, vol. 1, 168.

19   See Debord, *Society of the Spectacle*; Vaneigem, *The Revolution of Everyday Life*.

20   Lefebvre, *Rhythmanalysis: Space, Time and Everyday Life*, 6.

21   Hardt and Negri, *Empire*.

22   Foucault, *Discipline and Punish*; Deleuze and Guattari, *A Thousand Plateaus* (London, 1988).

23   Hardt and Negri, *Multitude*, 100.

24   Ibid., 221.

25   See Negri, *Subversive Spinoza*.

26   Davis, *Planet of Slums*, 201–2.

27   Harvey, *A Brief History of Neoliberalism*, 44–48.

28   Castells, *The Informational City*.

29   Giddens, *Runaway World*.

Bibliography

Adkins, A. W. D. *From the Many to the One*. Ithaca, N.Y.:
Cornell University Press, 1970.

Adorno, Theodor. *The Culture Industry: Selected Essays on
Mass Culture*. London: Routledge, 1991.

Adorno, Theodor, and Max Horkheimer. *Dialectic of Enlightenment*. Translated by John Cumming. London: Verso, 1997.

Agamben, Giorgio. *Homo Sacer: Sovereign Power and Bare
Life*. Stanford, Calif.: Stanford University Press, 1998.

———. *The Open: Man and Animal*. Stanford, Calif.: Stanford University Press, 2004.

Ahmed, Sara. "Imaginary Prohibitions: Some Preliminary Remarks on the Founding Gestures of the New Materialism."
European Journal of Women's Studies 15, no. 1 (2008), 23–39.

———. *Queer Phenomenology: Orientations, Objects, Others*.
Durham, N.C.: Duke University Press, 2006.

Althusser, Louis. "Contradiction and Overdetermination." *For
Marx*, 87–128. London: Verso, 1990.

———. *For Marx*. Translated by Ben Brewster. London:
Verso, 1990.

———. "Ideology and Ideological State Apparatuses (Notes
towards an Investigation)." *Essays on Ideology*, 1–60. London:
Verso, 1984.

———. *Lenin and Philosophy and Other Essays*. Translated by
Ben Brewster. New York: Monthly Review Press, 1971.

———. *Philosophy of the Encounter: Later Writings, 1978–1987*.
Edited by François Matheron and Oliver Corpet. London:
Verso, 2006.

Althusser, Louis, and Étienne Balibar. *Reading Capital*. Translated by Ben Brewster. London: Verso, 1997.

de Angelis, Massimo. "Neoliberal Governance, Reproduction and Accumulation." *Commoner* 7 (Spring/Summer 2003), www.thecommoner.org.

Ansell-Pearson, Keith. *Viroid Life: Perspectives on Nietzsche and the Transhuman Condition*. London: Routledge, 1997.

Appadurai, Arjun, ed. *The Social Life of Things: Commodities in Cultural Perspective*. Cambridge: Cambridge University Press, 1998.

Archer, Margaret. *Being Human: The Problem of Agency*. Cambridge: Cambridge University Press, 2000.

Arendt, Hannah. *Eichmann in Jerusalem: A Report on the Banality of Evil*. New York: Viking Press, 1963.

Aronson, Ronald, and Adrian van den Hoven, eds. *Sartre Alive*. Detroit: Wayne State University Press, 1991.

Baer, Susan. "In Vitro Fertilization, Stem Cell Research Share Moral Issues," *Baltimore Sun*, 4 June 2005, 5A.

Bakhtin, Mikhail. "Contemporary Vitalism." *The Crisis in Modernism: Bergson and the Vitalist Controversy*, edited by Frederick Burwick and Paul Douglass, 76–97. New York: Cambridge University Press, 1992.

Balibar, Etienne. "Eschatology versus Teleology: The Suspended Dialogue between Derrida and Althusser." *Derrida and the Time of the Political*, edited by Pheng Cheah and Suzanne Guerlac, 57–73. Durham, N.C.: Duke University Press, 2009.

———. *Politics and the Other Scene*. London: Verso, 2002.

Balsamo, Anne. *Technologies of the Gendered Body: Reading Cyborg Women*. Durham, N.C.: Duke University Press, 1996.

Banfield, Ann. *The Phantom Table: Woolf, Fry, Russell, and the Epistemology of Modernism*. New York: Cambridge University Press, 2000.

Barad, Karen. "Posthumanist Performativity: Toward an Understanding of How Matter Comes to Matter." *Signs: Journal of Women in Culture and Society* 28, no. 3 (2003), 801–33.

Battersby, Stephen. "Messenger from the Multiverse." *New Scientist* 199 (2008), 36–39.

Beauvoir, Simone de. *Old Age*. London: Weidenfeld and Nicolson, 1972.

———. *The Second Sex*. Translated by H. M. Parshley. Introduction by Deirdre Bair. New York: Vintage, 1989. Originally published as *Le deuxième sexe*, 2 vols. Paris: Gallimard, 1949.

Beck, Ulrich. *The Risk Society: Towards a New Modernity*. London: Sage, 1992.

———. "The Terrorist Threat: World Risk Society Revisited." *Theory, Culture and Society* 19, no. 4 (2002), 39–55.

Benhabib, Seyla. *The Claims of Culture: Equality and Diversity in the Global Era*. Princeton, N.J.: Princeton University Press, 2002.

Benjamin, Walter. *The Arcades Project*. Translated by Howard Eiland and Kevin McLaughlin. Cambridge, Mass.: Harvard University Press, 2002.

Bennett, Jane. *The Enchantment of Modern Life: Attachments, Crossings, and Ethics*. Princeton, N.J.: Princeton University Press, 2001.

———. "The Force of Things: Steps toward an Ecology of Matter." *Political Theory* 33, no. 3 (2004), 347–72.

Berger, Peter, and Thomas Luckmann. *The Social Construction of Reality*. Middlesex: Penguin, 1966.

Bergson, Henri. *Creative Evolution*. Translated by Arthur Mitchell. New York: Dover, 1998.

———. *The Creative Mind*. Translated by Mabelle L. Addison. New York: Philosophical Library, 1946.

———. *Matter and Memory*. Translated by Nancy M. Paul and W. Scott Palmer. New York: Zone Books, 1988.

———. *Mind-Energy*. London: Macmillan, 1921.

———. *Time and Free Will: An Essay on the Immediate Data of Consciousness*. Translated by F. L. Pogson. London: George Allen and Unwin, 1959.

Best, Robert. "Testimony of Robert A. Best, President, the Culture of Life Foundation." Submitted to the Committee on Commerce, Science, and Transportation, Subcommittee on Science, Technology, and Space, United States Senate Hearing on Cloning, Washington, D.C., 2 May 2001. http://commerce.senate.gov.

Bittner, Rudiger. "Masters without Substance." *Nietzsche's Postmoralism: Essays on Nietzsche's Prelude to Philosophy's Future*, edited by Richard Schacht, 34–46. New York: Cambridge University Press, 2001.

Blits, Jan. "Hobbesian Fear." *Political Theory* 17, no. 3 (1989), 417–31.

Bordo, Susan. *Flight to Objectivity: Essays on Cartesianism and Culture*. New York: SUNY Press, 1987.

Bourdieu, Pierre. *Outline of a Theory of Practice*. Translated by Richard Nice. Cambridge: Cambridge University Press, 1977.

Braidotti, Rosi. *Metamorphoses: Towards a Materialist Theory of Becoming*. Cambridge: Polity Press, 2002.

———. *Patterns of Dissonance: A Study of Women and Contemporary Philosophy*. Cambridge: Polity Press, 1991.

Brennan, Teresa. *The Transmission of Affect*. Ithaca, N.Y.: Cornell University Press, 2004.

Brown, Andrew, Steve Fleetwood, and John Michael Roberts, eds. *Critical Realism and Marxism*. New York: Routledge, 2002.

Bryson, Bill. *A Short History of Nearly Everything*. London: Black Swan, 2004.

Bukatman, Scott. *Terminal Identity: The Virtual Subject In Postmodern Science Fiction*. Durham, N.C.: Duke University Press, 1993.

Burwick, Frederick, and Paul Douglass, eds. *The Crisis in Modernism: Bergson and the Vitalist Controversy*. Cambridge: Cambridge University Press, 1992.

———. "Introduction" to *The Crisis in Modernism: Bergson and the Vitalist Controversy*. Cambridge: Cambridge University Press, 1992.

Butler, Judith. *Bodies That Matter: On the Discursive Limits of "Sex."* New York: Routledge, 1993.

——. *Gender Trouble: Feminism and the Subversion of Identity*. New York: Routledge, 1990.

——. "Imitation and Gender Insubordination." *The Second Wave: A Reader in Feminist Theory*, edited by Linda Nicholson, 300–315. New York: Routledge, 1997.

——. "Performative Acts and Gender Constitutions: An Essay in Phenomenology and Feminist Theory." *Writing on the Body: Female Embodiment and Feminist Theory*, edited by Katie Conboy, Nadia Medina, and Sarah Stanbury, 401–18. New York: Columbia University Press, 1997.

——. *Precarious Life*. London: Verso, 2004.

Calder, Nigel. *Magic Universe: A Grand Tour of Modern Science*. Oxford: Oxford University Press, 2003.

Canguilhem, Georges. "Aspects du vitalisme." *La connaissance de la vie*, 105–27. Paris: Hachette, 1952.

Capra, Fritjof. "Complexity and Life." *Theory, Culture and Society* 22, no. 5 (2005), 33–44.

Carman, Taylor, and Mark Hansen, eds. *The Cambridge Companion to Merleau-Ponty*. Cambridge: Cambridge University Press, 2005.

Carsten, Janet. *After Kinship*. Cambridge: Cambridge University Press, 2004.

Castells, Manuel. *The Informational City: Information Technology, Economic Restructuring, and the Urban Regional Process*. Oxford: Blackwell, 1989.

——. *The Rise of the Network Society*. Oxford: Blackwell, 1996.

Catalano, Joseph S. *Thinking Matter: Consciousness from Aristotle to Putnam and Sartre*. New York: Routledge, 2000.

Certeau, Michel de. *The Practice of Everyday Life*. Berkeley: University of California Press, 1984.

Cheah, Pheng. *Inhuman Conditions: On Cosmopolitanism and Human Rights*. Cambridge, Mass.: Harvard University Press, 2006.

——. *Spectral Nationality: Passages of Freedom from Kant to Postcolonial Literatures of Liberation*. New York: Columbia University Press, 2003.

——. "The Untimely Secret of Democracy." *Derrida and the Time of the Political*, edited by Pheng Cheah and Suzanne Guerlac, 74–96. Durham, N.C.: Duke University Press, 2009.

Chesters, Graeme, and Ian Welsh. *Complexity and New Social Movements: Masses on the Edge of Chaos*. London: Routledge, 2006.

Chiari, Joseph. "Vitalism and Contemporary Thought." *The Crisis in Modernism*, edited by Frederick Burwick and Paul Douglass, 245–73. Cambridge: Cambridge University Press, 1992.

Chow, Rey. *The Age of the World Target: Self-Referentiality in War, Theory, and Comparative Work*. Durham, N.C.: Duke University Press, 2006.

———. "Poststructuralism: Theory as Critical Self-Consciousness." *The Cambridge Companion to Feminist Literary Theory*, edited by Ellen Rooney, 195–210. Cambridge: Cambridge University Press, 2006.

———. "Sacrifice, Mimesis, and the Theorizing of Victimhood." *Representations* 94 (Spring 2006), 131–49.

Cohen, Gerald Allan. *Karl Marx's Theory of History: A Defence*. Princeton, N.J.: Princeton University Press, 1978.

Cole, Ethan. "Bush Stands against 'Temptation to Manipulate Life.'" *Christian Post Reporter*, Friday, 13 April 2007. www.christianpost.com.

Conboy, Katie, Nadia Medina, and Sarah Stanbury, eds. *Writing on the Body: Female Embodiment and Feminist Theory*. New York: Columbia University Press, 1997.

Connolly, William. "Experience and Experiment." *Daedalus* 135 (Summer 2006), 67–75.

———. *Neuropolitics: Thinking, Culture, Speed*. Minneapolis: University of Minnesota Press, 2001.

Coole, Diana. "Experiencing Discourse: Gendered Styles and the Embodiment of Power." *British Journal of Politics and International Relations* 9, no. 3 (2007), 413–33.

———. *Merleau-Ponty and Modern Politics after Anti-humanism*. Lanham, Md.: Rowman and Littlefield, 2007.

———. *Negativity and Politics: Dionysus and Dialectics from Kant to Poststructuralism*. London: Routledge, 2000.

———. "Rethinking Agency: A Phenomenological Approach to Embodiment and Agentic Capacities." *Political Studies* 53 (2005), 124–42.

Coward, Rosalind, and John Ellis. *Language and Materialism: Developments in Semiology and the Theory of the Subject*. London: Routledge and Kegan Paul, 1977.

Cox, Christopher. *Nietzsche: Naturalism and Interpretation*. Berkeley: University of California Press, 1999.

Crary, Jonathan, and Sanford Kwinter, eds. *Incorporations*. New York: Zone Books, 1992.

Damasio, Antonio. *Looking for Spinoza: Joy, Sorrow and the Feeling Brain*. New York: Harcourt, 2003.

Daniels, Cynthia. *At Women's Expense: State Power and the Politics of Fetal Rights*. Cambridge, Mass.: Harvard University Press, 1993.

Davidson, Arnold, ed. *Foucault and His Interlocutors*. Chicago: University of Chicago Press, 1998.

Davies, Karen. "Responsibilities and Daily Life: Reflections Over Timespace." *Timespace: Georgraphies of Temporality*, edited by Jon May and Nigel Thrift, 133–48. London: Routledge, 2001.

Davis, Mike. *Planet of Slums*. London: Verso, 2006.

Debord, Guy. *Society of the Spectacle*. Detroit: Black and Red, 1977.

Deleuze, Gilles. "The Actual and the Virtual." *Dialogues II*, by Gilles Deleuze and Claire Parnet, translated by Hugh Tomlinson and Barbara Habberjam, 148–52. 2nd edn. New York: Columbia University Press, 2002.

——. *Cinema II: The Time Image*. Translated by Hugh Tomlinson. New York: Athlone Press, 1989.

——. *Difference and Repetition*. Translated by Paul Patton. New York: Columbia University Press, 1994.

——. *Essays Critical and Clinical*. Translated by Daniel W. Smith and Michael A. Greco. Minneapolis: University of Minnesota Press, 1997.

——. "Ethnology: Spinoza and Us." *Incorporations,* edited by Jonathan Crary and Sanford Kwinter, 628–33. New York: Zone Books, 1992.

——. *Expressionism in Philosophy: Spinoza*. Translated by Martin Joughin. New York: Zone Books, 1990.

——. *The Fold*. London: Continuum, 2006.

——. *Foucault*. Minneapolis: University of Minnesota Press, 1988.

——. "Immanence: A Life." *Pure Immanence: Essays on A Life*, translated by Anne Boyman, 25–33. New York: Zone, 2001.

——. "L'immanence: Une vie. . . ." *Philosophie* no. 47 (1995), 3–7.

——. *The Logic of Sense*. Translated by Mark Lester and Charles Stivale. New York: Columbia University Press, 1990.

——. *Logique du sens*. Paris: Minuit, 1969.

——. *Negotiations*. New York: Columbia University Press, 1995.

——. *Spinoza et le problème de l'expression*. Paris: Minuit, 1968.

Deleuze, Gilles, and Félix Guattari. "Capitalisme énurgumène." *Critique* no. 306 (November 1972), 923–56.

——. *Mille plateaux: Capitalisme et schizophrénie II*. Paris: Minuit, 1980.

——. *A Thousand Plateaus: Capitalism and Schizophrenia*. Translated by Brian Massumi. Minneapolis: University of Minnesota Press, 1987.

——. *A Thousand Plateaus: Capitalism and Schizophrenia*. Translated by Brian Massumi. London: Athlone, 1988.

Deleuze, Gilles, and Claire Parnet. "The Actual and the Virtual." *Dialogues II*, 2nd edn., translated by Hugh Tomlinson and Barbara Habberjam, 148–52. New York: Columbia University Press, 2002.

Derrida, Jacques. "As If It Were Possible, 'Within Such Limits' . . ." *Negotiations: Interviews and Interventions 1971–2001*. Translated by Elizabeth Rottenberg, 343–70. Stanford, Calif.: Stanford University Press, 2002.

——. "The Double Session." *Dissemination*. Translated by Barbara Johnson, 173–286. Chicago: University of Chicago Press, 1983.

——. "Not Utopia, the Im-possible." *Paper Machine*. Translated by Rachel Bowlby, 121–35. Stanford, Calif.: Stanford University Press, 2005.

——. *Politics of Friendship*. Translated by George Collins. New York: Verso, 1997.

———. *Positions*. Chicago: University of Chicago Press, 1981.

———. *Rogues: Two Essays on Reason*. Translated by Pascale-Anne Brault and Michael Naas. Stanford, Calif.: Stanford University Press, 2005.

———. *Specters of Marx: The State of the Debt, the Work of Mourning, and the New International*. Translated by Peggy Kamuf. New York: Routledge, 1994.

———. "Structure, Sign and Play in the Human Sciences." *Writing and Difference*, 351–70. London: Routledge, 2002.

———. "Typewriter Ribbon: Limited Ink (2)." *Without Alibi*, edited and translated by Peggy Kamuf, 71–160. Stanford, Calif.: Stanford University Press, 2002.

Descartes, René. *Principles of Philosophy*. Translated by Reese P. Miller. Dordrecht: Kluwer Academic Publishers, 1991.

De Veaux, Alexis. *Warrior Poet: A Biography of Audre Lorde*. New York: W. W. Norton, 2004.

Diamond, Irene, and Lee Quinby, eds. *Feminism and Foucault: Reflections on Resistance*. Boston: Northeastern University Press, 1998.

Dobson, Ken, David Grace, and David Lovett. *Physics*. 2nd edn. London: Harper Collins, 2002.

Driesch, Hans. *The History and Theory of Vitalism*. London: Macmillan, 1914.

———. *The Problem of Individuality: A Course of Four Lectures Delivered before the University of London in October 1913*. London: Macmillan, 1914.

———. *The Science and Philosophy of the Organism: The Gifford Lectures Delivered before the University of Aberdeen in the Year 1907–8*. 2 vols. London: Adam and Charles Black, 1908.

Durie, Bruce. "Doors of Perception." *New Scientist*, 29 January–4 February 2005, 34–37.

Ebert, Teresa L. *Ludic Feminism and After: Postmodernism, Desire, and Labor in Late Capitalism*. Ann Arbor: University of Michigan Press, 1996.

Eldon, Stuart. *Understanding Henri Lefebvre: Theory and the Possible* London: Continuum, 2004.

Elliott, Anthony. "Foreword." *Ethnicity and Everyday Life*, edited by Christian Karner, viii. London: Routledge, 2007.

Engels, Friedrich. *The Condition of the Working Class in England*. Oxford: Oxford University Press, 1993.

———. "Socialism: Utopian and Scientific." *The Marx-Engels Reader*. 2nd edn., edited by Robert C. Tucker, 683–717. New York: Norton, 1978.

Epstein, Mark. *Going to Pieces without Falling Apart: A Buddhist Perspective on Wholeness*. New York: Broadway Books, 1999.

Esposito, Roberto. *Bios: Politiche della vita e filosofia dell'impersonale*. Torino: Einaudi, 2004.

Fausto-Sterling, Anne. "The Bare Bones of Sex: Part 1 — Sex and Gender." *SIGNS* 30, no. 2 (2005), 1491–1527.

Featherstone, Mike, and Nicholas Gane, eds. "Annual Review." Special issue, *Theory, Culture and Society* 23, nos. 7–8 (2006).

Fingarette, Herbert. "The Ego and Mystic Selflessness." *Identity and Anxiety: Survival of the Person in Mass Society*, edited by Maurice R. Stein, et al., 552–81. Glencoe, Ill.: Free Press, 1960.

Fisher, Philip. "The Aesthetics of Fear." *Raritan* 18, no. 1 (Summer 1998), 40–72.

Foucault, Michel. *Discipline and Punish*. Translated by Alan Sheridan. New York: Pantheon Books, 1977.

——. *Discipline and Punish: The Birth of the Prison*. Harmondsworth: Penguin, 1991.

——. *The History of Sexuality*. Vol. 1. New York: Random House, 1978.

——. "Nietzsche, Genealogy, History." *Language, Counter-Memory, Practice: Selected Essays by Michel Foucault*, edited by Donald F. Bouchard, 139–64. Ithaca, N.Y.: Cornell University Press, 1980.

——. *Power/Knowledge*. New York: Pantheon, 1972.

Franklin, Jane, ed. *The Politics of Risk Society*. Cambridge: Polity Press, 1998.

Franklin, Sarah, Celia Lury, and Jackie Stacey. *Global Nature, Global Culture*. London: Sage, 2000.

Fraser, Mariam, Sarah Kember, and Celia Lury, eds. *Inventive Life: Approaches to the New Vitalism*. London: Sage, 2006.

——, eds. "Inventive Life: Approaches to the New Vitalism." Special issue, *Theory, Culture and Society* 22, no. 1 (2005).

Freud, Sigmund. *The Standard Edition of the Complete Psychological Works*. 24 vols. London: Hogarth Press, 1964.

Frost, Samantha. "Hobbes and the Matter of Self-Consciousness." *Political Theory* 33, no. 4 (2005), 495–517.

——. *Lessons from a Materialist Thinker: Hobbesian Reflections on Ethics and Politics*. Stanford, Calif.: Stanford University Press, 2008.

Fukuyama, Francis. *Our Posthuman Future: Consequences of the Biotechnology Revolution*. New York: Picador, 2003.

Gatens, Moira, and Genevieve Lloyd. *Collective Imaginings: Spinoza, Past and Present*. London: Routledge, 1999.

Giddens, Anthony. *Runaway World*. London: Routledge, 2000.

Gilman, Charlotte Perkins. *The Home: Its Work and Influence*. Walnut Creek, Calif.: AltaMira, 2002.

Gilroy, Paul. *Against Race: Imagining Political Culture beyond the Color Line*. Cambridge, Mass.: Harvard University Press, 2000.

Gladwell, Malcolm. *The Tipping Point: How Little Things Can Make a Big Difference*. Boston: Back Bay Books, 2002.

Gleick, James. *Chaos: Making a New Science*. New York: Penguin, 1987.

Glissant, Edouard. *Poetics of Relation*. Translated by Betsy Wing. Ann Arbor: University of Michigan Press, 1997.

——. *Poetique de la relation*. Paris: Gallimard, 1990.

Glucksmann, André. "A Ventriloquist Structuralism." *Western Marxism: A Critical Reader*, edited by Gareth Stedman Jones, 282–314. London: Verso, 1978.

Goffman, Erving. *The Presentation of Self in Everyday Life*. Harmondsworth: Penguin, 1990.

Goodwin, Brian. *How the Leopard Changed Its Spots*. Princeton, N.J.: Princeton University Press, 1994.

Goodwin, Michele. *Black Markets: The Supply and Demand of Body Parts*. Cambridge: Cambridge University Press, 2006.

Gould, Stephen Jay. *The Structure of Evolutionary Theory*. Cambridge, Mass.: Harvard University Press, 2002.

Greco, Monica. "On the Vitality of Vitalism." *Theory, Culture and Society* 22, no.1 (2005), 15–27.

Grosz, Elizabeth. *The Nick of Time: Politics, Evolution and the Untimely*. Durham, N.C.: Duke University Press, 2004.

——. *Space, Time and Perversion*. St. Leonards: Allen and Unwin, 2005.

——. *Volatile Bodies: Toward a Corporeal Feminism*. Sydney: Allen and Unwin, 1994.

Guattari, Félix. *Chaosmosis: An Ethico-aesthetic Paradigm*. Sydney: Power Publications, 1995.

Guha, Ranajit. *History at the Limit of World-History*. New York: Columbia University Press, 2002.

Habermas, Jürgen. *The Future of Human Nature*. Cambridge: Polity Press, 2003.

Hampton, Jean. *Hobbes and the Social Contract Tradition*. Cambridge: Cambridge University Press, 1986.

Hansen, Mark B. N. *New Philosophy for New Media*. Cambridge, Mass.: MIT Press, 2004.

Haraway, Donna. "The Biopolitics of Postmodern Bodies." *Feminist Theory and The Body*, edited by Janet Price and Margit Shildrick, 203–14. New York: Routledge, 1999.

——. "A Cyborg Manifesto: Science, Technology, and Socialist-Feminism in the Late Twentieth Century." *Simians, Cyborgs, and Women: The Reinvention of Nature*, 149–82. London: Routledge, 1991.

——. *Modest_Witness@second_Millennium: FemaleMan©_Meets_OncoMouse™*. London: Routledge, 1997.

Hardt, Michael, and Antonio Negri. *Empire*. Cambridge, Mass.: Harvard University Press, 2000.

——. *Multitude: War and Democracy in the Age of Empire*. London: Penguin, 2004.

Harrington, Anne. *Reenchanted Science: Holism in German Culture from Wilhelm II to Hitler*. Princeton, N.J.: Princeton University Press, 1996.

Harvey, David. *The Condition of Postmodernity*. Oxford: Blackwell, 1989.

——. *A Brief History of Neoliberalism*. Oxford: Oxford University Press, 2007.

——. *Spaces of Capital: Towards a Critical Geography*. Edinburgh: Edinburgh University Press, 2001.

——. *Spaces of Global Capitalism: Towards a Theory of Uneven Geographical Development*. London: Verso, 2006.

Hayles, N. Katherine. "Computing the Human." *Theory, Culture and Society* 22, no. 1 (2005), 131–51.

——. *How We Became Posthuman: Virtual Bodies in Cybernetics, Literature, and Informatics*. Chicago: University of Chicago Press, 1999.

——. "Unfinished Work: From Cyborg to Cognisphere." *Theory, Culture and Society* 23, nos. 7–8 (2006), 159–66.

Heath, Robert. *The Hidden Power of Advertising*. Henley-on-Thames: Admap Publications, 2005.

Heidegger, Martin. *Ontology — The Hermeneutics of Facticity*. Bloomington: Indiana University Press, 1999.

Heinämaa, Sara. *Toward a Phenomenology of Sexual Difference*. Lanham, Md.: Rowman and Littlefield, 2003.

Hennessy, Rosemary. *Profit and Pleasure: Sexual Identities in Late Capitalism*. New York: Routledge, 2000.

Hill, Rebecca. "Interval, Sexual Difference." *Hypatia: A Journal of Feminist Philosophy* 23, no. 1 (Winter 2008), 119–31.

Hindess, Barry, and Paul Hirst. *Mode of Production and Social Formation*. London: MacMillan, 1977.

Hirst, Paul. *Space and Power: Politics, War and Architecture*. Cambridge: Polity, 2005.

Hobbes, Thomas. *Behemoth, or the Long Parliament*. Edited by S. Holmes. Chicago: University of Chicago Press, 1990.

——. *De Cive*. Vol. 2, *The English Works of Thomas Hobbes*, edited by Sir William Molesworth. London: John Bohn, 1841.

——. *De Corpore*. Vol. 1, *The English Works of Thomas Hobbes*, edited by Sir William Molesworth. London: John Bohn, 1839. First published 1655.

——. *De Homine. Thomas Hobbes: Man and Citizen*. Edited by Bernard Gert. Indianapolis: Hackett, 1991.

——. *Human Nature. Thomas Hobbes: The Elements of Law Natural and Political: Human Nature and De Corpore Politico*. Edited by J. C. A. Gaskin. Oxford: Oxford University Press, 1994. First published 1640.

——. *Leviathan*. Edited by C. B. Macpherson. New York: Penguin, 1968. First published 1651.

——. *Of Liberty and Necessity*. Vol. 4, *The English Works of Thomas Hobbes*, edited by Sir William Molesworth. London: John Bohn, 1840. First published 1655.

——. *The Questions Concerning Liberty, Necessity, and Chance*. Vol. 5, *The English*

Works of Thomas Hobbes, edited by Sir William Molesworth. London: Richard Bohn, 1841.

Hollis, James. *The Middle Passage: From Misery to Meaning in Midlife*. Toronto: Inner City Books, 1993.

——. *Swamplands of the Soul: New Life in Dismal Places*. Toronto: Inner City Books, 1996.

Honneth, Axel. "The Intellectual Legacy of Critical Theory." *The Cambridge Companion to Critical Theory*, edited by Fred Rush, 336–60. Cambridge: Cambridge University Press, 2004.

Husserl, Edmund. *The Crisis of the European Sciences and Transcendental Phenomenology: An Introduction to Phenomenological Philosophy*. Translated by David Carr. Evanston, Ill.: Northwestern University Press, 1970.

——. *Ideas: General Introduction to Pure Phenomenology*. Translated by W. R. Boyce Gibson. London: George Allen and Unwin, 1969.

——. *Ideas Pertaining to a Pure Phenomenology and to a Phenomenological Philosophy, Second Book*. Translated by Richard Rojcewicz and André Schuwer. Dordrecht: Kluwer, 1989.

Irigaray, Luce. "Equal to Whom?" *differences* 1, no. 2 (1989), 59–76.

——. *An Ethics of Sexual Difference*. Translated by Carolyn Burke and Gillian C. Gill. Ithaca, N.Y.: Cornell University Press, 1993.

——. "Is the Subject of Science Sexed?" *Hypatia* 2, no. 3 (1987), 65–87.

——. *Marine Lover: Of Friedrich Nietzsche*. Translated by Gillian Gill. New York: Columbia University Press, 1991.

——. *Speculum of the Other Woman*. Translated by Gillian Gill. Ithaca, N.Y.: Cornell University Press, 1985.

——. *This Sex Which Is Not One*. Translated by Catherine Porter with Carolyn Burke. Ithaca, N.Y.: Cornell University Press, 1985.

Israel, Jonathan. *Radical Enlightenment: Philosophy and the Making of Modernity 1650–1750*. New York: Oxford University Press, 2001.

Jackson, Richard, and Neil Howe. *The Graying of the Great Powers: Demography and Geopolitics in the 21st Century*. Washington: CSIS, 2008.

Jameson, Frederic. *Postmodernism, or, The Cultural Logic of Late Capitalism*. London: Verso, 1991.

Jasanoff, Sheila. *Designs on Nature: Science and Democracy in Europe and the United States*. Princeton, N.J.: Princeton University Press, 2005.

Jennings, Herbert Spencer. "Doctrines Held as Vitalism." *American Naturalist* 47, no. 559 (1913), 385–417.

——. "Driesch's Vitalism and Experimental Indeterminism." *Science* 36, no. 927 (1912), 434–35.

Jones, G. Stedman, ed. *Western Marxism: A Critical Reader*. London: New Left Books, 1978.

Kant, Immanuel. *Critique of Judgment*. Translated by Werner Pluhar. Indianapolis: Hackett, 1987.

Kelly, Sean Dorrance. "Seeing Things in Merleau-Ponty." *The Cambridge Companion to Merleau-Ponty*, edited by Taylor Carman and Mark Hansen, 74–110. Cambridge: Cambridge University Press, 2005.

Kolakowski, Leszek. Vol. 2 of *Main Currents of Marxism*. Oxford: Oxford University Press, 1978.

Kopytoff, Igor. "The Cultural Biography of Things: Commoditization as Process." *The Social Life of Things*, edited by Arjun Appadurai, 64–94. Cambridge: Cambridge University Press, 1998.

Kruks, Sonia. "Beauvoir's Time / Our Time: The Renaissance in Simone de Beauvoir Studies." *Feminist Studies* 31, no. 2 (2005), 286–309.

———. "Simone de Beauvoir: Teaching Sartre about Freedom." *Sartre Alive*, edited by Ronald Aronson and Adrian van den Hoven, 285–300. Detroit: Wayne State University Press, 1991.

Lanchester, John. "Cityphilia." *London Review of Books*, 3 January 2008, 9–12.

———. "Cityphobia." *London Review of Books*, 23 October 2008, 3–5.

Lashley, Karl Spencer "The Behavioristic Interpretation of Consciousness." Part 1. *Psychological Bulletin* 30 (1923), 237–72.

———. "The Behavioristic Interpretation of Consciousness." Part 2. *Psychological Bulletin* 30 (1923), 329–53.

Latour, Bruno. *Politics of Nature: How to Bring the Sciences into Democracy*. Cambridge, Mass.: Harvard University Press, 2004.

Lavin, Chad. "Fear, Radical Democracy, and Ontological Methadone." *Polity* 38, no. 2 (2006), 254–75.

Lear, Jonathan. *Happiness, Death, and the Remainders of Life: The Tanner Lectures on Human Values*. Cambridge, Mass.: Harvard University Press, 2000.

Lefebvre, Henri. *Critique of Everyday Life*. Vol. 1, translated by John Moore. London: Verso, 1991.

———. *Critique of Everyday Life*. Vol. 3, *From Modernity to Modernism: Towards a Metaphilosophy of Daily Life*, translated by Gregory Elliott. London: Verso, 2005.

———. *The Production of Space*. Translated by Donald Nicholson-Smith. Oxford: Blackwell, 1991.

———. *Rhythmanalysis: Space, Time and Everyday Life*. Translated by Stuart Eldon and Gerald Moore. London: Continuum, 2004.

Lenin, Vladimir I. *Materialism and Empirio-Criticism*. Vol. 14 of *V. I. Lenin: Collected Works*. London: Lawrence and Wishart, 1968.

LeVay, Simon. *Queer Science: The Use and Abuse of Research into Homosexuality*. Cambridge, Mass.: MIT Press, 1996.

Loewald, Hans. *Sublimation: Inquiries into Theoretical Psychoanalysis*. New Haven, Conn.: Yale University Press, 1988.

Lorde, Audre. *Sister Outsider: Essays and Speeches*. Trumansburg, N.Y.: The Crossing Press, 1984.

Lovejoy, Arthur O. "The Import of Vitalism." *Science* 43, no. 864 (1911), 75–80.

——. "The Meaning of Driesch and the Meaning of Vitalism." *Science* 36, no. 933. (1912), 672–75.

——. "The Meaning of Vitalism." *Science* 33, no. 851 (1911), 610–14.

Lutzow, Thomas H. "The Structure of the Free Act in Bergson." *Process Studies* 7, no. 2 (Summer 1977), 73–89.

Lyotard, Jean-François. *Le Différend*. Paris: Editions de Minuit, 1983.

MacIntyre, Alasdaire. *Dependent Rational Animals: Why Human Beings Need the Virtues*. Peru, Ill.: Carus, 2001.

Magnus, George. *The Age of Aging: How Demographics Are Changing the Global Economy and Our World*. Singapore: John Wiley and Sons (Asia), 2009.

Maienschein, Jane. "What's in a Name: Embryos, Clones, and Stem Cells." *American Journal of Bioethics* 2, no. 1 (2002), 12–19.

Marcuse, Herbert. *One-Dimensional Man: Studies in the Ideology of Advanced Industrial Society*. 2nd edn. Boston: Beacon Press, 1991.

Markell, Patchen. *Bound by Recognition*. Princeton, N.J.: Princeton University Press, 2003.

Marks, Laura U. *The Skin of the Film*. Durham, N.C.: Duke University Press, 2000.

Martin, Biddy. "Feminism, Criticism, and Foucault." *Feminism and Foucault: Reflections on Resistance*, edited by Irene Diamond and Lee Quinby, 3–20. Boston: Northeastern University Press, 1988.

Marx, Karl. *Capital: A Critical Analysis of Capitalist Production*. Vol. 1. Moscow: Progress Publishers, 1887.

——. *Capital*. Vol. 1. Harmondsworth: Penguin, 1990.

——. "Economic and Philosophical Manuscripts" (third manuscript). *Karl Marx: Early Writings*, translated by Thomas Bottomore. New York: McGraw-Hill, 1964.

——. *The Eighteenth Brumaire of Louis Bonaparte. Surveys From Exile: Political Writings*, vol. 2, edited by David Fernbach. Harmondsworth: Penguin, 1973.

——. *Karl Marx: Early Writings*. Edited by Thomas Bottomore. New York: McGraw Hill, 1964.

——. Preface (1859) to *A Contribution to the Critique of Political Economy. Selected Works*. London: Lawrence and Wishart, 1947.

——. Preface to *An Introduction to the Critique of Political Economy. Karl Marx: Early Writings*, translated by Thomas Bottomore. Harmondsworth: Penguin, 1992.

——. *Theses on Feuerbach. Ludwig Feuerbach and the Outcome of Classical German Philosophy*, edited by Friedrich Engels, 82–84. The Marxist-Leninist Library. London: Lawrence and Wishart, 1941.

Marx, Karl, and Friedrich Engels. *The German Ideology*. Edited by C. J. Arthur. New York: International Publishers, 1970.

——. *The German Ideology. The Marx-Engels Reader*, edited by Robert Tucker, 146–200. New York: W. W. Norton, 1975.

Massey, Doreen. *For Space*. London: Sage, 2005.

Massumi, Brian. *Parables for the Virtual: Movement, Affect, Sensation*. Durham, N.C.: Duke University Press, 2002.

Masters, Roger, and Myron Coplan. "Water Treatment with Silicofluorides and Lead Toxicity." *International Journal of Environmental Studies* 56, no. 4 (1999), 435–49.

Masters, Roger, Brian Hone, and Anil Doshi. "Environmental Pollution, Neurotoxicity, and Criminal Violence." *Environmental Toxicology: Current Developments*, edited by J. Rose, 13–48. London: Taylor Francis, 1998.

May, Jon, and Nigel Thrift, eds. *Timespace: Geographies of Temporality*. London: Routledge, 2001.

Mead, George Herbert. *Mind, Self, and Society*. Chicago: University of Chicago Press, 1997.

Merleau-Ponty, Maurice. *Adventures of the Dialectic*. London: Heinemann, 1974.

———. "Indirect Language and the Voices of Silence." *Signs*, 39–83. Evanston, Ill.: Northwestern University Press, 1964.

———. *In Praise of Philosophy*. Evanston, Ill.: Northwestern University Press, 1963.

———. *Nature: Course Notes from the Collège de France*. Compiled and with notes by Dominique Séglard. Translated by Robert Vallier. Evanston, Ill.: Northwestern University Press, 2003.

———. *Phenomenology of Perception*. London: Routledge, 1962.

———. *The Primacy of Perception*. Evanston, Ill.: Northwestern University Press, 1964.

———. *Sense and Non-Sense*. Evanston, Ill.: Northwestern University Press, 1964.

———. *Signs*. Evanston, Ill.: Northwestern University Press, 1964.

———. *The Visible and the Invisible*. Translated by Alfonso Lingis. Evanston, Ill.: Northwestern University Press, 1968.

Mitchell, Don. *The Right to the City: Social Justice and the Fight for Public Space*. New York: Guildford Press, 2003.

Moi, Toril. *Sexual/Textual Politics: Feminist Literary Theory*. London: Methuen, 1985.

———. *What Is a Woman?* New York: Oxford University Press, 1999.

Moss, Jeremy, ed. *The Later Foucault: Politics and Philosophy*. London: Sage, 1998.

National Institutes of Health. *Stem Cells: Scientific Progress and Future Research Directions*. 2001. Available at the website for the National Institutes of Health, Stem Cell Information, http://stemcells.nih.gov/.

Negri, Antonio. *Subversive Spinoza: (Un)Contemporary Variations*. Manchester: Manchester University Press, 2004.

Nelson, Dana. "The President and Presidentialism." *South Atlantic Quarterly* 105, no. 1. (Winter 2006), 1–17.

New York Times News Service. "U.S. Policy Directive Might Open Door to Space Weapons." *Baltimore Sun*, 18 May 2005, 6A.

Nicholson, Linda, ed. *The Second Wave: A Reader in Feminist Theory*. New York: Routledge, 1997.

Nietzsche, Friedrich. *Beyond Good and Evil*. Translated by Walter Kaufmann. New York: Vintage, 1966.

———. *The Gay Science*. Translated by Walter Kaufmann. New York: Vintage, 1974.

———. *On the Genealogy of Morals*. Translated by Walter Kaufmann. New York: Vintage, 1967.

———. *Thus Spoke Zarathustra*, in *The Portable Nietzsche*, translated by Walter Kaufmann. New York: Penguin, 1954.

———. *Twilight of the Idols*, in *The Portable Nietzsche*, translated by Walter Kaufmann. New York: Penguin, 1954.

Olkowski, Dorothea. "The End of Phenomenology: Bergson's Interval in Irigaray." *Hypatia* 15, no. 3 (2000), 73–91.

Orlie, Melissa A. "The Art of Despising Oneself: The Slavish Roots of Nietzsche's Asceticism." *International Studies in Philosophy* 32, no. 3 (2000), 71–82.

Oyama, Susan. *Evolution's Eye: A Systems View of the Biology-Culture Divide*. Durham, N.C.: Duke University Press, 2000.

———. *The Ontogeny of Information: Developmental Systems and Evolution*. Durham, N.C.: Duke University Press, 2000.

Panagia, Davide. "The Effects of Viewing: Caravaggio, Bacon, and *The Ring*." *Theory and Event* 10, no. 4 (2007).

Parisi, Luciana. "For a Schizogenesis of Sexual Difference." *Identities* 3, no. 1 (2004), 67–93.

Patton, Paul. *Deleuze and the Political*. New York: Routledge, 2000.

———. "Foucault's Subject of Power." *The Later Foucault*, edited by Jeremy Moss, 64–77. London: Sage, 1998.

Paul II, John. "Evangelium Vitae: To the Bishops, Priests and Deacons, Men and Women, Religious, Lay, Faithful, and All People of Good Will, on the Value and Inviolability of Human Life." Encyclical of 25 March 1995 available from the website of the Holy See, http://www.vatican.va/holy_father/john _paul_ii/index.htm.

Phillips, Adam. *The Beast in the Nursery: On Curiosity and Other Appetites*. New York: Vintage, 1998.

———. *Darwin's Worms: On Life Stories and Death Stories*. New York: Basic Books, 2000.

———. *Terrors and Experts*. Cambridge, Mass.: Harvard University Press, 1995.

———. *Winnicott*. Cambridge, Mass.: Harvard University Press, 1998.

Plekhanov, George. "The Materialist Conception of History." *Essays in Historical Materialism: The Materialist Conception of History, The Role of the Individual in History*. New York: International Publishers, 1940.

Price, Janet, and Margit Shildrick, eds. *Feminist Theory and the Body: A Reader*. New York: Routledge, 1999.

Prigogine, Ilya. *Is the Future Given?* New Jersey: World Scientific Press, 2003.

Quirk, Tom. *Bergson and American Culture: The Worlds of Willa Cather and Wallace Stevens*. Chapel Hill: University of North Carolina Press, 1990.

Rabinow, Paul. *Anthropos Today*. Princeton, N.J.: Princeton University Press, 2003.

Rajan, Kaushik Sunder. *Biocapital: The Constitution of Postgenomic Life*. Durham, N.C.: Duke University Press, 2006.

Ramachandran, V. S. *Phantoms in the Brain*. New York: William Morrow, 1998.

Rich, Adrienne. *Of Woman Born*. London: Virago, 1991.

Rizzolatti, Giacomo, and Corrado Sinigaglia. *Mirrors in the Brain: How Our Minds Share Actions and Emotions*. London: Oxford University Press, 2008.

Robin, Corey. *Fear: The History of a Political Idea*. New York: Oxford University Press, 2004.

Rooney, Ellen, ed. *The Cambridge Companion to Feminist Literary Theory*. Cambridge: Cambridge University Press, 2006.

Rose, Nikolas. "The Politics of Life Itself." *Theory, Culture and Society* 18, no. 6 (2001), 1–30.

———. *The Politics of Life Itself: Biomedicine, Power, and Subjectivity in the Twenty-first Century*. Princeton, N.J.: Princeton University Press, 2007.

Rush, Fred, ed. *The Cambridge Companion to Critical Theory*. Cambridge: Cambridge University Press, 2004.

Ruyer, Raymond. *Néo-finalisme*. Paris: Presses Universitaires de France, 1952.

Sartre, Jean-Paul. *Critique of Dialectical Reason*. Vol. 1. Translated by Alan Sheridan-Smith. London: New Left Books, 1976. Originally published as *Critique de la raison dialectique*, tome 1. Paris: Gallimard, 1960.

———. "Jean-Paul Sartre répond." *L'Arc* 1 no. 30 (1966), 87–96.

———. *Search for a Method*. Translated by Hazel E. Barnes. New York: Vintage Books, 1968.

Saussure, Ferdinand de. *Course in General Linguistics*. Introduced by Jonathan Culler. Edited by Charles Bally and Albert Sechehaye in collaboration with Albert Reidlinger. Translated by Wade Baskin. London: Fontana, 1974.

Schacht, Richard, ed. *Nietzsche's Postmoralism: Essays on Nietzsche's Prelude to Philosophy's Future*. New York: Cambridge University Press, 2001.

Schiller, Claire H., ed. *Instinctive Behavior: The Development of a Modern Concept*. New York: International University Press, 1957.

Schutz, Alfred, and Thomas Luckmann. *The Structure of the Lifeworld*. Translated by Richard M. Zaner and H. Tristram Engelhardt. London: Heinemann Educational Books, 1974.

Searle, John. *Freedom and Neurobiology: Reflections on Free Will, Language, and Political Power*. New York: Columbia University Press, 2007.

Serres, Michel. *The Birth of Physics*. Translated by Jack Hawes. Manchester: Clinamen Press, 2001.

Shapiro, Ian. *The Flight from Reality in the Human Sciences*. Princeton, N.J.: Princeton University Press, 2005.

Shapiro, Ian, Rogers M. Smith, and Tarek E. Masoud, eds. *Problems and Methods in the Study of Politics*. Cambridge: Cambridge University Press, 2004.

Sharp, Lesley. *Bodies, Commodities, and Biotechnologies: Death, Mourning, and Scientific Desire in the Realm of Human Organ Transfer*. New York: Columbia University Press, 2007.

———. *Strange Harvest: Organ Transplants, Denatured Bodies, and the Transformed Self*. Berkeley: University of California Press, 2006.

Sheets-Johnstone, Maxine. *The Roots of Power: Animate Form and Gendered Bodies*. Chicago: Open Court, 1994.

Shiva, Vandana. *Biopiracy: The Plunder of Nature and Knowledge*. Boston: South End Press, 1997.

Simondon, Gilbert. "The Genesis of the Individual." *Incorporations*, edited by Jonathan Crary and Sanford Kwinter, 296–319. New York: Zone Books, 1993.

Smith, Adam. *The Wealth of Nations*. Books 1–3. Harmondsworth: Penguin, 1986.

Smith, John, and Chris Jenks. "Complexity, Ecology, and the Materiality of Information." *Theory, Culture and Society* 22, no. 5 (2005), 141–63.

Smolin, Lee. *The Trouble with Physics: The Rise of String Theory, the Fall of a Science, and What Comes Next*. London: Penguin, 2006.

Sohn-Rethel, Alfred. *Intellectual and Manual Labour: A Critique of Epistemology*. Translated by Martin Sohn-Rethel. Atlantic Highlands, N.J.: Humanities Press, 1978.

Sokoloff, William. "Politics and Anxiety in Thomas Hobbes's *Leviathan*." *Theory and Event* 5, no. 1 (2001).

Sokolowski, Robert. *Introduction to Phenomenology*. Cambridge: Cambridge University Press, 2000.

Soló, Richard, and Brian Goodwin. *Signs of Life: How Complexity Invades Biology*. New York: Basic Books, 2000.

Spike, Jeffrey. "Open Commentary: Bush and Stem Cell Research: An Ethically Confused Policy." *American Journal of Bioethics* 2, no. 1 (2002), 45–46.

Springer, Claudia. *Electronic Eros: Bodies and Desire in the Postindustrial Age*. Austin: University of Texas Press, 1996.

Stein, Maurice, Arthur J. Vidich, and David Manning White, eds. *Identity and Anxiety: Survival of the Person in Mass Society*. Glencoe, Ill.: Free Press, 1960.

Steinbock, Anthony. *Home and Beyond: Generative Philosophy after Husserl*. Evanston, Ill.: Northwestern University Press, 1995.

Stolberg, Sheryl Gay. "House Approves a Stem Cell Bill Opposed by Bush." *New York Times*, 25 May 2005, 1.

Strasser, Anne. "La vieillesse comme mutilation: Essai et autobiographie." *Simone de Beauvoir Studies* 22 (2005–6), 38–52.

Strauss, Leo. *The Political Philosophy of Thomas Hobbes*. Translated by Elsa Sinclair. Chicago: University of Chicago Press, 1952. First published 1936.

Sumner, Francis B. "Review." *Journal of Philosophy, Psychology and Scientific Methods* 13, no. 4. (1916), 103–9.

Sunstein, Cass, and Martha Nussbaum, eds. *Animal Rights: Current Debates and New Directions*. Oxford: Oxford University Press, 2005.

Timpanaro, Sebastiano. *On Materialism*. Translated by Lawrence Garner. London: Verso, 1980.

Tuck, Richard. *Philosophy and Government, 1572–1651*. Cambridge, Mass.: Harvard University Press, 1993.

Uexküll, Jakob von. "A Stroll through the World of Animals and Men." *Instinctive Behavior: The Development of a Modern Concept*, edited by Claire H. Schiller, 6–80. New York: International University Press, 1957.

——. *Theoretical Biology*. London: Kegan Paul, 1926.

Urry, John. "The Complexity Turn." *Theory, Culture and Society* 22, no. 5 (2005), 10–14.

Van Buren, John. "Translator's Notes" to Martin Heidegger, *Ontology — The Hermeneutics of Facticity*. Bloomington: Indiana University Press, 1999.

Vaneigem, Raoul. *The Revolution of Everyday Life*. Translated by Donald Nicholson-Smith. London: Rebel Press, 1994.

Veyne, Paul. "Foucault Revolutionizes History." *Foucault and His Interlocutors*, edited by Arnold Davidson, 146–82. Chicago: University of Chicago Press, 1997.

Waldby, Catherine, and Robert Mitchell. *Tissue Economies: Blood, Organs, and Cell Lines in Late Capitalism*. Durham, N.C.: Duke University, 2006.

White, Stephen. *Sustaining Affirmation: The Strengths of Weak Ontology in Political Theory*. Princeton, N.J.: Princeton University Press, 2000.

White House. "President Bush, Ambassador Bremer Discuss Progress in Iraq." Press release, 27 October 2003. Available at http://georgewbush-whitehouse.archives.gov/.

——. "President Bush Discusses Iraq War Supplemental." Press release, 16 April 2007. Available at http://georgewbush-whitehouse.archives.gov/.

——. "Remarks by President and Mrs. Bush in Interview by Television of Spain." Press release, 12 March 2004. Available at http://georgewbush-white house.archives.gov/.

Williams, Caroline. "Thinking the Political in the Wake of Spinoza: Power, Affect and Imagination in the *Ethics*." *Contemporary Political Theory* 6, no. 3 (2007), 349–69.

Woolf, Virginia, *A Room of One's Own* (London: Hogarth Press, 1991).

Wynne, Brian. "Reflexing Complexity: Post-genomic Knowledge and Reductionist Returns in Public Science." *Theory, Culture and Society* 22, no. 5 (2005), 67–94.

Young, Iris M. "Gender as Seriality: Thinking about Women as a Social Collective." *Intersecting Voices*, 12–37. Princeton, N.J.: Princeton University Press, 1997.

——. "Lived Body vs. Gender: Reflections on Social Structure and Subjectivity." *On Female Body Experience*, 12–26. New York: Oxford University Press, 2005.

——. *On Female Body Experience*. New York: Oxford University Press, 2005.

Zeman, Adam. *Consciousness: A User's Guide*. New Haven, Conn.: Yale University Press, 2002.

Žižek, Slavoj. *The Sublime Object of Ideology*. London: Verso, 1989.

Contributors

SARA AHMED is a professor of race and cultural studies at Goldsmiths College, University of London. Her books include *Differences That Matter: Feminist Theory and Postmodernism* (1998); *Strange Encounters: Embodied Others in Post-Coloniality* (2000); *The Cultural Politics of Emotion* (2004); *Queer Phenomenology: Orientations, Objects and Others* (2006); and *The Promise of Happiness* (2010).

JANE BENNETT teaches political theory at The Johns Hopkins University, where she is also the chair of the Department of Political Science. Her latest book is *Vibrant Matter: A Political Ecology of Things* (2010).

ROSI BRAIDOTTI is Distinguished Professor in the Humanities at Utrecht University and founding director of the Centre for Humanities. She has published extensively in feminist philosophy, epistemology, poststructuralism, and psychoanalysis. Her books include *Patterns of Dissonance* (1991); *Nomadic Subjects: Embodiment and Sexual Difference in Contemporary Feminist Theory* (1994); and *Metamorphoses: Towards a Materialist Theory of Becoming* (2002); and *Transpositions: On Nomadic Ethics* (2006).

PHENG CHEAH is a professor of rhetoric at the University of California, Berkeley. He writes on postcolonial theory and postcolonial literatures, eighteenth-century to contemporary continental philosophy and critical theory, theories of globalization, cosmopolitanism and human rights, and social and political thought. He is the author of *Spectral Nationality: Passages of Freedom from Kant to Postcolonial Literatures of Liberation* (2003) and

Inhuman Conditions: On Cosmopolitanism and Human Rights (2006). He has recently coedited *Grounds of Comparison: Around the Work of Benedict Anderson* (2003) and *Derrida and the Time of the Political* (2009). He is currently working on a book on world literature and another book on the concept of instrumentality.

REY CHOW is the Anne Firor Scott Professor at Duke University. She is the author of seven books on literature, film, and cultural theory and politics, including, most recently, *The Age of the World Target* (2006) and *Sentimental Fabulations, Contemporary Chinese Films* (2007). Her publications in English have been widely anthologized and translated into major Asian and European languages. *The Rey Chow Reader*, edited by Paul Bowman, is forthcoming in 2010.

WILLIAM E. CONNOLLY is Krieger-Eisenhower Professor at The Johns Hopkins University where he teaches political theory. His recent publications include *Neuropolitics: Thinking, Culture, Speed* (2002); *Pluralism* (2005); *Capitalism and Christianity, American Style* (2008); and *A World of Becoming* (2010).

DIANA COOLE is a professor of political and social theory at Birkbeck College, University of London. Her most recent books are *Negativity and Politics: Dionysus and Dialectics from Kant to Poststructuralism* (2000) and *Merleau-Ponty and Modern Politics after Anti-Humanism* (2007). She is currently researching the population question, funded by the Leverhulme Major Research Fellowship.

JASON EDWARDS is a lecturer in politics at Birkbeck College, University of London. He is the author of *The Radical Attitude and Modern Political Theory* (2007) as well as numerous essays. He is currently working on a book provisionally entitled "War Pursued by Other Means."

SAMANTHA FROST is an associate professor in the Department of Political Science, the Gender and Women's Studies Program, and the Unit for Criticism and Interpretive Theory at the University of Illinois, Urbana-Champaign. Her book *Lessons from a Materialist Thinker: Hobbesian Reflections on Ethics and Politics* (2008) was selected for the First Book Award by the Foundations Section of the American Political Science Association. She is currently completing a book titled "Hobbes and Heteronomy: Essays on Materialism and Politics."

ELIZABETH GROSZ teaches in the Women's and Gender Studies Department at Rutgers University. She is also a continuing visiting professor at the University of Bergen and the University of Sydney. She is the author, most recently, of *Chaos, Territory, Art: Deleuze and the Framing of the Earth* (2008).

SONIA KRUKS is the Danforth Professor of Politics at Oberlin College, where she teaches political theory and philosophy. Her publications include *Retrieving Experience: Subjectivity and Recognition in Feminist Politics* (2001) and numerous essays on existential social and political theory. She is currently writing a study of Simone de Beauvoir's political thinking.

MELISSA A. ORLIE teaches political theory at the University of Illinois, Urbana-Champaign. She is currently completing two books, one on the politics of good after Nietzsche, from which this essay is drawn, and another on the need for a new concept of the political if we are to effectively respond to ecological crises.

Index

Library of Congress Cataloging-in-Publication Data

New materialisms : ontology, agency, and politics /
Diana Coole and Samantha Frost, eds.
p. cm.
Includes bibliographical references and index.
ISBN 978-0-8223-4753-8 (cloth : alk. paper)
ISBN 978-0-8223-4772-9 (pbk. : alk. paper)
1. Materialism.
2. Ontology.
3. Agent (Philosophy)
4. Materialism — Political aspects.
I. Coole, Diana H.
II. Frost, Samantha.
B825.N49 2010
146'.3 — dc22   2010017237